Outlaws and Spies

Available or forthcoming titles
Imagined States: Law and Literature in Nigeria
Katherine Isobel Baxter

Judging from Experience: Law, Praxis, Humanities
Jeanne Gaakeer

Schreber's Law: Jurisprudence and Judgment in Transition
Peter Goodrich

Outlaws and Spies: Legal Exclusion in Law and Literature
Conor McCarthy

Living in Technical Legality: Science Fiction and Law as Technology
Kieran Tranter

edinburghuniversitypress.com/series/ecsllh

Outlaws and Spies

Legal Exclusion in Law and Literature

Conor McCarthy

EDINBURGH
University Press

Edinburgh University Press is one of the leading university presses in the UK. We publish academic books and journals in our selected subject areas across the humanities and social sciences, combining cutting-edge scholarship with high editorial and production values to produce academic works of lasting importance. For more information visit our website: edinburghuniversitypress.com

Edinburgh University Press Ltd
The Tun – Holyrood Road
12 (2f) Jackson's Entry
Edinburgh EH8 8PJ

First published in hardback by Edinburgh University Press 2020

Typeset in 11/13pt Adobe Garamond Pro by
Servis Filmsetting Ltd, Stockport, Cheshire
and printed and bound by CPI Group (UK) Ltd, Croydon, CR0 4YY

A CIP record for this book is available from the British Library

ISBN 978 1 4744 5593 0 (hardback)
ISBN 978 1 4744 5594 7 (paperback)
ISBN 978 1 4744 5595 4 (webready PDF)
ISBN 978 1 4744 5596 1 (epub)

Contents

Acknowledgements

This book has been a long time in the making, and I am grateful to family and friends for their enduring support and encouragement. Thanks in particular to Deidre Brollo, Caoimhe Brollo McCarthy and Isabella Brollo McCarthy, and thanks in general to my parents Nuala and Michael, my brothers Michael and David, Anne van den Dungen, Phillipa Dunne, Margot Durcan, Dario and Julie Brollo, Darren and Emily Brollo, and all of the McCarthy and Brollo families.

Many thanks too to William MacNeil, series editor of Edinburgh Critical Studies in Law, Literature and the Humanities, and to Laura Williamson and all at Edinburgh University Press, for strongly supporting this project and steering it safely into print.

Several people have generously offered advice on work in progress. Members of the Advisory Board for Edinburgh Critical Studies in Law, Literature and the Humanities offered early feedback; Tony O'Connor and Ross Moore commented on draft chapters; and two referees for Edinburgh University Press read and commented upon the entire text. All have made this a better book.

Parts of chapter one were presented at the 32nd Irish Conference of Medievalists (ICM) in 2018 and the 12th Australian and New Zealand Association for Medieval and Early Modern Studies (ANZAMEMS) conference in 2019, and I am grateful to conference participants for their engagement and advice.

For use of their collections and resources, I am grateful to the National Library of Australia, the University of Newcastle's Auchmuty Library, and the University of Sydney's Fisher Library. Quotations from Ciaran Carson's *Collected Poems* are made by kind permission of Gallery Press. Quotations from other works are made under fair dealing conventions, with thanks to their authors and publishers.

Finally, some of the texts discussed below are works I first read a quarter of a century ago at Trinity College, Dublin, and I acknowledge those debts once again.

Conor McCarthy
Newcastle, NSW
July 2019

Introduction

Article six of the Universal Declaration of Human Rights declares that 'everyone has the right to recognition everywhere as a person before the law'.[1] Implicit here is the idea that the law offers protection; article six states that availing of such protection is an automatic condition of being human. The Universal Declaration dates from 1948, and does not in itself have legal force; the right to recognition as a person before the law is a right that has often been ignored in the years before and since. This book is about the practice that article six seeks to abolish: exclusion from law. It discusses some of the ways in which individual persons, groups, places, states and nations have been considered to exist outside the law, and offers readings of a range of literary texts in English, from the Middle Ages to the present day, that represent such exclusion.

In the English legal system, from early medieval times until relatively recently, a person could be placed outside the law, deprived of the law's protection, through a legal process that declared them an outlaw.[2] An outlawed person became a fugitive, and the word *outlaw* had the related senses of a person banished, or proscribed, or in exile,[3] or of a person who lived without regard for the law, a person on the run.[4] There is a sense of the outlaw being bestial in being compared to the wolf: the outlaw 'bear(s) the wolf's head'.[5] Outlawry bears some similarity to the related concepts of exile and banishment,[6] both long-standing legal punishments.[7] Its ecclesiastical equivalent is excommunication.[8]

---

[1] 'The Universal Declaration of Human Rights'. On the construction of the 'person' in the UDHR, see Slaughter, *Human Rights, Inc.*, pp. 57–63. On approaches to literature and human rights more broadly, see McClennen and Moore, 'Aporia and Affirmative Critique', pp. 1–20.

[2] *OED*, s.v. *outlaw*, n., A. 1a.

[3] *OED*, s.v. *outlaw*, n., A. 1c.

[4] *OED*, s.v. *outlaw*, n., A. 1b.

[5] *Bracton*, ed. Woodbine, trans. Thorne, II, 354.

[6] *Bracton*, ed. Woodbine, trans. Thorne, II, 361, says that to be outlawed is to forfeit the country and the realm.

Legally, outlawry is now an historical phenomenon. In English law, outlawry was abolished for civil proceedings in 1879, and for criminal proceedings in 1938.[9] But it was not entirely moribund in the centuries before its abolition. As we shall see, outlawry in its strict legal sense was still in use against bushrangers in nineteenth-century Australia, where the New South Wales Felons Apprehension Acts of 1865–99 and related legislation in Victoria and Queensland allowed outlawed persons who were armed (or believed to be armed) to be apprehended alive or dead by any person.[10] The formal abolition of outlawry notwithstanding, the discussion below will argue that the practice of placing individuals outside the law is very much an enduring tactic of state power.

Ever since Aristotle's *Politics*, it has been possible to classify exclusion from law in two ways: exclusion above the law, and exclusion below it. Exclusion beneath the law is exclusion from the law's protection, as when someone is declared an outlaw. Exclusion above the law is exclusion from legal punishment. In Aristotle's discussion, humans, in general, are deemed to be within the law. Gods (or men deemed akin to gods) are excluded from the law as being superior to it, and animals (or humans considered to be subhuman) are excluded from the law as being beneath it.[11] This double sense of exclusion (taken up again most recently by Jacques Derrida in *The Beast & the Sovereign*)[12] remains a useful model for thinking about the limits of law and what lies outside it. And so this book considers exclusion from law in both of these senses – exclusion from the protection offered by law, and exclusion from the reach of its chastisement – arguing that these are related concepts, usefully discussed together, and sometimes seen to work in tandem.

There is a long-standing historical idea that may be investigated here: the notion of sovereign immunity. Here the sovereign (akin to a god in Aristotle, divinely appointed by God or acting as his substitute in medieval political thought) is declared to be above the law, immune from legal action, and able

[7] Isidore of Seville, *Etymologies*, p. 124, cites Cicero in listing eight kinds of legal punishment: 'fines, fetters, lashes, compensation in kind, disgrace, exile, slavery, and death'. *Magna Carta* (1215) c. 39 pairs outlawry and exile as possible punishments: *Select Charters*, ed. Stubbs, rev. Davis, p. 297.

[8] 8 Æthelred 42 describes the excommunicate as 'God's outlaw': *Gesetze der Angelsachsen*, ed. Liebermann, I, 218.

[9] Civil Procedure Acts Repeal Act 1879, Administration of Justice (Miscellaneous Provisions) Act 1938.

[10] Felons Apprehension Act (NSW) 1865.

[11] Aristotle, *The Politics*, trans. Sinclair, rev. Saunders, pp. 59–61, 213–14, 215–16 (1253a1–39, 1284a3–17, 1284b22–34).

[12] Derrida, *The Beast & the Sovereign*.

to suspend the law if required. The notion that the sovereign was above the law was, of course, also a contested idea, and the discussion below contrasts historical arguments for sovereign immunity with competing discourses against tyranny.

While sovereign immunity continues to have standing as a legal concept today, its scope is reduced from historical examples where it represents a line of absolutist thinking about monarchy and government: many democratic governments may now be sued in court by their citizens, for instance.[13] But even in a modern republic such as the United States, where the people, not the President, are sovereign, the President enjoys immunity from damages predicated on his official acts.[14] Modern political theory also suggests that in a state of emergency, the sovereign may act extralegally (John Locke, Carl Schmitt and Giorgio Agamben propose very different versions of this idea).[15] The discussion below suggests that in fact contemporary states continue to licence themselves to act extralegally in a number of ways, not only at moments of extreme crisis when the state faces an existential threat, but also in ways that are far more regular and institutionalised.

The actions of the state outside the law are of course most visible in those totalitarian states governed primarily by other means than the rule of law, where exception from the law is the rule. There are some extreme examples from the twentieth and twenty-first centuries. As Ai Weiwei wrote in 2012, following his two months of secret detention the previous year:

> China has not established the rule of law and if there is a power above the law there is no social justice. Everybody can be subjected to harm.[16]

In Nazi Germany, the creation of a 'state of exception' which left the constitution in place but ineffective, created a space without law, both in theory (as discussed by Giorgio Agamben),[17] and in practice (as described by Tony Judt):

---

[13] The Crown Proceedings Act 1947 allowed civil actions to be brought against the UK government for the first time (the monarch remains immune).

[14] The Supreme Court ruled in *Nixon* v. *Fitzgerald* (1982) that the President enjoyed absolute immunity from damages predicated on his official acts. Dissenting opinions suggested that 'attaching absolute immunity to the Office of the President, rather than to particular activities that the President might perform, places the President above the law. It is a reversion to the old notion that the King can do no wrong'. Questions on the President's legal immunity or otherwise are again topical at the time of writing: see Feldman, 'Crooked Trump?'.

[15] For differences between Locke and Schmitt's versions of the exception, see Gross and Ní Aoláin, *Law in Times of Crisis*, pp. 119–23, 162–70.

[16] Ai, 'Ai Weiwei: to live your life in fear'.

[17] Agamben, *State of Exception*, pp. 48–51.

> For most Europeans in the years 1939–45 *rights* – civil, legal, political – no longer existed. The state ceased to be the repository of law and justice; on the contrary, under Hitler's New Order government itself was the leading predator.[18]

While acknowledging the very real differences between totalitarian states and the democracies of the contemporary West, the discussion below proceeds on the basis (after a suggestion of Jacques Derrida, discussed in more detail below)[19] that in fact all states act outside the law.

One of the most obvious and significant ways in which the modern state moves to institutionally embody its ability not only to exclude people from law, but also itself to act extralegally, is in the creation of secret services. Such agencies may play a particularly important role in totalitarian states,[20] but they are also near-ubiquitous: Wikipedia lists intelligence agencies for more than 120 contemporary states.[21] But the activities, and in some cases existence, of these services are at some remove from legal norms, in ways that are discussed in detail during the argument below. If the first part of this book, then, is broadly concerned with outlawry, where individuals are excluded from the protection of the law, the second is broadly concerned with espionage, where the state may licence itself to act extralegally with impunity.

In its discussion of both outlawry and espionage, this book is concerned with exclusion from law as a method of support for sovereign power; as a means through which the state seeks to maintain or extend its reach (I use the word 'state' here in a qualified sense, conscious that the modern concept is an emergent one in the medieval period, and that the medieval uses of *status, état, estate* reflect a broader, but relevant, set of concepts).[22] It argues that the state's exclusion of individuals from the protection of the law is usefully read in relation to other forms of legal exclusion. It also takes the position that outlawry is only notionally an historical phenomenon: that legal exclusion in various forms remains an enduring tactic of state power.

Before turning to the discussion proper, however, it may be useful to briefly survey some of the most influential contemporary studies of outlawry and legal exclusion within the humanities.

---

[18] Judt, *Postwar*, p. 38.
[19] Derrida, *Rogues*, p. 102.
[20] Arendt, *Origins of Totalitarianism*, pp. 548–73.
[21] 'List of intelligence agencies' and cf. 'List of secret police organizations'.
[22] Harding, *Medieval Law and the Foundations of the State*, pp. 1–9.

Eric Hobsbawm and the 'Social Bandit'

A substantial part of the literature on outlawry has come from disciplines such as history, literary studies and folklore studies, and has tended to focus on the figure of the outlaw hero as a challenge to the authorities, and the qualities characteristic of such a figure. The work of Eric Hobsbawm has been influential in setting the terms for these discussions.

In a short book first published in 1969, Hobsbawm defined 'social bandits' as 'peasant outlaws whom the lord and state regard as criminals, but who remain within peasant society, and are considered by their people as heroes, as champions, avengers, fighters for justice, perhaps even leaders of liberation, and in any case as men to be admired, helped, and supported'.[23] Hobsbawm's social bandit is an archetypal figure who represents justice for his community, and who exhibits certain defining characteristics. The social bandit is criminalised as the result of an injustice, or an action which the authorities (but not the community) regard as criminal; he rights wrongs; he takes from the rich and gives to the poor; he kills only in self-defence or revenge; if he survives, he returns to his community as an honourable citizen; he is admired and supported by his people; if he is defeated, it is by means of betrayal; he seems invisible and invulnerable; and finally, he does not oppose the sovereign and the sovereign's justice, but rather the oppression of local enforcers.[24] Walter Benjamin argued in 'Critique of Violence' that the secret admiration of the public for a 'great' criminal arises not from his deeds, but from the violence involved. The law conventionally seeks to appropriate violence to itself: the spectacle of someone transgressing this norm and challenging the claim that the state and the law make for their own monopoly on violence arouses admiration from the populace.[25] But for Hobsbawm's reading of the outlaw, the public's admiration is based rather on the bandit's commitment to social justice in contrast to the oppression of the authorities.

Hobsbawm's work initiated a large amount of subsequent work on bandits and outlaws, and his social bandit archetype has remained influential. In 2011, Graham Seal (whose own work on outlawry is influenced by Hobsbawm) wrote that 'Hobsbawm's basic contention that certain individuals transcend the merely criminal to be accepted by their own social group, and so are to some extent justified in their violence and defiance of authority,

---

[23] Hobsbawm, *Bandits*, p. 20.
[24] Hobsbawm, *Bandits*, pp. 47–8. Seal, 'The Robin Hood Principle', pp. 74–5, offers a slightly revised list of characteristics.
[25] Benjamin, 'Critique of Violence', p. 281.

has stood the test of time as a seminal and still valuable approach to a broad socio-political phenomenon'.[26]

Hobsbawm's model of the 'social bandit' has also been subjected to modification and critique from a number of different perspectives. Anton Blok argues that Hobsbawm's model omits various categories of bandits from consideration, ignores the ways in which bandits may help to support existing power structures, and places an emphasis on social protest that Blok sees as intrinsic to the mythology of banditry, but not necessarily its reality.[27] Gillian Spraggs constructs a cultural history of robber heroes in England over many centuries which suggests ideological roots in aristocratic codes of behaviour, not peasant protest.[28] Hobsbawm, in turn, acknowledges that his 'social bandit' is not representative of all outlaw behaviour, and in particular acknowledges a tradition of bandit gentry distinct from the social bandit tradition.[29] Spraggs also argued that the work of Hobsbawm and subsequent work by Seal presents a syncretised view of the outlaw hero: she suggests that not all characteristics of Hobsbawm's archetypal social bandit are simultaneously present at any given time.[30] In particular, she argues that the motif of taking from the rich to give to the poor, associated with Robin Hood, may be a late development, perhaps as late as the sixteenth century.[31]

Other writers have suggested that while outlawry is inevitably the result of conflict, more nuance is required in determining the nature of the conflict at stake in each particular instance. A recent study of medieval outlawry by Timothy Jones, while acknowledging Hobsbawm's work, argues that there are ways in which its focus needs to be expanded: rather than primarily representing economic injustice and dissatisfaction, outlaws and outlaw narratives may 'embody all sorts of conflicts and appeal to all sorts of frustrations in a variety of potential audiences'.[32]

While Hobsbawm and other cultural historians of outlawry have been primarily (though not exclusively) concerned with the figure of the outlaw,

---

[26] Seal, *Outlaw Heroes*, pp. 3–4.

[27] Blok, 'The Peasant and the Brigand', 494–503. Hobsbawm continued to defend his original thesis. Blok's original article is followed by a reply from Hobsbawm, and the fourth edition of *Bandits* contains a postscript defending Hobsbawm's position against this and other criticisms (pp. 167–85).

[28] Spraggs, *Outlaws and Highwaymen*, p. 278.

[29] Hobsbawm, *Bandits*, pp. 19–20, 41–2.

[30] Spraggs, *Outlaws and Highwaymen*, p. 278.

[31] Spraggs, *Outlaws and Highwaymen*, pp. 51–2, 279; cf. Hobsbawm, *Bandits*, pp. 46–8. Knight, *Robin Hood: A Mythic Biography*, pp. 199–200, also critiques Hobsbawm on this point, but nonetheless discusses Robin Hood at length as a 'social bandit'.

[32] Jones, *Outlawry in Medieval Literature*, p. 4.

and particularly with the outlaw as a hero figure who challenges the authorities, from the 1990s onwards there has also been a line of discussion coming from philosophy which has looked at outlawry in relation to questions of sovereignty and the state. These discussions give much more substantial consideration to the implications of outlawry for our thinking not only about the individual who is placed outside the law, but about the workings of power within the state that excludes them.

Giorgio Agamben's *Homo Sacer*

In a book published in 1995 (translated into English in 1998), Giorgio Agamben offered an examination of sovereign power defined in terms of exception and exclusion, a study which took as its focus the figure of the *homo sacer*, an enigmatic figure from Roman law, who is called *sacer*, 'sacred', and yet may be killed by anyone, but not sacrificed. Agamben sees the *homo sacer* as defined not by the 'originary ambivalence of the sacredness that is assumed to belong to him', but rather the double exclusion of his violent death from the categories of homicide and ritual sacrifice. Violence against the *homo sacer* subtracts itself 'from the sanctioned forms of both human and divine law'.[33] The *homo sacer* is excluded from the protection of the law, and akin therefore to the outlaw or bandit of ancient Germanic and medieval law (and the related figure of the werewolf).[34] But he also resembles two other figures. One is the sovereign himself, who Agamben sees (drawing on Carl Schmitt) as occupying the paradoxical position of being 'at the same time, both outside and inside the juridical order', because the sovereign is defined by his ability to suspend the law, to create a state of exception.[35] And the second figure the *homo sacer* resembles is the occupant of the twentieth-century concentration camp, the camp being a space that is made possible only through the creation of a state of exception to the law which then becomes the rule.[36]

Agamben's reading of the person excluded from the law as a *homo sacer* or bandit is very different from that of historians and cultural critics who read the outlaw as a challenge to the authority of the state. For Agamben, the outcast is an abjected and vulnerable figure:

> His entire existence is reduced to a bare life stripped of every right by virtue of the fact that anyone can kill him without committing homicide; he can save himself only in perpetual flight or a foreign land. And yet he is in a

[33] Agamben, *Homo Sacer*, p. 82.
[34] Agamben, *Homo Sacer*, pp. 104–11.
[35] Agamben, *Homo Sacer*, p. 15, and cf. Schmitt, *Political Theology*, p. 5.
[36] Agamben, *Homo Sacer*, pp. 168–80.

continuous relationship with the power that banished him precisely insofar as he is at every instant exposed to an unconditional threat of death.[37]

Agamben's argument seeks to build on the work of Michel Foucault (while also drawing substantially on Walter Benjamin and Hannah Arendt). For Agamben, Foucault's work on power followed two lines of enquiry: one into the political techniques through which the state begins to concern itself with 'care of the natural life of individuals', and a second through which technologies of the self 'bring the individual to bind himself to his own identity and consciousness and, at the same time, to an external power'.[38] Agamben seeks to build on Foucault's work by looking for what he terms 'the zone of indistinction (or, at least, the point of intersection) at which techniques of individualization and totalizing procedures converge', or, in another formulation, what Agamben suggests should be 'the hidden point of intersection between the juridico-institutional and the biopolitical models of power'.[39]

Homo Sacer, then, treats exclusion from the law, the creation of a state of exception, not in any way as an archaism or an historical phenomenon, but as a fundamental part of the workings of political power. In the three theses that Agamben offers as provisional conclusions to the volume, he argues that the ban is the original political relation; that the fundamental activity of sovereign power is the production of bare life; and that the camp is the fundamental biopolitical paradigm of the West.[40] Exclusion, exception, the creation of persons and spaces outside the law, then, are for Agamben not just historical phenomena, but rather sit at the heart of and form the basis for contemporary political structures. Such thinking about outlawry and sovereignty would come to seem timely given the turns taken by global politics in the late twentieth and early twenty-first century.

Outlaw States and the 'War on Terror'

Following the end of the Cold War, US administrations, beginning with the Clinton administration and continuing with the Bush administration, began to describe certain states which it opposed as 'rogue states', 'outlaw states', or 'pariah states': states which consistently acted outside the accepted norms of international law and politics.

---

[37] Agamben, *Homo Sacer*, p. 183. The idea of 'bare life' (*bloßes Leben*) is from Benjamin, 'Critique of Violence'; Jephcott's English translation gives 'mere life' (p. 297).

[38] Agamben, *Homo Sacer*, p. 5.

[39] Agamben, *Homo Sacer*, p. 6.

[40] Agamben, *Homo Sacer*, p. 181.

As President George W. Bush's 2002 State of the Union speech put it:

> Thousands of dangerous killers, schooled in the methods of murder, often
> supported by outlaw regimes, are now spread throughout the world like
> ticking time bombs, set to go off without warning.

Bush then named three of these outlaw regimes – North Korea, Iran and
Iraq – going on to say, in a famous phrase, that:

> States like these, and their terrorist allies, constitute an axis of evil, arming
> to threaten the peace of the world.[41]

In US foreign policy of the late twentieth and early twenty-first century, then,
the concept of outlawry applies not just to individual persons, but to states. As
rogues, these states are inherently dangerous. As outlaws, they can (and perhaps
should) be attacked with impunity. And as we shall see, such tactics are not
entirely novel: the non-recognition of the sovereign status of other nations, territories and legal systems has a long-standing role in the service of state power.

The Clinton/Bush notion of 'rogue states' was subject to contemporary
critique, not least by Noam Chomsky and Jacques Derrida, both of whom
argued that the United States was itself in many senses a rogue or outlaw
state. In a book entitled *Rogue States*, Chomsky suggested that the term had
two uses: 'a propagandistic use, applied to assorted enemies, and a literal use
that applies to states that do not regard themselves as bound by international
norms'.[42] Chomsky agreed that Iraq under Saddam Hussein was indeed a
criminal regime, but argued that the United States itself could be described as
a rogue state in this second sense of the term in its disregard for international
institutions and norms, in particular the United Nations and the Universal
Declaration of Human Rights.[43]

In a pair of essays from 2002 that builds upon the arguments of Chomsky
among others, published as a book under the title *Rogues*, Jacques Derrida
contended that the US tactic of accusing others of being 'rogue states' was
effective from the end of the Cold War up to 11 September 2001. In doing
so, the US itself acted as a rogue state. As, he suggests, do all other states:

> As soon as there is sovereignty, there is abuse of power and a rogue state ...
> There are thus only rogue states. Potentially or actually. The state is a voyou,
> a rogue, roguish. There are always (no) more rogue states than one thinks.[44]

---

[41] *The Iraq Papers*, ed. Ehrenberg et al., p. 60.
[42] Chomsky, *Rogue States*, p. 1.
[43] Chomsky, *Rogue States*, pp. 12–33, 108–55.
[44] Derrida, *Rogues*, p. 102.

Derrida contended that on 11 September 2001, it became clear that non-state actors could pose an existential threat to state power, and so what he calls the 'epoch' of the rogue state – the rogue state, that is, in Chomsky's first, propagandistic, sense – came to an end.[45] Derrida's argument here is from 2002, and so precedes the 2003 invasion of Iraq, the justification of which would seem to be constructed firmly upon the idea of the 'rogue state'. In any case, it is not this first, propagandistic, sense of 'rogue state' (or 'outlaw state') that concerns us, but rather the second. If Agamben suggested in *Homo Sacer* that exclusion and exception were at the heart of contemporary political structures, Derrida now suggests in *Rogues* that all states are rogue or outlaw states in this sense of acting outside legal norms.

Giorgio Agamben, *State of Exception*

In 2003, Agamben published a further study in his *Homo Sacer* series, entitled *State of Exception*.[46] Starting from Carl Schmitt's definition of the sovereign as 'he who decides on the state of exception', Agamben argued for the importance of the state of exception in understanding the nature of sovereignty. He also argued for the contemporary relevance of such a discussion given President Bush's order of 13 November 2001 authorising the indefinite detention and trial by military commission of non-US citizens suspected of involvement in terrorist activities.[47]

For Agamben:

> What is new about President Bush's order is that it radically erases any legal status of the individual, thus producing a legally unnameable and unclassifiable being. Not only do the Taliban captured in Afghanistan not enjoy the status of POWs as defined by the Geneva Convention, they do not even have the status of persons charged with a crime according to American laws. Neither prisoners nor persons accused, but simply 'detainees,' they are the object of a pure de facto rule, of a detention that is indefinite not only in the temporal sense but in its very nature as well, since it is entirely removed from the law and from judicial oversight.[48]

Detainees were held at Guantánamo Bay in Cuba, where the United States exercises territorial control and operates a naval base, originally established in 1898 during the Spanish-American War, and continued under treaties of

---

[45] Derrida, *Rogues*, pp. 103–7.
[46] The *Homo Sacer* series now has several additional volumes: Agamben, *The Use of Bodies*, has been announced as the last of the sequence.
[47] Bush, 'Military Order of November 13, 2001'.
[48] Agamben, *State of Exception*, pp. 3–4.

1903 and 1934, despite the objections of the Cuban government subsequent to the country's mid-century revolution.

The force of Agamben's analysis would only be strengthened by subsequent events. The detention of captured Taliban at Guantánamo in an effort to place them outside the law would in fact be only one of the ways in which the United States would seek to place both its own actions, and the status of its opponents in the 'War on Terror' outside the law. From 2001 onwards, the CIA operated programmes of 'extraordinary rendition', transferring detainees to the custody of foreign governments whose legal protections differed from those of the United States. They also operated a secret prison programme at 'black sites' outside the United States, 'designed to place detainee interrogations beyond the reach of the law'.[49] Further to this, the US would engage in targeted killings of its opponents, a programme expanded under the Obama regime, which would eventually include the targeted killings of US citizens.[50]

These measures were possible because the Bush administration determined that the War on Terror could occur within what Gabriella Blum and Philip Heymann have called 'a No-Law Zone':[51]

> The Bush administration adopted a theory of 'no law' for detention: it began with the determination that *only* the law of war, as opposed to any constitutional or domestic law, was relevant to the detention of terrorists … and it then proceeded to conclude that there was no law of war literally applicable to the detention of terrorists, as the latter did not meet the conditions of lawful combatancy. It thus left detainees stripped of all legal protections …[52]

The Bush administration also argued that the nature of this conflict with terror groups as a war also gave the President, as Commander-in-Chief at

---

[49] *Globalizing Torture*, p. 5.

[50] Scahill, *Dirty Wars* discusses US covert actions post-2001, focusing on the story of Anwar Awlaki and his son Abdulrahman, US citizens killed in separate incidents in 2011. Anwar Awlaki's daughter was later killed in a US raid in Yemen in 2017. Scahill quotes a 2012 speech by Pentagon general counsel Jeh Johnson which argues that US practices of 'capture, detention and lethal force' should be 'viewed within the context of conventional armed conflict' and are therefore legal (Scahill, *Dirty Wars*, p. 519, quoting from Wittes, 'Jeh Johnson Speech at the Oxford Union').

[51] Blum and Heymann, *Laws, Outlaws, and Terrorists*, p. xiii.

[52] Blum and Heymann, *Laws, Outlaws, and Terrorists*, p. 97. The legal status of detainees and the President's powers to detain combatants and establish military commissions were the subject of subsequent Supreme Court cases, particularly *Hamdi* v. *Rumsfeld* (2004), *Rasul* v. *Bush* (2004), *Hamdan* v. *Rumsfeld* (2006) and *Boumediene* v. *Bush* (2008). For the Obama administration's responses to the ongoing issue of detainees, see Savage, *Power Wars*, pp. 101–61, 293–349, 475–554.

a time of war, the power to act outside the law. The Office of the Attorney General assured President Bush that his powers under Article II of the US Constitution were sufficient to override statutory prohibitions in time of war, and Congress did not have competing powers to limit his actions.[53]

All of these measures that the United States has taken to place its opponents outside the law – the detention programme at Guantánamo, extraordinary rendition, black sites, assassinations – would seem to represent the return of outlawry in a new and extraordinary sense in the twenty-first century.

Jacques Derrida, *The Beast & the Sovereign*

These discussions by Chomsky, Derrida and Agamben published in the decade between 1995 and 2005 may be supplemented by Derrida's *The Beast & the Sovereign*, the title for seminars given at the *École des hautes études en sciences sociales* in the academic years 2001–2 and 2002–3, but published only after Derrida's death, with a two-volume English-language edition appearing in 2009 and 2011. Here Derrida argues that the beast and the sovereign resemble one another in that both may be seen to reside outside the law: 'both share that very singular position of being outlaws'.[54]

The first volume of *The Beast & the Sovereign* meditates at length on the figure of the wolf (Derrida refers to this seminar more than once as a *genelycology*),[55] who is of course a beast, and a dangerous one. The wolf is traditionally an excluded figure, a figure associated with the outlaw. But the wolf is also a figure for the sovereign, particularly in the text that Derrida opens with, La Fontaine's fable of the Wolf and the Lamb. Its opening lines read:

> The reason of the strongest is always the best
> As we shall shortly show.[56]

The problematic of sovereignty, and the related issues of force and right, form a substantial concern in Derrida's seminar (among a wide range of others, impossible to summarise here). In discussing a broad range of texts that bear upon this dynamic of the beast and the sovereign, Derrida makes reference also to contemporary events, suggesting (in line with the argument he makes around the same time in *Rogues*) that:

---

[53] Blum and Heymann, *Laws, Outlaws, and Terrorists*, pp. 11–12.
[54] Derrida, *The Beast & the Sovereign*, I, 32.
[55] Derrida, *The Beast & the Sovereign*, I, 96, 98; Derrida, *Rogues*, p. 69.
[56] Derrida, *The Beast & the Sovereign*, I, 7. La Fontaine's French text is 'La raison du plus fort est toujours la meilleure: | Nous l'allons montrer tout à l'heure'. In the fable, the Wolf deploys various arguments for taking the Lamb's life; the Lamb refutes them all, but to no avail, for the Wolf is strong enough to impose his will.

It is the most powerful sovereign states which, making international right
and bending it to their interests, propose and in fact produce limitations
on the sovereignty of the weaker states, sometimes, as we were saying at
the beginning of the seminar, going so far as to violate or not respect the
international right they have helped institute and, in so doing, to violate
the institutions of that international right, all the while accusing the weaker
states of not respecting international right and of being rogue states, i.e.
outlaw states, like those animals said to be 'rogue' animals, which don't
even bend to the law of their own animal society? Those powerful states
that always give, and give themselves, reasons to justify themselves, but are
not necessarily right, have reason of the less powerful; they then unleash
themselves like cruel, savage, beasts, or beasts full of rage. And this is just
how La Fontaine describes the sovereign wolf in the fable.[57]

The exercise of sovereign power, then, on the part of the strongest, can be less
about reason and law,[58] than it is about strength:

The sovereign (or the wolf in the fable) acts as if he had reason to judge just
and legitimate the reason he gives because he is the strongest, i.e. because,
in the relation of force that here makes right, that here gives reason, the
strongest one, the sovereign, is he who, as we say in French, *a raison des
autres* [prevails over the others], who wins out over the less strong, and
treads on the sovereignty or even the reason [or sanity] of the others.[59]

For Derrida, then, the power of the sovereign is not constrained by law: the
powerful bend reason to their will, and act outside the law. All states are,
in some sense, rogue states. But also, he suggests, sovereignty is also not as
all-powerful as it pretends to be: sovereignty is 'said and supposed to be indi-
visible but always divisible'.[60] Derrida's discussion, then, like Agamben's, sees
the sovereign and the outlaw as related figures, who exist outside the law,[61]

---

[57] Derrida, *The Beast & the Sovereign*, I, 208–9. As the translator notes elsewhere (I, 16 n. 22),
French *droit* can mean both 'law' and 'right', and as is clear from the next quotation to
'have reason' (*avoir raison*) can also mean to 'prevail over'. Cf. also the discussion at I, 70–6,
where Derrida discusses Carl Schmitt's claims that humanitarian interventions that seek
to override nation-state sovereignty always do so from hidden political motives; Derrida
exercises a certain caution (I, 75) regarding Schmitt's argument here.

[58] On the interrelation of reason and law from Cicero through the Middle Ages, see Alford,
'The Idea of Reason in *Piers Plowman*', pp. 200, 201, 204 and n. 24.

[59] Derrida, *The Beast & the Sovereign*, I, 208. As the translator notes, Derrida uses the French
word *raison* here in several senses: *raison*, 'reason'; *avoir raison*, 'to be right'; *avoir raison de*,
'to prevail' (I, 208, n. 3).

[60] Derrida, *The Beast & the Sovereign*, I, 291.

[61] Because the dynamic in Derrida's analysis is between the beast and the sovereign, not the

although he rejects Agamben's argument (after Foucault) for a *biopolitics* (or *zoopolitics*) as something new, arguing that this is a notion already present in political theory as early as Aristotle.[62] The discussion below is concerned with legal exclusion, rather than these larger questions of biopolitics and its origins, though I am inclined to agree with Derrida (against Agamben and Foucault) that the biopolitical itself is likely neither modern nor new, though new things may manifest within it over time.[63]

Despite their differences, what these works by Agamben and Derrida offer us is a series of recent studies where exclusion from law (whether above or below) is read as being bound up with questions of sovereignty, power and the state. In contrast to the work of cultural historians, these studies are focused less on the outlaw as an individual who challenges the authority of the state and embodies certain characteristics in doing so, but rather on the implications of exclusion from law for questions of sovereign and state power. These are also studies that engage with recent events in global politics in ways which suggest that far from being an idea of purely historical interest, outlawry – exclusion from law – in several senses is very much in force today.

This Book

The discussion here begins from a point of agreement in Derrida and Agamben – that exclusion from law is a tactic of sovereign or state power. It proceeds from this starting point to engage in readings of a variety of texts, primarily literary texts in the English language, from the Middle Ages to the present day. In doing so, this discussion seeks to identify the ways in which the state uses exclusion from law, in a variety of forms, to further its own interests, and to explore how such actions are represented across a range of texts. In approaching these texts from this perspective, this study differs from

---

outlaw and the sovereign, he is also greatly concerned with the figure of the beast, defini-tions of the bestial, and issues of animal rights in a challenge to Cartesian thinking and its derivatives that falls outside the scope of our discussion here. For a recent discussion of exclusion and animal rights, see Creed, *Stray*.

[62] Derrida, *The Beast & the Sovereign*, I, 305–34, 348–9. For Foucault, biopolitics is a new form of power over life, beginning in the seventeenth century, in a break with what Aristotle means in his definition of man as a *politikon zōon* in the *Politics* (Foucault, *History of Sexuality*, pp. 139–43; Foucault, '*Society Must Be Defended*', pp. 239–64). Agamben, argu-ing for a distinction between two Greek words for life, constructs an opposition between *zoē*, 'bare life', and *bios*, 'the form or way of living proper to an individual or a group', and draws on Foucault's identification of biopolitics with modernity in his construction of a dynamic between *zoē* and *bios*, bare life and political existence, exclusion and inclusion (Agamben, *Homo Sacer*, pp. 1, 8).

[63] Derrida, *The Beast & the Sovereign*, I, 329–30.

most previous readings of outlaw literature. Hobsbawm's own work acknowledged that the history of banditry could not be understood except as part of
the history of political power, though, like others, he emphasises banditry as a
consequence of the weakness of state power – a 'weak state' thesis challenged
in the discussion below.[64] There have also been readings of banishment and
outlawry in literary texts that have drawn on or engaged with Agamben's
work (I am particularly conscious of Ruth Evans's discussion of *Sir Orfeo*,
Helen Phillips's introduction to the essay collection *Bandit Territories*, and
Joseph Taylor's reading of *A Gest of Robyn Hode*).[65] However, it is still the
case, I think, that discussion is generally focused around the figures of individual outlaws, and has not generally approached the question of outlawry as
one of a range of tactics designed to expand or maintain state power.

This is primarily a book about literature, rather than a discussion of politics, history or law (much as it may draw on these subjects in the discussion
below). It focuses on two extensive bodies of literature in English: the literature of outlawry, which extends from the Middle Ages to the present day,
and the literature of espionage, which emerges in the twentieth-century from
roots in detective fiction and the nineteenth-century literature of terrorism.
These are two reasonably coherent bodies of literature, not conventionally
discussed in tandem; in treating them together, the discussion here suggests
they share a concern with the subject of legal exclusion and its consequences.

Outlawry has a substantial literature across a long time period and a
range of cultures. While this book in no way attempts to survey the literature
of outlawry, it does take a long view, longer than is conventional in contemporary scholarship. There are gains as well as risks in looking across a long
timeline, however, and there have been moves in that direction elsewhere: Jo
Guldi and David Armitage's book *The History Manifesto* recently argued the
case for the return of the *longue durée* as remediation for a short-termism that
has come to dominate so many aspects of contemporary thinking.[66] Taking
a long view, however, does not mean neglecting historical difference, and the
discussion below also takes a broadly historicist approach: legal exclusion and
its representation are seen to be enduring, but by no means unchanging.

If the subject of outlawry has a long literary history, that history is also a
diverse one. Something of a canon of outlaw texts for medieval England was
established by Maurice Keen's book *The Outlaws of Medieval Legend*, first

---

[64] Hobsbawm, *Bandits*, pp. 11–17.
[65] Evans, '*Sir Orfeo* and Bare Life'; Phillips, 'Bandit Territories and Good Outlaws', pp. 14–15;
Taylor, 'Me longeth sore to Bernysdale'.
[66] Guldi and Armitage, *The History Manifesto*.

published in 1961.[67] Well-known post-medieval examples of outlawry include British highwaymen (of whom Dick Turpin remains the best-remembered example), and the outlaws of the American West and their representation in twentieth-century American cinema. Some outlaw figures have remained culturally potent, with their stories reworked over and over again across long periods of time.[68] But those outlaw figures who are well known in modern Anglophone popular culture – Robin Hood from medieval England, Dick Turpin from eighteenth-century England, Jesse James and Billy the Kid from the nineteenth-century American West, Ned Kelly from nineteenth-century Australia – may be supplemented with less well-known outlaws from the same contexts, and with outlaw figures from a variety of other cultures.[69] And while the cultural representation of outlawry is conventionally associated with popular forms such as the oral ballad and, in the contemporary era, the cinema (particularly the Western), the subject of outlawry appears in the work of a wide range of writers and a variety of forms, extending from medieval romance, through Walter Scott's portrayals of Rob Roy and Robin Hood, to contemporary literary works such as Michael Ondaatje's *The Collected Works of Billy the Kid* and Paul Kingsnorth's reworking of the Hereward story in *The Wake*.[70] Despite its diversity, there are some visible continuities to be found across this literature of outlawry. If the medieval literature of outlawry offers a vision of solidarity and resistance akin to that of Hobsbawm's 'social bandit' (albeit with qualifications), Ned Kelly's self-representation centuries later draws on the enduring cultural archetype of the outlaw to portray himself in recognisably similar terms.

The opening three chapters of this book offer a series of case studies that seek to discuss the continuities, contrasts and tensions within various representations of outlawry, grounded in specific historical circumstances. Texts considered include a variety of texts from medieval England (and, to a certain extent, its neighbours), the second tetralogy of Shakespeare's history plays, and finally various versions of the story of Ned Kelly, particularly Kelly's own *Jerilderie Letter* and Peter Carey's *True History of the Kelly Gang*.

These opening chapters outline a diversity of ways in which outlawry is represented. If medieval legal texts offer a view of the outlaw akin to Agamben's *homo sacer*, medieval literary texts offer us a view closer to Hobsbawm's 'social

[67]   Keen, *Outlaws of Medieval Legend*.
[68]   For a long view of the Robin Hood phenomenon, see Knight, *Robin Hood: A Mythic Biography*; for Ned Kelly, see *Kelly Culture*.
[69]   *Outlawed!*, ed. Weber, offers a broad view.
[70]   Scott, *Rob Roy*; Scott, *Ivanhoe*; Ondaatje, *The Collected Works of Billy the Kid*; Kingsnorth, *The Wake*.

bandit'. The actions of the real outlaw gangs of medieval England, we discover, are different again. Elsewhere, we find outlawry employed as a political tactic against the medieval English crown's political opponents across the archipelago, where leaders with genuine claims to sovereign authority are reduced to the status of outlaws. We find the outlaw's exclusion beneath the law doubled by the sovereign's exclusion above it, though we also find the monarch's claim to extralegal status repeatedly challenged by a tradition of writing against tyranny. And, as in Derrida and Agamben, we find a parallel drawn between the sovereign and the outlaw in a variety of outlaw texts – a parallel found at the heart of Shakespeare's *Richard II*.

As well as this motif of double exclusion, above and below the law, these early chapters further suggest that the exclusion of individuals from legal recognition may also intersect with broader tactics of legal exclusion: the non-recognition of the sovereign status of other nations, territories and legal systems. This application of the concept of outlawry not just to individual persons, but also to entire states, familiar from the contemporary discussion of 'rogue states', is visible in the English crown's actions from medieval Britain and Ireland to colonial Australia.

From Chapter 4 onwards, the discussion below turns away from the historical practice of outlawry to consider legal exclusion in the contemporary literature of espionage. This book is not the first to argue that legal exclusion is an important feature of espionage and its literature. Timothy Melley describes the covert as 'the institutional sedimentation of what Giorgio Agamben calls "the state of exception" – the paradoxical suspension of democracy as a means of saving democracy'.[71] Eva Horn likewise argues that the modern secrets of the state 'amount to an ongoing state of exception, a permanent (self-) suspension of the rule of law that introduces the possibility of pure, "extralegal" violence'.[72]

Espionage literature has its origins in both detective fiction and a literature concerned with terrorism. Detective fiction evolves from the 1840s in the work of Edgar Allan Poe, Wilkie Collins and Arthur Conan Doyle. 'Terrorism', though it has its precursors, dates as a term from the late eighteenth century,[73] and as a systematic practice from the second half of the nineteenth.[74] Even at this early stage, the term covers a variety of forms of political violence; later, 'the term has been used in so many different senses

---

[71] Melley, *The Covert Sphere*, p. 5.
[72] Horn, *The Secret War*, p. 95.
[73] *OED*, s.v. *terrorism*, n., *terrorist*, n.; Laqueur, *Terrorism*, p. 6.
[74] Laqueur, *Terrorism*, p. 11.

as to become almost meaningless'.[75] With the growth of the phenomenon of terrorism in the second half of the nineteenth century comes a literature of terrorism, which in English includes as early examples Henry James's *The Princess Casamassima*, Joseph Conrad's *The Secret Agent* and *Under Western Eyes*, and G. K. Chesterton's *The Man Who Was Thursday*.[76] Indebted to – and sometimes crossing over with – both of these genres, the espionage novel is generally considered to emerge in the early years of the twentieth century with the publication of Rudyard Kipling's *Kim* and Erskine Childers's *The Riddle of the Sands*.[77] The genre's emergence in English in the early twentieth century is roughly contemporary with the formation (and perhaps influences the growth) of the modern British intelligence services.[78] There have been an enormous number of spy thrillers produced in the years since, and the subject has influenced a wide range of writers.

The discussion below does not attempt a survey of the literature of espionage, any more than it attempts such for the literature of outlawry. It extends beyond the boundaries of the spy thriller in offering readings of texts by four very different contemporary English-language writers – John le Carré, Don DeLillo, Ciaran Carson and William Gibson – only one of whom (le Carré) is what we might call an espionage novelist. These texts play out against different historical contexts, including the construction of the Berlin Wall; the exposure of the Cambridge spy ring; the Kennedy assassination; the Northern Ireland Troubles; the Iran hostage crisis; the rise of the internet; and the War on Terror. But there are recurring themes to be found nonetheless.

We find state agencies acting outside the law throughout. Such actions range from le Carré's description of murder, kidnapping and blackmail as common currency in the early days of the Cold War to the suggestion of state collusion with terrorists in Carson. They extend through the use of extraordinary rendition to allow the secret torture of suspected terrorists in le Carré and DeLillo to the secretive deployment of mass surveillance in both Carson

---

[75] Laqueur, *Terrorism*, p. 6; cf. Richardson, *What Terrorists Want*, p. 3. For the difficulty in defining terrorism legally, see Gross and Ní Aoláin, *Law in Times of Crisis*, pp. 366–71.

[76] James, *The Princess Casamassima*; Conrad, *The Secret Agent*; Conrad, *Under Western Eyes*; Chesterton, *The Man Who Was Thursday*. Laqueur, *Terrorism*, pp. 149–74, offers a survey of terrorism and literature to the 1970s.

[77] Kipling, *Kim*; Childers, *The Riddle of the Sands*.

[78] Andrew, *Defence of the Realm*, pp. 4–21, discusses in passing the role of Kipling in promoting the myth of a British intelligence network, and of William Le Queux in propagating a fear of German espionage that contributed to the creation of the modern secret services. Espionage is not, of course, a twentieth-century invention, and espionage in seventeenth-century England is briefly discussed in Chapter 2 below.

and Gibson. All of these works, then, are interested in extralegal action by the state, its agencies, and its contractors, as a tactic of power.

We also encounter a wide range of marginalised and excluded figures. Alec Leamas in *The Spy Who Came in from the Cold* is an agent exiled and abandoned, as vulnerable as any *homo sacer*. In Don DeLillo's *Libra* it is 'an outlawed group' of CIA agents that plots the assassination of President Kennedy. William Gibson's hacker protagonists are described as 'high-tech outlaws'. If some of these marginal figures are, as in Hobsbawm, figures of resistance, there are also repeated attempts here by the powerful to co-opt the marginal. Here, too, the medieval parallel between the sovereign and the outlaw, excluded above and below the law, is reconfigured as parallels are drawn between the spy and the terrorist, the political assassin, the hacker and the refugee.

Overall, then, this book pursues two broad lines of enquiry. The first is the theme of legal exclusion as an enduring tactic (or, rather, a set of tactics) of state or sovereign power. This involves the exclusion of individuals from legal protection via a range of measures, from outlawry to extraordinary rendition. These tactics of exclusion beneath the law may be paired with the related practice of exclusion above it. Here, the sovereign or the state claims the ability to act with legal impunity, by a variety of means, from the historical notion of sovereign immunity, executive approval of covert actions by modern-day intelligence agencies, or the implementation of emergency powers. Furthermore, the exclusion of individuals from legal recognition may be usefully compared and aligned with circumstances where the legal status and legal practice of other nations or states are disregarded.

Our second line of enquiry investigates the enduring role of literature in both representing and critiquing such legal exclusion. The literature of outlawry and the literature of espionage do, of course, create a certain mythology and mystique for their archetypal protagonists, the outlaw and the spy. But as the discussion below argues at length, both bodies of literature also serve an important purpose in representing and critiquing the state's enduring use of legal exclusion as a tactic of power. A desire for justice is a key characteristic of Hobsbawm's 'social bandit'.[79] As we shall see, there are many reasons to qualify this suggestion: historical studies suggest that real outlaws are enmeshed in power relations in complex ways, and may be participants in the corruption of law, rather than ethical outsiders. But if Hobsbawm's comments cannot always be upheld for the practice of outlawry, they have a certain validity when applied to its literature. As the discussion below suggests, outlaw

---

[79] Hobsbawm, *Bandits*, pp. 29–30, 46–51, 58–62.

literature's critique of the medieval English justice system aligns these works with the very extensive tradition of medieval satire and complaint and that tradition's critique of injustice. The contemporary literature of espionage, in turn, plays an unusually important role in both portraying and questioning the workings of the state, given both the secrecy that surrounds such activities, and the state's ongoing efforts to influence, censor or suppress factual accounts of its extralegal actions.

In pursuing these two broad lines of enquiry, the discussion here makes four key arguments. First, it suggests that these various forms of legal exclusion – the exclusion of individuals from the law's protection, the exclusion of the state's own actions from legal punishment, and the non-recognition of the sovereign status of other nations, territories and legal systems – are related means of defending, consolidating or extending state or sovereign power. Secondly, it argues that legal exclusion, far from being an historical curiosity, is an enduring phenomenon that is alive and well in disturbing new combinations in the twentieth and twenty-first century West. Thirdly, it seeks to show that exclusion from law is a shared concern for the literatures of outlawry and espionage, and hence a key theme in writing about the state and its actions at the heart of a wide range of literary texts in English from the Middle Ages to the present day. Finally, it suggests that the role of literature in relation to such exclusion is often to offer critique, a critique that implicitly carries within it a demand for justice.

1

Outside the Law in the Middle Ages

The 'Lawless Man' in Medieval English Law

Outlawry is a phenomenon found in legal texts from across the medieval period. It is a commonplace amongst commentators that in part, at least, the resort to exclusion from law may be explained by the weakness of legal authority. 'Outlawry is the last weapon of ancient law', writes F. W. Maitland, 'but one that it must often use'. However, 'as the power of the state and the number of its weapons increase, outlawry loses some of its gravity'. Outlawry is reduced from being a substantive punishment to becoming mere process, a means of compelling the accused to attend trial.[1] A sentence of outlawry, says Maurice Keen, 'implied an admission of weakness on the part of the law itself'. 'It revealed', he suggests, 'a failure on the part of the government; the sentence uncovered the inability of medieval society to curb its own unruly elements'. But when law and government become strong enough, outlawry fades away.[2]

In this view, outlawry is a supplement to the formal legal system of a weak or emerging state, a remedy for its failings, and in fact we do find exclusion from law regularly described in early medieval texts in terms that may justify such a view: those who will not answer to the law, or submit to it, are placed outside it. The sixth-century Germanic *Lex Salica* describes how a man who refuses to come to court or obey a judgment, after being summoned on specified subsequent occasions, may be placed outside the king's protection (*extra sermonem suum*); his life and property then belong to the *fisc* until he has paid composition for his offence.[3] The subsequent Edict of Chilperich

---

[1] Pollock and Maitland, *History of English Law*, I, 476.
[2] Keen, *Outlaws of Medieval Legend*, p. 10.
[3] *Laws of the Salian Franks*, trans. Drew, p. 119. Jones, *Outlawry in Medieval Literature*, p. 19, notes that while the meaning of *sermonum* is a matter for debate, the procedure is clearly related to outlawry. 'Composition' is a specified monetary payment for an offence (*Laws of the Salian Franks*, trans. Drew, pp. 35–6).

describes how an 'evil man' who has committed an 'evil deed', and does not have the means to make composition but has fled to the forest, will be placed outside the king's protection (*nostro sermone*): whoever finds him can kill him without fear.[4]

In the Early English laws, the earliest potential references to outlawry involve thieves caught in the act, who may be killed with impunity.[5] This practice endures into the later medieval period, where a thief caught in the act may be killed, or, if captured, brought before a hastily convened court 'and without being allowed to say one word in self-defence, he will be promptly hanged, beheaded, or precipitated from a cliff'.[6] As Maitland comments, 'there is hardly room for doubt that this process had its origin in days when the criminal taken in the act was *ipso facto* an outlaw'.[7]

Outlawry may be applied to escapees: in the laws of Alfred, if an oath-breaker escapes from prison, 'he shall be banished (*afliemed*), and excommunicated from all the churches of Christ'.[8] It may be used against those who sit outside the regular social and legal order: in the laws of Æthelstan, lordless men from whom no legal satisfaction can be obtained, whose situation is not satisfactorily resolved by settling them in a fixed place and finding them a lord, are declared *flyma*. Anyone encountering them subsequently may assume them to be thieves, and kill them.[9] Again, it may be used against those who seek to avoid judgment: in the laws of Æthelred, a thief who steals for a second time is liable to execution; if the accused flees, his pledge man pays compensation to the accuser and his *wergeld* to his lord. If, however, the accused's lord is himself accused of advising him to flee, and the lord cannot clear himself by the oaths of five men, the king receives the *wergeld*, and the thief 'will be an outlaw with all people' (*beo se þeof utlah wið eall folc*).[10] Outlawry may even be imposed upon those recidivist criminals who have somehow survived judgment: the Assize of Clarendon (1166) specifies that a person whose bad reputation is the subject of widespread testimony, even if cleared by judicial ordeal, shall

---

[4] *Laws of the Salian Franks*, trans. Drew, p. 152.

[5] Wihtred 25, Ine 16, Ine 35, 2 Æthelstan 1 in *Laws of the Earliest English Kings*, ed. and trans. Attenborough, pp. 28, 29, 40, 41, 46, 47, 126, 127.

[6] Pollock and Maitland, *History of English Law*, II, 579.

[7] Pollock and Maitland, *History of English Law*, II, 580; Bellamy, *Crime and Public Order*, p. 134, comments that by the mid-fourteenth century, such suspects were assured of a trial.

[8] Alfred 1.7 in *Laws of the Earliest English Kings*, ed. and trans. Attenborough, pp. 64–5.

[9] 2 Æthelstan 2 in *Laws of the Earliest English Kings*, ed. and trans. Attenborough, pp. 128–9.

[10] 1 Æthelred 1.9a in *Gesetze der Angelsachsen*, ed. Liebermann, I, 218; discussed in Jones, *Outlawry in Medieval Literature*, pp. 22–3.

nonetheless be outlawed.[11] Outlawry, then, is often a method of enforcing justice in the absence of other means.

We also find outlawry prescribed for particular breaches of the law. These are offences whose nature, as Timothy Jones puts it, 'suggests that the guilty party is not fit to live in the human community'.[12] The Salic laws, then, prescribe that a person who digs up or despoils a dead body is declared an outlaw (specifically, a *wargus*);[13] a woman who marries her own slave will be outlawed (*aspellis*);[14] a person who commits *raptus* (rape, or more broadly abduction) is to be killed or outlawed (*forbatuous*).[15] The penalty of outlawry for despoiling the dead also appears in the Old English text *Walreaf*: here corpse-robbery is the act of a *niðing* (a person stigmatised by *nið* and so deserving of exclusion as an outlaw).[16] In the laws of Æthelred, witches, diviners, perjurers, poisoners and adulteresses are to be driven from the land or killed.[17] Persons who commit crimes such as these are outlawed as a means of exclusion from society; in a parallel process of ecclesiastical exclusion, the excommunicate was 'God's outlaw'.[18]

The outlaw's exclusion from human society is emphasised by the use of wolf imagery. Various legal texts describe the outlaw as a wolf's head,[19] as do literary texts such as the later medieval poem *Gamelyn* (*Gamelyn*, 706).[20] The outlaw is a beast to be hunted: the wolf, like the outlaw, might be killed with impunity, and its death rewarded.[21] Equating the outlaw with the wolf, then, is to render the man into a beast, to place the outlaw, like an animal, beneath the law. As Derrida reminds us, however, the wolf is also a powerful

---

[11] *Assize of Clarendon*, ed. Vincent.

[12] Jones, *Outlawry in Medieval Literature*, pp. 25–6.

[13] *Laws of the Salian Franks*, trans. Drew, pp. 37–8, 188. Jones, *Outlawry in Medieval Literature*, p. 26 and n. 66, notes that 'wargus' here is a Latin adaptation of a Germanic term leading to Old English *wearg*, Old Norse *vargr*, meaning 'criminal', 'outlaw' and 'wolf'.

[14] *Laws of the Salian Franks*, trans. Drew, pp. 37–8, 144.

[15] *Laws of the Salian Franks*, trans. Drew, pp. 37–8, 157.

[16] *Walreaf* in *Gesetze der Angelsachsen*, ed. Liebermann, I, 392. *OED*, s.v. *nithing*, n. and adj. A. 1. offers the definition 'a coward, a villain; a person who breaks the law or a code of honour; an outlaw'.

[17] 6 Æthelred 7 in *Gesetze der Angelsachsen*, ed. Liebermann, I, 248.

[18] 8 Æthelred 42 in *Gesetze der Angelsachsen*, ed. Liebermann, I, 218. For excommunication and exile as forms of penance in the early Middle Ages, see *Medieval Handbooks of Penance*, ed. McNeill and Gamer.

[19] *Leges Edwardi Confessoris*, ed. O'Brien; *Bracton*, ed. Woodbine, trans. Thorne, II, 354.

[20] *The Tale of Gamelyn* in *Robin Hood and Other Outlaw Tales*, ed. Knight and Ohlgren, pp. 184–226.

[21] Jones, *Outlawry in Medieval Literature*, p. 27.

creature, one to be feared, and dangerous for humans (while also resembling them, for, in the phrase derived from Plautus, and much repeated, *homo homini lupus*, 'man is a wolf to man').[22] For Agamben, reading specifically the English description of the outlaw as a 'wolf's head', the outlaw is not a wolf, but a werewolf: he occupies a zone of indistinction between human and animal.[23] The outlaw, then, is not merely excluded, but may be hunted down and killed, like a beast, or (as with the werewolf) a monster.

Outlawry endures into the later Middle Ages, though *Magna Carta* (1215) insists that outlawry or exile shall not occur without judicial process.[24] Despite Maitland's view of its diminishing force in the later medieval period, the power of outlawry is still such that Wat Tyler, leader of the English rising of 1381, reportedly included its abolition among his demands for change.[25]

The thirteenth-century English legal text *Bracton* describes the procedure for outlawry in detail. A person accused of homicide or another crime, summoned to appear in court, who fails to appear within five months, is declared an outlaw:

> If he does not appear within that time he will be regarded as an outlaw, since he obeys neither the prince nor the law, and will thenceforth be outlawed, that is, one who is outside the law, that is, a 'lawless man'.[26]

By *Bracton*'s time, the ability to kill an outlaw with impunity is qualified. The outlaw who flees from or resists arrest may be killed without consequence; not so the outlaw who surrenders or is arrested:

> Henceforth they bear the wolf's head and in consequence perish without judicial inquiry; they carry their judgment with them and they deservedly perish without law who have refused to live according to law. This is so if they take to flight or resist when they are to be arrested; if they are arrested alive or give themselves up, their life and death will be in the hands of the lord king.[27]

---

[22] Derrida, *The Beast & the Sovereign*, I, 58–62.

[23] Agamben, *Homo Sacer*, pp. 105–6; for thinking about hybridity and metamorphosis around the year 1200, with specific reference to werewolves, see Bynum, *Metamorphosis and Identity*.

[24] *Select Charters*, ed. Stubbs, p. 297.

[25] As described by the *Anonimalle Chronicle*: *Crime, Law and Society*, ed. Musson with Powell, p. 61.

[26] *Bracton*, ed. Woodbine, trans. Thorne, II, 352. For an early fifteenth-century case demonstrating the process, see *Crime, Law and Society*, ed. Musson with Powell, p. 162.

[27] *Bracton*, ed. Woodbine, trans. Thorne, II, 354.

In a case from 1323, William le Kyng and Robert de Haldeleghes appear in court accused of killing John son of John de Clayton. Their defence is that John was an outlaw. By this period, John's outlawry in itself is not sufficient to secure their release: the jurors have to testify that William and Robert would not have been able to take John alive before the pair are allowed to go free.[28]

In *Bracton*, the outlaw forfeits both the realm and the assistance of his friends:

> It is clear that he first forfeits the country and the realm and is made an exile, such as the English call an 'outlaw'; in ancient times he used to be called by another name, that is, 'friendless man', from which it is apparent that he forfeits his friends.[29]

The outlaw forfeits his legal standing;[30] those who assist outlaws are liable to share their punishment.[31] Outlawry is common in the later Middle Ages. 'We are speaking of no rarity', says Maitland. 'The number of men outlawed at every eyre is very large; ten men are outlawed for one who is hanged'.[32]

Though by the thirteenth century the earlier sense that the outlaw was to be killed with impunity has been softened, the portrayal of outlawry in medieval English legal texts is one we can align in general terms with that of Agamben's *homo sacer*. Outlaws are excluded from the protection of the community and the law, and, in *Bracton*'s words, 'deservedly perish without law'. As we shall see, however, there are very different accounts of outlawry in medieval England to be found in the literary texts of the later medieval period, and different implications again to be gathered from the real actions of medieval outlaw gangs.

Outlawry and Resistance in Medieval English Writing

Outlawry is a substantial theme in the literature of later medieval England. In his survey of outlaw literature, Maurice Keen suggested that in England, the traditional three subjects of medieval romance, the matter of Britain, the matter of France, and the matter of Rome, might be supplemented by a fourth: 'the matter of the Greenwood'.[33] Keen's survey demonstrated continuities within a literature that begins by reworking the narratives of historical

---

[28] *English Historical Documents 1042–1189*, ed. Douglas and Greenaway, p. 559.
[29] *Bracton*, ed. Woodbine, trans. Thorne, II, 361.
[30] *Bracton*, ed. Woodbine, trans. Thorne, II, 362–3.
[31] *Bracton*, ed. Woodbine, trans. Thorne, II, 361–2.
[32] Pollock and Maitland, *History of English Law*, I, 477–8.
[33] Keen, *Outlaws of Medieval Legend*, p. 1.

figures such as Hereward, Eustace the Monk and Fouke Fitz Waryn, and progresses to the later medieval fictions of Robin Hood and his companions. There are broad continuities here in that early literary outlaws like Hereward and Fouke are figures of resistance, motivated by injustice to struggle against the powers-that-be, just as Robin Hood is in later medieval literature.[34] But minute continuities are also visible in specific motifs found repeated across very different tales. Hereward, the Englishman engaged in guerrilla warfare against the occupying Normans in the eleventh century, disguises himself at one stage as a potter to infiltrate the enemy camp; a similar story is later told of Eustace the Monk, of William Wallace and of Robin Hood.[35]

If medieval English legal texts portray the outlaw in terms reminiscent of Agamben's *homo sacer*, the outlaw literature of later medieval England does not. Medieval English literature has many examples of vivid description of the harshness of an exposed life out of doors, from the Old English poems *The Wanderer* and *The Seafarer*[36] to the Middle English romances *Sir Orfeo* and *Sir Gawain and the Green Knight*.[37] But these are not the descriptions found in the literature of outlawry. As Helen Phillips writes, 'in late medieval fiction the outlaw's territory is a fantasy of luxury rather than Lear-like nakedness: it is not the opposite of aristocratic life but (notably in *A Gest of Robyn Hode*) more like an alternative court, a sylvan Land of Cockaigne'.[38]

Neither, for the most part, is the outlaw of medieval English literature a solitary figure; rather, he is a 'good fellow' and a member of a company. This also seems the case for actual outlaws: 'there is plenty of evidence', writes Richard Firth Green, 'that the outlaw bands thought of themselves as unified confederacies'.[39] John Bellamy notes several reasons for criminals working in groups. First, some forms of crime – seizing land, committing mayhem, abduction, highway robbery, feuding – required strength in numbers for success, and in an era where most men were armed, numbers were a substantial advantage. Secondly, the importance of kinship bonds in the Middle Ages meant that criminals could usually count on assistance from their families, and many gangs contained groups of family members. Finally, the system of outlawry was itself responsible for the creation of gangs as the excluded joined

---

[34] Keen, *Outlaws of Medieval Legend*, pp. 51–2.
[35] Keen, *Outlaws of Medieval Legend*, pp. 18–19, 23–4; Jones, *Outlawry in Medieval Literature*, p. 100.
[36] In *A Choice of Anglo-Saxon Verse*, ed. and trans. Hamer, pp. 172–95.
[37] *Sir Orfeo*, ed. Bliss, pp. 22–4; *Sir Gawain and the Green Knight*, ed. Tolkien and Gordon, rev. Davis, lines 726–32.
[38] Phillips, 'Bandit Territories and Good Outlaws', p. 15.
[39] Green, *A Crisis of Truth*, p. 189.

together for mutual support.[40] Many later medieval outlaw narratives contain a rescue of the threatened or captured outlaw by his companions. William of Cloudesley's outlaw companions rescue him from the gallows;[41] in *Robin Hood and the Monk*, Little John and Much the Miller's son rescue Robin from the Sheriff of Nottingham's jail.[42]

The outlaws survive not only through mutual assistance, but also through support from their communities. In *Adam Bell, Clim of the Clough and William of Cloudesley*, the small boy who is the town swineherd has often seen William in the woods and given him food; when William is captured by the sheriff, this little boy alerts the other outlaws (*Adam Bell*, 173–84). In *The Tale of Gamelyn*, the hero relies on his brother's servant, Adam, to rescue him, while his loyal brother Sir Ote relies on Gamelyn himself for deliverance at the end of the poem. Far from presenting outlaws as entirely excluded figures, then, the literature of outlawry suggests a social context for support of outlaws, present in the tales themselves and implicit also in the fact that these tales find a contemporary audience (however much the nature of that audience is debated).

Medieval outlaw literature has elements of wish-fulfilment: forest life is idyllic, companions are eternally loyal, the outlaws always defeat their enemies despite impossible odds, and so on. But the harshness and danger of the outlaw life is a latent presence in these tales whose manifest meaning is a celebration of outlaw resistance. If the idyllic portrait of forest life is the norm in outlaw narratives, there are exceptions: in one episode, the sheriff, having sampled forest life, would rather be beheaded than spend another night there (*A Gest of Robyn Hode*, 785–800).[43] In the sixteenth-century ballad *The Nut-Brown Maid*, a young man tests his lover by pretending that he is outlawed, and describing the hardships she would endure should she join him in the forest (*The Nut-Brown Maid*, 85–90).[44]

Nor are outlaws always idealised figures. If Robin Hood is often portrayed as both ethical and pious, poems such as *The Hermit and the Outlaw* offer a very different view of outlawry. Here, the outlaw has never attended

---

[40] Bellamy, *Crime and Public Order*, pp. 69–70.

[41] *Adam Bell, Clim of the Clough, and William of Cloudesley* in *Robin Hood and Other Outlaw Tales*, ed. Knight and Ohlgren, pp. 235–67.

[42] *Robin Hood and the Monk* in *Robin Hood and Other Outlaw Tales*, ed. Knight and Ohlgren, pp. 31–48.

[43] *A Gest of Robyn Hode* in *Robin Hood and Other Outlaw Tales*, ed. Knight and Ohlgren, pp. 80–148.

[44] *Specimens of English Literature*, ed. Skeat, pp. 96–107; discussed in Jones, *Outlawry in Medieval Literature*, pp. 38–9.

mass during his twenty years in the wilderness. On the outlaw's death, his brother the hermit is outraged that his penance has gained him salvation, given the extent of his wrongdoing: the outlaw 'neuer wrou3t wel', but 'al hys lyfe hadde ladde amys', as a defiler of women (*The Hermit and the Outlaw*, 82–90, 295–303).[45] There are occasional episodes in the Robin Hood ballads also where a murderous pragmatism unsettles any outlaw claim to ethical superiority. This is particularly so for the episode in *Robin Hood and the Monk* where John and Much kill not only the monk, but also his page (emphatically a 'litul page', a child), who is killed 'for ferd lest he wolde tell' (*Robin Hood and the Monk*, 154, 205, 206).

Outlaw solidarity is important because of the dangers faced by the excluded. Agamben's construction of the *homo sacer* as the man who may be killed without consequence is counterbalanced rather than negated in these texts by loyalty between outlaws: the outlaws still face certain death if captured. William of Cloudesley visits his family despite the warnings of his companions, and is betrayed by an old woman whom he has taken into his household out of charity. In his nostalgia for his family, he has endangered their lives, for the sheriff is prepared not only to kill William, but also to burn his wife and children alive. In *Robin Hood and the Monk*, Robin's capture follows a falling-out with Little John at the tale's outset. The tale emphasises the dangers of conflict within the group and the vulnerability of the isolated outlaw, a message reinforced by the recognition of Little John's fidelity at the end of the ballad by no less a figure than the king himself.[46]

In general, however, literature and law offer very different perspectives on outlawry. In the legal texts, the narrative of outlawry is about exclusion, negation and abjection. But the narrative – and perhaps also the practice – of outlawry also offers the opportunity for a reversal in perspective: outlawry can allow the wanted man to put himself outside the reach of the law. 'Just as the practice of outlawry offers the opportunity for self-help', Timothy Jones suggests, 'the narrative of outlawry offers the opportunity for reinterpretation and self-fashioning'.[47]

It also provides an opportunity for resistance. 'The weakness of power', as Hobsbawm puts it, 'contained the potential for banditry'.[48] But if Hobsbawm's model of the social bandit is a potentially useful one, it requires some qualification. In particular, Hobsbawm's social bandit, with its debts

---

[45] Green, '*The Hermit and the Outlaw*: An Edition'; for a modern English translation, see *The Hermit and the Outlaw*, trans. Kaufman in *Medieval Outlaws*, ed. Ohlgren, pp. 338–55.

[46] As discussed in *Robin Hood and Other Outlaw Tales*, ed. Knight and Ohlgren, p. 33.

[47] Jones, *Outlawry in Medieval Literature*, p. 17.

[48] Hobsbawm, *Bandits*, p. 16.

to twentieth-century Marxism, is a figure from and of the peasantry.[49] While the figure of Robin Hood fulfils Hobsbawm's model in many ways (and is explicitly the archetypal figure that Hobsbawm is thinking of in constructing the social bandit model),[50] the Robin Hood of the early texts is not a peasant, but a yeoman, a somewhat more flexible category.

As Richard Almond and A. J. Pollard observe, Robin Hood's own yeomanry is consistently depicted as that of a yeoman of the forest, a forester, but in the later Middle Ages yeomanry had become an intermediate social category between husbandman and gentleman. This social category below the gentry was swollen by both upward and downward mobility, as both substantial tenants seeking to leave behind their servile origins, and the younger sons and especially grandsons of gentlemen, found positions within this social group.[51]

There is some evidence in early Robin Hood texts for the broad use of the term yeoman. Two of the texts make in passing a broad distinction between two social categories: yeoman and knave (*Robin Hood and the Monk*, 292; *A Gest of Robyn Hode*, 1714). The term *yeoman* is given to tradespersons: the potter of *Robin Hood and the Potter*, and the cook who takes up with Little John in *A Gest of Robyn Hode* (*A Gest of Robyn Hode*, 709).[52] In *Robin Hood and the Potter*, both the yeoman Robin and the ballad's yeoman audience are given the chivalric attribute of being *corteys*, 'courteous'; Robin himself is also *fre*, 'generous' (*Robin Hood and the Potter*, 6, 10).[53] Perhaps most surprisingly, Robin's enemy Sir Guy of Gisborne is described as a 'wight yeoman' (*Robin Hood and Guy of Gisborne*, 25).[54] The honorific 'sir' was used outside

[49] Hobsbawm, *Bandits*, p. 20.
[50] Hobsbawm, *Bandits*, pp. 46–62.
[51] Almond and Pollard, 'The Yeomanry of Robin Hood', p. 53. Discussion of the social context for the literature of Robin Hood has been concerned substantially with defining yeomanry. For Hilton, 'The Origins of Robin Hood', linking the ballads with fourteenth-century agrarian tensions, a yeoman was 'simply a peasant of free personal status' (p. 204). Holt, 'The Origins and the Audience', emphasised the social fluidity of yeomanry, while imagining a social context for the dissemination of the Robin Hood ballads in the halls of the gentry (pp. 224–5) (and cf. Holt, *Robin Hood*, pp. 116–28). Keen's view, originally similar to Hilton's, subsequently agreed with Holt that the yeoman Robin Hood occupied an intermediate state between the peasantry and knighthood, while arguing for a broader context for the ballads' reception than Holt had allowed (Keen, *Outlaws of Medieval Legend*, p. xvii).
[52] Tardif, 'The "Mistery" of Robin Hood', notes the prominence of urban craftsmen in the yeomanry of the Robin Hood ballads.
[53] *Robin Hood and the Potter* in *Robin Hood and Other Outlaw Tales*, ed. Knight and Ohlgren, pp. 57–79.
[54] *Robin Hood and Guy of Gisborne* in *Robin Hood and Other Outlaw Tales*, ed. Knight and Ohlgren, pp. 169–83.

the knightly class,[55] though Robin's opponent is explicitly a knight in the analogous narrative of *Robyn Hod and the Shryff off Notyngham*.[56] Describing Sir Guy as a yeoman extends the definition of yeomanry across a broad social spectrum, as Almond and Pollard suggest.

In *Robin Hood and the Potter*, Robin's sense of social solidarity is initially lacking: he is not above ambushing his fellow yeoman, the potter, at the start of the tale. But when the potter defeats him and rebukes him for a lack of courtesy in obstructing a yeoman at his work, Robin is forced to agree (*Robin Hood and the Potter*, 85–92). The potter's words are *god yemenrey*, 'good yeomanry', and Robin will not obstruct him again (implicitly accepting that class solidarity means he should never have done so in the first place). The two now join in fellowship to outwit a much more appropriate target, the Sheriff of Nottingham. The repeated emphasis on yeomanry and yeoman values in the Robin Hood texts lend an air of class solidarity, certainly, but that class is not the peasantry.

If the social position of the medieval Robin Hood does not quite match Hobsbawm's 'social bandit' archetype, it is also true that not all of the other characteristics of the 'social bandit' apply straightforwardly to medieval outlaw texts. All early Robin Hood texts describe the outlaw hero (in line with Hobsbawm's formulation) as a righter of wrongs. But Gillian Spraggs argues that the specific motif of taking from the rich and giving to the poor may be a late development in the Robin Hood tradition, perhaps as late as the sixteenth century.[57] That motif is explicitly present in John Major's *Historia Majoris Brittaniae* of 1521.[58] It is also present in *A Gest of Robyn Hode*, but here we have the problem of dating. The existing text of the *Gest* is from the early sixteenth century; the date of composition is unclear, but may be mid-fifteenth century; it is, in any case, something of a compilation of previous material.[59] In the *Gest*, Robin instructs his outlaws lying in wait for passers-by as follows:

> Whether he be messengere,
> Or a man that myrthes can,
> Of my good he shall have some,
> Yf he be a pore man. (*A Gest of Robyn Hode*, 837–40)

---

[55] Discussed in *Robin Hood and Other Outlaw Tales*, ed. Knight and Ohlgren, p. 169, citing *Reliques of Ancient English Poetry*, ed. Percy, I, 86.

[56] *Robyn Hod and the Shryff off Notyngham* in *Robin Hood and Other Outlaw Tales*, ed. Knight and Ohlgren, pp. 269–80.

[57] Spraggs, *Outlaws and Highwaymen*, pp. 51–2, 279; cf. Hobsbawm, *Bandits*, pp. 46–8.

[58] *Robin Hood and Other Outlaw Tales*, ed. Knight and Ohlgren, p. 27.

[59] Knight, *Robin Hood: A Complete Study*, pp. 46–9; *Robin Hood and Other Outlaw Tales*, ed. Knight and Ohlgren, pp. 80–1.

The ballad closes with:

> For he was a good outlawe,
> And dyde pore men moch god. (*A Gest of Robyn Hode*, 1823–4)

Where the narrative of the *Gest* actually tells of Robin helping the poor, however, the beneficiary is a knight reduced to penury: here, Robin's actions are a restoration of an idealised social order rather than a challenge to it. However, as Stephen Knight suggests, these last-quoted lines need not be read as suggesting financial support for 'the poor' as a social category. 'Like other social bandits from Ned Kelly to Salvatore Giuliano', says Knight, 'the early Robin Hood takes from the rich to give not to some loosely identified poor, but to protect those who are his own affiliates'. Rather, Robin's generosity is shown in that 'he welcomes people to his service, provides them with food, clothing and protection'.[60]

The struggle against injustice is the motivating factor for medieval outlaw heroes such as Hereward and Fouke Fitz Waryn from the outset of the tradition. In the later medieval period, the corruption of justice is a substantial motif. In *The Tale of Gamelyn*, we see the use of public office to settle private scores when Gamelyn's brother becomes sheriff and outlaws Gamelyn, indicting him, and declaring him 'wolfshead' (*Gamelyn*, 705–6). In *A Gest of Robyn Hode*, an impoverished knight faces a chief justice of England in the pay of his opponent (*A Gest of Robyn Hode*, 371–4, 425–6) – an example of the widespread contemporary problem of maintenance (private networks of loyalty to powerful individuals which conflicted with the public administration of justice).[61] Here, it is Robin Hood, not the courts, who will do justice.

This critique of the justice system aligns the literature of outlawry with the extensive tradition of satire and complaint in later medieval literature. As Anthony Musson and Mark Ormrod rightly observe, the fourteenth century was an age of complaint,[62] and there is a great deal of late medieval complaint about the law and its administration. Hostility towards the law and lawyers finds substantial expression in literature, in preaching,[63] and even in social revolt. The rising of 1381, prompted not only by the 1380 poll tax but by the judicial commissions which follow it,[64] sees not only attacks on lawyers

---

[60] Knight, *Robin Hood: A Complete Study*, p. 79.
[61] Keen, *English Society in the Later Middle Ages*, p. 207.
[62] Musson and Ormrod, *Evolution of English Justice*, p. 189.
[63] See Owst, *Literature and Pulpit*, pp. 338–49.
[64] Harding, 'The Revolt Against the Justices'; Musson and Ormrod, *Evolution of English Justice*, p. 97.

and the release of prisoners, but radical demands for legal reform.[65] Literary satire of contemporary justice complains particularly about the partiality of judges aligned with the powerful and the financial corruption of the legal system. Sometimes, as in Chaucer's *General Prologue to the Canterbury Tales*, that satire is circumspect (at least regarding officials of the secular courts).[66] Elsewhere, as in Langland's *Piers Plowman*, it is forcefully direct: here, the contemporary administration of law is attacked as corrupt, especially in those early passages of the poem dealing with the allegorical figure of Mede, or reward.[67] The literature of outlawry likewise offers a social critique. As Joseph Nagy puts it, 'the world of Robin Hood is based on essential social values such as truth, loyalty, honesty, reciprocity, and religiosity' – values seen to be lacking in the world outside.[68]

In some late medieval texts, satire against the failings of the legal system has political implications. In *Richard the Redeless* (a poem in the 'Piers Plowman tradition' written after Richard II's deposition), the failings of law are attributable to the monarch's own lawlessness (*Richard the Redeless*, I, 88–9).[69] In *Mum and the Sothsegger*, the legal system is still corrupt, but the verdict on the king is more politic: the lack of a *sothsegger*, a truth-teller, leaves the king unaware of the corruption and manipulation of the legal system. If the king only knew what the common people said, he would amend the situation (*Mum and the Sothsegger*, 133–8).[70] This belief that the king will do justice is also found in the literature of outlawry. In line with Hobsbawm's definition of the social bandit, the outlaw of medieval literature is not usually opposed to the sovereign and the sovereign's justice, but rather to the oppression of local enforcers.[71] This is a characteristic found in medieval political verse generally, where the king is conventionally a friend of the oppressed against unjust officials.[72] We see the king grant mercy to the outlaws, for instance, in *A Gest of Robyn Hode* and in *Adam Bell, Clim of the Clough and William of Cloudesley*. Sometimes, though, that mercy seems tentative and fragile. In *Robin Hood and the Monk*, Little John has tricked the king (*Robin Hood and the Monk*, 331–54). In *Adam Bell, Clim of the Clough and*

---

[65] *Crime, Law and Society in the Later Middle Ages*, ed. Musson with Powell, p. 61.

[66] McCarthy, 'Injustice and Chaucer's Man of Law'.

[67] Langland, *Piers Plowman*, ed. Pearsall.

[68] Nagy, 'The Paradoxes of Robin Hood', p. 424; cf. Gray, 'The Robin Hood Poems', p. 36.

[69] *Richard the Redeless* in *The Piers Plowman Tradition*, ed. Barr.

[70] *Mum and the Sothsegger* in *The Piers Plowman Tradition*, ed. Barr. For further examples of the satirical treatment of lawlessness and injustice in fifteenth-century literature, see Scattergood, *Politics and Poetry*, pp. 316–25.

[71] Hobsbawm, *Bandits*, p. 48.

[72] Scattergood, *Politics and Poetry*, p. 360.

William of Cloudesley, the king's mercy is obtained through a combination of fast work and the queen's intervention: had the messengers from the north arrived earlier, the outlaws would have hanged (*Adam Bell*, 544–51). In fact, the king still seems minded to hang them if William does not succeed in his subsequent feat of archery (*Adam Bell*, 616–23). Elsewhere, however, the king and the outlaws have, as Helen Phillips puts it, something approaching a symbiotic relationship.[73]

Medieval outlaw literature, then, offers a vision of outlaw solidarity and resistance, a vision akin to that of Hobsbawm's social bandit (albeit with qualifications). The outlaw appears here not as a solitary outcast, but as a member of a confederacy, supported by his companions and by elements of the mainstream community. Some texts, the Robin Hood texts in particular, carry a strong sense of class solidarity (though amongst the yeomanry rather than the peasantry). The outlaw is also an ethical figure whose belief in justice contrasts with the corruption of the king's officials, a portrayal that aligns the literature of outlawry with anti-legal satire elsewhere. If outlaw literature offers a strong contrast to the representation of outlawry in medieval legal texts, however, it qualifies rather than contradicts that representation. Beneath the overt narratives where the outlaws thrive in the greenwood, and constantly win against impossible odds, there lurks a latent sense of the dangers and hardships faced by the excluded. But in its portrayal of the outlaw as a figure of resistance, the medieval literature of outlawry offers an important modification of the representation offered in the legal texts.

Folville's Laws: Criminality in Later Medieval England

If literary texts complicate the legal perspective on outlawry, matters become more complex still when we turn to evidence of actual practice. There is certainly evidence of a contemporary sense of a crisis of lawlessness in later medieval England.[74] 'We have clear and abundant evidence of a contemporary sense of crisis', writes Richard Kaeuper of the early fourteenth century, 'and what makes this evidence all the more impressive is the variety of witnesses in agreement'.[75]

That sense of a crisis of lawlessness is not separable, of course, from the other shocks to afflict later medieval England, economic, demographic and political. The famines of 1315–17 and 1323–33 and the Black Death from 1348 onwards brought population collapse, economic recession and

---

[73] Phillips, 'Bandit Territories and Good Outlaws', p. 11.
[74] Bellamy, *Crime and Public Order*, pp. 3–10.
[75] Kaeuper, 'Law and Order in Fourteenth-Century England', p. 735.

substantial social change.[76] Politically, the fourteenth century saw the deposition of Edward II, the revolts of 1381, and the deposition of Richard II, before the country's eventual slide into the civil wars of the fifteenth century. Ongoing intermittent warfare with France through the Hundred Years War was supplemented by war with Scotland, and conflict in both Ireland and in Wales.

Some of the perceived crisis of criminality in later medieval England was certainly associated with outlaw bands. These groups differed from literary outlaws in some key ways. First, some prominent bandit groups draw their personnel from the gentry, rather than the yeomanry of the literary texts. John Bellamy's study of medieval crime suggests that gang leaders were often drawn from the gentry, with a wide variety of lower status individuals making up the remaining membership.[77] As Barbara Hanawalt's study of upper-class crime in the fourteenth century emphasises, there is a fine line between upper-class lawbreaking and a long tradition of the upper class asserting its perceived rights through force.[78] Secondly, the victims of criminal gangs were more broadly based in real life than in outlaw literature. While ambushing travelling merchants, clergy, nobles and government officials was potentially lucrative for outlaws, in reality bandits also stole extensively from the peasantry to obtain everyday goods, and violent robberies of households meant that women and children were more likely to be killed by bandits than by ordinary homicide.[79] Outlaw groups could contribute to a sense of disorder on a larger scale: later medieval bandit gangs were capable not only of ambushing individuals and groups, and attacking individual dwellings, but sometimes of attacking ports, market towns and fairs.[80] Finally, if literary outlaws are sometimes ethically exemplary figures who stand apart from the corruption of local law enforcement, real outlaws are sometimes participants in the local conflicts for power which undermine later medieval justice: they are participants in the corruption of the law rather than a remedy for it. Lords, as Bellamy observes, were by no means above maintaining outlaws as part of their households, or hiring outlaw gangs for specific purposes.[81]

Two fourteenth-century gangs, the Folvilles and the Coterels, have been

---

[76] See Hanawalt, 'Economic Influences' for increases in crime during famine years in the early fourteenth century.

[77] Bellamy, *Crime and Public Order*, pp. 72–3.

[78] Hanawalt, 'Fur-Collar Crime'.

[79] Hanawalt, 'Ballads and Bandits', pp. 276–8.

[80] Hanawalt, 'Ballads and Bandits', p. 278.

[81] Bellamy, *Crime and Public Order*, pp. 70, 73–4.

studied in detail.[82] The Folville brothers were gentry, as were some of their associates, and had influence in higher circles.[83] Their long career extended from the 1320s to the 1340s, and their notoriety – and possibly a certain sympathetic outlook – is suggested by Langland's late fourteenth-century reference to 'Folville's laws'. The legal weapons of outlawry and trailbaston[84] were largely ineffective against them, and their crimes included attacks on prominent persons: in 1332, with the aid of accomplices, they kidnapped a justice, Sir Richard Willoughby, who later served as Chief Justice of the king's bench.[85] The Coterel gang were contemporaries of the Folvilles, and occasionally their collaborators: they, too, were involved in the Willoughby kidnapping. The core of such gangs was often quite small: the Folville gang had four brothers at its core; the Coterels a larger group of perhaps twenty.[86] But they relied upon a broader network for support: 175 people were accused of supporting the Coterels in Derbyshire,[87] and, like the Folvilles, they too had influential supporters.[88]

If the reality of medieval outlawry substantially complicates the literary portrayal of the outlaw, some crossover is visible nonetheless. We can sometimes see a slippage between fiction and real life when real outlaws either appropriate or are assigned the names of fictional outlaws.[89] David Crook notes the early use of the name 'Robin Hood' (in 1262) to describe an outlaw: an outlawed man named William son of Robert le Fevere has his name altered in a document where he appears as William 'Robehod'. A clerk who knew something of the Robin Hood legend has renamed William after the fictional outlaw.[90] In 1417, we find Robert Stafford, a chaplain from Lindfield, in Sussex, adopting the name 'Frere Tuk' as an outlaw persona.[91] A 1439 parliamentary petition names Piers Venables, a gentleman, fifteen other named yeomen who wear his livery, and 'many other unknowyn' who

---

[82] Stones, 'The Folvilles'; Bellamy, 'The Coterel Gang'.

[83] Stones, 'The Folvilles', pp. 118, 121, 124, 128–9.

[84] Judicial commissions instituted in 1305.

[85] Stones, 'The Folvilles', p. 122; *Crime, Law and Society*, ed. Musson with Powell, pp. 75–9.

[86] There are occasional references to much larger groups: Bellamy, *Crime and Public Order*, pp. 70–2.

[87] Bellamy, 'Coterel Gang', p. 715.

[88] Bellamy, 'Coterel Gang', pp. 701, 702–4.

[89] I am grateful to several people for noting that 'Outlaw' is itself a surname, prominent in an early fourteenth-century Irish case where Alice Kyteler is accused of sorcery. Alice's first husband and son are both named William Outlaw; her brother-in-law, the king's chancellor in Ireland, is Roger Outlaw: Williams, 'Sorcery Trial'.

[90] Crook, 'Some Further Evidence'.

[91] *Crime, Law and Society*, ed. Musson with Powell, p. 62.

have taken to the woods 'like as it hadde be Robynhode and his meyne', from where they cause havoc in Scropton and neighbouring areas as far as Cheshire.[92] In 1441, we find a group of Norfolk labourers blocking the highway, threatening to murder Sir Geoffrey Harsyk, and singing 'We arn Robynhodesmen, war, war, war'.[93] Many people in the later Middle Ages play at being outlaws via the various plays and games of Robin Hood that were common in later medieval England:[94] sometimes, that play crosses over with the serious business of medieval crime.

Medieval English Law and its Exceptions

The later Middle Ages had a theoretically unified model of law. There were three different types of law: divine, natural and positive. All were interrelated. Divine law was the will of God. Natural law consisted of fundamental notions of right and wrong, reason informed by the will of God. The sinful nature of postlapsarian humanity meant that natural law needed to be supplemented by a third form of law, positive law: laws explicitly formulated by God or man. But positive law did not exist separately from the two higher forms of law: if legislation differed from divine or natural law, it was not law at all.[95] The implicit interrelation of the legal and the theological here is visible in the nature of the Bible as legal text, a text that prescribes laws that Christians must adhere to, and a text that, in its Latin translation, was filled with Roman legal terminology: the Bible entered Latin culture clothed in the language of law.[96]

In contrast to this theoretically unified legal universe, however, actual practice in later medieval England strikes us as fragmented. The country had 'a palimpsest of jurisdictions': as well as the king's courts (ruling by the common law, or via the king's prerogative in the conciliar courts), there were ecclesiastical courts (ruling via ecclesiastical law) and customary courts (communal and manorial courts ruling by local custom).[97] As S. F. C. Milsom puts it, 'in the fourteenth century there was no law of England, no body of rules complete in itself with known limits and visible defects; or if there was it was not the property of the common law courts or any others'.[98]

---

[92] *Rotuli Parliamentorum*, ed. Strachey, V, 16.

[93] Knight, *Robin Hood: A Mythic Biography*, p. 8.

[94] Knight, *Robin Hood: A Mythic Biography*, pp. 8–13.

[95] Alford, 'Literature and Law in Medieval England', pp. 942–3.

[96] Ullmann, *Law and Politics in the Middle Ages*, pp. 42–6; Ullmann, 'Historical Jurisprudence'.

[97] Musson and Ormrod, *Evolution of English Justice*, p. 8.

[98] Milsom, *Historical Foundations of the Common Law*, p. 83. To a large degree, different business was transacted in different courts: Musson and Ormrod, *Evolution of English Justice*, p. 9.

These fragmented legal structures created a variety of visible exceptions and exclusions. First, not everyone in England had access to justice in the king's courts. Villeins – unfree tenants, who numbered perhaps half the rural population in 1300 – could receive legal redress only in their lords' courts, not in the king's.[99] Married women, too, could not take legal action in common law courts without their husbands (customary courts and customary law sometimes afforded them a different status).[100] In theory, women could not be outlawed: *Bracton* claims that as they are not under the law to begin with, women are 'waived', abandoned as waifs rather than outlaws (though actual practice differs).[101] Conflict could arise between the jurisdictions of church and state:[102] in a 1342 case, a royal clerk outlaws some clergy, and is himself excommunicated for doing so.[103] Various marginal figures also had their legal rights curtailed. The separate legal position of England's Jewish community, initially a sign of the king's protection, came over time to stand for restriction rather than privilege, and the entire Jewish population of England was finally expelled on the king's authority in 1290.[104]

The king's own legal status adds an additional layer of complexity. The long-standing idea that the king was above the law endures in this period in the sense that no legal action may be taken against him. There was, nonetheless, a sense that the king ought to be law-abiding: hence Ernst Kantorowicz's formula for the medieval English monarch as *rex infra et super legem*, a king both under and above the law.[105] The exceptional legal position of the king extended beyond his person to the geographical space around him: from about 1290 the court of the verge exercised a special jurisdiction involving the crown's domestic servants, certain acts affronting the royal dignity, and breaches of the king's peace within a twelve-mile radius of the sovereign's presence.[106]

---

[99] Musson and Ormrod, *Evolution of English Justice*, p. 9. On the decline of villeinage from the mid-fourteenth century, see Bailey, *The Decline of Serfdom*, pp. 4–5, 10–11, 285–306.

[100] McCarthy, *Marriage in Medieval England*, pp. 60–2.

[101] *Bracton*, ed. Woodbine, trans. Thorne, II, 353–4. I am grateful to Bridgette Slavin for the observation that, in practice, court records do show women being outlawed.

[102] I am grateful to Sybil Jack for this point.

[103] Gosling, *Church, State, and Reformation*, pp. 115–16.

[104] Brand, 'Jews and the Law'.

[105] Kantorowicz, *The King's Two Bodies*, pp. 143–64. Sovereign immunity is discussed at length in Chapter 2, below.

[106] Jones, 'The Court of the Verge'. McIntosh, 'Immediate Royal Justice', suggests that, in practice, the court exceeded its jurisdiction by hearing private disputes of people unconnected with the royal household, providing litigants with swift justice and the crown with a small, but regular, income stream.

The king also had several other courts not governed by the common law and its procedures. The king's council, and other courts associated with it, offered judgment via the king's prerogative justice rather than the common law. Chancery had an emerging jurisdiction as a court of conscience, or equity, rather than law. Finally, in addition to its other functions, parliament also acted as a high court, and increasingly became the necessary venue for state trials concerned with matters such as treason or impeachment.[107]

Aside from this fragmentation of legal venues and forms of law, there were a number of ways in which wrongdoers might escape legal punishment. First, fugitives from justice (with certain specified exceptions) could seek sanctuary in consecrated buildings or land (and some secular liberties in northern England and the Welsh Marches).[108] Secondly, anyone in holy orders could claim benefit of clergy in the secular courts (with crimes such as treason excepted). If their claim to clerical status was accepted, the prisoner would be transferred to the ecclesiastical jurisdiction for trial: for those accused of felonies, this meant imprisonment and penance rather than hanging. *The Outlaw's Song of Trailbaston* alludes to the possibility of claiming clerical status for those who are literate and tonsured, but nonetheless suggests that outlawry in the woods is preferable to the bishop's prison.[109] While the minimum requirement for claiming clerical status was literacy (specifically the ability to read verses from Psalm 51), stricter requirements might be imposed: a tonsure, clerical clothing, and acceptance by a representative of the ordinary that the accused was a genuine cleric.[110] Be that as it may, benefit of clergy could provide a loophole for literate prisoners to escape secular punishment.[111]

In other instances, the king employed political rather than judicial means to restore public order, employing the prerogative of mercy rather than legal process.[112] Pardons were purchased for money or through performance of military service, and criminals sometimes seem to have been offered inducements, such as appointment to office, to lure them from crime. The extensive use of pardons was a cause for contemporary concern: the crown agreed to statutory limitations on the use of pardons in 1328, 1330, 1336 and 1340, but parliamentary complaint endured into the 1350s.[113]

---

[107] Musson and Ormrod, *Evolution of English Justice*, pp. 20–8.
[108] Bellamy, *Crime and Public Order*, pp. 106–14.
[109] *Political Songs*, ed. and trans. Wright, pp. 231–6; English translation, *The Outlaw's Song of Trailbaston*, trans. Revard in *Medieval Outlaws*, ed. Ohlgren, pp. 151–64.
[110] *Crime, Law and Society*, ed. Musson with Powell, pp. 179–80.
[111] Bellamy, *Crime and Public Order*, pp. 151–5. Hanawalt, 'Ballads and Bandits', p. 269, notes high participation rates for clergy in bandit gangs and suggests this as an explanation.
[112] Bellamy, *Crime and Public Order*, pp. 85–7.
[113] Musson and Ormrod, *Evolution of English Justice*, pp. 79–80.

Finally, there were geographical qualifications to the operation of the common law. In addition to the customary jurisdictions of boroughs and liberties, forests were governed specifically by forest law, rather than common law.[114] Border areas were subject to the laws of the March (discussed further below), as well as the common law. In a practical sense, the majesty of the law was considerably less potent in the remoter parts of the kingdom. Remote and impoverished areas, says Gerald Harriss, 'were bandit country'.[115] Musson and Ormrod, similarly, suggest that incidents such the 1317 hold-up where Sir Gilbert Middleton robbed two cardinals and kidnapped the Bishop of Durham-elect, 'highlighted the degree to which the north had fallen beyond the effective reach of the crown'.[116]

Law, Outlawry, Sovereignty and the State

If the medieval English legal system was a fragmentary one, an increasing coherence and expansion of royal justice are nonetheless of fundamental importance in creating the later medieval English state.[117] If Richard Kaeuper has argued that a thirteenth-century 'law state' is forced to give way to a fourteenth-century 'war state', Musson and Ormrod suggest that the late thirteenth and fourteenth centuries saw an ongoing evolution of English justice, with royal justice eroding the jurisdiction of the customary courts in what they term 'a veritable "nationalisation" of English justice'.[118] Royal justice was growing in scope in the later medieval period, and outlawry beginning to decline in effectiveness: evidence from fifteenth-century petitions suggests that by this period, outlawry could be held in contempt.[119] We might assume, then, as suggested by the 'weak state' thesis of Maitland and Keen, that legal exclusion is a tactic of power that is superseded as the state grows in authority.

---

[114] This separate jurisdiction is asserted in the late twelfth century by FitzNigel, *Dialogus de Scaccario*, pp. 59–60. Henry II's Charter of the Forest 1217 conceded that 'no one shall henceforth lose life or limb because of our venison' (*English Historical Documents, 1189–1327*, ed. Rothwell, pp. 329–31). On the medieval forest more broadly, see Saunders, *The Forest of Medieval Romance*, pp. 1–10.

[115] Harriss, *Shaping the Nation*, p. 201.

[116] Musson and Ormrod, *Evolution of English Justice*, pp. 78; *Crime, Law and Society*, ed. Musson with Powell, pp. 74–5; discussion in Prestwich, 'Gilbert de Middleton and the Attack on the Cardinals, 1317'.

[117] As argued in different ways by Kaeuper, *War, Justice, and Public Order* and Harding, *Medieval Law and the Foundations of the State*.

[118] Kaeuper, *War, Justice, and Public Order*; Musson and Ormrod, *Evolution of English Justice*, pp. 9–10.

[119] Bellamy, *Crime and Public Order*, pp. 116–17.

This is not quite what happens. First, we should not assume that the increased scope of royal justice was effective: Kaeuper argues that the medieval state's ambitions to provide justice raised expectations it could not meet.[120] Perceptions of lawlessness endured. There was a sense that the judiciary were both corrupt and punitive, and that the powerful successfully employed financial resources and legal guile in tandem with the previously available method of brute force in pursuit of their interests.[121] There was, as we have seen, substantial satire of the legal system in later medieval English writing. And while unrest from the lower classes, most obvious in the rising of 1381, has often been read in terms of economic tensions, there may also be a legal dimension, with a sense that traditional rights were being infringed by a growing national legal system.[122] If royal justice grows in scope, then, this does not lead to an increased confidence in the justice system.

Nor does the expansion of royal justice necessarily lead to the disappearance of exclusion from law. To explain why, we must qualify the 'weak state' explanation for the employment of outlawry. Outlawry is not only a reactive tactic of a weak state to enforce its legal authority over resistant elements of its population. Exclusion from law can also be a proactive tactic of a growing state power designed to destabilise internal and external opponents, and any alternative claims to sovereignty they might pose. In other words, it can be a political weapon. As well as the direct use of outlawry against those deemed rebels or traitors,[123] John Bellamy suggests that from the mid-thirteenth century, to be formally reputed a traitor 'must have been roughly the same as being outlawed', allowing rebels to be hanged immediately on capture.[124] This is by no means a late medieval phenomenon only: Timothy Jones notes early English examples where individuals are *flymed* (put to flight, exiled or outlawed) for political rather than criminal reasons: the *Anglo-Saxon Chronicle* describes Ine of Wessex's conflict with Ealdberht, a claimant to his throne, whom he had previously exiled.[125]

Outlawry is paradoxical, after all. A declaration of exclusion is both an acceptance of the weakness of the sovereign's position, and an attempt to enforce the sovereign's power. The sovereign seeks to *include* the excluded

---

[120] Kaeuper, *War, Justice, and Public Order*, pp. 2–3.
[121] McFarlane, *The Nobility of Later Medieval England*, p. 115.
[122] Musson and Ormrod, *Evolution of English Justice*, p. 98; Harding, 'The Revolt against the Justices'; Green, *A Crisis of Truth*, pp. 198–9.
[123] Bellamy, *Law of Treason*, pp. 28, 33–9, 49–50, 53, 171–2, 196, offers several examples.
[124] Bellamy, *Law of Treason*, p. 28, and cf. the discussion of attainder, pp. 177–205.
[125] Jones, *Outlawry in Medieval Literature*, pp. 21–2, citing *The Anglo-Saxon Chronicle*, ed. Cubbin, p. 11.

person within their authority to punish by *excluding* them from their power to protect. Agamben describes this paradox of exclusion/inclusion as follows: the *homo sacer* 'is in a continuous relationship with the power that banished him precisely insofar as he is at every instant exposed to an unconditioned threat of death'.[126] The paradox of outlawry is that in excluding the outlaw from the law, it simultaneously insists on the outlaw's inclusion under the power of the sovereign. Expansion *of* law and exclusion *from* law, then, may serve the interests of state power in tandem.

Finally, if sovereign power expands substantially in the later medieval period, it remains far from absolute. The English crown is remarkably successful in expanding the extent and the depth of its authority through the central and later Middle Ages. As Robin Frame comments, in 1100 Britain and Ireland have many and varied kings; by 1270 the kings of England and of Scots have eliminated some of the other kingships and are posing hard questions for those others still hanging on.[127] But, as Helen Phillips writes, English monarchs of the fourteenth and fifteenth centuries 'often lacked secure sovereignty in the sense in which continental theorists like Foucault or Agamben conceive it'.[128] The medieval English sovereign could not claim a monopoly on law and violence within his lands. The king's sovereignty was relative, not absolute: it existed in varying degrees of intensity across a flexible range of territories and peoples. Joseph Strayer suggests that by the thirteenth century, notions of external sovereignty, where a monarch had no external superior, were entrenched (even this, as we shall see, requires qualification for the Anglo-Scottish relationship), but acceptance of internal sovereignty in an absolute sense was contested through the Middle Ages.[129] If Derrida suggests that we might, in the twenty-first century, begin to deconstruct sovereignty by recognising its divisible and contested nature,[130] we can also recognise that the fragmented and contested nature of sovereignty is clearly on show in the premodern state.

We can also see that outlawry and its literature are places where tensions around sovereignty are made visible. In *The Deeds of Hereward* (*Gesta Herewardi*), an early outlaw text, an English outlaw avenges himself on the Normans who have murdered his younger brother, and joins a group of Englishmen who are holding out against the conquest. The challenge that

---

[126] Agamben, *Homo Sacer*, p. 183.
[127] Frame, *Political Development of the British Isles*, p. 98.
[128] Phillips, 'Bandit Territories and Good Outlaws', p. 15.
[129] Strayer, 'The Historical Experience of Nation-Building in Europe', pp. 344–5; cf. Canning, 'Law, Sovereignty and Corporation Theory', pp. 464–9.
[130] Derrida, *The Beast & the Sovereign*, I, 76, 290–1.

such resistance poses to the legitimacy of the powers-that-be is obvious.[131] Likewise, in *The Romance of Fouke Fitz Waryn*, Fouke, like Hereward an historical figure, asserts his feudal rights and dissolves his allegiance to King John before taking up arms against him.[132] Oaths of fealty, like earlier medieval oaths of loyalty, incur mutual obligations. A king's failure to meet his obligations allows his vassal to renounce his homage, to perform *diffidatio*, and therefore to engage in open conflict against his former lord the king, in a way that becomes impossible from the late thirteenth century as treason begins to be defined not simply as a personal betrayal, a breach of oath, but as a crime against the sovereign.[133]

Such straightforward political frameworks for armed resistance against an unjust monarch or an unjust state are mostly lacking for later medieval English outlaws, literary or real (although, as we shall see in the next chapter, one way of reading Henry Bolingbroke is as just such an outlaw). But there are several examples of later medieval outlawry that render vulnerable the claims to authority of those in power. Extensive lawlessness itself may be seen as a threat to royal authority: Richard Kaeuper notes Edward I's characterisation of the trailbaston ordinance of 1305 as enacted 'to suppress the disorders, tumults and outrages of the past, which were like the start of war and which flouted the lordship of the king'. This, Kaeuper notes, is not a declaration for public effect, but a private communication recorded on the King's Remembrancer Memoranda Roll.[134]

In some later medieval texts, the outlaws have their own king and their own justice. When Gamelyn takes to the forest, he asks the outlaws who their master is; they reply that 'Oure maister is crowned of outlawe king' (*Gamelyn*, 655). Shortly afterwards, Gamelyn himself is crowned king of the outlaws (*Gamelyn*, 689–90). In *A Gest of Robyn Hode*, Robin Hood is implicitly compared to King Arthur by the motif of refusing to eat until he hears of some adventure (*Gest*, 19–28). Such parallels or parodies of authority are also found among real outlaw gangs, who adopt the royal style in sending letters of extortion, hold quasi-formal assembles, and in the case of at least one fourteenth-century outlaw, Lionel 'king of the rout of raveners', adopting

[131] *The Deeds of Hereward*, trans. Swanton in *Medieval Outlaws*, ed. Ohlgren, pp. 28–99.

[132] *Two Medieval Outlaws*, ed. and trans. Burgess, p. 151.

[133] Bellamy, *Law of Treason*, pp. 23–39; Green, *A Crisis of Truth*, pp. 208–21.

[134] Kaeuper, 'Law and Order in Fourteenth-Century England', p. 737. The trailbaston ordinances are 'une especial ordenance faite pur redrescer les riotes e les outrages faitz que feurent come comencement de guerre, e a la desobeissance de la seignureie le roi' (*Calendar of Close Rolls: Edward I. Vol. V. A. D. 1302–1307*, p. 454).

a title parodying monarchical authority.[135] These are almost carnivalesque figures: bandits exiled to the margins of society who parody royal authority as a means of challenging it.

There are also examples of groups taking the law into their own hands, either in parody or with real intent. In 1344, the conclusion of judicial sessions in Ipswich is followed by a parodic re-enactment where those indicted and their accomplices take on the judicial role and summon the two justices and those appearing for the crown to appear in turn before them, 'in contempt of the king and in mockery of the aforesaid justices and ministers of the lord king'.[136] A similar reversal occurs at the conclusion of *The Tale of Gamelyn*, where the outlaw Gamelyn, rescuing his brother from a corrupt trial, himself sits in the judge's seat, and has the judge, the sheriff (also his brother), and the jurors hanged (*Gamelyn*, 831–82). As John Scattergood puts it, 'Gamelyn and his followers have not only exacted vengeance, but have also subverted royal power in this instance and appropriated it to themselves, albeit temporarily'.[137] Outside the realm of parody, in the later medieval period we find that the killing of outlaws may come close to being viewed as usurpation of royal authority. A Leicester gaol delivery case from 1408 describes how six individuals imprisoned two men, Richard Bradford and Robert Webster. Two, acting as judges, condemned Bradford and Webster to death; they were beheaded, and their heads sent to Leicester. The six are in prison for usurping royal power without legal authority, acting 'against the crown and dignity of the lord king and to the manifest weakening and detriment of his laws'. What they may have been doing, however, was exercising summary justice against outlaws: their later appearance in court with royal pardons may indicate that this was indeed the case.[138]

We must be careful not to make too much of these examples. If outlawry can pose a challenge to sovereignty, in practice, sovereigns are also capable of exploiting the liminal position of outlaws to their own purposes. A useful example might be Eustace the Monk, who again is both an historical figure and protagonist of a thirteenth-century romance. A nobleman from the Boulonnais in northern France, Eustace is driven to outlawry after a dispute with his lord, the Count of Boulogne, a dispute linked in the romance

---

[135] *Crime, Law and Society*, ed. Musson with Powell, pp. 45–6; Bellamy, *Crime and Public Order*, pp. 76–8; Keen, *Outlaws of Medieval Legend*, pp. 200–2.

[136] *Crime, Law and Society*, ed. Musson with Powell, pp. 46–7.

[137] Scattergood, '*The Tale of Gamelyn*', p. 88; Scattergood reads the poem as representing the values of the provincial gentry, 'a set of attitudes and a voice not so much from the greenwood as from the backwoods, resistant to a centralism it mistrusts' (p. 99).

[138] *Crime, Law and Society*, ed. Musson with Powell, pp. 35–7.

account to ongoing tensions between Eustace and his father's murderer, Hainfrois de Heresinghen.[139] From about 1205, Eustace is found in the service of England's King John, whose loss of territory in northern France will lead to the end of the 'Angevin empire'. Eustace serves John in helping to capture the Channel Islands, and raiding in France, but he also maintains a parallel career as a pirate, causing losses to French and English alike. John, at least for a time, is prepared to turn a blind eye to Eustace's piracy and its effects on his subjects – political expediency trumps legality here.[140] Around a decade later, however, things have changed. By 1214, Eustace has escaped from England and transferred his allegiance to France;[141] John, the romance tells us, retaliates by killing, burning and disfiguring Eustace's daughter.[142] Eustace himself is killed by the English at the Battle of Sandwich in 1217.

In the literary texts, too, these latent alternative sovereignties are always safely absorbed into a model of ultimate loyalty to the monarch. Gamelyn, for instance, having served as king of the outlaws, and having hanged a judge, sheriff and jury, makes peace with the king immediately thereafter, and he and his brother are subsequently appointed to real judicial offices (*Gamelyn*, 883–99). 'Alle his wight yonge men', we are told, 'the king foryaf her gilt' (*Gamelyn*, 889), and this forgiveness and appointment to office annuls any potential threat to royal sovereignty. If literary texts are often visibly keen to downplay the challenges outlawry might pose to ideologies of sovereignty, and sovereign power is perfectly capable of exploiting the outlaw's exceptional status to its own ends, outlawry and outlaw texts nonetheless remains a location where tensions around sovereign authority are visibly played out.

Archipelagic Outlawry

Outlawry, we are suggesting here, is not just a reactive gesture by a weak state but also a way in which sovereign power is asserted. Exclusion from law is sometimes a proactive tactic of the state intended to destabilise opponents, and this proactive tactic is of particular use in contesting alternative claims to forms of sovereignty, in an era where the sovereign power of the monarch is expanding. If this is so, it is especially visible in the protocolonial context of medieval England's dealings with Scotland, Ireland and Wales, where questions of law and legal exclusion in several senses are visibly used to political ends.

---

[139] *Two Medieval Outlaws*, ed. and trans. Burgess, pp. 53–5.
[140] *Two Medieval Outlaws*, ed. and trans. Burgess, pp. 16–17.
[141] For his possible motivation, see *Two Medieval Outlaws*, ed. and trans. Burgess, pp. 22–31, 76).
[142] *Two Medieval Outlaws*, ed. and trans. Burgess, p. 77.

England regularly asserted overlordship over Wales, Scotland and Ireland through the later medieval period, but the realisation of these claims ebbed and flowed. English dominance reached a peak in 1175, when Henry II received a delegation of Welsh leaders at Gloucester, imposed the treaty of Falaise on the king of Scotland, and the treaty of Windsor on the representatives of the Irish high-king. It reached another after Edward I's conquest of Wales in 1282–3 and political ascendancy over the Scots in the 1290s.[143] Only Wales was definitively conquered in the medieval period, and even then, its complete annexation to England did not occur until the sixteenth century; the final conquest of Ireland and the union of crowns between England and Scotland did not occur until the seventeenth century. But England exercised a claim to possession, an ongoing physical presence, and a substantial political, cultural and legal influence in these neighbouring territories across the later medieval period.

If the English monarchy's long-term strategy in the central and later Middle Ages was one of overlordship across the archipelago, it employed a flexible but interlocking range of tactics – military, political and cultural – in pursuit of this goal. Over the long term, these tactics involved the non-recognition of the sovereign status of neighbouring territories, their rulers, and their legal systems, rendering these subservient to, and ultimately replaceable by, the legal and governmental systems of the emerging English state.

If, as we have just seen, outlaw literature and practice in the later Middle Ages threw up several outlaw 'kings' and parodies of royal justice within England itself, the growth of English power across medieval Britain and Ireland faced as obstacles some very real alternative rulers and legal systems. Initially, the English monarchy, growing dominant in the archipelago, recognised these alternative rulers while asserting its overlordship. In doing so, however, it prepared the ground for later, more extensive claims. The Treaty of Falaise between Henry II and William, king of Scots, referred to Scotland as a land (*terra*) not a kingdom (*regnum*), and gave Henry II the title of the lord king (*dominus rex*), where William was king of Scots (*rex Scottorum*), a hierarchy of naming which, as Rees Davies notes, anticipates by over a century Edward I's vocabulary of demotion as he makes his move to a more substantial appropriation of Scotland.[144] In Ireland, Ruaidrí Ua Conchobair's lack of genuine authority over his fellow Irish kings saw his recognition as high-king in 1175 replaced a mere two years later with Henry II's grant of the title of lord of Ireland to his son, John.[145] Recognition endured as a tactic

[143] Davies, *First English Empire*, pp. 4–10, 14, 22–9, 83–7.
[144] Davies, *First English Empire*, pp. 13–14.
[145] Martin, 'Overlord becomes Feudal Lord'.

as late as 1267, a year when Henry III was prepared to recognise Llywelyn ap Gruffudd as Prince of Wales, albeit a prince clearly subject to an English king who had agreed to pay 25,000 marks for the title.[146] Following Edward I's defeat of Llywelyn in 1284, the title of Prince of Wales endured, but only as the title of the heir to the English throne.

In the contrary direction, there were occasional (unsuccessful) attempts to resurrect or reappropriate titles that might challenge the authority of the English monarch. Brian Ó Néill in 1258 and Edward Bruce in 1315 both claimed the high-kingship of Ireland in a challenge to the English monarch's title of Lord of Ireland.[147] Owain Glyn Dŵr declared himself Prince of Wales in 1400, challenging the English royal family's appropriation of the title to themselves.[148] While English claims to overlordship over the entire archipelago were ultimately to prove successful, the English were not the only ones to entertain such a vision: medieval Welsh prophecy and mythology also envisaged the possibility that Britain would once again be ruled by the Britons, that is the Welsh themselves.[149] As late as 1405, the 'tripartite indenture' of Henry Percy, Edmund Mortimer and Owain Glyn Dŵr (if genuine) suggests Owain's vision for an expanded Wales reaching to the Severn.[150]

If England's expansion into medieval Wales, Ireland and Scotland was a partial, stop-start process, the early result was a variety of jurisdictional compromises. *Magna Carta* (1215) declared that English law applied in England, Welsh law in Wales, but the law of the March for tenements in the March.[151] The 'March of Wales' was a malleable term referring to the conquest lordships created in Wales between the late eleventh and late thirteenth centuries, along the Anglo-Welsh border and the southern Welsh coast.[152] March law was, Rees Davies suggests, a law of compromise between the will of the lord and the custom of the lordship, defined in part by folk memory and in part by the legislative will of individual Marcher lords.[153] Judicially immune from the crown and from each other, the Marcher lordships developed a distinctive legal tradition that saw the endurance of feudal institutions and customs in these territories prepared for war, a significant role for the law of Wales, but

---

[146] Frame, *Political Development of the British Isles*, pp. 115, 122.
[147] Frame, *Political Development of the British Isles*, pp. 46, 131.
[148] Davies, *Revolt of Owain Glyn Dŵr*, pp. 159–66.
[149] Davies, *First English Empire*, pp. 39–41, 44–6, 48–9. See, for instance, the thirteenth-century 'Song of the Welsh', in *Political Songs*, ed. Wright, pp. 56–8.
[150] Davies, *Revolt of Owain Glyn Dŵr*, pp. 166–73.
[151] *Select Charters*, ed. Stubbs, p. 300.
[152] Lieberman, *Medieval March of Wales*, pp. 2–5.
[153] Davies, 'Law of the March', pp. 7–11.

also the influence of English legal practice.[154] Nor did the plural nature of March law cease at the boundaries of each lordship, for separate customs might exist for differing localities, and Marcher lordships were frequently divided into Englishries and Welshries, areas under the jurisdiction of English and Welsh courts.[155] 'The March seemed to be a criminal's paradise', says Davies, 'a land of multiple bolt-holes and loopholes'.[156] Such administrative complexity, combined with long-term social disruption, meant, as Adrian Price suggests, that 'Wales became a breeding ground for outlawry'.[157]

But questions of law were also important for the expansion of English power into Wales. The Welsh rising of 1282 that marked a decisive turning point in Anglo-Welsh relations had a legal context. The rising was preceded by legal conflicts involving both the Prince of Wales, Llywelyn ap Gruffudd, and his brother Dafydd, where diversity of law was at issue. Llywelyn claimed that in his litigation over Arwystli, he had been denied the law of Wales in contravention of the treaty of Aberconwy. His opponent in the case, the Marcher lord Gruffudd ap Gwenwynwyn, arguing against diversity of laws, suggested that the various nations should be governed in the king's court by a single common law. The case was referred back to Edward I, who opted for delay, and it remained unresolved by 1282. Similarly, Llywelyn's brother Dafydd ap Gruffudd, asked to answer under English law in Chester for a case concerning lands in Wales, protested that Welsh law should apply, claiming 'it was right, since the king was lord of several countries (*patrie*) whose several languages and several laws were administered and remained unchanged, that the laws of Wales should be left unchanged like the laws of other nations (*nationes*)'. Llywelyn's list of grievances against the crown, compiled shortly before his death, gives the denial of Welsh law in the Arwystli dispute a prominent place.[158]

The substance of Edward I's overlordship was not in dispute here. What was at issue was the sort of state that Edward was presiding over. Llywelyn and Dafydd ap Gruffudd were arguing that Edward's state was (or should have been) a federative state with a variety of laws for its various nations and territories. This had certainly seemed a possibility earlier: as Rees Davies suggests, periodically in the late twelfth and early thirteenth centuries it seemed possible that high kingship of the British Isles might become 'a federative,

---

[154] Davies, 'Law of the March', pp. 12–23, 28–9.
[155] Davies, 'Law of the March', pp. 11, 25.
[156] Davies, 'Frontier Arrangements in Fragmented Societies', p. 93.
[157] Price, 'Welsh Bandits', p. 58.
[158] Smith, *Llywelyn ap Gruffudd*, pp. 462, 469–89, 533–4; see also Prestwich, *Edward I*, pp. 184–8.

loose-limbed, composite monarchy', with various peoples and territories presided over by a single multi-titled ruler.[159] Gruffudd ap Gwenwynwyn was arguing on the contrary that a single common law should apply (in this instance at least). There were also other influential parties, not least John Peckham, the archbishop of Canterbury, who offered substantial criticisms of Welsh law. While the positions of all concerned here reflected their particular interests, the dispute reflects a tendency by the late thirteenth century for a promotion of English legal systems to the detriment of others. Nor was Llywelyn ap Gruffudd the last Welsh noble provoked into an unsuccessful rebellion in this way: in 1287, Rhys ap Maredudd of Deheubarth was likewise provoked to arms by the insistence he plead certain cases by English law.[160]

The Welsh defeat in 1282 was followed by the Statute of Wales in 1284, which imposed English criminal law in Wales. It was, however, the subsequent rising of 1294–5 that saw much more severe ordinances imposed against the native Welsh. These ordinances were built on further in the four-teenth century, culminating in the anti-Welsh legislation issued by Henry IV in 1401–2 that imposed restrictions on freedom of movement, freedom of assembly, access to public posts, and legal status, in the context of Owain Glyn Dŵr's revolt.[161]

Expansion into Ireland, likewise, had a legal context. The bull *Laudabiliter*, Pope Adrian IV's grant of Ireland to Henry II (possibly granted at the instiga-tion of John of Salisbury), suggested that Henry desired: 'to enter the island of Ireland in order to subject its people to law and to root out from them the weeds of vice'.[162] When Henry did eventually enter Ireland, he did so as a reactive move to pre-empt Richard de Clare from building a competing power base on the island, but *Laudabiliter* provided justification.[163] In 1317, *The Remonstrance of the Irish princes to Pope John XXII* recalled *Laudabiliter*, and complained that rather than being subjected to the rule of law, the Irish were being excluded from it:[164] English law was indeed extended to Ireland, but not, in general, for the native Irish.

The imposition of English law in the conquered territories of both Ireland

---

[159] Davies, *First English Empire*, pp. 140–1.
[160] Frame, *Political Development of the British Isles*, pp. 159–60.
[161] Davies, *Revolt of Owain Glyn Dŵr*, pp. 281–92. Glyn Dŵr is often included in discussions of medieval outlawry: Mica Gould reads a reference to Henry IV's grant of Owain's lands to Lord Grey of Ruthin in 1400 as suggesting that Glyn Dŵr has been outlawed (*Two Tales of Owain Glyndwr*, trans. Gould, in *Medieval Outlaws*, ed. Ohlgren, p. 254 n. 3).
[162] *Irish Historical Documents*, ed. Curtis and McDowell, pp. 17–18.
[163] Martin, 'Diarmait Mac Murchada', pp. 57–8.
[164] *Irish Historical Documents*, ed. Curtis and McDowell, p. 41.

and Wales was partial and inconsistent. English law applied for English set-tlers and/or English-held territories in Ireland and Wales. English law might also be granted to other individuals or groups. But in general, the native populations were not recognised under English law. To some extent this was pure pragmatism: the English conquests were partial, and it made no sense to unsuccessfully attempt to impose English law upon people and territories that were, in reality, outside English control. But it also meant the native populations of Ireland and Wales were legally disadvantaged in those zones where English jurisdiction was effective.

The 1317 *Remonstrance* stated the effects of legal exclusion in strong terms. Irishmen could not bring actions in the king's courts, 'refused all recourse to law by the very fact [of being Irish]'. Nor was it a felony in English law to kill an Irishman: 'nay more, the better the murdered man was and the greater the place he held among his people, the more his murderer is honoured and rewarded by the English.'[165]

This view of the situation is not entirely inaccurate, but it is polemical, and some qualifications are needed. In general, Irishmen could not bring actions in the king's courts. Because of this legal disadvantage, accusing someone of being Irish was a defamatory statement, for which legal action could be taken. Irish defendants, however, were not under any formal legal disability, except exclusion from wager at law.[166] Irishmen could receive remedy if their lords took action on their behalf.[167]

Killing an Irishman was not a felony, and the courts would, as the *Remonstrance* suggests, acquit someone accused of killing an Irishman. This does not entirely mean that an Irishman might be killed with impunity: in line with Irish legal practice, the lord of an Irishman (but not their kin) might sue the killer for compensation. There were, however, many lordless Irish in the Marches: in the absence of a lord to seek compensation, their killing would go unpunished. Killing of an Englishman *was* a felony, but generally lords did not hang Irish felons, and, again in line with Irish practice, usually fined or ransomed them instead.[168]

Exclusion had its exceptions. Access to English law was granted to the royal families of the five provinces, and on an ongoing basis by specific grants to named individuals.[169] A 1277 ecclesiastical initiative that proposed

---

[165] *Irish Historical Documents*, ed. Curtis and McDowell, p. 41.
[166] Hand, *English Law in Ireland*, pp. 188, 198–201.
[167] Otway-Ruthven, 'The Native Irish and English Law', p. 11.
[168] Hand, *English Law in Ireland*, pp. 188, 202–4. For interaction between Irish law and the common law, see MacNiocaill, 'The Contact of Irish and Common Law', pp. 16–23.
[169] Hand, *English Law in Ireland*, pp. 206–8.

the extension of English law to all of the Irish was positively received by the king, but failed to proceed.[170] Those individually admitted to English law sometimes seem to have accrued the advantages of admission while escaping the penalties; hence the king's instruction in 1321 that the Irish admitted to English law should be subject to the same penalties as the English.[171] In November 1330, the English parliament decided that the Irish in English-controlled areas should be admitted to English law, but that decision has left no practical trace, and individual charters of liberty continue to be granted into the fifteenth century.[172]

Within the English-controlled areas of medieval Ireland, then, English law applied, but only the English had full rights within it; effectively, a mixture of territorial and personal law applied, with the Irish mostly excluded from initiating legal complaint within English territory.[173] Outside the English-controlled areas, Brehon law continued to prevail amongst the Irish, and, in the March, the border-zones between Irish and English territory, disputes between Irish and English might be settled by the negotiated compromise of March law.[174] But the March was also portrayed as an ungoverned landscape, where the Irish 'confiding in the thickness of the woods and the depth of the adjacent bogs' could escape capture, 'especially when the King's highway in very many places is now so closed up and obstructed by the thickness of quickly growing wood, that scarcely any person, even on foot, can pass through them'.[175] This was a landscape of lawlessness not unlike the descriptions found in the literature of outlawry, with the substantial difference that the Irish March was, of course, effectively a war-zone.

As in Wales, any potential equilibrium between the various legal systems at work in medieval Ireland was problematised by the regular resurgence of an English (and ecclesiastical) sense that Irish law was not really law at all. This was something implicit as early as *Laudabiliter*'s statement that Henry II wished to enter Ireland to subject its people to law: the Irish here were implicitly a lawless race.[176] It was explicit in Edward I's statement of 1277

---

[170] Otway-Ruthven, 'The Request of the Irish for English Law'.
[171] Hand, *English Law in Ireland*, pp. 209–10; *Irish Historical Documents*, ed. Curtis and McDowell, pp. 47–8.
[172] Watt, 'The Anglo-Irish Colony under strain', p. 395.
[173] Otway-Ruthven, 'The Native Irish and English Law', p. 5, and Hand, *English Law in Ireland*, p. 187 and n. 3, both argue to differing degrees for a distinction between what they see as the imposition of territorial laws in Wales and personal laws in Ireland.
[174] Smith, 'The Concept of the March in Medieval Ireland', p. 264.
[175] *Irish Historical Documents*, ed. Curtis and McDowell, pp. 36–7.
[176] For medieval English representations of Irish barbarism, see Leerssen, *Mere Irish and Fíor-Ghael*, pp. 32–7.

that 'the laws which the Irish use are detestable to God and contrary to all law so much so that they ought not to be deemed law'.[177] The king (as Robin Frame suggests) might have been quoting directly from the Irish prelates who petitioned him to see those Irish laws superseded,[178] but Edward was similarly inclined to substantially modify the laws of the Scots and the Welsh, if not to condemn them so absolutely. By the time of the Statutes of Kilkenny in 1366, the Irish colony was under pressure: now diversity of law was explicitly an evil, March and Brehon law 'by right ought not to be called law but bad custom', and Englishmen who agreed to be subject to such were to be imprisoned as traitors.[179] Such identification of law with English law, and rejection of other legal traditions, was a tactic recognised by contemporaries, and medieval Welsh and Scottish legal collections may well have been compiled 'in repudiation of English legal imperialism', as Alan Harding puts it.[180]

In Scotland, the crisis in succession to the Scottish crown in the 1280s saw Edward I attempt to expand his power northwards. Initially, this involved a planned union of crowns through a marriage between his heir, the future Edward II, and the infant Matilda of Norway, the Scottish heir, with the proposed arrangements for the union careful to demarcate the rights of Scotland. Matilda's death saw a change in tactics. Called upon to adjudicate the contested succession to the Scottish throne in 1291–2, Edward now pressed his claim to be overlord of the king of Scots, with jurisdiction ultimately belonging to him. Following John Balliol's accession as King of Scots, Edward enforced his claim to overlordship by hearing appeals in Scottish legal cases, and issuing a feudal summons for Scots to support him militarily. These claims to practical (rather than theoretical) overlordship in Scotland were a substantial contributory factor to the outbreak of Anglo-Scottish military conflict from 1296.[181] In some senses, this was a legal claim: Edward's invasion of Scotland and removal of John Balliol as king treats Scotland (as he also treated the principality of Wales) as a fief that has escheated to the crown after a subject's rebellion.[182] But that is to assume that his sovereignty and legal authority already extended over Scotland and Wales, a political tactic of non-recognition of any claims to sovereignty or legal authority that those countries might wish to claim.

---

[177] *Irish Historical Documents*, ed. Curtis and McDowell, p. 32.
[178] Frame, *Political Development of the British Isles*, p. 143.
[179] *Irish Historical Documents*, ed. Curtis and McDowell, p. 53.
[180] Harding, *Medieval Law and the Foundations of the State*, p. 199; likewise Neville, *Violence, Custom and Law*, p. 3.
[181] Prestwich, *Edward I*, pp. 356–75.
[182] Frame, *Political Development of the British Isles*, pp. 143–4.

Edward I's pressing of English claims to sovereignty over Scotland also led to a change in the ability of Scots to seek legal redress against Englishmen. A body of custom governing cross-border legal disputes between England and Scotland is first documented in 1249, but based on earlier practice. These customary laws, the laws of the March, were suppressed by Edward I in tandem with his insistence upon his superior jurisdiction in Scotland itself. These laws remained in abeyance under both Edward I and Edward II while the relationship between the kingdoms was in dispute. In the context of the Anglo-Scottish wars and English occupation of Scotland from 1296, legal grievances by Scots against English went largely without remedy. Although subsequently revived, the laws of the March were again suspended when Henry IV and Henry V revived claims to overlordship over Scotland; here, again, an insistence on sovereignty required a suppression of law.[183] In practice, then, Scots were treated alternately as neighbours, rebellious subjects, or enemies, with differing positions vis-à-vis English law, as the political occasion demanded. What we see here is the tactical extension or withdrawal of differing forms of recognition for Scots under English law in line with the circumstantial interests of English power.

Recognition before the law, or exclusion from it, then, was a tactic of power for the medieval English crown across the archipelago. This was a tactic that extended to declaring the crown's political opponents to be outside the law.[184] Consequently, the canon of outlaw literature in English includes alongside the fictional yeoman Robin Hood the surprising figures of the guardian of Scotland, William Wallace, and Scotland's eventual king, Robert Bruce. These are unusual figures in the canon of medieval outlawry, for two reasons. First, unlike the carnivalesque outlaw kings discussed earlier, they have real claims to sovereign authority. And, secondly, their individual exclusion from legal redress occurs in parallel with another, larger, act of legal exclusion – England's non-recognition of the status of Scotland as a sovereign nation.

The Bruce, John Barbour's fourteenth-century poetic account of Robert Bruce's career, sees the king in hiding from the English regime as an outlaw:[185]

---

[183] Neville, *Violence, Custom and Law*, pp. 1–7, 9–11, 15–19, 100; Musson and Ormrod, *Evolution of English Justice*, p. 83.

[184] Excommunication, outlawry's ecclesiastical equivalent, might also be used to political ends – James IV of Scotland was excommunicated for breach of his oath in invading England in 1513. I owe this point to Sybil Jack.

[185] Bruce was declared a traitor rather than formally outlawed, but Bellamy, *Law of Treason*, pp. 28, 44, suggests an equivalence between the two measures.

As utelawys went mony day
Dreand in the Month thar pyne,
Eyte flesch and drank water syne. (*The Bruce*, II. 493–5)

In Blind Harry's fifteenth-century *The Wallace*, William Wallace displays a variety of outlaw characteristics.[186] His extraordinarily violent antipathy to the English is caused not only by the loss of Scotland, but also by personal loss: his early actions are reportedly motivated in part by a desire to avenge his father and brother's deaths at Loudoun Hill (*The Wallace*, 1. 319–26, 3. 111–14, 3. 241–3), and later to avenge the killing of his wife (*The Wallace*, 6. 191–4, 209–24).[187] Like other medieval outlaws, real and imaginary, he moves between taking refuge with sympathisers and hiding in forests, and Blind Harry's borrowings from his literary predecessors extend to disguising his hero (like Robin Hood) as a potter (*The Wallace*, 6. 430–96).

In the poem, as in real life, Wallace's story ends with his execution. An early fourteenth-century expenses claim gives us a description:

As expenses and payments made by the same sheriffs for William Wallace, as a robber, a public traitor, an outlaw, an enemy and rebel against the king (*Willelmo le Waleys, latrone, proditione puplico, utlagato, inimico et rebellione regis*), who in contempt of the king had, throughout Scotland, falsely sought to call himself king of Scotland, and slew the king's officials in Scotland, and also as an enemy led an army against the king, by sentence of the king's court at Westminster being drawn, hanged, beheaded, his entrails burned, and his body quartered, whose four parts were dispatched to the four principal towns of Scotland.[188]

In Blind Harry's poem, Wallace is the chosen leader of the Scots:

Thus Wallace straiff agayne that gret barnage.
Sa he begane with strenth and stalwart hand
To chewys agayne sum rowmys of Scotland.
The worthi Scottis that semblit till him thar
Chesit him for cheyff, thar chyftayne and ledar. (*The Wallace*, 6. 269–73)

---

[186] For Wallace's exclusion from the peace terms of 1304 and outlawry by the St Andrews parliament, and legal proceedings following his capture, see Bellamy, *Law of Treason*, pp. 32–9.

[187] Anne McKim casts doubt on both the deaths of Wallace's brother and father (Wallace's brother was alive in 1299) and the supposed location (the site of a Bruce victory in 1307) (Blind Harry, *The Wallace*, nn. to 1. 319–21 and 3.78).

[188] Pipe Roll of 33 Edward I (Michaelmas 1314–15) cited in Davies, 'The Execution of William Wallace'.

To the English, such a claim is illegitimate.[189] Scotland rightfully belongs to King Edward, not the Scots, and Wallace is therefore guilty of the litany of crimes listed above: he is a robber, a traitor, an outlaw, an enemy, a rebel. He is, accordingly, subjected to a variety of the most extreme physical punishments: drawn, hanged, beheaded, disembowelled, and quartered.[190] Sometime leader of a country whose sovereignty has been subsumed, he is, in short, an entirely abjected figure.

---

[189] See Bellamy, *Law of Treason*, pp. 37–8.
[190] In Blind Harry's version, Edward I would even have denied him confession before his execution, but this episode, McKim notes, is an invention (Blind Harry, *The Wallace*, 12. 1312–37 and nn.).

2

Sovereign Outlaws:
Shakespeare's Second Tetralogy

'**O**ure maister is crowned of outlawe king', Gamelyn is told when he takes to the forest, and, as we saw in the last chapter, there are a variety of outlaw kings to be found across medieval texts. Some, like the fictional Gamelyn or the factual Lionel, 'king of the rout of raveners', are almost carnivalesque: bandits exiled to the margins of society who parody royal authority as a means of challenging it. Others are leaders like William Wallace, who may have genuine claims to sovereign authority, but are reduced to the status of outlaws by the political use of legal exclusion. Despite their differences, all of these outlaw kings are to be found at the margins of power, the traditional location for the outlaw. The work of both Agamben and Derrida, however, suggests that exclusion from law exists not only at the margin, but also at the very centre of the state. This chapter, then, looks at the idea that the sovereign exists above or outside the law, and in doing so revisits the portrayals of embattled sovereignty in the second tetralogy of Shakespeare's history plays.

The King Outside the Law

In their discussions of sovereignty, both Derrida and Agamben focus upon the sovereign's power, in Derrida's words, 'to *give*, to *make*, but also to *suspend* the law'.[1] In doing so, each draws upon Carl Schmitt's definition of sovereignty: 'sovereign is he who decides on the exception'.[2] For Schmitt, this ability to decide on the exception, an ability that for him defines sovereignty, paradoxically places the sovereign both within and outside the legal system. 'Although he stands outside the normally valid legal system', Schmitt writes,

---

[1] Derrida, *The Beast & the Sovereign*, I, 16.
[2] Schmitt, *Political Theology*, p. 5. Strong, 'Foreword. The Sovereign and the Exception', pp. xi–xiii, discusses the translation of *ausnahmezustand*, here 'exception', but also possibly (and more narrowly) 'state of emergency'. For a brief history of states using emergency powers, see Agamben, *State of Exception*, pp. 11–22. For a critique of Schmitt in light of other possible models of legal exception, see Gross and Ní Aoláin, *Law in Times of Crisis*, pp. 162–70.

the sovereign 'nevertheless belongs to it, for it is he who must decide whether the constitution needs to be suspended in its entirety'.[3]

The notion that the sovereign is above the law is both long-standing and surprisingly enduring. In *The Politics*, Aristotle suggests that men who surpass all others in their virtue and capacity for statecraft are akin to gods among men: there is no law that embraces them, for they are themselves law. He goes on to say that in democratic states, such men are likely to suffer ostracism and removal from the state, if their excess of wealth or power threatens the equality of others.[4] In the civil law tradition, Ulpian's statements *princeps legibus solutus est*, 'the sovereign is not bound by the laws' (*Digest*, 1.3.31) and *quod principi placuit, legis habet vigorem*, 'what pleases the prince has the force of law' (*Digest*, 1.4.1) were influential for centuries.[5]

In the later Middle Ages, we find the argument that the king is above the law, in the sense that legal action may not be taken against him. We see practical expressions of the king's ability to act outside formal legal process in the ability of his conciliar courts to offer forms of justice that stand apart from the common law.[6] We even see the king explicitly asserting his right to override the law because of his supralegal status: in the Calendar of Welsh Rolls (1291), we read of a group of reluctant magnates told on behalf of the king (here Edward I) that 'no one in this behalf can have a march from the king (*habere marchiam domino regi*), who for the common advantage (*utilitate*) is by his prerogative in many cases above the laws and customs used in his realm'.[7]

But we also find thinking in this period seeking a balance between the notion that the king was above the law and a sense that the sovereign might not be entirely free from constraint. In Thomas Aquinas's *Summa Theologiae*,

[3] Schmitt, *Political Theology*, p. 7. Kantorowicz, *The King's Two Bodies*, p. 149, discussing the *rex infra et super legem* in *Bracton*, likewise suggests that the king's status above the law was itself perfectly 'legal' and guaranteed by law. Agamben, *State of Exception*, pp. 50–1, argues against Schmitt that the state of exception cannot be a state of law, but rather must be a space without law.

[4] Aristotle, *The Politics*, trans. Sinclair, rev. Saunders, pp. 213–14.

[5] *Iustiniani Digesta*, ed. Mommsen. *Digest of Justinian*, ed. Watson, I, 13, 14, translates: 'The emperor is not bound by statutes', and 'a decision given by the emperor has the force of a statute'. For the distinction between the Greek philosophical tradition which sees the king as above the law and the state (as in Aristotle's *Politics*) and the Roman law tradition of the king above the law to which the medieval period is indebted, see Schulz, 'Bracton on Kingship', p. 157.

[6] Musson and Ormrod, *Evolution of English Justice*, p. 20.

[7] *Calendar of Various Chancery Rolls*, A.D. *1277–1326*, p. 336, discussed in Davies, 'Kings, Lords and Liberties in the March of Wales', p. 55.

the sovereign can change the law, and dispense the law, and cannot be judged by the coercive powers of the law: in these senses he is above or exempt from the law. But he is not exempt from the law in the judgment of God, and though he cannot be coerced, Aquinas argues, he should obey the law of his own free will.[8]

In Ernst Kantorowicz's discussion of *rex infra et super legem* in the thirteenth-century English legal text *Bracton*, the king is under the law of the land, but nonetheless in a unique position against whom law could not legally be set in motion: he is both under and above the law.[9] *Bracton* certainly stresses that the king is under the law: 'the king must not be under man but under God and under the law, because law makes the king' (*Bracton*, II, 33). *Bracton* also cites Ulpian. *Bracton*'s comments on kingship rest heavily on prior authority; they are, as Fritz Schulz puts it, 'an artificial tissue of quotations'.[10] But quotations that might seem to support an absolutist view of monarchical power are carefully qualified. So the will of the prince may have the force of law, as per Ulpian (*Digest*, 1.4.1), but the will of the prince does not mean 'anything rashly put forward of his own will'. Rather, according to *Bracton*, it means 'what has rightly been decided with the counsel of his magnates, deliberation and consultation having been had thereon, the king giving it *auctoritas*' (*Bracton*, II, 305). Here, as Brian Tierney says, we have 'an odd conjunction of an apparently absolutist text and a constitutionalist sentiment'.[11] We might add that visible tensions between absolutist and constitutionalist interpretations of authoritative statements on monarchy might seem to embody the challenges posed by the doctrine of a king theoretically positioned both above and under the law.

If *Bracton*'s thirteenth-century interpretation of Ulpian offers one example of such tension, another might be seen in the articles of Richard II's deposition at the end of the fourteenth century. These accuse Richard of saying 'that the laws were in his mouth, or, at other times, that they were in his breast, and that he alone could change or make the laws of his kingdom'.[12] Kantorowicz argues that this is a legal maxim, intended to mean that the sovereign when legislating was expected to have all the relevant laws present

---

[8] Aquinas, *Summa Theologiae*, 1a2ae, q. 96 art. 5. Tierney, 'Bracton on Government', pp. 303–5, suggests similarities between Aquinas's position here and that of *Bracton*.

[9] Kantorowicz, *The King's Two Bodies*, pp. 143–64.

[10] Schulz, 'Bracton on Kingship', p. 145; Schulz offers a detailed analysis of the sources for Bracton's discussion of kingship.

[11] Tierney, 'Bracton on Government', p. 298.

[12] *Chronicles of the Revolution*, trans. and ed. Given-Wilson, pp. 177–8; Latin text in *Rotuli Parliamentorum*, ed. Strachey, III, 419.

in his mind. Furthermore, medieval Italian jurists interpreted the phrase to mean that the king should consult his councillors: for them, having the laws in the prince's mouth or in his breast means consulting expert advice when legislating.[13] But if Kantorowicz can cite Italian evidence to support this constitutionalist interpretation, Walter Ullmann cites French use of the same phrase in support of a theocratic and absolutist model of kingship.[14] Richard and/or his accusers similarly seem to take an absolutist view of the phrase as meaning that the king alone is the source of law: Richard is portrayed as using the phrase to support 'his own arbitrary will', ignoring his justices and his council.[15] As with *Bracton*'s use of *quod principi placuit*, this text from the articles of Richard's deposition seems to give expression to an ongoing contest about the nature of the king's legislative power.[16]

Kantorowicz stresses that 'Bracton's expansion of the king's status "under the Law" did not abolish a status of the king also "above the Law."'[17] As Tierney puts it:

> No person in the realm was the equal or superior of the king, and so no judge could dispute his acts. No writ ran against the king. He was indeed *sub lege* in that he had a duty to live according to the laws; nothing in his position licenced him to disobey them; but his observance of the law could be ensured only by his own good will, not by judicial coercion.[18]

This idea of the king simultaneously under and above the law endures into the late sixteenth century. James VI of Scotland (later James I of England), writes in *The True Law of Free Monarchies* (1598) that while 'a good king will not only delight to rule his subjects by the law but even will conform himself

---

[13] Kantorowicz, *The King's Two Bodies*, p. 28 n. 15 and pp. 153–4.

[14] Ullmann, *A History of Political Thought*, pp. 155–6; Ullmann also quotes the thirteenth-century French jurist Beaumanoir here as citing Ulpian's *quod principi placuit* in support of the king's right to make law without his council.

[15] *Chronicles of the Revolution*, ed. Given-Wilson, pp. 177–8; Latin text in *Rotuli Parliamentorum*, ed. Strachey, III, 419.

[16] On which see Green, *A Crisis of Truth*, pp. 237–47.

[17] Kantorowicz, *The King's Two Bodies*, p. 149. For a contrary view, see Lewis, 'King Above Law?'. More recently, Halpern, 'The King's Two Buckets', p. 73, cites Lewis to suggest (incorrectly, it seems to me) that 'claims about the king's supralegal status seem to be Kantorowicz's invention, with no real supporting evidence in Bracton'. A possible exception to the king's supralegal status in *Bracton* is a (disputed) portion of text known as the *addicio de cartis* that seems to modify the king's status above the law (*Bracton*, ed. Woodbine, trans. Thorne, II, 110); for readings that seek to reconcile the *addicio* with the rest of *Bracton*, see Tierney, 'Bracton on Government', p. 316, Nederman, *Lineages of European Political Thought*, p. 91.

[18] Tierney, 'Bracton on Government', p. 303.

in his own actions thereunto', he conforms to the law 'of his own free will, but not as subject or bound thereto', for 'the king is above the law'.[19]

King or Tyrant?

This long-standing tradition that placed the sovereign above the law was challenged by a tradition of writing against tyranny. In the twelfth century, John of Salisbury argued against the notion of the king above law:

> Now may the whitewashers of rulers proceed, now may they whisper or, if this is too little, publicly proclaim that the prince is not subject to law, and that his will has the force of law not only in establishing legal right according to the form of equity, but in establishing anything whatsoever. If they wish and they dare, they may make the king, whom they remove from the bonds of law, an outlaw (*exlegem*), yet I assert that kings must keep this law – protesting this loudly not only against their denials but to the world.[20]

For John, failure to rule by the laws is the definition of a tyrant.[21] The tyrant oppresses the people by violent domination; the prince rules by the laws.[22]

Bracton is indebted to John's *Policraticus* for its definition of tyranny.[23] The king is called *rex* from ruling well, an etymological definition indebted (as Schulz shows) to a proverbial tradition expressed in Isidore of Seville and a long line of literary descendants.[24] Furthermore, in *Bracton*, *rex est, dum bene regit*: someone is king not *if* they rule well (as in Isidore), but *while* they rule well.[25] A ruler governing to the detriment of their people is a tyrant, not a king (*Bracton*, II, 305–6). As Chaucer puts it at the end of the fourteenth century (and as John of Salisbury does two centuries earlier), a tyrant may be considered a sort of outlaw:

> Right so bitwixe a titlelees tiraunt
> And an outlawe or a theef erraunt,
> The same I seye: ther is no difference. (*The Canterbury Tales*, IX. 223–35)[26]

---

[19] James I, *The True Law of Free Monarchies and Basilokon Doron*, p. 72.
[20] John of Salisbury, *Policraticus*, pp. 47–8.
[21] John of Salisbury, *Policraticus*, p. 28.
[22] John of Salisbury, *Policraticus*, p. 190.
[23] Schulz, 'Bracton on Kingship', pp. 140, 153.
[24] Schulz, 'Bracton on Kingship', pp. 140, 151–3; Isidore of Seville, *Etymologies*, pp. 55, 200.
[25] Schulz, 'Bracton on Kingship', pp. 152–3 uses this 'dum' clause to identify *Bracton*'s source here.
[26] *Titlelees* here means 'without title, usurping' (Davis et al., *A Chaucer Glossary*). As Jones, *Outlawry in Medieval Literature*, pp. 35–8, observes, Chaucer plays it safe here by comparing tyrant and outlaw; other versions of the story equate robbers and kings.

But who may act against an unjust king? John of Salisbury argues in the *Policraticus*, on Biblical evidence, that while praying to God for relief is the best policy, tyrants may be lawfully killed by those who are not obligated to them by oath or fealty.[27] But if John of Salisbury (and some later writers, including George Buchanan in the sixteenth century)[28] would justify tyrannicide, the authoritarian James VI would have none of it. His *True Law of Free Monarchies* denies any justification for rebellion against tyranny; punishment for wrongs committed by kings should be remitted, by right, only to God.[29]

Sovereign Immunity and *Richard II*

To read the second tetralogy of Shakespeare's history plays in light of *Bracton*'s comments on kingship is to participate in a discussion that is now more than fifty years old.[30] That discussion reflects Kantorowicz's influence upon Shakespeare scholarship, but also his book's broader reach (Foucault's *Discipline and Punish*, Agamben's *Homo Sacer* and Derrida's *The Beast & the Sovereign* all cite *The King's Two Bodies*).[31] But if Kantorowicz's thinking about *Bracton*, kingship and Shakespeare has been influential, there are, perhaps, still further things to say about exclusion from law in the second tetralogy.

The first play of the sequence, *Richard II*, begins with a dramatisation of a recognisable medieval judicial process in its opening scenes.[32] The issues at stake, though, seem uncertain at first, as characters trade accusations about events preceding the action of the play.[33] When Bolingbroke and Mowbray appear on stage, it becomes clear that each has accused the other of treason (*Richard II*, 1.1.27), though it is not yet clear on what grounds. When Bolingbroke's accusations are eventually made, they are a mixture of the

---

[27] John of Salisbury, *Policraticus*, pp. 206–10; cf. Nederman, 'A Duty to Kill'.

[28] Buchanan, *De Jure Regni aped Scotos*.

[29] James I, *The True Law of Free Monarchies and Basilokon Doron*, pp. 72–82.

[30] Reference to the history plays is to the Arden Shakespeare: *King Richard II*, ed. Forker; *King Henry IV Part I*, ed. Kastan; *The Second Part of King Henry IV*, ed. Humphreys; *King Henry V*, ed. Craik.

[31] On Kantorowicz's influence, cf. Jussen, '*The King's Two Bodies* Today', pp. 105–6.

[32] For unsupported accusations of treason being resolved through trial by battle in the court of chivalry during Richard II's reign, with Richard's support but to the commons' concern, see Bellamy, *Law of Treason*, p. 143. On the legal process and its representation in Shakespeare's play, see Gohn, '*Richard II*: Shakespeare's Legal Brief', pp. 946–8, 959–64.

[33] Chris Given-Wilson comments that the background to the Mowbray-Bolinbroke quarrel 'is notoriously difficult to disentangle' and likely arose from wider disagreements about the direction of policy (*Chronicles of the Revolution*, ed. Given-Wilson, p. 17 and cf. pp. 11–24).

general and the specific. Most importantly, he accuses Mowbray of being responsible for the Duke of Gloucester's death (*Richard II*, 1.1.87–108). Mowbray, in reply, admits a previous plot against John of Gaunt, but denies murdering Gloucester (*Richard II*, 1.1.124–51).[34]

What is crucial but not at all manifest during this opening scene is that primary responsibility for Gloucester's death lies with Gloucester's nephew, the king. We discover this from Gaunt, who later accuses Richard directly; the accusation is independently confirmed by York (*Richard II*, 1.2.4–5, 1.2.37–41, 2.1.126–31, 2.2.100–2). Richard seems to be responsible for an action that would be a crime were he not the monarch, but, being king, he is immune to legal challenge. Richard cannot be accused in court; uttering words of accusation is potentially dangerous in any context.[35] Nor is there any viable authority to try him. As Carlisle puts it much later: 'What subject can give sentence on his king?' (*Richard II*, 4.1.122).

Bolingbroke's accusation of Mowbray effectively accuses Richard by proxy, and comes far too close to putting Richard himself on trial. In Lorna Hutson's reading of act one, 'everyone quietly *knows* that the person on trial at Coventry on St Lambert's Day will not be Mowbray, but the king himself'; the play's second scene exists to demonstrate the other characters' expectations that the trial will proceed, and justice will manifest itself.[36] Richard, acting as judge in his own case, has been understandably keen to draw the matter to a premature close, but has been unsuccessful in doing so. His initial attempt to impose peace between Bolingbroke and Mowbray fails: 'be ruled by me' he says (*Richard II*, 1.1.152), a request refused by both. What follows is a trial by combat, aborted at the last moment (*Richard II*, 1.3.118). Richard moves to maintain his status above the law – to remove the possibility of his effectively being tried by proxy – by suspending the legal process he has set in train.[37] He then resorts to exiling both men, suspicious of the dangers that this contest may pose to his state (*Richard II*, 1.3.123–39). The banishment of Bolingbroke is described in the articles of the historical

---

[34] Historically, the widespread assumption was that Mowbray, as captain of Calais (where Gloucester died), was Richard's agent in arranging Gloucester's death (*Chronicles of the Revolution*, ed. Given-Wilson, pp. 14–15).

[35] Speaking against the monarch is explicitly treasonous by the late sixteenth century: Lemon, *Treason by Words*, pp. 8–9; cf. pp. 61–2 on *Richard II*.

[36] Hutson, 'Imagining Justice', pp. 136–77.

[37] Gohn, '*Richard II*: Shakespeare's Legal Brief', p. 947 and nn. 17, 18, suggests that Richard was within his rights to suspend the proceedings, but that his use of the Parliamentary Committee's advice 'added a taint of illegality to the proceedings'.

Richard's deposition as 'contrary to all justice, to the laws of and customs of his kingdom, and to the law of arms pertaining thereto'.[38] This temporary exile, furthermore, seems likely to be permanent (*Richard II*, 1.4.20–2).

At the end of act one of *Richard II*, then, it is already clear that questions around the king's status relative to the law constitute an important set of issues within the play. These come into sharper focus with Richard's decision to prevent Bolingbroke from inheriting. This is a decision informed both by need (a pending war in Ireland) and opportunity (the imminent demise of John of Gaunt). The nation's finances are in a perilous state under Richard,[39] for which Gaunt offers the king a rebuke from his deathbed:

> Landlord of England art thou now, not king.
> Thy state of law is bondslave to the law (*Richard II*, 2.1.113–14)[40]

On Gaunt's death, Richard moves immediately to seize his uncle's property, disinheriting his exiled cousin, Gaunt's heir. That Richard's disregard for law here undermines his own position as sovereign is made explicit to Richard by York:

> For how art thou a king
> But by fair sequence and succession? (*Richard II*, 2.1.198–99)

Bolingbroke will later make exactly the same point to York in justifying his return:

> If that my cousin king be King in England,
> It must be granted I am Duke of Lancaster. (*Richard II*, 2.3.123–4)

As *Bracton* puts it, the king ought to obey the law, 'for the law makes him king' (*Bracton*, II, 305–6). By meddling with the law of inheritance, Richard threatens to undo himself.

Historically, disregard for the law was a significant factor in Richard's deposition. The 'Record and Process', the official (and therefore Lancastrian) version of Richard's deposition, quotes Henry, claiming the throne, as stating that the realm 'was in poynt to be undone for defaut of Governance

---

[38] *Chronicles of the Revolution*, ed. Given-Wilson, p. 176, Latin text in *Rotuli Parliamentorum*, ed. Strachey, III, 419. Gohn, '*Richard II*: Shakespeare's Legal Brief', p. 947 n. 19, also suggests that the banishments may be viewed as 'an abuse of the royal prerogative', citing *Magna Carta* c. 39, which suggests that no freeman may be exiled without the lawful judgment of his peers.

[39] The historical Richard was accused at his deposition of disinheritance of the Crown itself: *Chronicles of the Revolution*, ed. Given-Wilson, p. 180; *Rotuli Parliamentorum*, ed. Strachey, III, 420; Kantorowicz, pp. 372–3.

[40] On which see Hamilton, 'The State of Law in *Richard II*'.

and undoyng of the gode Lawes'.[41] The articles of deposition in that document are preceded by a text of Richard's coronation oath, and the articles themselves can be read in part as describing breaches of that oath.[42] The oath (taken again at the end of his disputes with the Lords Appellant) obliged Richard to uphold, defend and enforce the laws and customs which the commons have chosen.[43] Edward II's deposition was likewise characterised as a response to his failure to keep the terms of his oath.[44] The 'Record and Process' is a problematic document, but its list of charges against Richard can in several instances be justified.[45] As a monarch acting against the interests of his subjects, and flouting the law in doing so, Richard may well be open to accusations of tyranny,[46] even if medieval and early modern political thinkers were divided on such questions as the deposition of tyrants and tyrannicide.

Bolingbroke as Outlaw

The conclusion of *Richard II*'s opening act sees Bolingbroke banished. *Banish*, in its original sense, means: 'to put to the ban, "proclaim" as an outlaw, to outlaw'.[47] We can see that even in its later refined sense, banishment, exile from the territory of the state and of the nation, is a category akin to outlawry, and the similarity is made concrete for the returned exile: unauthorised return from banishment automatically places an exile outside the law.[48] On Bolingbroke's return, then, he is literally 'a poor unminded outlaw sneaking home' (*1 Henry IV*, 4.3.58).

If Bolingbroke's return sees him both in breach of the law ('even in condition of the worst degree' as York tells him (*Richard II*, 2.3.108)), and placed outside it, he nonetheless repeatedly justifies his return by claiming he comes only to regain his legal rights. Bolingbroke insists on his own status before the law: 'I am a subject', he says, 'And I challenge law' (*Richard II*, 2.3.133–4).

---

[41] *Rotuli Parliamentorum*, ed. Strachey, III, 423 (modern English text in *Chronicles of the Revolution*, ed. Given-Wilson, p. 186).

[42] *Chronicles of the Revolution*, ed. Given-Wilson, pp. 172–84; *Rotuli Parliamentorum*, ed. Strachey, III, 417–22; Green, *A Crisis of Truth*, p. 234.

[43] For the text of the oath as reported prior to the articles of deposition, see *Rotuli Parliamentorum*, ed. Strachey, III, 417.

[44] Green, *A Crisis of Truth*, p. 233.

[45] *Chronicles of the Revolution*, ed. Given-Wilson, p. 168.

[46] Not all readers would agree: Tillyard, *Shakespeare's History Plays*, p. 261, held that 'Richard's crimes never amounted to tyranny'.

[47] *OED*, s.v. *banish*, v. (1).

[48] *Shakespeare's Legal Language*, ed. Sokol and Sokol, p. 248, comments: 'the notion that an exile who returns without leave becomes an outlaw is made clear in the case of Bolingbroke'.

This is a status which he assumes grants him rights, and particularly the right to inherit his father's property.

As a returned exile, and therefore an outlaw, however, Bolingbroke has no claim to challenge law. *Bracton*'s discussion of outlawry asks what a man forfeits through being outlawed. The outlaw forfeits the country and the realm, and he forfeits his friends, who may themselves be punished as outlaws for assisting him. But he also forfeits the law:

> *He [forfeits] the things pertaining to law.*
>
> He also forfeits the things pertaining to law, for if, greatly daring, he returns after outlawry, without the king's grace, he will perish without law and judicial enquiry. <Nor may he appeal others because he has lost all law.> For he bears his judgment with him on his own head and in consequence will have no defence when his outlawry is manifest. For it is a just judgment that he who has refused to live by the law should perish without law and without judgment.[49]

Bolingbroke has returned to claim his legal rights, he says, but paradoxically, his unauthorised return from exile renders him an outlaw: a man without legal rights, a man outside the law.

Bolingbroke's return to press a legal claim also seems to imply that the law may act as a check upon the actions of the king: that Richard's move to disinherit him may be subject to challenge before the law. This, in a sense, is a repetition of the action that led to his exile in the first place: an attempt to make the king legally answerable for his actions. By invoking what he supposes to be his legal rights against the king's decision, Bolingbroke is challenging the king's extralegal status, and seeking to bring the king under the law. He makes this claim to law in contradiction of the possibility that both he and Richard are in fact outside it: the king because of his sovereign immunity, Bolingbroke because of his status as a returned exile, and hence an outlaw. But Bolingbroke's invocation of law also has the dual effect of highlighting both his own extralegal status (and hence the ineffectiveness of his legal claims), and the justice of his demand to inherit. His lineal rights are being denied by a king who uses his extralegal status to breach the law, while Bolingbroke's own extralegal status now prevents him from obtaining justice, in a striking instance of both the parallel that is sometimes visible between the sovereign and the outlaw, and of the challenge that the excluded may pose to the power of the sovereign.

Bolingbroke's question to York, 'What would you have me do?' (*Richard*

---

[49] *Bracton*, ed. Woodbine, trans. Thorne, II, 362–3.

II, 2.3.123) is a fair one. In the face of Richard's actions, he is otherwise without redress: medieval English law lacks a legal remedy against a king who acts against the law. But, their questionable legal validity aside, Bolingbroke's claims are also somewhat problematised within the play by a sense that his disinheritance is a convenient pretext rather than a motivating force. The fiction that Bolingbroke seeks only his inheritance – his 'lineal royalties' in Northumberland's fruitfully ambiguous phrase (*Richard II*, 3.3.113) – evaporates quickly as Richard's power dissipates. Few, if any, seemed to believe it in the first place. By the middle of the play, Bolingbroke has moved a long way towards becoming king himself.

Legal Fictions, Deposition and Regicide

In act three of *Richard II*, Bolingbroke is already king *de facto* despite his protests to the contrary, and all parties are adjusting to the realities of the shift in power. But moving to legitimate this *de facto* position is a problem, and nowhere does the play make a case for the possibility of valid deposition of the king.[50] The third and fourth acts of *Richard II* are a reminder that we should qualify or supplement Schmitt's statement that it is the sovereign who decides on the state of exception, for a similar state may also be created by the revolutionary who seizes power.[51] They also illustrate the extent to which the premodern English state may be seen to be incapable of defending and reproducing its own power structures through the peaceful instruments of law and politics.

Bolingbroke's action in seizing the throne was by no means unprecedented. Medieval English kingship was hereditary, but also regularly contested: Gerald of Wales memorably described the Norman and Angevin kings as princes who succeeded one another 'by killing and slaughtering their own'.[52] But if inheritance was not the only way of becoming king of England, the suggestion that force was a legitimate means of acquiring the throne, even if historically true, was seen by contemporaries to be fundamentally destabilising. The version of the 'Record and Process' contained in Thomas Walsingham's chronicle places objections to such a claim in the mouth of Justice Thirning: here Thirning allegedly says that a claim to the throne based on conquest would make it appear that Henry had the broader power to disinherit anyone at will, and to change the laws, whereby no one would be

---

[50] Saul, *Richard II*, pp. 418–19, argues that the case for the historical Richard's deposition was based in canon, rather than common, law.

[51] Agamben, *State of Exception*, pp. 1–2, notes that the state of exception is difficult to define in part because of its similarity to civil war, insurrection and resistance.

[52] Cited in Bartlett, *England Under the Norman and Angevin Kings*, p. 7.

secure in their possessions.[53] This is almost a reversal of the Shakespearean Bolingbroke's complaint against Richard II. In the play, Bolingbroke asks how Richard can claim to hold his hereditary office as king if Bolingbroke's own hereditary entitlements can be set aside? If Bolingbroke can claim the crown by force, however (as in fact he does), then the entire legal basis for inheritance and property holding might be seen as vulnerable. There is an opposition implicit here between force and law.[54] Bolingbroke's accession to the throne therefore needs to be re-presented to support the fiction of a legitimate (rather than revolutionary) transfer of power.[55]

In *Richard II*, Bolingbroke's eventual means of becoming king *de jure* as well as *de facto*, in appearance at least, is to have Richard abdicate and designate him as heir. The possibility of heirship gets an early, ironic, mention in the play. In Richard's unconvincing statement of impartiality in the opening scene, he says of Bolingbroke, 'were he my brother, nay, my kingdom's heir', he would not be swayed towards him, whereas, in fact, the relationship is more distant, 'as he is but my father's brother's son' (*Richard II*, 1.1.116–17). Intended at face value as an insult to Bolingbroke, these words are potentially expressive of a latent nervousness on Richard's part that Bolingbroke already seeks the crown (potentially also expressed at 1.1.109 and 1.3.130). These early references to 'my kingdom's heir' in act one carry an ironic awareness that by the play's conclusion Bolingbroke will indeed have 'inherited' the crown.

The artificiality of this solution is highlighted in the play by its awkwardness: Richard's resignation of the crown and nomination of Bolingbroke as his heir is a process that takes place in fits and starts. At the beginning of act four, we see a reworking of the play's opening events, with Bolingbroke now playing Richard's part. At 4.1.107 Bolingbroke is already using the royal 'we'. His sudden move to ascend the throne in act four following his acclamation by York (*Richard II*, 4.1.112, 114) seems premature, a possible false start: Richard has reportedly resigned, but not yet in public, and if York acclaims Bolingbroke as king, Carlisle immediately denounces him as 'a foul traitor' to

---

[53] *Chronicles of the Revolution*, ed. Given-Wilson, pp. 186–7. For the presentation of Thirning's role in the events of 1399, see Giancarlo, 'Murder, Lies, and Storytelling'.

[54] Cf. Agamben's comment (*State of Exception*, p. 39) that 'the state of exception is an anomic space in which what is at stake is a force of law without law'.

[55] Gohn, '*Richard II*: Shakespeare's Legal Brief', outlines five alternative methods through which the crown might (historically) be claimed: conquest, divine designation, inheritance, acclamation or parliamentary designation (p. 949); Gohn suggests that historically Henry sought, with varying degrees of plausibility, to claim inheritance, parliamentary acclamation and divine designation (p. 952). For Chaucer's description of Henry's claim in *To his Purse*, 22–4, see Strohm, 'Saving the Appearances'.

Richard (*Richard II,* 4.1.136).[56] On appearing, Richard, asked repeatedly to resign his crown, proceeds to undo himself, as he puts it (*Richard II,* 4.1.180, 190, 200, 203). He gives Bolingbroke the symbols of office, and renounces his kingship, though he will not read the accusations from the Commons, his language is often equivocal and double edged, and he repeatedly disputes the possibility of valid deposition, continuing to call himself king with his final words (*Richard II,* 5.5.110). For all of this, Bolingbroke is still not king until act five scene three when he first appears as King Henry.

The awkward deposition of Richard and accession of Henry in act four may give a veneer of legitimacy to events, but the narrative of resignation and heirship runs intertwined with a narrative of deposition and usurpation, and it is force, not legal process, that determines the direction of events. All of this makes Henry vulnerable. As David Kastan puts it, having deposed Richard, Henry IV 'has no meaningful access to the powerful rhetoric of legitimacy that had surrounded the throne',[57] and the first of what will be a succession of plots against him appears in act five scene three of *Richard II*. The plot is foiled, but in the subsequent scene, we hear Exton reporting what he takes to be Henry's wishes to be rid of Richard. Exton fulfils these wishes,[58] but the murder of Richard does not solve the problem: in the opening act of *Henry IV Part 1*, Henry is wary of Mortimer as Richard's intended heir (*1 Henry IV*, 1.3.144–56).[59]

Even now, at the play's end, there is a surfeit of kings: 'This dead King', Exton says, 'to the living King I'll bear' (*Richard II,* 5.5.117). Henry's response to Richard's death is complex (*Richard II,* 5.6.38–40), but, whatever his regrets, he does not deny his involvement. 'I did wish him dead' he says (*Richard II,* 5.6.39); he will go on pilgrimage 'to wash this blood off from my guilty hand' (*Richard II,* 5.6.50). By initiating Richard's death, Henry has effectively repeated the crime at the heart of the play's opening dispute:

---

[56] As Charles Forker notes, his move to ascend the throne has justification in the historical sources, though it is not clear from the text whether Bolingbroke actually does ascend the throne at 115 when invited to do so, or whether Carlisle's interjection interrupts his ascent (*King Richard II*, ed. Forker, 4.1.114n.). *Chronicles of the Revolution*, ed. Given-Wilson, pp. 190–1, questions the historical accuracy of Carlisle's supposed protest.

[57] *King Henry IV Part 1*, ed. Kastan, p. 27.

[58] Given-Wilson suggests that the story that Exton and his accomplices murder Richard on Henry's orders is 'obviously spurious'; Richard is either starved to death by his captors or starves himself (*Chronicles of the Revolution*, ed. Given-Wilson, p. 51 and n. 80).

[59] As Kastan notes, Shakespeare is confusing two Edmund Mortimers here, uncle and nephew, and is indebted to Holinshed both for the error and the claim that Edmund Mortimer earl of March was designated heir by Richard (*King Henry IV Part 1*, ed. Kastan, 1.3.84–5n. and 1.3.144–5n.).

the king moving to have his opponent furtively murdered. Having deposed Richard for disregard of the law, Henry has now repeated Richard's own offence of acting outside the law to secure his state.

Hal as Bandit

If Henry IV begins his path to the crown by being banished, and on return from banishment is immediately an outlaw, we first meet Hal playing the role of bandit: his opening appearance in *Henry IV Part 1* is at the planning of the Gadshill robbery. Despite the soliloquy with which he ends the scene, distancing himself from his companions, and his initial insistence that he will not join in the robbery (*1 Henry IV*, 1.2.131), Hal participates in the raid, if only to rob the robbers. As Falstaff puts it later, imitating the king, Hal's father: 'Shall the son of England prove a thief and take purses?' (*1 Henry IV*, 2.4.399–400). After the robbery, Hal joins Falstaff and the others at the tavern, where he, like the others, is praised with 'all the titles of good fellowship' (*1 Henry IV*, 2.4.269–70): a euphemism for outlawry.[60]

When the sheriff arrives in pursuit of the perpetrators, telling Hal 'a hue and cry | Hath followed certain men unto this house' (*1 Henry IV*, 2.4.493–94), Hal lies to him, twice. First, he tells the sheriff that Falstaff is not present (*1 Henry IV*, 2.4.499–500). Second, he gives his word that he will send Falstaff to the sheriff to face any charges; and if Falstaff has robbed the carriers (which he has), then 'he shall be answerable' (*1 Henry IV*, 2.4.501–4, 508–9). But this is not what happens. Earlier, Falstaff pleaded with Hal in their introductory scene 'Do not thou, when thou art king, hang a thief' (*1 Henry IV*, 1.2.58–9). Although as king, Henry V will indeed see thieves hanged, friends of his or no, at this juncture he will help Falstaff to evade justice. 'The money shall be paid back again with advantage', he declares (*1 Henry IV*, 2.4.533–4), but he will rescue Falstaff. 'I'll procure this fat rogue a charge of foot', Hal says (*1 Henry IV*, 2.4.531–2). That may seem an effort to force some remedy on Falstaff, but the direct effect is rather different, if not immediately apparent. In the subsequent play, the Lord Chief Justice reminds Falstaff that he sent for him after the robbery 'when there were matters against you for your life' (*2 Henry IV*, 1.2.131–2). Falstaff replies that 'As I was then advised by my learned counsel in the laws of this land-service, I did not come' (*2 Henry IV*, 1.2.133–4). Military service makes Falstaff temporarily immune from civilian prosecution:[61] far from being made answerable, Hal

---

[60] Spraggs, *Outlaws & Highwaymen*, pp. 123–4; Green, *A Crisis of Truth*, pp. 188–91.
[61] *The Second Part of King Henry IV*, ed. Humphreys, 1.2.134n.

uses his royal power to place Falstaff, at least for a time, beyond the long arm of the law.[62]

Both Hal's pretence at banditry and his accommodation of Falstaff and his like are, of course, temporary, and in *Henry IV Part 2*, Hal is reconciled with both his dying father and with his Lord Chief Justice. Both still express fears of the prodigal ascending the throne. Henry IV worries that when he is gone, under his son England will become a wilderness, 'peopled with wolves' (*2 Henry IV*, 4.5.137); the Lord Chief Justice that his service of Henry IV 'hath left me open to all injuries' (*2 Henry IV*, 5.2.8). Hal's conflict with the representatives of the law clearly goes further than his play-acting at Gadshill and his protection of Falstaff. Shakespeare's play describes (though unlike *The Famous Victories of Henry the Fifth* it does not show)[63] an incident where Hal, seeking to free Bardolph, his retainer, assaulted the Lord Chief Justice and was temporarily committed to prison as a result. The Lord Chief Justice recollects the incident in speaking to the (now) king Henry V (*2 Henry IV*, 5.2.76–83). Henry, in reply, quotes his late father, who reports himself gladdened to have both a justice bold enough to imprison a prince, and a son who will submit to justice (*2 Henry IV*, 5.2.108–12). But this is clearly Henry IV's retrospective spin-doctoring of events: the episode's more obvious meaning is that Hal's disregard for law has extended as far as physical assault upon the justice administering it. Certainly his enmity towards that justice is assumed by all to endure long afterwards.

Following his father's death, however, Henry does submit to the law. He confirms the Lord Chief Justice in office, and in the following play, when Bardolph finds himself once again on the wrong side of the law, Henry speaks to condemn him, not to save him. In tandem with his submission to justice, Henry banishes Falstaff, an action perhaps predicted in the earlier play, when Falstaff (playing at being Henry IV) pleads on his own behalf against banishment (*1 Henry IV*, 2.4.461–7), to which Hal, of course, replies 'I do; I will'. But if Henry V in his first actions as king submits to law and banishes the accessories of his former lawlessness, we can nonetheless read him in the subsequent play as an outlaw of a different sort, engaged in potentially extralegal actions in defence of his state.

War and Law in *Henry V*

There is much discussion at the beginning of *Henry V* about the legitimacy of Henry's claim to the throne of France, a claim he will seek to enforce

---

[62] Medieval practice did see the king offer pardons to prisoners and outlaws in return for military service: Bellamy, *Crime and Public Order*, pp. 192–3, 197.

[63] *Narrative and Dramatic Sources of Shakespeare*, ed. Bullough, IV, 307–10.

through arms and negotiation for the remainder of the play. The Archbishop of Canterbury offers a lengthy justification of Henry's claim to the French throne, through his great-grandmother, Isabella, wife of Edward III, and daughter of Philip IV of France. The Archbishop's advice is unambiguous (even if there are questions about his motives in offering it), and Henry's prior warning to tell the truth is clear. Canterbury's speech offers Henry the justification he needs to go to war in France.

But, as with the opening of *Richard II*, there is a great deal here left unsaid. Henry claims France as heir to Edward III of England. The unspoken question is not whether he is rightful heir to France, but whether he is rightful heir to England? Was Henry IV really heir to Richard II? If not, Canterbury's justification of the English claim to the French throne by inheritance might well relate not to Henry, but to the Mortimers. 'No king of England, if not king of France!' declares Henry as he departs for war (*Henry V*, 2.2.194). The reverse is also true. Although Shakespeare's text conceals it, as Andrew Gurr notes, the conspiracy against Henry (exposed some lines earlier in act two scene two) is based upon the Mortimer claim to the throne.[64]

Henry IV's deathbed advice to his heir at the end of *Henry IV Part 2* is very specifically related to the 'by-paths and indirect crook'd ways' by which he gained the crown (*2 Henry IV*, 4.5.184), and the dangers yet posed by those who helped him to gain it, one-time allies who might have undone him after. Henry's advice to his son is to use 'foreign quarrels' as a distraction (*2 Henry IV*, 4.5.213–14): advice that Henry V takes.

Richard II's death and the rightness of Henry V's claim to France are raised again on the eve of Agincourt. The king, disguised under Sir Thomas Erpingham's cloak, is in conversation with three soldiers. When Henry says he would be content to die beside the king, 'his cause being just and his quarrel honourable' (*Henry V*, 4.1.126–8), Williams replies 'That's more than we know' (*Henry V*, 4.1.129). Perhaps it is more than Henry knows too: later in the same scene he kneels and prays that God will ignore his father's fault 'in compassing the crown' (*Henry V*, 4.1.290–1). The means by which Henry IV gained the crown of England still cast their shadow over his son, as the younger Henry prepares to do battle for a second crown, that of France. His claim to one depends on his shaky right to the other.

The portrayal of Henry's French campaign proceeds from an early confrontation, at Harfleur, to a concluding one, at Agincourt. In each, there are questions to be asked about the king's conduct in relation to law. The historical Henry V issued military ordinances in 1415, 1417 and 1419 (or possibly

---

[64] *King Henry V*, ed. Gurr, pp. 19–21.

1421) to govern the conduct of his soldiers in France. Surviving texts have not proved precisely datable, but, as Anne Curry comments, 'when considering the possible content of Henry's ordinances in both 1415 and 1417, we must remember he was not working from scratch', and chronicle evidence suggests Edward III's ordinances issued in 1346 for his own campaign in France forbade the burnings of towns or manors, the sacking of churches or holy places, the harming or molesting of children or women, the threatening of people or doing any kind of wrong.[65]

Curry's compiled text from five versions of ordinances associated with Henry includes the following:

> c. Not to rob or pillage a church, nor to attack man of church or woman, nor to take prisoner unless armed, nor to rape a woman: hanging.[66]
> ff. If any country or lordship is won or by free will offered to the king's obedience, no one should rob or pillage there after peace is proclaimed: penalty death.[67]

Shakespeare's Henry, too, is rigid in enforcing such discipline upon his army. Approving the order to execute his sometime companion Bardolph for robbery of a church, he says:

> We would have all such offenders so cut off; and we give express charge that in our marches through the country there be nothing compelled from the villages, nothing taken but paid for, none of the French upbraided or abused in disdainful language; for when lenity and cruelty play for a kingdom, the gentler gamester is the soonest winner. (*Henry V*, 3.6.106–12)

Before the gates of Harfleur a few scenes earlier, however, we see a very different side to Henry, as he threatens the civilian population with a gory vision of their fate if they resist him (*Henry V*, 3.3.10–21). Harfleur, Henry says, must surrender 'whiles yet my soldiers are in my command' (*Henry V*, 3.3.29):

> If not, why, in a moment look to see
> The blind and bloody soldier with foul hand
> Defile the locks of your shrill-shrieking daughters,
> Your fathers taken by the silver beards,
> And their most reverend heads dashed to the walls,
> Your naked infants spitted upon pikes,
> Whiles the mad mothers with their howls confused

---

[65] Curry, 'Military Ordinances', p. 229.
[66] Curry, 'Military Ordinances', p. 240.
[67] Curry, 'Military Ordinances', p. 247.

Do break the clouds, as did the wives of Jewry
At Herod's blood-hunting slaughtermen. (*Henry V*, 3.3.33–41)

Contrasting these threats with the 'existing and emerging norms protecting women and others from the ravages of war', norms of the sort documented in the historical Henry's own ordinances, and suggested by the Shakespearean Henry's own ruthlessness towards Bardolph some scenes later, Theodor Meron makes a distinction between 'the treatment of both combatants and civilians in captured territory or on the battlefield, on the one hand, and their treatment in a besieged city or fortress that was taken by "assault," on the other hand'. In the latter context, we are told, 'unmitigated brutality' was the expected norm (albeit a norm challenged by Renaissance writers on *jus gentium*).[68]

Unmitigated brutality might be expected, but the language of Henry's speech to the defenders of Harfleur invokes the notion of the protection of innocents by threatening the opposite. If the city is sacked, Henry says, women, children and the elderly will be raped and killed. Some of this imagery is recurrent in the play – in Andrew Gurr's reading, 'the war is imaged as dog-hearted soldiers raping the daughters of France'[69] – but here the Biblical parallels suggest an even greater extreme: these actions will be the 'fell feats' of 'the prince of fiends', and the killing of children will be like Herod's slaughter of the innocents.[70]

What we see in Henry's speech before Harfleur is the ability of the king to give, to make, but also to suspend the law: the licensing of exception. Normally, women, children and the elderly are vulnerable in wartime, but the law-enforcing king, in issuing ordinances to restrain his soldiers, seeks to protect them. Here, Henry's soldiers remain in his command for now, but if the town does not surrender, Henry will release them from that command. The captured town will then become a space where legal norms protecting innocents are deemed not to apply, and slaughter, describable in Biblical terms, will ensue. In the play, the town surrenders, and Henry tells Exeter to 'use mercy' to the population (*Henry V*, 3.3.54): the massacre of Harfleur is one conjured only in words. But that is not to say we do not believe Henry's threats. We do.[71]

---

[68] Meron, *Henry's Wars and Shakespeare's Laws*, pp. 101–3; cf. the similar argument in Keen, *Laws of War*, pp. 121–4.

[69] *King Henry V*, ed. Gurr, p. 13.

[70] We can see comparisons with Herod used elsewhere to condemn the killing of non-combatants: see Blind Harry, *The Wallace*, 1.165–6.

[71] Meron, *Henry's Wars*, pp. 77–81, 85–7, notes the emphasis on mercy, not in Holinshed or Hall; historically, the population of Harfleur was expelled and replaced with English

The second instance where Henry's military decisions are open to legal question is the killing of French prisoners at Agincourt. The French have had the worst of the battle, but still outnumber the English (*Henry V*, 4.5.19–21). The French rally, and Henry notes that 'the French have reinforced their scattered men' (*Henry V*, 4.6.36). He then orders the English troops to kill their prisoners (*Henry V*, 4.6.37). In the next scene, Fluellen and Gower reveal that a French attack upon the English camp, guarded only by boys, has seen the boys killed and the luggage plundered. This action by the French, Fluellen says, is 'expressly against the law of arms' (*Henry V*, 4.7.2),[72] and Gower retrospectively interprets Henry's order to kill the prisoners as given in retaliation for this action by the French (*Henry V*, 4.7.7–10).

Meron notes these two potential justifications for Henry's killing of the prisoners: reprisal for the French attack on the English servants in the rear, or the danger of the French prisoners rejoining the renewed battle. He finds both unconvincing, but goes on to say that killing prisoners, though condemned by some writers, cannot be shown to have 'clearly violated contemporary standards'.[73] The historical Henry's ordinances have plenty to say about prisoners, but primarily in relation to their economic value and secure quarantine with their captors; there is nothing here to say prisoners cannot be killed.[74] But the killing of prisoners is not so easily passed over.

The treatment of prisoners recurs in different ways as an issue across the tetralogy. In *Henry IV Part 1*, prisoners are valuable in a variety of ways: economically, politically and symbolically. The play opens with a dispute over King Henry's demand that Hotspur give up his recently captured Scottish prisoners.[75] Hotspur holds out, seeking a return on any such surrender: he wants Henry to fund the ransom of his brother-in-law, Edmund Mortimer. Henry refuses, alleging treason by Mortimer (who in the play is Richard II's designated heir, and as such a threat to Henry's throne),[76] and repeats the

settlers; Meron draws the contrast with the widespread killing of the population during Henry's conquest of Caen.

[72] Meron, *Henry's Wars*, pp. 157–60, questions Fluellen's assertion.

[73] Meron, *Henry's Wars*, pp. 154–69. Keen, *Laws of War*, does not discuss the killing of prisoners at Agincourt, but discusses surrender in general as a contractual condition made in order to save the prisoner's life, which rendered the prisoner a non-combatant (pp. 156–60). For a defence of Henry's killing of the prisoners from an ethical perspective, see Condren, 'Understanding Shakespeare's Perfect Prince', pp. 202–4.

[74] Curry, 'Military Ordinances', pp. 240–9.

[75] On the legal basis for the demand and refusal, see Rauchut, 'Hotspur's Prisoners'.

[76] Historically, the Edmund Mortimer sent to Wales was the uncle of the Edmund Mortimer, Earl of March, supposedly designated Richard II's heir (*King Henry IV Part 1*, ed. Kastan, 1.3.84–5n., 1.3.144–5n.).

demand that Hotspur surrender his prisoners. This dispute is the spark for rebellion, and one of the first decisions the conspirators make is to return the disputed prisoners without ransom as a prelude to gaining Scottish support against Henry (*1 Henry IV*, 1.3.254–61). The treatment of noble prisoners is again a key issue at the end of the play. The Douglas (in the play, though not historically, the father of Murdoch, earl of Fife, captured by Hotspur at the outset)[77] is released without ransom by Hal after the battle of Shrewsbury, in recognition of his actions on the battlefield (*1 Henry IV*, 5.5.27–31). Shakespeare's allocation of this action – the noble treatment of a noble prisoner – to Hal, rather than his father, is a mark of Hal's emerging maturity and fitness to rule,[78] but it also stands in sharp contrast with the very different choices he makes towards the end of *Henry V*.

Prisoners are treated much more harshly by Hal's brother Prince John of Lancaster in *Henry IV Part 2*. Having promised rebel leaders that their complaints will be redressed, and having persuaded them to disband their forces, John has Hastings, York and Mowbray arrested and sent to execution (*2 Henry IV*, 4.2.106–23). These rebel leaders were not formally prisoners in the same way Douglas was, but Coleville of the Dale, who surrenders to Falstaff in the next scene, and is therefore a prisoner, is likewise sent to execution by John (*2 Henry IV*, 4.3.71–3). John breaks no laws here, but his actions show a ruthlessness not seen in the first Henry IV play (in keeping, perhaps, with the general tendency for the second play to adopt a darker tone).

In *Henry V*, the stage direction at the beginning of act four scene six has Henry and his train arrive on stage with prisoners, and there is a debate as to whether or not these prisoners should be killed onstage in front of the audience once Henry gives his order.[79] Even if not, Gower reports the action in vivid terms, saying 'the King most worthily hath caused every soldier to cut his prisoner's throat' (*Henry V*, 4.7.8–10).[80] This image of throat-cutting recurs as a refrain throughout the play, in the mangled French phrase 'couple a gorge' (*Henry V*, 2.1.72), '*couper votre gorge*' (*Henry V*, 4.4.35–6), 'cuppele gorge' (*Henry V*, 4.4.37). Up until Henry's order, this phrase has been played for (grim) laughs. Now the cutting of throats recurs in deadly earnest. The

---

[77] *King Henry IV Part 1*, ed. Kastan, 1.1.71–3n.
[78] *King Henry IV Part 1*, ed. Kastan, p. 5, and 5.5.27–30n.
[79] *Henry V*, ed. Craik, 4.6.35–38n.
[80] Holinshed is even more graphic: 'When this dolorous decree, and pitifull proclamation was pronounced, pitie it was to see how some Frenchmen were suddenlie sticked with daggers, some were brained with pollaxes, some slaine with malls, other had their throats cut, and some their bellies panched, so that in effect, having respect to the great number, few prisoners were saved' (*Narrative and Dramatic Sources of Shakespeare*, ed. Bullough, IV, 397).

cutting of throats has criminal associations: a cutthroat is 'one who cuts throats; a ruffian who murders or does deeds of violence; a murderer or assassin by profession', a phrase attested in *OED* as early as 1535, and used of Shakespeare's Shylock (*Merchant of Venice*, 1.3.108).[81] Gower's praise of the decision notwithstanding, the transfer of the language of cutting throats from the cut-throat Pistol to the monarch, Henry, is an unsettling one, and in the Quarto text, the scene does not end with Henry's order: the last words are Pistol's, and the words are 'couple gorge'.[82]

When, some scenes later, Henry threatens once more to kill his prisoners, there is again a reference to the cutting of throats. Henry directs a herald to tell the remaining French on a nearby hillside either to come down or to void the field. If they will not, the English will come to them, but:

> Besides, we'll cut the throats of those we have,
> And not a man of them that we shall take
> Shall taste our mercy. Go and tell them so. (*Henry V*, 4.7.62–4)

Here, Meron's balancing of Shakespearean texts against early modern legal norms does find fault with Henry. The threat to kill his remaining prisoners and refuse quarter to any further prisoners taken should the French remain in the field 'was most likely in violation of the contemporary laws of war'.[83] Necessity has no law, perhaps, but here again we see Henry prepared to step outside legal bounds. And Henry's killing of prisoners to save his army (and his threat to repeat the action) also offers an unsettling resonance with the first play of the tetralogy, where Henry IV secures his state at the end of the play through the killing of a prisoner: Richard II.

Henry triumphs at Agincourt, and ends the play not just as King of England, but also heir to France. But if *Henry V* is a play about English triumph, it is also a play filled with concerns about the internal tensions within Henry's unstable state. Henry IV's advice to his son was to pursue 'foreign quarrels' in pursuit of domestic objectives: to keep the state intact. But what is Henry's state? The rhetoric of the opening scene of war, at Harfleur, is about England (*Henry V*, 3.1.1–2,17, 25–7, 34), but Henry's state (and person) notionally includes France, Wales and Ireland too. 'Macmorris is not the only one confused about cultural identity', writes Willy Maley, 'Henry V thinks he's England, France, Wales, Ireland, and he has a point, or a claim'.[84] Scotland, too, a separate kingdom and 'a giddy neighbour' (*Henry*

---

[81] *OED*, s.v. *cutthroat, cut-throat*, n., 1 (a), 6; *The Merchant of Venice*, ed. Halio.
[82] *Henry V*, ed. Craik, 4.6.35–8n.
[83] Meron, *Henry's Wars*, p. 170.
[84] Maley, 'Irish Text and Subtext', p. 118.

V, 1.2.145) is nonetheless represented in this hybrid English army: John Kerrigan suggests that James VI's likely succession to the English throne may inform the play's portrayal of the Scottish Captain Jamy as a peacemaker among the army's fractious collection of nationalities.[85] Along with these multinational tensions, we also have class issues and threats of aristocratic revolt within England itself canvassed at length in the Henry IV plays. If Henry succeeds in (temporarily) stabilising his state through his victorious campaign in France, the plays also reminds us at length of just how substantial those internal tensions are.

If Stephen Greenblatt's powerful reading of these plays suggested that 'Shakespeare's plays are centrally, repeatedly concerned with the production and containment of subversion and disorder'[86] (a formulation somewhat reminiscent of Aristotelian catharsis: subversion, rather like pity and fear in the *Poetics*, is created but safely contained within the theatre), we might argue here that containment, even where achieved, is not at all easily won. *Henry V* and the preceding plays in the tetralogy seem to offer an examination of historical power politics in which tensions within the state threaten repeatedly to consume it. Even if not all of these threats are what they seem (both the Lancastrian and Elizabethan regimes were capable of producing a state of 'managed insecurity' for political purposes),[87] the state here appears remarkably unstable, even in territorial terms. We see Richard II losing his campaign in Ireland, the contemplation of a redrawing of political boundaries within England and Wales in *Henry IV Part 1*, and a claim to France (eventually lost) in *Henry V*. As well as turmoil at the head, there are violent ebbs and flows here in what constitutes the physical, territorial body of the state. Such threats to the state, both body and head, are hardly alien to the Elizabethan regime. Act V of *Henry V* makes mention of the 'General of our Gracious Empress' (either Essex or Mountjoy) fighting Hugh O'Neill's Irish rebellion (*Henry V*, 5.0.30–2). Not long afterwards, *Richard II* became something of a politically dangerous text via its (likely unintended) association with Essex's rebellion.[88]

In counterpoint to such threats, the sovereign repeatedly acts outside the law to defend, and sometimes expand, the scope of his power. There are repeated instances in *Henry V* where we might suggest this is the case: if none

---

[85] Kerrigan, *Archipelagic English*, p. 15

[86] Greenblatt, 'Invisible Bullets', p. 40.

[87] Strohm, *England's Empty Throne*, pp. 63–100, discusses Lancastrian manufacture of (supposed) opposition precisely in order to contain it; the creation of a similar 'managed insecurity' in the Elizabethan era is discussed in Greenblatt, 'Martial Law in the Land of Cockaigne', pp. 136–8.

[88] For a recent discussion, see Scott-Warren, 'Was Elizabeth I Richard II?'.

are unambiguous, then we must acknowledge that *Henry V* is a play rich with uncertainties ('impossibly ambivalent' says Andrew Gurr of the Folio text).[89] But whether it is Henry's claim to the French throne (compromised by his weak claim to the English one), his threats to suspend the protection of the vulnerable should he take Harfleur by force, approving the hanging of his onetime companion Bardolph, or ordering the deaths of his French prisoners (with a threat to repeat the action a second time), we see Shakespeare's Henry V prepared either to use or suspend the law in his own interests and in the interests of his state, in a military campaign where both are very much at hazard.

Sovereign Outlaws: Plantagenet, Lancastrian, Elizabethan and Shakespearean

Outside of the plays, extralegal action in defence of the state is visible also in Elizabethan England. Stephen Greenblatt describes Queen Elizabeth as 'a ruler whose power is constituted in theatrical celebrations of royal glory and theatrical violence visited upon the enemies of that glory'. He continues by saying (in words that echo Foucault's *Discipline and Punish*):

> Power that relies upon a massive police apparatus, a strong middle-class nuclear family, an elaborate school system, power that dreams of a panopticon in which the most intimate secrets are open to the view of an invisible power – such power will have as its appropriate aesthetic form the realist novel; Elizabethan power, by contrast, depends upon its privileged visibility.[90]

All of this may be true, but the Elizabethan state is also not without recourse to invisible power. It does after all have an invisible network of spies and informers that deliver people up to this theatrical violence on the gallows or at the stake.[91] Greenblatt himself recalls this in his talk to the Iranian Shakespeare Congress in 2014, a talk where he seeks to explore the ways in which Shakespeare's work, with its characteristics of honesty, openness and freedom, is possible in a society as unfree as that of Elizabethan England (and contemporary Iran, too, he reminds us, is a state which spies upon and tortures its own people).[92]

---

[89] *King Henry V*, ed. Gurr, p. 63.
[90] Greenblatt, 'Invisible Bullets', p. 64.
[91] On which there is now a substantial literature; recent studies include Cooper, *The Queen's Agent*, and Alford, *The Watchers*. The English word *spy* seems to date from the mid-thirteenth century at least: see *OED*, s.v. *spy*, n. (1a), *MED*, s.v. *spie*. For a survey of espionage in later medieval England, see Arthurson, 'Espionage and Intelligence'.
[92] Greenblatt, 'Shakespeare in Tehran'.

We occasionally catch glimpses in the plays of these procedures of invisible power, in moments such as Hotspur's complaint that Henry IV 'sought to entrap me by intelligence' (*1 Henry IV* 4.3.98),[93] or the king's unexpected knowledge of the plot against him in act two scene two of *Henry V*.[94] Outside the theatre, these are also procedures that may have impinged on Shakespeare's life. The Elizabethan state's search for fugitive Catholic priests led to the capture and execution of Thomas Cottam, brother of the Stratford schoolteacher John Cottam; if the young Shakespeare spent time in Lancashire in the early 1580s, there are suggestions he did so (as Stephen Greenblatt, again, tells us) in the houses of families clinging to Catholicism.[95] Later in Shakespeare's life, the world of espionage and the world of the London theatre are connected in various ways. The authorities, we know, were keen to spy on any public gatherings, so there was always the possibility of spies in the audience.[96] But there were also several playwrights who may have worked on behalf of the Elizabethan secret state, or died because of it. Anthony Munday infiltrated the English College in Rome as a young man and later gave evidence against Edmund Campion.[97] Christopher Marlowe may or may not have been a spy, and his murder may or may not have been related to his possible sideline in espionage.[98] Thomas Kyd was questioned under torture by the state, dying soon afterwards.[99] Both the plays and Shakespeare's life, then, occasionally reveal the state's secret workings.

Furthermore, the violence that the early modern state enacts against its opponents is not always public and theatrical. Sometimes, both historically and theatrically, the state has people quietly murdered in secret, as we hear or see at both the beginning and end of *Richard II*. While, as Foucault has eloquently and persuasively shown, the modern state extends and refines these approaches enormously, it is not quite the case that the early modern state lacks these modes of power. Equally, neither is it the case that the modern

---

[93] *King Henry IV Part 1*, ed. Kastan, 4.3.98n glosses 'intelligence' here as 'spies'; cf. *OED*, s.v. *intelligence*, n. 6 (c).

[94] For the possible role of intelligence in the discovery of the Southampton plot, see Strohm, *England's Empty Throne*, p. 97.

[95] Greenblatt, *Will in the World*, pp. 97–8, 103–17.

[96] Greenblatt, *Will in the World*, pp. 187–8.

[97] Alford, *The Watchers*, pp. 56–68, 113–16, 316; coincidentally, Munday, the spy turned writer, plays a substantial role in the transformation of Robin Hood into a noble exile in his two plays about the outlaw (Knight, *Robin Hood: A Mythic Biography*, pp. 52–62; Knight and Ohlgren, pp. 296–440).

[98] On Marlowe and espionage, see Riggs, *World of Christopher Marlowe* and Honan, *Christopher Marlowe*, but cf. the contrary views of Bossy, 'Trust the Coroner'.

[99] Mulryne, 'Kyd, Thomas (bap. 1558, d. 1594)'.

state is so all-powerful that it has ceased to make use of the extrajudicial methods we have been looking at under the label of 'outlawry'. In fact, as we shall see, quite the contrary seems to be true.

3

The Endurance of Exclusion:
Versions of Ned Kelly

If enforcing the law in the medieval period often meant resorting to exclusion outside it, long after the autumn of the Middle Ages fugitives from justice continued to defy the law. Some of these fugitives were simply criminals: England boasts a tradition of highway robbers into the late eighteenth century, Dick Turpin being the most famous, who remain the subject of nineteenth-century nostalgia.[1] In other instances, banditry emerges from a context of broader conflict. In seventeenth-century Ireland, the bandits known as 'tories' and 'rapparees' are active in the aftermath of the Irish Confederate Wars.[2] Two centuries later on the other side of the Atlantic, Jesse James starts out serving with the guerrilla group known as Quantrill's Raiders during the American Civil War, and Billy the Kid's career takes place against the backdrop of the New Mexico factional conflict known as the Lincoln County War.[3]

To a certain extent, outlawry endures less as a legal practice than as a cultural phenomenon, for the word 'outlaw' has both a legal and a figurative sense.[4] Legally, an outlaw was a person declared to be outside the law and deprived of its benefits and protection. Figuratively, a person living without regard for the law, and particularly a fugitive from justice, might also be described as an outlaw, while not formally meeting the legal definition.

The Constitution of the United States did not either endorse or forbid outlawry, but outlawry was allowed in the constitutions of several individual states. Outlawry remained legal in New York, Pennsylvania and North Carolina into the 1970s: North Carolina outlawed an escaped prisoner in 1960. For the most part, however, states began to abolish outlawry in the

---

[1] Spraggs, *Outlaws and Highwaymen*, pp. 234–57.
[2] Ó Ciardha, 'Tóraíochas is Rapairíochas'; Corish, 'The Cromwellian Regime', p. 375, cites Major Anthony Morgan as describing the tory, the wolf and the priest as 'three beasts that lay burthens upon us' who are consequently hunted down.
[3] Seal, *The Outlaw Legend*, pp. 85–7, 103–9.
[4] *OED*, s.v. *outlaw*, n. and adj., A. n. 1. a and b.

aftermath of the Civil War. Mostly, then, the term is used of the American West not to describe individuals formally placed outside legal protection, but rather notorious fugitives from justice, few of whom were ever formally outlawed. However, the common law power of *posse comitatus* was used to mobilise citizens alongside lawmen in pursuit of criminals, and was often construed to authorise widespread manhunts.[5]

Outlawry in its legal sense of exclusion from law, however, does endure in nineteenth-century Australia. Both banditry and legal exclusion are present in colonial Australia from its foundation. Watkin Tench's account of the colony's earliest days records an escaped convict declared an outlaw as early as June 1788.[6] By 1791, there are at least thirty-eight escaped convicts living in the woods by day and raiding the colony's farms for subsistence by night.[7] In the early years, convicts attempting to escape overland almost inevitably died (in the gruesome case of Alexander Pearce and his fellow escapees from Macquarie Harbour, desperation led to cannibalism).[8] But as the nineteenth century progressed, bushrangers, as they were known, became a serious problem. In 1815, martial law was declared in Van Diemen's Land (Tasmania) in response to concern that bushrangers might form an alliance with the convict population against the authorities.[9] In 1830, the Bushranging Act, renewed in 1832 and 1834, allowed anyone in New South Wales to search and apprehend men suspected of being escaped convicts who could not prove otherwise.[10] By 1865, the authorities were declaring outlawry against bushrangers: the Felons Apprehension Acts 1865–99 in New South Wales, and related legislation in Victoria and Queensland, allowed outlawed persons who were armed (or believed to be armed) to be apprehended alive or dead by any person.[11] In the meantime, a small number from the hundreds and perhaps thousands of Australian bushrangers active during the nineteenth century – Jack Donohue, Frank Gardiner, Ben Hall, Daniel Morgan, Frederick Ward and Joseph Johns – became folk heroes.[12] One, Ned Kelly, would eventually become a kind of national icon.

---

[5] Prassel, *The Great American Outlaw*, pp. 106–10.
[6] Tench, *1788*, p. 67.
[7] Tench, *1788*, p. 212.
[8] Hughes, *Fatal Shore*, pp. 219–26.
[9] Hughes, *Fatal Shore*, p. 228.
[10] An Act to Suppress Robbery and Housebreaking and the Harbouring of Robbers and Housebreakers 1830; discussion in Hughes, *Fatal Shore*, pp. 236–7, Seal, *Outlaw Legend*, pp. 125–6.
[11] Felons Apprehension Act (NSW) 1865.
[12] Seal, *Outlaw Legend*, pp. 119–46.

'Any Amount of Injustice to be Had': Ned Kelly as Social Bandit

Many of the attributes of Hobsbawm's 'social bandit' can be made to fit the story of Ned Kelly, and may be seen both in Kelly's own self-presentation in *The Jerilderie Letter* and elsewhere and in his representation in popular culture.[13] This is not accidental. Kelly had the influence of real-life exemplars to follow (in particular his apprenticeship to the bushranger Harry Power). But there were also cultural constructions of banditry available to him, including books he is known to have read such as *Lorna Doone*, and a tradition of outlaw songs and ballads.

If such constructions helped to shape the actions of Ned Kelly and his companions, the outlaws sought in turn to fit the mould. This was partly pragmatism: in seeking to construct a support base, the Kellys relied on family loyalties, adherence to an ethical code, the distribution of money, and the exploitation of both social tensions and hostility towards the police. The guerrilla campaign the Kellys waged against the authorities in North-East Victoria was not fought only through concealment and direct action. They also sought, with mixed success, to further their case through the courts, in print (Kelly unsuccessfully attempted to print a defence of his position, the text now known as *The Jerilderie Letter*, in 1879), and via popular culture (there are Kelly songs and ballads contemporary with the gang's activities, some attributed to Joe Byrne).[14] In doing so, they presented themselves and their actions in familiar terms. In particular, the events that led to Kelly's outlawry in 1878 were, for Kelly and his supporters, the result of injustice: the first of Hobsbawm's 'social bandit' criteria.

The context is complex. The Kellys had a substantial criminal background: Ned Kelly had acted for a time as an apprentice to the bushranger Harry Power, and was subsequently involved in horse-theft with his step-father George King (in his own words, 'wholesale and retail horse and cattle dealing' (*Jerilderie Letter*, p. 21)).[15] More broadly, Ellen Kelly's family, the Quinns, had been the focus of intense police scrutiny since 1856.[16] Against that, there is also plenty of evidence of police harassment[17] (the Victorian police in these years were plagued by poor reputation, poor morale and

---

[13] Kelly, *Jerilderie Letter*. For the attributes of the 'social bandit', see Hobsbawm, *Bandits*, pp. 47–8, and cf. Seal, 'The Robin Hood Principle', pp. 74–5.

[14] 'Songs and Ballads', in Corfield, *Ned Kelly Encyclopaedia*, pp. 442–3.

[15] Jones, *Ned Kelly*, pp. 40–5, 50–72, 110–32.

[16] McQuilton, *Kelly Outbreak*, pp. 70–4.

[17] Jones, *Ned Kelly*, pp. 46–7, 101, 116–17.

insecure tenure).[18] Such harassment includes three possible instances of Ned Kelly being set up. The first was by Senior Constable Edward Hall in collaboration with Kelly's uncle Jack Lloyd: Lloyd, having previously betrayed Harry Power, now testified against his nephew, and the young Kelly was sentenced to six months in prison.[19] In the second instance, Kelly was convicted for receiving a stolen horse, and jailed for three years: Kelly alleged that Senior Constable Hall bribed a James Murdock to give evidence against him (*Jerilderie Letter*, p. 15).[20] The third involved Constable Alexander Fitzpatrick, who may have drugged Kelly's drink as a pretext for arresting him.[21]

Kelly complained too of police corruption: while he was in prison, he claimed, his own horses were stolen by Constable Ernest Flood (*Jerilderie Letter*, p. 19). Flood was probably also the father of Annie Kelly's child, born while her husband was in prison, the birth tragically followed by Annie's death.[22] Kelly suggested, too, that former Constable Michael Farrell had stolen a horse from Kelly's stepfather, George King.[23] This theft, Kelly says, and various false allegations against him by James Whitty and John Farrell, 'was the cause of me and my step-father George King taking their horses and selling them to Baumgarten and Kennedy' (*Jerilderie Letter*, pp. 23–4). This theft from Whitty and Farrell was the crime for which Alexander Fitzpatrick would later try to arrest Dan Kelly; that attempted arrest would ultimately lead to the Kelly gang's outlawry.

Fitzpatrick was a sometime friend of Kelly with a romantic interest in his sister Kate. He had nonetheless been involved in one previous incident where he arrested Ned Kelly, and another where he arrested his brother Dan Kelly and two cousins.[24] In the incident that would ultimately lead to Kelly's outlawry, Fitzpatrick attempted to arrest Dan Kelly at the family home. Receiving an injury to his hand in the resulting brawl, Fitzpatrick claimed that Ned had shot him. Ned Kelly denied being present, and denied too that Fitzpatrick had been shot (*Jerilderie Letter*, pp. 34, 38–9).[25] He also noted the

---

[18] McQuilton, *Kelly Outbreak*, pp. 64–8.

[19] Jones, *Ned Kelly*, pp. 74–9.

[20] Jones, *Ned Kelly*, p. 84, suggests Hall also perjured himself at the trial.

[21] Jones, *Ned Kelly*, pp. 122–5.

[22] Kelly, *Jerilderie Letter*, ed. McDermott, p. 19n.; Jones, *Ned Kelly*, pp. 86–9, 94.

[23] Jones, *Ned Kelly*, p. 120, suggests that this alleged theft might have been a fabrication by King.

[24] Jones, *Ned Kelly*, pp. 122–8.

[25] Much has been made of evidence by the treating doctor, who was not certain that the injury was a bullet wound (Kelly, *Jerilderie Letter*, p. 34n). Jones, *Ned Kelly*, pp. 137–8, 144–5, suggests this is professional caution rather than doubt.

flaw in Fitzpatrick's evidence where Fitzpatrick named William Skillion as being present at Eleven Mile Creek (*Jerilderie Letter*, pp. 29–31). Fitzpatrick had mistaken Joe Byrne for Skillion.[26]

Subsequent accounts by others suggest that Ned Kelly was present at the altercation, and that he did shoot and wound Fitzpatrick. These accounts, however, suggest that Kelly was provoked by the advances of Fitzpatrick, who had been drinking, towards his young sister Kate, and a heated argument between Fitzpatrick and Ned's mother Ellen Kelly, which saw Fitzpatrick draw his revolver.[27] The latter aspect of the incident appears in Kelly's version (*Jerilderie Letter*, p. 32). In these accounts, then, Kelly was not innocent of injuring Fitzpatrick, but was unjustly provoked into acting as he did. The authorities themselves were not inclined, subsequently, to stand in defence of Fitzpatrick, who was dismissed from the police force: the Royal Commission established after the Kelly outbreak described Fitzpatrick as 'a very indifferent character in the force'; Commissioner Chomley described him as 'a liar and a larrikin'.[28]

Whatever the truth of the Fitzpatrick incident, it saw Ellen Kelly, Brickey Williamson and William Skillion imprisoned for aiding and abetting an attempted murder, and caused Ned Kelly, Dan Kelly and Joe Byrne to flee as fugitives. The prison sentences were seen as harsh even by Captain Standish, the Chief Commissioner of Police.[29] Skillion, it seems, was entirely innocent, convicted by Alexander Fitzpatrick's perjury. On the other hand, it seems likely that Kelly, provocation notwithstanding, did shoot Fitzpatrick, and in doing so, as Ian Jones puts it, 'blundered into a capital crime'.[30]

In popular retellings of the Kelly story, these events are reshaped to align more closely with the 'social bandit' archetype. In the song 'Kelly Was Their Captain', the Fitzpatrick shooting is recast to present Kelly and his companions as chivalrous defenders of his mother against the hostility of the state: here, the Governor is Ned Kelly's enemy, multiple troopers come to take Dan, and Ned Kelly stands in defence of his mother's home.[31] The first Ned Kelly film, *The Story of the Kelly Gang* (1906) also portrays Ned Kelly's shooting of Fitzpatrick in defence of his mother and sister.[32] In both

[26] Jones, *Ned Kelly*, pp. 138–9.
[27] Jones, *Ned Kelly*, pp. 139–47. The story of Fitzpatrick's advance to Kate Kelly first appears in the Melbourne *Herald* of 7 February 1879, based on the report of a conversation between Kate Kelly and a group of travellers visiting the Kelly home.
[28] *Second Progress Report of the Royal Commission of Enquiry*, p. x.
[29] *Royal Commission on Police*, p. 1.
[30] Jones, *Ned Kelly*, p. 150.
[31] Seal, *The Outlaw Legend*, p. 165.
[32] *Story of the Kelly Gang*, dir. Tait.

Kelly's own (probably unreliable) account, then, and in sympathetic popular accounts since, Ned Kelly is criminalised as the result of an injustice.

Kelly's self-portrayal also meets the second of Hobsbawm's 'social bandit' criteria, for he was, by his own lights, a righter of wrongs. Kelly repeatedly demanded justice for his mother, his friends, and himself. 'If I get justice I will cry a go', he says in *The Cameron Letter*.[33] In *The Jerilderie Letter*, too, he demanded justice be done: 'it will pay Government to give those people who are suffering innocence, justice and liberty' (*Jerilderie Letter*, p. 27). If he stole horses from wealthy local landowners, Kelly protested, this was no more than payback for their impounding the animals of poor farmers (*Jerilderie Letter*, pp. 23–4). A very real ongoing antagonism between large and small landholders in North-East Victoria reflected the failure of the selection process introduced by the Land Acts of 1860–84;[34] the drought of 1876–7 exacerbated tensions.[35] The rewards offered by Stock Protection Associations (representing wealthy squatters) to members of the police for arrests and convictions relating to stock theft helped to align the police and the squatters in opposition to the impoverished selector class, contributing to the latter's sense of injustice.[36]

The third of Hobsbawm's criteria, taking from the rich and giving to the poor, requires some qualification. As Stephen Knight suggests, social bandits from Robin Hood onwards take from the rich 'to give not to some loosely identified poor', but to protect their own affiliates.[37] With that qualification, Kelly meets this requirement too.[38] Certainly there were some grand gestures towards liberating mortgageholders from their obligations to the banks via the destruction of bank papers at Euroa and Jerilderie,[39] and Kelly instructed his opponents that they should withdraw their funds from the stock protection society and give it to 'the widows and orphans and poor of Greta district' (*Jerilderie Letter*, p. 81). In general, though, the proceeds from Kelly gang robberies went to reward their supporters. When the police arrested a large number of suspected Kelly sympathisers in January 1879, the gang paid for their defence in court.[40]

---

[33] Kelly, *Cameron Letter*. Jones, *Ned Kelly*, p. 201, suggests that the phrase 'cry a go' here is an offer to give up bushranging, but is not an offer to surrender.
[34] McQuilton, *Kelly Outbreak*, pp. 24–47.
[35] Jones, *Ned Kelly*, pp. 111–12.
[36] McQuilton, *Kelly Outbreak*, pp. 61, 64.
[37] Knight, *Robin Hood: A Complete Study*, p. 79.
[38] Jones, *Ned Kelly*, pp. 215, 250.
[39] McQuilton, *Kelly Outbreak*, pp. 111, 119.
[40] Jones, *Ned Kelly*, p. 221.

Hobsbawm's suggestion that the outlaw should kill only in self-defence or revenge is paralleled by Kelly's insistence that he is no murderer. The Kellys and Joe Byrne were fugitives before the killing of three policemen at Stringybark Creek, but these deaths saw the Kellys and their companions outlawed. Kelly was adamant that he acted in self-defence. In October 1878, two parties of police set out from Greta and Mansfield to hunt for the Kellys in the Wombat ranges. The Mansfield group set up camp at Stringybark Creek. The Kellys, together with Joe Byrne and Steve Hart,[41] decided on a pre-emptive strike (*Jerilderie Letter*, pp. 44–5) and ambushed the camp with two policemen present, Thomas Lonigan and Thomas McIntyre. McIntyre surrendered; Lonigan broke for cover and was shot by Ned Kelly. Kelly claimed self-defence:

> he had just got to the logs and put his head up to take aim when I shot him that instant or he would have shot me as I took him for Strachan the man who said he would not ask me to stand he would shoot me first like a dog. (*Jerilderie Letter*, p. 46)

Kelly's account acknowledges errors made in the heat of events: the Kellys mistook Lonigan and McIntyre for their enemies Strachan and Flood (*Jerilderie Letter*, pp. 45–6), and that misidentification informed their actions. McIntyre later gave multiple, contradictory accounts of the incident: these predominantly suggested that Lonigan was either running towards cover or about to draw his revolver when shot, but not, as Kelly claimed, about to fire from cover.[42]

The arrival of the remaining two policemen from the party, Michael Scanlan and Michael Kennedy, saw a second gunfight. Scanlan fired and missed, Ned Kelly returned fire and wounded him (Joe Byrne may have fired the fatal shot that killed Scanlan).[43] McIntyre escaped on Kennedy's horse. Kennedy fired several times and retreated into the bush, with Ned Kelly in pursuit (*Jerilderie Letter*, p. 60). Here, Kelly admitted a second error: he did not realise that Kennedy had dropped his revolver and was about to

---

[41] As McDermott notes, Kelly attempts to avoid incriminating Byrne and Hart in his account (Kelly, *Jerilderie Letter*, p. 57n.).

[42] Jones, *Ned Kelly*, pp. 164–5, and cf. Phillips, *Trial of Ned Kelly*, pp. 47–50. Burnside, 'R v Edward (Ned) Kelly', while of the opinion that Kelly did not receive a fair trial, questions a potential claim of self-defence. Burnside suggests that Kelly fired one shot that passed through Lonigan's left forearm (raised defensively) and into his right eye, and that Lonigan's thigh wound could have been caused by the accidental discharge of his holstered weapon.

[43] Jones, *Ned Kelly*, p. 168.

surrender when he fired at Kennedy, wounding him fatally (*Jerilderie Letter*, p. 60).

But as Kelly repeatedly emphasises in *The Jerilderie Letter*, there was much to suggest that the police had come not to apprehend the Kellys, but to kill them:

> I asked him what they carried spenceir rifles and breech loading fowling pieces and so much ammunition for as the Police was only supposed to carry one revolver and 6 cartridges in the revolver but they had eighteen rounds of revolver cartridges each three dozen for the fowling piece and twenty one spenceir-rifle cartridges and God knows how many they had away with the rifle this looked as if they meant not only to shoot me only to riddle me. (*Jerilderie Letter*, p. 54)[44]

In addition to the extra armaments, the police also carried long straps specially made to carry bodies back on their packhorse.[45] Kelly's protests of self-defence suggest that his position prior to Stringybark Creek was already akin to that of an outlaw: that the police did not intend to capture him for trial, but to execute him with impunity.

At Kelly's trial for the murder of Lonigan, Sir Redmond Barry rejected the idea that Kelly could have acted in self-defence, telling the jury that the police party 'had a double protection: that of the ordinary citizen and that of being ministers of the law'. As executive officers of the law, 'no person had any right to stop them or question them'.[46] This, John Phillips suggests, may have been misdirection by Barry: if the demonstrated purpose of the police was to shoot Kelly down rather than arrest him, and he acted in proportionate self-defence, Kelly might have been acquitted on the murder charge.[47]

Hobsbawm's social bandit also receives popular support, and such support, overt or tacit, helped the Kelly gang to evade the authorities for twenty months. *The Jerilderie Letter* threatens those tempted by the proffered reward (*Jerilderie Letter*, pp. 74, 76), but as Redmond Barry remarks at the end of Kelly's trial, no one in the community seems to have been moved by it.[48] The network of sympathisers included around eighty members of the family, and spread out through friends and relatives. Anti-Kelly sentiment, prominent at first, declined after the Euroa robbery.[49] Sympathy or support for the

---

[44] Cf. also Kelly, *Jerilderie Letter*, pp. 39, 56, 63.
[45] Jones, *Ned Kelly*, p. 163.
[46] Quoted in Jones, *Ned Kelly*, p. 376.
[47] Phillips, *Trial of Ned Kelly*, pp. 89–94.
[48] 'Trial of Ned Kelly (1880)', in Corfield, *Ned Kelly Encyclopaedia*, pp. 472–81 (p. 478).
[49] Jones, *Ned Kelly*, pp. 216–17.

group, active or passive, was widespread through North-East Victoria.[50] The extent to which the Kellys are identified with the territory that sustains them is clear from the term 'Kelly country', used to describe the area by police evidence and the Royal Commission itself.[51] Active supporters kept them supplied with provisions and intelligence, and in some instances rode with the outlaws: the 'Kelly Gang', John McQuilton suggests, may have been less a fixed entity of four outlaws hiding in the bush, than varying combinations of outlaws and friends moving freely and sometimes separately about the country.[52] At the end, the number of people prepared to actually stand with the Kellys may have been substantial: a number of sympathisers (estimated at anything between thirty and 150) were armed and mustered near the gang's final stand at Glenrowan, but stayed away on Kelly's instructions as his plans went disastrously awry.[53] In the aftermath of Ned Kelly's death, apprehension of another, similar, outbreak, informed an effective policy of moderation by at least some within the Victorian police.[54]

The outlaw seems invisible and invulnerable, says Hobsbawm, and again, there is a long literary tradition of the outlaw as a trickster, or a shape-shifter.[55] Early in his career, there were misleading reports of Kelly's appearance;[56] later, Aaron Sherritt would describe Ned Kelly to the police as 'an extraordinary man', 'superhuman', 'invulnerable'.[57] What appears to be the incompetence of the police in the hunt for the Kellys might in part be explained by their terror. All this was before Kelly's appearance in the bulletproof armour that would become emblematic. At Glenrowan, faced with an armoured Kelly, the police were mystified by their opponent's identity: was he a madman, a ghost, the devil, bulletproof, the bunyip?[58]

But Kelly does not meet the last of Hobsbawm's criteria. In Hobsbawm's formula, the outlaw does not oppose the sovereign and the sovereign's justice, but only the oppression of local enforcers. Kelly complains at length about local oppression, but he departs from Hobsbawm's posited archetype in that he is critical too of the monarch and the entire English legal system. In doing so, he uses the rhetoric of Irish nationalism:

---

[50] McQuilton, *Kelly Outbreak*, pp. 144–51.
[51] *Second Progress Report of the Royal Commission of Enquiry*, pp. xiii–ix.
[52] McQuilton, *Kelly Outbreak*, pp. 143, 148.
[53] Jones, *Ned Kelly*, p. 309.
[54] McQuilton, *Kelly Outbreak*, pp. 176–85.
[55] Jones, *Outlawry in Medieval Literature*, pp. 90–104.
[56] Jones, *Ned Kelly*, pp. 57, 59, 68, 69.
[57] Jones, *Ned Kelly*, p. 254.
[58] Jones, *Ned Kelly*, pp. 317–18.

there never was such a thing as justice in the English laws but any amount of injustice to be had. (*The Jerilderie Letter*, pp. 16–18)

and rise old Erins isle once more, from the pressure and tyrannism of the English yoke. which has kept it in poverty and starvation. and caused them to wear the enemys coat. What else can England expect. (*Jerilderie Letter*, pp. 71–2)

Australia is not Ireland, as Kelly well knows: he refers to himself and those like him as *creoles* (*Jerilderie Letter*, p. 56), persons of European descent born in the colonies.[59] Furthermore, this is a drama where the Irish are protagonists on both sides:[60] the police at Stringybark Creek were all Irish, two Catholic and two Protestant.[61] But ideas of Irish oppression and resistance provide an ideology and rhetoric to express local grievances. As Patrick O'Farrell puts it, 'the atmosphere of the Kelly outbreak is Irish, its grievances and conditions local'.[62]

Hobsbawm notwithstanding, as we saw earlier in texts such as *The Tale of Gamelyn* and real-life examples of medieval English outlaws who either parody or temporarily usurp royal authority, it is possible for those excluded from law to pose a challenge to the authority of the sovereign. There are earlier Australian examples also: Michael Howe, leader of a gang of Tasmanian bushrangers until his death in 1818, styled himself 'Lieutenant-Governor of the Woods'.[63] Toward the end of *The Jerilderie Letter*, Ned Kelly too appropriates the sovereign's authority in a reversal of roles where he declares outlawry for his opponents:

those who would be so deprived as to take blood money will be outlawed and declared unfit to be allowed human buriel their property either consumed or confiscated and them theirs and all belonging to them exterminated off the face of the earth, the enemy I cannot catch myself I shall give a payable reward for. (*Jerilderie Letter*, pp. 74, 76)

The Jerilderie Letter is a defence of the Kelly gang's actions, certainly, submitted to the court of public opinion, but it is also something of a manifesto. It opens, after all, promising to describe occurrences past, present *and* future, and Ian Jones suggests that prior to Glenrowan, Kelly may have gone so far as to declare a vision for the future: a republic of North-East Victoria,

---

[59] *OED*, s.v. *creole*, n. and adj., A n. (a).
[60] McDermott, 'Apocalyptic Chant', p. xxx.
[61] Jones, *Ned Kelly*, p. 162.
[62] O'Farrell, *Irish in Australia*, p. 138.
[63] Hughes, *Fatal Shore*, p. 229.

'a wild, vague dream of justice for all'.[64] The Glenrowan campaign, Jones writes, is inexplicable without the central (but carefully obscured) plan to declare a republic.[65] McQuilton agrees: Kelly's attempt may have lacked the theoretical sophistication and political organisation of a successful revolutionary movement, but the 'emotional political symbol' of a republic gives a rationale for Kelly's actions at Glenrowan, and explains police concerns that the Kelly outbreak could lead to a much more substantial crisis of authority in North-East Victoria.[66] Towards the end of his campaign, then, Ned Kelly may have been moving towards a real challenge to the Victorian state akin to his rhetorical assumption of authority posed at the end of *The Jerilderie Letter*. This assumed authority, ironically enough, is rooted in exclusion: 'I am a widows son outlawed and my orders *must* be obeyed' (*Jerilderie Letter*, p. 83).

'As Helpless and Degraded as a Wild Beast of the Field': Ned Kelly as *Homo Sacer*

If Kelly fits Hobsbawm's 'social bandit' archetype in many respects, there are also several reasons for reading him, like all outlaws, as a version of Agamben's *homo sacer*. This begins even before his formal outlawry, for Kelly's justification in killing three policemen at Stringybark Creek was that they had come not to apprehend him, but to execute him with impunity. If Kelly fears this might have been his position prior to Stringybark Creek, it is unequivocally his position thereafter. The state of Victoria passed legislation authorising the Governor to proclaim individuals as outlaws, after which anyone could apprehend them dead or alive:

> And if after proclamation by the Governor, with the advice of the Executive Council, of the fact of such adjudication shall have been published in the Government Gazette, and in one or more Melbourne and one or more country newspapers, such outlaw shall be found at large armed, or there being reasonable ground to believe that he is armed, it shall be lawful for any of Her Majesty's subjects, whether a constable or not, and without being accountable for using of any deadly weapon in aid of such apprehension, whether its use be preceded by a demand of surrender or not, to apprehend or take such outlaw alive or dead.[67]

---

[64] Jones, *Ned Kelly*, pp. 275–6, 280, and cf. Brown, *Australian Son*, p. 12, 'Republic of North-Eastern Victoria', in Corfield, *Ned Kelly Encyclopaedia*, pp. 408–9.
[65] Jones, *Ned Kelly*, p. 277.
[66] McQuilton, *Kelly Outbreak*, pp. 168–70.
[67] Text of the The Felons Apprehension Bill 1878, reported in *The Argus*, 31 October 1878.

Having failed to surrender, Ned Kelly, Dan Kelly and their two unnamed accomplices are duly outlawed.[68]

Sir Redmond Barry's speech after Ned Kelly's trial gives us a portrait of the outlaw as outcast from society, reduced to the status of a wild animal. Here, again, is the outlaw as a sort of *homo sacer*:

> *Barry:* A felon who has cut himself off from all decencies, all the affections, charities, and all the obligations of society is as helpless and degraded as a wild beast of the field. He has nowhere to lay his head, he has no-one to prepare for him the comforts of life. He suspects his friends, he dreads his enemies, he is in constant alarm lest his pursuers should reach him, and his only hope is that he might use his life in what he considers a glorious struggle for existence. That is the life of the outlaw or felon …
> *Kelly:* An outlaw![69]

If this is Redmond Barry imagining the life of a fugitive cast out from the law, Robert Drewe's novel *Our Sunshine* gives us a much more vividly conceived version of Ned Kelly as *homo sacer*.[70] Here, Kelly has conducted a secret affair with the wife of a squatter, Mrs C. Later, at their most desperate, the gang appears on her croquet lawn:

> This was a week or two after Hare's men poisoned our dam with three strychnine-baited pigs and a decomposed roo or two, then set alight our hideout country to flush us out. (*Our Sunshine*, p. 70)

Kelly is by now 'a scorched beast-creature' (*Our Sunshine*, p. 72). The gang have killed their horses to drink their blood, eaten goannas and an anteater, chewed on gum leaves and sucked on rocks. Kelly has eaten his own chin-strap. They are caked in blood, humming with flies. Steve Hart is beginning to sprout maggots. Mrs C. wonders 'if I should shoot you for humanity's sake' (*Our Sunshine*, p. 72).

Such imagined portraits of outlaws desperately attempting to escape from a hostile society are really only true of the Kellys in the initial days of their outlawry in late October and early to mid-November of 1878: Drewe's novel is explicitly 'a chronicle of the imagination' (*Our Sunshine*, p. 183). On 1 November, the outlaws were hiding in a clump of reeds, up to their necks in water, to avoid the police. On 2 November, Kelly told Mary Vandenberg of the Victoria Hotel, Everton that 'my men are in rags and must be fed'.[71]

---

[68] Jones, *Ned Kelly*, pp. 196–7.
[69] 'Trial of Ned Kelly' in Corfield, *Ned Kelly Encyclopaedia*, p. 478.
[70] Drewe, *Our Sunshine*.
[71] Jones, *Ned Kelly*, pp. 180–1.

But desperation of this sort is short-lived. Escaping the immediate pursuit of police, the gang returned to their home area, where they were concealed by community support.

Redmond Barry's subsequent comments show the extent to which his portrait of the outlaw as entirely excluded from society is a callous sort of wishful thinking. Barry comments:

> The love of country, the love of order, the love of obedience to the law, have been set aside for reasons difficult to explain, and there is something extremely wrong in a country where a lawless band of men, you and your associates, are able to live 18 months disturbing society.[72]

The outlaws are not solitary figures of abjection, as Barry might wish them to be. They are a 'band of men', and in fact they are more than that, for their survival for such a length of time means they are a band of men supported by their community. Such support leads Barry to comment that 'there is something extremely wrong' in a country where fugitives can survive for this length of time. In outlawing the Kelly gang, then, the state might wish to render them *homines sacri*. But community support means they are protected from the full force of such exclusion.

In attempting to undermine such support, the police arrested twenty-one relatives and associates of the Kellys in January 1879 under the outlawry legislation, and, in the absence of evidence, repeatedly remanded them in custody for a period of months, in what amounted to a policy of interning supporters.[73] Describing his opposition to this policy at the Royal Commission, Superintendent Sadleir declared it unlawful: 'It would have been a very good step if it had been lawful, and if we could have kept them right enough, but it was both unlawful and we could not keep them; I knew that'.[74]

If the Kelly gang are placed outside the protection of the law, we also see the authorities' disregard for the lives of others. The police employed spies in an effort to apprehend the gang: these agents, funded by secret service monies, assisted 'at the risk of their lives', in the words of Assistant Commissioner Nicolson.[75] One such agent was Aaron Sherritt, murdered by the gang as a prelude to the events at Glenrowan. Ian Jones suggests that Sherritt might not have been a traitor to the gang, but the loser in a game of double-bluff. If Sherritt was merely pretending to aid the police, joining in futile surveillance exercises, it is possible that the police, and in particular

---

[72] 'Trial of Ned Kelly' in Corfield, *Ned Kelly Encyclopaedia*, p. 479.
[73] Jones, *Ned Kelly*, pp. 219–21.
[74] *Royal Commission on Police*, p. 120.
[75] 'Captain Standish to the Chief Secretary'.

Detective Michael Ward, were less interested in Sherritt as an informer than as bait to draw the Kellys out.[76] If so, they were prepared to sacrifice Sherritt's life to gain advantage over the Kellys.

Further lives were taken during the gang's final stand at Glenrowan, this time by the police, who fired extensively on the hotel occupied by the Kellys despite the presence of a large number of local citizens detained by the gang. As described by the Royal Commission:

> After the first volley some of the female prisoners in the hotel escaped; but at the time Sergeant Steele took up his position, close to the rear of the hotel, Mrs. Reardon and some members of her family endeavored to make their escape. Mrs. Reardon, who had a child in her arms covered with a shawl, states distinctly that Sergeant Steele deliberately fired at her, and produced, before the Commission, a shawl perforated apparently by a bullet. Steele denies the allegation; but admits having shot young Reardon, who, it is asserted, neglected, when ordered, to put up his hands. The ball or pellet fired entered his breast, and lodged beneath the ribs, but did not cause death. Indeed, the firing at this time, by all accounts, seems to have been indiscriminate, the blacks particularly being industrious in potting away at the premises. The prisoners, in a state of terror, arranged to hold out a white handkerchief, at which several shots were immediately fired, a proceeding highly reprehensible, as the most untutored savage is supposed to respect the signal of surrender. The order was given to fire high, but not before one of Mrs. Jones' children and a man named Martin Cherry were wounded, the latter fatally.[77]

In fact, Martin Cherry was not the only death, for two of Ann Jones's children were wounded, one fatally. Fifteen-year-old Jane Jones was grazed by a bullet. Thirteen-year-old John 'Jack' Jones was shot in the hip, and died in hospital. Here we see that in the pursuit of the Kelly gang, it is not just the outlaws themselves, three of whom die at Glenrowan, but also innocent civilians who are at risk of being killed with impunity.

'Australian Son': Ned Kelly as Foundational Myth

Ned Kelly, says Robert Drewe, is 'a man whose story outgrew his life' (*Our Sunshine*, p. 183). There have been many Australian outlaws, but the story of Ned Kelly, through repeated retellings, has become something of a national myth. As well as Kelly's own writings, the accounts of contemporaries, and

---

[76] Jones, *Ned Kelly*, pp. 264–5, 272–4. Cf. 'Sherritt, Aaron (1854–80)' in Corfield, *Ned Kelly Encyclopaedia*, pp. 430–4.

[77] *Second Progress Report of the Royal Commission of Enquiry*, p. xxvii.

a range of factual historical and biographical studies,[78] Kelly's story has been repeatedly retold in a variety of forms. The earliest Kelly songs, some attributed to Joe Byrne, were published in 1879,[79] and through the twentieth century and into the twenty-first, there have been musical, artistic, dramatic, fictional and cinematic versions of the Kelly story.[80] Some contributors to Kelly culture have done so on both sides of the dividing line between fiction and non-fiction: Ian Jones was co-writer of the screenplay for Tony Richardson's film version of Kelly's life,[81] and later co-writer and executive producer for the television series *The Last Outlaw*,[82] but also the author of what remains the most substantial biography of Kelly.

Interest in Kelly becomes more pronounced at particular moments in time. John McQuilton notes that J. J. Kenneally's sympathetic and influential book, *The Inner History of the Kelly Gang and Their Pursuers*, 'coincided with the Great Depression when the Kelly story achieved both a new lease of life and a new significance'.[83] As the curators of the State Library of Victoria's *Kelly Culture* exhibition observed, 'key periods of Kelly culture have occurred at times when Australia has been consciously examining itself in an international context'. Such moments include the 1980 centenary of the Kelly outbreak, certainly, but also during and after the wartime period of the 1940s – Max Brown is perfectly conscious of this as the context for his own writing on Kelly[84] – and again in the early 2000s, in the aftermath of a debate around national identity centred on the possibility of an Australian republic.[85]

Particularly important or influential versions of the Kelly story include Douglas Stewart's verse play *Ned Kelly*,[86] Sidney Nolan's *Ned Kelly* paintings where Kelly is abstracted into an archetypal masked figure,[87] and two very

---

[78] McQuilton, *Kelly Outbreak*, pp. 202–9, offers a review of the biographical literature to 1987.

[79] 'Songs and Ballads', in Corfield, *Ned Kelly Encyclopaedia*, pp. 442–3.

[80] *Kelly Culture*, pp. 13–31; see also 'Films on Ned Kelly', in Corfield, *Ned Kelly Encyclopaedia*, pp. 151–62, 'Novels on the Kelly Outbreak', in Corfield, *Ned Kelly Encyclopaedia*, pp. 373–4, and 'Plays on the Kelly Outbreak', in Corfield, *Ned Kelly Encyclopaedia*, pp. 392–3. For a variety of responses to the Kelly story by contemporary artists, see Curtin, Fitzgibbon and Quinlan, *Imagining Ned*.

[81] Richardson, *Ned Kelly*.

[82] Dobson and Miller, *The Last Outlaw*.

[83] McQuilton, *Kelly Outbreak*, p. 204.

[84] Brown, *Australian Son*, p. 9.

[85] *Kelly Culture*, pp. 8, 30–1.

[86] Stewart, *Ned Kelly*.

[87] *Sidney Nolan's Ned Kelly*.

different novels: Robert Drewe's lush, hallucinatory *Our Sunshine* and Peter Carey's *True History of the Kelly Gang*.

'The Language of the Outlaw': Peter Carey's *True History of the Kelly Gang*

Peter Carey published his *True History of the Kelly Gang* in 2000.[88] The novel was widely praised; it won the 2001 Booker Prize, and in 2015 Robert McCrum included it as the final entry in *The Observer*'s list of the English language's one hundred greatest novels.[89] One of the most striking achievements of Carey's novel is its ability to give voice to exclusion: an act of literary ventriloquism that echoes Kelly's own *Jerilderie Letter*.

Carey comments in interview on the Hiberno-English background to the voice of the novel:

> When I got to *True History of the Kelly Gang*, I let myself do something that goes back to the beginning of my reading. I was nineteen and just discovering literature. I was reading Joyce, and at the same time I read the Jerilderie Letter, a letter written by Ned Kelly in a town where he was robbing a bank. It's a very Irish voice. I know it's not Joyce, but it does suggest even to a nineteen-year-old the possibility of creating a poetic voice that grows out of Australian soil, that is true to its place and hasn't existed before. I had that in my mind from very, very early. It was astonishing to me that I could finally do it.[90]

Aside from the coincidence in Carey's reading both texts at around the same time, there are perhaps two ways in which the language of *The Jerilderie Letter* might be described as Joycean. First, as McDermott suggests, the text's flow, in long streams of lightly punctuated free association, seems to prefigure modernism's attempts to bridge the gap between spoken and written language.[91] Secondly, though the letter is written in English, it is, as Carey says, 'a very Irish voice'.

There are several places in Joyce's work where language, and in particular the standard English that Joyce increasingly distances himself from as his work progresses, is associated with exclusion. Best-known is the episode in *A Portrait of the Artist as a Young Man* where Stephen Dedalus comes to the uneasy realisation that English will always be 'an acquired speech' for him, a

[88] Carey, *True History of the Kelly Gang*.
[89] McCrum, 'The 100 best novels: No 100 – True History of the Kelly Gang'.
[90] Jones, 'Peter Carey, The Art of Fiction'.
[91] McDermott, 'Apocalyptic Chant', p. xxix.

non-English speaker of the English language.[92] Another example, potentially useful for our purposes here, occurs in the 'Aeolus' episode of *Ulysses*. Here, in a speech on the Irish language revival movement, the barrister John F. Taylor compares the Irish to the Israelites in their Egyptian exile. Had Moses submitted to the superiority of the Egyptians, Taylor concludes, he would never have come down from Mount Sinai 'bearing in his arms the tables of the law, graven in the language of the outlaw'.[93]

Joyce's source for this speech, and for the phrase 'the language of the outlaw', is a pamphlet by Roger Casement.[94] In Taylor's speech, 'the language of the outlaw' clearly means the Irish language, but in the context of *Ulysses*, it may also mean something else. Joyce's unease with standard English does not see him turn to Irish as the outlaw language in which the tables of the law might nonetheless be written. Rather, as Declan Kiberd says, the phrase 'the language of the outlaw' 'might be taken to indicate a new dispensation for literature, written, however, in the experimental language of the rebel'.[95] It is perhaps a dispensation of this sort that lies behind Carey's use of language in the *True History of the Kelly Gang*, a novel written in a sort of Australian Hiberno-English that is, quite literally, the language of the outlaw.

Kelly's language might be regarded as impoverished: *The Argus* described *The Jerilderie Letter* as 'written by a clever illiterate person'.[96] On the other hand, as with Joyce's employment of Hiberno-English, Kelly's language has a vigour and richness of its own. Aside from its non-standard grammar, and lack of punctuation, Kelly's language is also unmistakably hybrid: as Carey says, it is 'true to its place'. Take this passage from *The Jerilderie Letter*:

> the ungrateful articles convicted my mother and an infant my brother-in-law and another man who was innocent and still annoy my brothers and sisters and the ignorant unicorns even threathen to shoot myself But as soon as I am dead they will be heels up in the muroo. (*Jerilderie Letter*, pp. 26–7)

We can hear Kelly's Irish accent here in 'threathen', with lenition of 't' to 'th' echoing Irish-language practice. But if that makes it, as Carey says, 'a very Irish voice', the language here is also distinctively Australian. The final word here, *muroo*, is not in any dictionary. But Michael Farrell suggests that it may

---

[92] Joyce, *A Portrait*, p. 189.

[93] Joyce, *Ulysses*, p. 117.

[94] The text of the pamphlet is printed in Casement, 'The Language of the Outlaw'; for discussion see Bender, 'The Language of the Outlaw: A Clarification'; Keane, 'Quotation Marks'.

[95] Kiberd, *Inventing Ireland*, p. 348, though note also Kiberd's qualification of this suggestion (pp. 348–9).

[96] 'The Mansfield Murderers'.

be *maroo*, a word found in Charles Harpur's poem 'The Kangaroo Hunt', an Indigenous Australian word for a sort of brush iron-wood.[97]

Carey's novel, in turn, employs plenty of Irish words, such as *poteen* (*True History,* p. 47), from Irish *poitín*, illicit spirits;[98] *shebeen* (*True History,* p. 54), from Irish *síbín*, an unlicensed liquor-house;[99] *banshee* (*True History,* p. 98), from Irish *bean sí*, a spirit woman;[100] *bruitin* (*True History,* p. 42), from Irish *brúitín*, a mashed potato dish; and *corrovat* (*True History,* p. 104), referring to a nineteenth-century secret society, the Caravats, from Irish *carabhat*, meaning 'cravat' or 'collar'.[101]

But there are also Australian words from other sources. When a young Dan Kelly, worse for wear, accuses his brother of having a *donah* (*True History*, p. 213), this word for a woman or a sweetheart is of Spanish origin.[102] When Ned Kelly describes his uncles as *shicker* (*True History*, p. 173), meaning drunk, the word is from Yiddish.[103] When they will not *kowtow* (*True History*, p. 173) or defer, the word is from Mandarin.[104] There are Australian colloquialisms of English origin, too, such as *skerrick*, a fragment.[105] Carey's version of Kelly's voice echoes the melting-pot that is nineteenth-century Australia.

Unsurprisingly, Carey's vernacular narrative is also leavened with the literary. In interview, Carey mentions William Faulkner as well as Joyce as a possible exemplar,[106] and quotes Faulkner for the novel's epigraph. The book alludes to outlaw narratives both literary and real: Robin Hood and Dick Turpin, *Rob Roy* and *Lorna Doone* (*True History*, pp. 79, 207–8, 325, 385). There is also a glance towards W. B. Yeats as well as James Joyce: Ned's comment that Mary Hearn 'were a gazelle although I never saw a gazelle she were a foal' (*True History*, p. 233), is reminiscent of Yeats's description of Eva Gore-Booth and Constance Markiewicz:

> Two girls in silk kimonos, both
> Beautiful, one a gazelle.[107]

[97] Farrell, *Writing Australian Unsettlement*, p. 56,
[98] *Dictionary of Hiberno-English*, ed. Dolan, s.v. *poitín*, n.
[99] *Dictionary of Hiberno-English*, ed. Dolan, s.v. *shebeen*, n.
[100] *Dictionary of Hiberno-English*, ed. Dolan, s.v. *banshee*, n.
[101] Ó Muirithe, *Words We Use* (Dublin: Gill & Macmillan, 2006), p. 277.
[102] *Macquarie Dictionary*, s.v. *donah*, n.
[103] *Macquarie Dictionary*, s.v. *shicker*, n., and *OED*, s.v. *shicker*, adj. and n.
[104] *Macquarie Dictionary*, s.v. *kowtow*, v., and *OED*, s.v. *kow-tow*, v.
[105] *OED*, s.v. *skerrick*, n. (2).
[106] O'Reilly, 'The Voice of the Teller', p. 164.
[107] Yeats, *Collected Poems*, pp. 241–2.

Finally, and remarkably, if Kelly in his armour is like Cuchulainn in his war-chariot (*True History*, p. 371 and cf. pp. 25, 178), he is also like Shakespeare's Henry V before Agincourt (*True History*, pp. 388–9), though the Kellys, of course, do not prevail against impossible odds.

If Carey's version of Kelly's story employs a 'language of the outlaw', its narrative is one that intertwines multiple forms of exclusion. Australia, Carey says in interview, is a country of orphans:

> I have the good fortune that my own personal trauma matches my country's great historical trauma. Our first fleet was cast out from 'home.' Nobody really wanted to be there. Convicts, soldiers were all going to starve or survive together. Later, the state created orphans among the aboriginal population through racial policies, stealing indigenous kids from their communities and trying to breed out their blackness. Then there were all these kids sent from England to Dr. Barnardo's Homes, which were institutions for homeless and destitute children, some of them run in the most abusive, horrible circumstances.[108]

The novel's opening words are 'I lost my own father at 12 yr. of age' (*True History*, p. 5).

In Carey's version, it is Ned Kelly, not his father Red, whose killing of a strayed calf delivers Red to a prison sentence he cannot endure, and after that to a premature death (*True History*, pp. 22–5, 36–7). The children's uncle seems for a brief moment a possible substitute father, but the family are scattered when, drunken and lecherous, the uncle burns their house down (*True History*, pp. 43–9). When the family is reunited, Ned literally stands in his father's shoes (*True History*, p. 56), but finds himself pushed out as other men are welcomed in: 'it were like an adjectival railway station' (*True History*, p. 64). Eventually, he is apprenticed to the bushranger Harry Power, another poor excuse for a substitute father, his mother having secretly paid Power fifteen pounds to take him (*True History*, p. 102).

Long before he is an adult, Carey's Kelly is deprived both of his childhood ('in truth I do not know what childhood or youth I ever had' (*True History*, p. 183)) and any sense of home (*True History*, p. 196). Shame is the defining characteristic of his early life: his first memory is of his humiliated mother delivering a ruined cake to her imprisoned brother (*True History*, pp. 5–7). More humiliations follow. When his mother rebuffs a sexual overture from Sergeant O'Neil, O'Neil tells the children the gruesome tale of Red

---

[108] Jones, 'Peter Carey, The Art of Fiction'.

Kelly's crimes of murder and betrayal (*True History*, pp. 8–11). Even in his moment of youthful triumph, his rescue of the drowning boy Dick Shelton, Kelly would have asked for a dress for his mother as a reward, but is incapable of doing so (*True History*, p. 32). His eventual reward is his father's release, arranged by Shelton's father, but Red Kelly barely speaks a dozen words to his son from then to his early death (*True History*, pp. 34–7).

From the early episode with Sergeant O'Neil, it is clear that the family's socially marginal status leaves the Kelly women sexually vulnerable. James Kelly's attempt at sexual relations with a widowed Ellen leads to their house burning down. When Ellen Kelly is 'taking in laundry' in Wangaratta, even a naïve young Ned is suspicious of how that can be profitable (*True History*, pp. 50, 51–2). He is shocked to discover that Alex Gunn is visiting, not for his mother, but for his 'skinny sister' (*True History*, p. 66); that same sister will later die having given birth to Constable Flood's child while her husband and brother are in prison (*True History*, p. 191).

Kelly's oedipal nightmare continues when Bill Frost, his mother's lover, deserts her. On the advice of Harry Power, the young Kelly shoots Frost, believing he has killed him (*True History*, pp. 131–6), only to find later that Frost is alive, and that Power, too, has been sleeping with his mother (*True History*, pp. 143–5). It continues further when he comes home from prison to meet his mother's new spouse George King: 'It disgusted me to see his age he were young enough to be myself' (*True History*, p. 193). Later, he takes up with Mary Hearn, only to discover that the father of her child is the self-same George King (*True History*, pp. 244–6). When Carey's Kelly finally comes to shoot Alexander Fitzpatrick, then, who has come to arrest his brother or seduce his sister, and has drawn a pistol on his mother in a house with young children present, it is at the end of a long series of humiliating failures to protect his vulnerable family from both police oppression and sexual exploitation.

Carey's novel is not the first Kelly narrative to claim the mantle of truth, but it does so with a knowing irony, for it is at precisely the point where Carey not only extrapolates from history but introduces a purely fictional main character, Mary Hearn, that he asserts the 'true' (and secret) nature of the narrative (*True History*, p. 227). This 'true & secret' narrative gives Kelly both a lover and a daughter (as well as giving us a rich and complex version of Constable Fitzpatrick). Carey says in interview that one of the problems with his initial draft, composed as an extended version of *The Jerilderie Letter*, was that *The Jerilderie Letter* is a sort of public rhetoric, unworkable at novel length. Carey's solution was to write something more personal and confessional, which required a (posited) reader: here, Kelly's daughter. The creation of a fictional daughter also offers a sense of optimism; in giving the doomed man a child, Carey suggests there is a possible sense of a better time ahead.[109]

Fictional versions of the Kelly story often include a sexual aspect, for which there is little biographical evidence. Clare Wright and Alex McDermott are scathing of the romance plotline in Gregor Jordan's 2003 film version as 'Lady Chatterley's lover transplanted to the Antipodes'[110] (this aspect of the film derives from Robert Drewe's novel). If Carey's novel gives Ned Kelly a (not uncomplicated) secret relationship, it also contains an extended motif of cross-dressing that suggests other forms of (excluded) sexuality in Australian outlawry.

Cross-dressing is not unusual in outlaw tradition: as Timothy Jones comments, in medieval outlaw narratives 'the outlaw invariably adopts disguises that cross social, ethnic, gender, and racial boundaries', and the Englishman Hereward the Wake and the Scotsman William Wallace both adopt female disguises.[111] But the cross-dressing motif in Carey's novel also echoes its main concerns in a number of ways. The costumes are a sign of defiance, but also of failure. Initially, they are a motif of shame. Sergeant O'Neil's suggestion that Red Kelly, wearing a dress, 'was off to be serviced by his husband' (*True History*, p. 14) is intended to humiliate his son. Later, Steve Hart attempts to appropriate the disguise as a symbol of resistance and pride: 'I aint a sissy', he tells Ned, 'I'm a Lady Clare boy' (*True History*, p. 222). Mary Hearn's brutal story of a horse being tortured turns this attempt at appropriation into another motif of failure: 'this costume is worn by Irishmen when they is weak and ignorant' (*True History*, p. 311). At the end of the Kelly story, Ned and the others will wear a different costume instead, one intended to suggest strength rather than weakness, though this too will fail. There are hints of homosexuality here too: Heather Smyth documents the extent to which the language of Carey's novel alludes to and evokes sexual ambiguities and anxieties.[112] In penal Australia, a society with very few women, homosexuality was both common and punishable by death,[113] and the suggested pairing of homosexuality and outlawry again joins different forms of exclusion (a real-life example is the bushranger couple Andrew Scott and James Nesbit).[114]

Like the historical Kelly, Carey's version of the outlaw demands justice

---

[109] O'Reilly, 'The Voice of the Teller', p. 164.
[110] Wright and McDermott, 'Ned's Women'; Jordan, *Ned Kelly*.
[111] Jones, *Outlawry in Medieval Literature*, pp. 90, 97, 100.
[112] Smyth, 'Mollies Down Under', pp. 209–12.
[113] Hughes, *Fatal Shore*, pp. 264–72, 529–32, 536–8.
[114] Wotherspoon, 'Gay Men'.

(as he sees it) from a state based on injustice. If *The Jerilderie Letter* is, among other things, a defence of his cause, in Carey's novel we also see Kelly pleading his case at Euroa, before what is effectively an informally constituted jury of his peers. 'In the hut at Faithfull's Creek', Kelly says, 'I seen proof that if a man could tell his true history to Australians he might be believed it is the clearest sight I ever seen and soon Joe seen it too' (*True History*, p. 342). The people of Euroa, having heard his case, applaud the departing bank robbers (*True History*, p. 343).

But Kelly's attempts to offer his defence publicly are repeatedly thwarted, and his failure to find a hearing drives Kelly further towards revolt:

> I wished only to be a citizen I had tried to speak but the mongrels stole my tongue when I asked for justice they give me none. (*True History*, p. 375)

It is a desire for justice that sees Carey's Kelly refuse to leave Victoria with Mary Hearn (*True History*, pp. 350–2). In part, the justice that he seeks is personal: on the eve of Glenrowan he dreams of freeing his mother from jail (*True History*, p. 383). But, as in Ian Jones's version of Kelly, Glenrowan also represents something broader, as Kelly begins to fashion suits of bulletproof armour, and gathers his supporters with the intention to revolt: 'We wasnt men with pikes no more and would not repeat the tragedies of Vinegar Hill or the Eureka Stockade' (*True History*, p. 375).

Sidney Nolan compares his painting, *Glenrowan*, to an opera's concluding act.[115] Carey's Glenrowan, too, has its dramatic comparisons, Shakespearean rather than operatic, as Curnow the schoolteacher recites Henry V's St Crispin's Day speech at Mrs Jones's hotel (*True History*, pp. 388, 389). In one sense, the inclusion of the speech elevates the Kellys' last stand by drawing a parallel with Henry and his troops facing impossible odds at Agincourt (*True History*, p. 389). If this seems unlikely, it is worth remembering again the Joycean subtext to Carey's Kelly narrative, for *Ulysses* is the great example of elevating the everyday and the vernacular to the status of epic.

In another sense, though, the inclusion of these lines from Shakespeare is filled with irony. Not only do the Kelly gang not triumph against the odds at Glenrowan, it is Curnow, the man reciting Shakespeare, who will betray them. Kelly feels that Curnow's face is 'that of a soldier by my side' (*True History*, p. 389), but the lines that Curnow begins with are telling:

> he who has no stomach for this fight,
> Let him depart; his passport shall be made,
> And crowns for convoy put into his purse. (*True History*, p. 388)

[115] *Sidney Nolan's Ned Kelly*, p. 70.

The man with no stomach for the fight, in fact the man fervently opposed to the Kellys, is Curnow, who will indeed depart, to warn the police. In Carey's version of the story, Curnow's passport is the manuscript we are reading, which he has undertaken to edit. Carey does not mention the crowns that Curnow receives by way of reward from the government: £550 initially, subsequently increased to £1,000.[116]

The Kelly gang's last stand at Glenrowan is a disaster, as the police fire on the hotel where both the outlaws and their captives are trapped. Curnow's wife accuses him of cowardice as the police shoot at children, but Kelly too bears the burden of responsibility (*True History*, pp. 394–5). Ned Kelly is not Prince Hal, bandit turned king, and the Kelly Gang do not triumph against impossible odds at Glenrowan, as the English do at Agincourt. But Henry does not tell his troops they will win; he tells them they will be remembered (*True History*, p. 389). Here, perhaps, we have the essential truth of the comparison. The Kelly gang fail, but they too are remembered, and not merely remembered, but elevated to the status of something approaching a national myth.

Australian Exclusions

Australia is founded in exclusion. The creation of a penal colony in Australia is based on the practice of transporting convicts and prisoners-of-war from Britain and Ireland in the seventeenth and eighteenth centuries to America and the Caribbean; 'banishment' in the terms of the Elizabethan legislation initiating the practice.[117] Transportation to America ended with the American revolution, but, Robert Hughes argues, the growth of the African slave trade had rendered convict transportation an economic irrelevance anyway: 'on the eve of the American Revolution, 47,000 African slaves were arriving in America every year: more than English jails had sent across the Atlantic in the previous half-century'.[118] The end of convict transportation to the New World led to pressure on the English prison system: the solution was transportation to Australia, and between 1787 and the end of transportation in 1868, more than 160,000 men, women and children were sent to Australia as convicts.[119]

But the forced exile of these convicts is based upon a second form of exclusion: that of Indigenous Australians. The legal basis on which Britain claimed sovereignty over Australia is the subject of debate, and under-

---

[116] Jones, *Ned Kelly*, p. 402.
[117] Hughes, *Fatal Shore*, pp. 40–1; An Acte for punishment of Rogues Vagabonds and Sturdy Beggars 1597.
[118] Hughes, *Fatal Shore*, p. 41.
[119] Hughes, *Fatal Shore*, pp. 2, 56–67.

standably so, for in claiming sovereignty, initially over New South Wales, Britain does not contest Indigenous sovereignty so much as simply ignore it. The instructions appointing Arthur Phillip as Governor of NSW mention Indigenous Australians twice: first, instructing Phillip to take measures against 'any attacks or Interruptions of the Natives of that Country'; and, secondly, to 'open an Intercourse with the Natives and to conciliate their affections, enjoining all Our Subjects to live in amity and kindness with them', meanwhile making an estimate of the population and reporting on how advantageous relationships may be established.[120]

In a landmark work, Henry Reynolds argued that British settlement of Australia was based upon the notion that prior to 1788, the continent was *terra nullius*, land belonging to no one, a term with two different meanings, often conflated: first, a country without a sovereign; and, secondly, a country without a system of property tenure.[121] Britain takes possession, then, on the assumption that the country is not legally governed, and has no recognisable system of property holding. Reynolds's application of the term *terra nullius* to the colonisation of Australia was and is influential. His work is important in the High Court's 1992 decision in the Mabo case that recognises native title in Australia.[122] The 2012 expert panel report on recognition of Aboriginal and Torres Strait Islander people in the Australian constitution refers to the idea of *terra nullius* as the basis for settlement.[123] Contemporary work in postcolonial studies continues to refer to the concept,[124] and Reynolds himself uses the term in later work.[125]

Reynolds's terminology has also been criticised: writing in 2007, Andrew Fitzmaurice suggests 'it is becoming widely acknowledged that the term *terra nullius* was not used in the eighteenth and nineteenth centuries to justify the dispossession of Australian Aborigines'.[126] But while criticising Reynolds's terminology, Fitzmaurice suggests that there is a broad concept that remains applicable: '*Terra nullius* was anachronistic history but what it described was an approximation of the positive use of the law of the first taker in natural law to justify dispossession'.[127]

---

[120] 'Governor Phillip's Instructions'.
[121] Reynolds, *Law of the Land*, p. 12.
[122] *Mabo* v. *Queensland (No 2)* (1992).
[123] *Recognising Aboriginal and Torres Strait Islander Peoples in the Constitution,* chapter 1. The report cites Blackstone rather than Reynolds as the authority for this claim (n. 53).
[124] See the entry for *terra nullius* in Nayar, *Postcolonial Studies Dictionary*, pp. 153–4.
[125] Reynolds, *Forgotten War*, pp. 50, 163, 191.
[126] Fitzmaurice, 'The genealogy of *Terra Nullius*', p. 1.
[127] Fitzmaurice, 'The genealogy of *Terra Nullius*', p. 14.

European colonisation of Australia was a matter of force as well as law. Sporadic conflict between Europeans and the Eora people begins within weeks of the first settlement in 1788, and conflict between Europeans and Indigenous Australians continued for some 140 years, though the history of Australian frontier conflict was long ignored or suppressed, and was subsequently the subject of heated debate in Australia's 'history wars' around the turn of the century.[128] On the Aboriginal side, the conflict involved intermittent but ongoing guerrilla warfare. On the European side, it involved a variety of tactics including the use of troops in punitive raids, the arming of civilian settlers, and the creation of paramilitary forces such as the Mounted Police.[129] It also extended to the imposition of martial law in 1824 against the Wiradjuri people of New South Wales, and from 1828 against the Palawa people of Tasmania.

There are questions about the legal status of both the conflict and its participants. Was this a war? Were the Indigenous Australians fighting against European occupation to be regarded as British subjects, rebelling against sovereign authority, or defenders of their country, subject to the laws of war?[130] These were questions debated by contemporaries, and answers varied. In 1825, the Secretary of State for the Colonies, Lord Bathurst, gave instructions that the colonists were 'to oppose force by force' just as if attacked 'by the subjects of any accredited State'.[131] Here, then, Indigenous Australians, where hostile, are akin to foreign enemies. But by 1837, the then Secretary of State for the Colonies, Lord Glenelg, takes the opposing position: Indigenous Australians are not aliens with whom a war can exist, but are rather protected by law.[132] If, as David Neal says, Aboriginal Australians have an ambiguous legal status as 'some hybrid of outlaw, foreign enemy and protected race' in the years prior to the 1830s,[133] in that decade this legal ambiguity seems to resolve in favour of inclusion in law. In 1838, seven white men were hanged for murdering approximately twenty-eight Aboriginal people in what was known as the Myall Creek Massacre.[134] But if this case suggested a willingness to enforce the rule of law in relation to settler-Indigenous conflict, another

---

[128] Reynolds, *Forgotten War*, pp. 15–20, 26–8, 49; Macintyre and Clark, *The History Wars*, pp. 142–70.

[129] Reynolds, *Forgotten War*, pp. 57–8, 64–9, 82–3, 131–2, 152–4; on the Mounted Police and Border Police in early NSW, see also Neal, *The Rule of Law in a Penal Colony*, pp. 144, 150–4.

[130] Reynolds, *Forgotten War*, pp. 9–14.

[131] Reynolds, *Forgotten War*, p. 62.

[132] Reynolds, *Forgotten War*, p. 72.

[133] Neal, *The Rule of Law in a Penal Colony*, p. 151.

[134] Neal, *The Rule of Law in a Penal Colony*, pp. 79–80.

case problematises such assumptions, for an 1839 enquiry into the killing of Aboriginal people by Mounted Police at Waterloo Creek the previous year was abandoned.[135] As conflict endured, massacres of Aboriginal people by both civilians and police would continue throughout the nineteenth century and into the twentieth without legal consequence.

Indigenous Australians, then, are excluded from law in the interests of colonial power in several senses. First, Britain's eighteenth-century claim to sovereignty over the eastern coast of Australia ignores Indigenous Australian sovereignty and tenure. Secondly, from 1788 until the 1830s, the status of Indigenous Australians within British law is ambiguous and debated: when conflict occurs, Indigenous people are deemed to occupy an indeterminate position between rebellious subjects and foreign enemies. Thirdly, the colonial authorities are prepared, on at least two occasions, to declare martial law during conflict with the Aboriginal population. Finally, even when cases in the 1830s such as the trial of the Myall Creek murderers establish that Aboriginal Australians should enjoy protection from the law, this has little practical effect on the ground, where ongoing colonial expansion sees Indigenous people treated as *de facto* outlaws.

To note this exclusion is not to conflate Indigenous Australians and Australian bushrangers. Carey's novel offers us an early reminder not to do so, in a brief episode where a group of Indigenous Australians ambush Red Kelly, who barely escapes with his life (*True History*, pp. 14–15). There are, of course, points of contact as well as conflict: Les Murray's poem 'Maryanne Bugg', for instance, celebrates the Aboriginal wife of the bushranger Frederick Ward, while noting his own family's connection with Ward,[136] and Deborah Bird Rose has described the incorporation of Ned Kelly into the stories of the Yarralin and Lingara people of the Northern Territory.[137] But in general, while these two groups are both subject to exclusion by the state, their exclusion occurs in very different contexts. Anna Boswell, reflecting on the inclusion of stories of Indigenous resistance in the National Museum of Australia's 2003 exhibition *Outlawed! Rebels, Revolutionaries and Bushrangers*, contemplates the extent to which outlaws are seen as culturally central to Australian identity, in contrast to the silence surrounding frontier conflict.[138]

---

[135] Neal, *The Rule of Law in a Penal Colony*, p. 80.

[136] Les Murray, 'Maryanne Bugg', in Murray, *Waiting for the Past*, p. 78.

[137] Rose, 'Ned Kelly Died for Our Sins'.

[138] Boswell, 'Cross-Cultural Comparison', p. 197; *Outlawed!* included exhibits on the Indigenous Australians Walyer and Musquito (remembered for tracking down the bushranger Michael Howe as well as his own resistance to the colonial state), and the Maori leader Honi Heke (*Outlawed!*, ed. Weber, pp. 34–47); for conservative attacks upon the

Such memorialising of one excluded group in tandem with erasing others has been a key issue in contemporary Australia's understanding of its own past.[139] As Ann Curthoys suggests, mainstream Australian culture's predominant view of its past in terms of victimhood creates a difficulty in understanding that this past also consists of oppression.[140] The same caution is required in discussing Irishness: writing on relations between Aboriginal and Irish-Australians, Ann McGrath warns that the prospect of any colonising group successfully maintaining the label of 'good colonisers' seems like wishful thinking.[141]

But what is illustrated by the exclusion of both bushrangers and Indigenous Australians from law is the continued state use of legal exclusion as a tactic of power. In a variety of ways – the proclamation of outlawry or martial law, the ignoring of sovereignty, the unwillingness to decide upon a legal status for Aboriginal Australians, the creation of *de facto* outlaw status through a consistent failure to implement the law as it applied to Indigenous people in particular – colonial Australia demonstrates the endurance of exclusion from law well into the modern era. As the remainder of this book will argue, such exclusions last long after outlawry in its formal, legal sense has fallen into disuse.

National Museum's presentation of Australian history in general and frontier conflict in particular, see Macintyre and Clark, *The History Wars*, pp. 191–215.

[139] Prassel, *The Great American Outlaw*, pp. 194–215, similarly notes that while the legendary American outlaw is white, and often of Irish descent, this cultural construct conceals a much more complex reality, particularly in relation to Native Americans, at times 'almost regarded as an outlaw race' (p. 198).

[140] Curthoys, 'Expulsion, Exodus and Exile'.

[141] McGrath, 'Shamrock Aborigines', p. 73.

4

'We're Not Policemen':
Espionage and Law in John le Carré

Our discussion until now has focused largely upon the historical practice of outlawry. We have seen that the exclusion of individuals from the protection of the law was a long-standing phenomenon, enduring in English law from the earliest medieval English legal texts through to colonial practice in nineteenth-century Australia. We have also found that the outlaw is a complex figure. Portrayed as a sort of *homo sacer* by the state and its legal texts, but perhaps claimed as a 'social bandit' by a literature celebrating his resistance to authority, the outlaw is capable of being both of these things, and more besides. The discussion so far has also emphasised that there is more to outlawry than the figure of the outlaw. We have argued that outlawry is not merely a reactive gesture by the state, but also a proactive tactic, a way in which sovereign power is asserted. Further to this, outlawry itself is only one of a variety of forms of legal exclusion employed by the state in the pursuit or defence of power. The sovereign may (and perhaps must) seek to act outside the law in defence of the state, and in that sense the sovereign is a figure who bears a surprising resemblance to the outlaw. Additionally, these exclusions of individuals from the law's protection or punishment may also intersect with broader tactics of legal exclusion aimed at entire nations, territories and legal systems.

From here on, we turn away from the historical practice of outlawry and towards the contemporary practice of espionage. On the face of it, this would seem a very different subject, and the literatures of outlawry and espionage are not conventionally considered together. But the discussion below suggests that the contemporary state too acts outside the law in the interests of power, and that one of the most significant ways in which it does so is via the creation of secret services. While not a new phenomenon, such agencies and their activities, from intelligence gathering to covert action, take on a substantial importance in the international politics of the twentieth and twenty-first centuries, particularly during the Cold War and its aftermath.

The following chapters consider ways in which the various intelligence agencies of the United Kingdom and the United States in particular may be considered to act outside the law. These include ambiguities in the legal status of the agencies themselves (in the UK, where domestic and foreign intelligence activities were properly governed by legislation only with the passage of relevant laws in 1989 and 1994) and of their covert actions (in the US, where the CIA conducted covert actions under the National Security Act in ways that may have exceeded legislative intent). They also include actions in breach of both domestic and foreign laws by the security agencies and their personnel: breaches of law that extend as far as suggestions of involvement in torture and collusion in terrorist killings.

In addition to the ability of state actors to operate with seeming impunity, we may also note tactics that seek to exclude the opponents of the state from legal recourse: tactics that range from the cancellation of citizenship to extralegal detention in remote and extraterritorial spaces. These tactics of exclusion from law serve to reinstate a sort of outlawry in a particularly twenty-first century form, and suggest an enduring relationship between exclusion above and below the law. Also, as we shall see, it is not merely the opponents of the state who find themselves expendable in the world of espionage: the agents of the state, too, find themselves as dehumanised and vulnerable as any *homo sacer*.

Contemporary literature that deals with extralegal action by the state is unusual in that, for the most part, when contemporary intelligence agencies act outside the law, they do so in secret, and disclosure of their actions is potentially prohibited by law. In the United States, the disclosure of classified information is prohibited by the Espionage Act of 1917,[1] and classified information is regulated under Executive Order 13526 of 29 December 2009.[2] In the United Kingdom, disclosure of classified information is prohibited by the Official Secrets Act,[3] and the DSMA-Notice system requires the media to consult the government before publishing certain material (DSMA-Notice 3 concerns Security and Intelligence Agency operations).[4] The sheer extent of fictional writing about the secret actions of contemporary Western states is particularly remarkable, then, given the ongoing efforts by these states to influence, censor or suppress accounts of their secret actions. Nor is this

---

[1] Espionage Act 1917.
[2] Obama, 'Executive Order 13526'. Savage, *Power Wars*, notes that in the US disclosure of classified information without authorisation is not a crime *per se*, but that government 'has begun exploiting the loose wording of the Espionage Act to turn the statute into a de facto Official Secrets Act' (pp. 364–5); Savage also surveys recent cases (pp. 350–414).
[3] Official Secrets Act 1989.
[4] 'DSMA – Notice 03'. For the Act and Notices in practice, see Cobain, *The History Thieves*, pp. 30–63.

commitment to secrecy in any way moribund. A useful reminder is apparent in two recent but very different books: Richard Immerman's history of the CIA,[5] and Mohamedou Ould Slahi's account of his detention at Guantánamo Bay.[6] Both of these books are printed with blacked-out passages representing redactions imposed upon the text.

In light of such restrictions on factual accounts, fictional representations become an important forum for public understanding and consideration of the activities of the state's secret services. As Timothy Melley puts it, 'fiction is one of the few permissible discourses through which writers can represent the secret work of the state'.[7] This is so in part because of its fictional status. As Melley writes:

> Unlike the 'serious' discourses of the rational-critical public sphere, fiction can reveal the public secrets of the covert state without appearing to reveal any 'real' secrets, for its knowledge is invented, not found.[8]

Eva Horn, likewise, suggests that fiction's insistence that it is not literal truth allows it to publicly discuss the secrets of the state: '"Invention" has always been a mask to reveal otherwise "unspeakable" facts'.[9] Such fictions, then, are also inherently political: in discussing subjects that are taboo in other forms of political discourse, literature, Horn says, becomes 'both part of the secretive structure of modern power and, at the same time, its most insightful critique'.[10]

Espionage and Abjection: *The Spy Who Came in from the Cold*

We are told early on in *The Spy Who Came in from the Cold* that ends justify means in the world of espionage:

> Intelligence work has one moral law – it is justified by results. Even the sophistry of Whitehall paid court to that law, and Leamas got results. Until Mundt came. (*The Spy*, p. 11)

Towards the end of the book, as Alec Leamas and Liz Gold are desperately trying to escape from East Germany, having fully realised the extent to which they have been used by British Intelligence, Leamas says something that recalls that phrase, telling Liz 'there's only one law in this game' (*The Spy*,

[5] Immerman, *The Hidden Hand*.
[6] Slahi, *Guantánamo Diary*.
[7] Melley, *Covert Sphere*, p. 9.
[8] Melley, *Covert Sphere*, p. 16.
[9] Horn, *Secret War*, p. 25.
[10] Horn, *Secret War*, p. 41.

p. 243). But the question of the balance between ends and means is at the heart of this novel, where a British plot to deceive the East Germans succeeds, but at a very high price in both moral equivocation and human life.

The plot of *The Spy Who Came in from the Cold* is complex, not least because of the level of deception involved; the narrative is full of blink-and-you'll-miss-it hints as to what might be going on. Alec Leamas is the Circus's man in Berlin, returning to London after his East German opponent, Hans-Dieter Mundt, destroys the network of agents he was running in East Berlin.[11] On his return, Leamas discovers that he is not to be put out to grass just yet: rather, Control, his boss, wishes to use him for one last job, a complex exercise in deception. Control's plan begins with Leamas's public decline and disgrace. Afterwards, Leamas will agree to work with the East Germans, disclosing the existence of an operation named Rolling Stone. This operation supposedly involves payments to an informer whom the East Germans will identify as Mundt.

Le Carré's spies are anti-heroes, explicitly the antithesis of figures such as James Bond who serve to embed Cold War oppositions, where le Carré himself could say in 1966 that 'there is no victory and no virtue in the Cold War, only a condition of human illness and a political misery'.[12] Cold War espionage requires that intelligence operatives should live without sympathy, as Control says to Leamas at the start. Control knows, of course, that this is impossible, and he asks Leamas to endure in a state of emotional frigidity for one last mission, after which he can 'come in from the cold' (*The Spy*, pp. 17, 56). That tantalising possibility is an unreal one: exile is endemic to espionage, as Phyllis Lassner writes, and le Carré's spies 'live and die in the Cold, never invited to be insiders, to belong'.[13] In le Carré, for the spy to be truly effective, they must be dehumanised, as David Monaghan puts it,[14] and Leamas's predicament demonstrates the need for the agent to be entirely subjected to the needs of the state, a figure completely abjected from social loyalties, a figure who can be sacrificed at will. Such a construction of the agent is a figure akin to Agamben's *homo sacer*, a figure as excluded as any outlaw. It is also remarkably similar to the definition of the revolutionary in nineteenth-century anarchism as 'a doomed man' who has 'no personal interests, no business affairs, no emotions, no attachments, no property,

[11] 'The Circus' is a fictionalised version of the UK's foreign intelligence agency, the Secret Intelligence Service (SIS or MI6); 'The Abteilung' is a fictionalised version of the German Democratic Republic's Ministry for State Security (the Stasi).

[12] Le Carré, 'To Russia, with Greetings', p. 6.

[13] Lassner, *Espionage and Exile*, pp. 3, 171.

[14] Monaghan, *The Novels of John le Carré*, p. 33.

and no name'.[15] This view of the agent need not be taken as a realist one – like the literature of outlawry, the literature of espionage creates a certain mythology for its protagonists. As Eva Horn describes it, 'the figure of the agent – defector, mole, traitor, seducer, bearer of secrets, hidden agitator, sleeper, partisan – remains a figure of modern political anthropology'.[16] But the fictional archetype of the agent as outcast (an alternative to the agent as superman) allows espionage literature to both represent and critique a real phenomenon – the state's tactics of exclusion.

Leamas himself is a somewhat uncertain figure. 'He looked like a man who could make trouble, a man who looked after his money, a man who was not quite a gentleman' (The Spy, p. 13). There are vague suggestions of Irishness, which we might take as a sign of rebelliousness, of not-quite-belonging.[17] As well as two explicit comments (The Spy, pp. 12, 47), there is a not-quite-spelled-out misspelling of his name by a hostile employer that might be read as 'Lemass' (The Spy, p. 34), the surname of Seán Lemass, Ireland's Taoiseach at the time when le Carré's book appeared in the early 1960s. Lemass was a former IRA member: a passing reference later on to an IRA-supporting prisoner (The Spy, p. 45) reminds us that the IRA was active in the late 1950s and into the early 1960s.

As planned, then, Leamas is disgraced, abandoned and imprisoned, with the intention of making him attractive to the enemy as a potential recruit. But the extent of his abandonment is greater than he had anticipated, for up to this point, he is merely feigning his role as an outcast. Things take a far more serious turn when he makes contact with the East Germans: the Circus unexpectedly has him declared a wanted man in Britain, and he is taken behind the Iron Curtain. But there is further abandonment to come. After his departure from the Circus in supposed disgrace, Leamas had embarked upon an affair with a young woman, Liz Gold, a communist. This affair was not part of the plan: or not, at least, in the minds of Leamas and his lover. But when the affair and subsequent payments by the Circus to Liz are revealed during a showdown at an East German legal tribunal between Mundt and his deputy head of security, Jens Fiedler, each accusing the other of treason, Leamas is exposed as acting for the Circus in seeking to frame Mundt. It is clear that the person responsible for this unravelling of the plot is Control's right-hand man, George Smiley.

---

[15] Nechayev, The Revolutionary Catechism, and see the discussion in Laqueur, Terrorism, pp. 29–30.

[16] Horn, Secret War, p. 355.

[17] Le Carré says his inspiration for Leamas was a man at London airport bar with a very slight Irish accent: Plimpton, 'John le Carré, The Art of Fiction No. 149', p. 149.

Control had told Leamas that Smiley was no longer with the Circus (*The Spy*, p. 19); that he was deliberately standing aside from the operation (*The Spy*, p. 55). There is a certain irony here in that Control delivers these latter lines in Smiley's house, but Leamas seems to believe it: he tells the East Germans later that Smiley's nerve has gone (*The Spy*, p. 225). But Smiley is constantly hovering in the background. It is he who briefs Leamas on Mundt's background as an East German spy in Britain (events described in le Carré's first novel, *Call for the Dead*).[18] It is he who is waiting as Leamas tries to escape over the Berlin Wall at the novel's end. And, in clumsily paying off Liz Gold and other parties associated with the cover story of Leamas's decline, it is he who exposes the whole operation as the work of British Intelligence.

When Leamas is confronted with news of Smiley's actions, he has difficulty understanding what has happened:

> It was insane, fantastic. What were they trying to do – kill Fiedler, kill their agent? Sabotage their own operation? Was it just Smiley – had his wretched little conscience driven him to this? (*The Spy*, p. 220)

Smiley, a previous book tells us, 'had been described by his superiors as possessing the cunning of Satan and the conscience of a virgin'.[19] Leamas at first interprets Smiley's actions as a grotesque error based upon a fit of conscience (the same conscience that has been played up by Control).[20] In fact, it is Smiley's other attribute, the cunning of Satan, that is on show here. Far from being an independent initiative to salve Smiley's conscience, this is a sequence of planned actions by the Circus that is insane and fantastic, certainly, but also deliberate and ruthless. Leamas finally realises, far too late, that Mundt is indeed London's agent. His mission, in which he has unwittingly succeeded, was not to destroy Mundt, but to save him.

'There's only one law in this game', as Leamas says, and London gets its result: it succeeds in preserving its agent at the very heart of the Abteilung. But in doing so, it pays a very high price in human lives. Preserving Mundt has already meant deliberately sacrificing the lives of Karl Riemeck and his entire network, along with various other agents sacrificed for Leamas's credibility ('here and there a little fish which we shall take out of the pool' (*The Spy*, p. 130)). Now it places the lives of Fiedler, Leamas himself, and finally Liz Gold (who has also been duped into travelling to East Germany) in jeop-

---

[18] Le Carré, *Call for the Dead*.
[19] Le Carré, *A Murder of Quality*, p. 83.
[20] Le Carré, *A Legacy of Spies*, revisiting the events of *The Spy Who Came in from the Cold*, again highlights Smiley's conscience: Control tells Guillam they have a plan, but Smiley cannot stomach it (p. 211).

ardy. Even if 'espionage is not a cricket game' (as Peters observes to Leamas) (*The Spy*, p. 120), there are some disturbing decisions here.

The tribunal where this drama eventually plays out also delves into the differences between the British state's legal processes, and the methods of its intelligence services. Part of Fiedler's case against Mundt is that his escape from England during the Fennan affair was unlikely, and that he was allowed to escape because he had been turned.[21] Leamas is asked what would have happened to Mundt had he been caught by the British. Mundt had no diplomatic immunity to hide behind because the UK did not recognise the GDR (*The Spy*, p. 190) (Leamas insists on calling East Germany 'the Zone', a non-country (*The Spy*, p. 132)).[22] Leamas's response is that it would depend on who caught him. If it was the police, they would report it to the Home Office, and he would have been charged. If the Circus caught him, however, he would have been interrogated, and the Circus would either have traded him for an East German prisoner, or 'given him a ticket'. Asked what this might mean, Leamas replies 'got rid of him'. Pressed on whether this meant execution, Leamas professes not to know (*The Spy*, pp. 193–4). Where the police would have done one thing, then, the Circus would have played by entirely different rules (trials, we are told in passing, can produce inconvenient truths (*The Spy*, pp. 148–9)). There is some irony here, of course, in that this dissection of the fault lines between the UK's overt legal process (represented by the police and the Home Office) and its covert actions (represented by the Circus) takes place at an East German legal tribunal which is not expected to deliver anything resembling justice. At the novel's end, Mundt, too, lets Leamas run rather than have him stand trial for espionage and murder.

If *The Spy Who Came in from the Cold* portrays the Circus as ruthless in its methods, it also poses hard questions about means and ends, and it does so particularly in Leamas's conversations with two interlocutors. One involves Fiedler's questioning of Leamas across a series of discussions about the moral or ethical positions of British Intelligence: how far they might go in sacrificing innocent individuals for the greater good (*The Spy*, pp. 138, 179). The other such conversation comes much earlier in the novel, in Control's initial discussion with Leamas. This is a conversation which Leamas finds difficult to navigate, and which he seems to have forgotten entirely by the time of his

---

[21] The Fennan affair takes place in *Call for the Dead*. Le Carré, *A Legacy of Spies*, suggests rather that Mundt is turned by Smiley when captured in a separate incident.

[22] Recognition of the German Democratic Republic (East Germany) by the United Nations came in 1973, after which the UK and USA also extended diplomatic recognition: Judt, *Postwar*, p. 499.

conversations with Fiedler. But it seems to foreshadow these later discussions in suggesting that there are no differences in method between the British and their opponents (*The Spy*, p. 18).[23] Control justifies such ruthlessness by arguing it is essentially defensive, though conceding 'of course, we occasionally do very wicked things' (*The Spy*, p. 17).[24]

In retrospect, we can see that Control is about to propose a plan to Leamas that includes a number of 'very wicked things' – sacrificing innocent individuals to protect a man who is reprehensible but useful – and that he is attempting to justify those actions. But in conceding that East and West use essentially the same methods, and that those methods are 'disagreeable', Control comes close here to Fiedler's later suggestion that there is no real difference between the sides. It is not that le Carré is not unflinching in his critique of the East, for he is: East Germany clearly appears in the novel as a police state built on hypocrisies and lies.[25] But le Carré critiques the West for pretending that it will not sacrifice the innocent to achieve its purposes. Such a critique was not welcomed by members of the CIA, which, as Frances Stonor Saunders has demonstrated at length, expended large amounts of money and effort in co-opting Western artists and intellectuals during the Cold War.[26]

These moral questions are further complicated because Fiedler is a Jew, where Mundt is, in Control's words, 'quite the other thing' (*The Spy*, p. 121), or, as Liz Gold says, a Nazi (*The Spy*, p. 243).[27] Jens Fiedler is German, and an intelligence agent. Liz Gold is British, and a civilian. Both are communists, and that, to a certain extent, might be thought to make them fair game: Liz

---

23 Cf. the discussions of means and ends in le Carré, *Tinker Tailor Soldier Spy*, p. 82; le Carré, *A Legacy of Spies*, p. 8. See also Vaughan, 'Le Carré's Circus', p. 57; Sisman, *John le Carré*, p. 233.

24 Le Carré, 'To Russia, with Greetings', p. 4, critiques each side's supposedly defensive posture as fictional.

25 For accounts of life under the Stasi in East Germany, see Garton Ash, *The File* and Funder, *Stasiland*.

26 Saunders, *Who Paid the Piper?*, p. 359, quotes the CIA's Frank Wisner as describing le Carré and Graham Greene as 'dupes'. All of le Carré's books up to *A Perfect Spy* were vetted for publication by MI5 and MI6, though some former colleagues were very critical of his work (Sisman, *John le Carré*, pp. 240, 250, 255, 403, 415–16, 446, 520, 593). CIA disapproval cannot have been uniform. *Reader's Digest* consulted CIA contacts before taking the book for its Condensed Book Club (Sisman, *John le Carré*, p. 257), and le Carré's defence against Soviet criticism that he was an apologist for the Cold War appeared in *Encounter*, a journal covertly funded by the CIA.

27 On recruitment of ex-Nazis to post-war intelligence roles, see Judt, *Postwar*, pp. 56, 57, 59–60, 61); for anti-Semitism in post-war Eastern Europe, see Judt, *Postwar*, pp. 181–7, 445 n. 15, 434–6, 804–8.

asks Leamas if that might be so in her case (*The Spy*, pp. 240–1). But both are also Jewish, which should have the opposite effect: the early 1960s are not so far from 1945 that the Holocaust could be ignored in favour of Cold War polarities. Anti-Semitism in post-war Germany is an important theme here and elsewhere in le Carré's work from this period; the world of the early novels is very much a post-war world. In *Call for the Dead*, Elsa Fennan is both a Jewish survivor of the Holocaust and an East German spy: for Phyllis Lassner's reading of le Carré's early work, Fennan is a crucial figure who represents the exile and exclusion shared by both Jewish refugees and Cold War spies.[28] Smiley's ally Inspector Mendel is also Jewish (he voices a brief outburst about the return of anti-Semitism in Germany (*Call for the Dead*, p. 47)), as is Dieter Frey, once Smiley's pupil and later his agent, now his enemy. *A Small Town in Germany* features the rise of a political figure, Klaus Karfeld, with a hidden Nazi past.[29] When Liz Gold asks Leamas, 'what side are you on?' she doesn't mean in the conflict between East and West, but rather another conflict that cuts across the Cold War divide (*The Spy*, p. 243).[30]

If arranging the death of Fiedler to protect his reprehensible boss is morally questionable, most problematic is the sacrifice of Liz Gold, because Liz is a civilian, an innocent abroad. The narrator's use of her first name, while using surnames for everyone else, marks her difference in status. As they attempt to escape at the end of the novel, Liz asks Leamas why Mundt would allow her to go free: 'a Party member knowing all this ... it doesn't seem logical that he should let me go' (*The Spy*, p. 241). As they enter the no-man's-land that surrounds the Berlin Wall, Leamas clearly has similar suspicions. Moving towards the Wall 'Leamas was determined to keep Liz very close to him, as if he were afraid that Mundt would not keep his word and somehow snatch her away at the last moment' (*The Spy*, p. 252).

Their instructions are explicitly that Leamas is to go first, and then pull Liz up after him (*The Spy*, p. 245). As they climb the Wall, they are caught in the searchlights, and Liz is shot (*The Spy*, pp. 252, 253). The sequence of events here (searchlights, sirens, orders, then shots) echoes the killing of Riemeck at the beginning of the novel (*The Spy*, p. 9), an echo that again suggests betrayal. Leamas now seems safe, but he climbs back down the Wall to Liz's body. The East Germans prove reluctant to shoot, perhaps suggesting that they have already achieved their objective:

[28] Lassner, *Espionage and Exile*, pp. 188–9.
[29] Le Carré, *A Small Town in Germany*.
[30] See le Carré, 'To Russia, with Greetings', p. 5; Piette, *The Literary Cold War*, p. 13.

They seemed to hesitate before firing again; someone shouted an order, and still no one fired. Finally they shot him, two or three shots. (*The Spy*, p. 253)

When Liz is shot, with Leamas still on the Wall, a voice calls to him in English from the Western side, urging him to jump. Then he hears Smiley's voice close by, asking an ambiguous question: 'The girl, where's the girl?' (*The Spy*, p. 253). In William Boyd's reading of the novel's final pages, 'what Smiley wants to know is not whether the girl is safe but whether the girl is *dead*'.[31] Leamas, realising this final betrayal, then climbs back down to die with her. This would not be the first Smiley novel where what seems an offer of assistance at the end of the story is merely a feint: at the end of *A Murder of Quality*, having exposed Fielding as the murderer, Smiley urges him to make his escape, where, in fact, it is already far too late for that (*A Murder of Quality*, p. 168). If Boyd's reading is right, British Intelligence has colluded with Mundt to kill a British civilian and (reluctantly) their own agent in order to preserve the tactical advantage that Mundt offers them. The ambiguity in Smiley's words, however, leaves the question open (and in Phyllis Lassner's reading, insoluble).[32] In *A Legacy of Spies*, both Guillam's lawyer Tabitha and Smiley himself offer versions of events where killing Leamas and Liz is Mundt's initiative alone, but these accounts are offered in a context where Guillam, Smiley and the Circus are accused of having arranged their murder (*A Legacy*, pp. 241, 260).

If *The Spy Who Came in from the Cold* posits a construction of the agent as abjected, perhaps dehumanised, and able to be sacrificed at will, in the end, the novel's main characters do not fit this mould. The Circus may be ruthless in its deception and abandonment of Leamas, but Leamas himself, rather than stay out in the cold, thaws along the way, first towards Liz, and later towards Fiedler. In the novel's final chapters, Leamas tries to sacrifice himself to save them, to place individual human lives above the machinations of political intrigue (*The Spy*, p. 220, 222, 225–6). He cannot do so, and, having failed, he chooses to die. But he has, in a sense, already come in from the cold.[33]

Something similar is true of Fiedler. Timothy Garton Ash notes the suggested similarities between Fiedler and the real figure of Markus 'Mischa' Wolf, the former head of East German foreign intelligence. Certainly

---

[31] Boyd, 'Introduction', p. x. Cf. Seed, 'Well-Wrought Structures', p. 151; Monaghan, *The Novels of John le Carré*, p. 33.

[32] Lassner, *Espionage and Exile,* p. 174.

[33] Cf. Boyd, 'Introduction', p. x, who comments: 'Leamas, in *refusing* to come in from the cold as a spy, does in fact come in from the cold as a person'.

the novel takes some of its general impetus from a real event in Cold War politics – the construction of the Berlin Wall in 1961[34] – but Garton Ash asks whether there were more specific influences. Fiedler was, he says, actually called 'Wolf' in an earlier draft of the novel, and the real Markus Wolf was reportedly 'amazed at the uncanny way in which the novelist had echoed, in the Fiedler-Mundt conflict, the tensions of his own relationship with his superior, Erich Mielke, the Minister for State Security'.[35] Le Carré has been emphatic in his denials that Wolf was a model for Fiedler.[36] Whether or not the 'wolf' that le Carré had in mind for those early drafts was a real wolf, the Markus Wolf of the Stasi, or a more abstract lupine figure, the figure of the wolf, a solitary predator (and a long-standing figure of the outlaw), seems an apt one to represent a spymaster in search of a traitor, for, in the phrase derived from Plautus, *homo homini lupus*, 'man is a wolf to man'.[37]

But if Fiedler was, in an earlier incarnation of le Carré's text, a wolf, here he is insufficiently lupine. Ruthless in his pursuit of Mundt, he is sympathetic in his treatment of Leamas, his vulnerable enemy, whom he will try to help (*The Spy*, p. 143). Later, faced with the collapse of his case against Mundt, he allows the innocent Liz Gold to leave the court without questions (*The Spy*, p. 223). His empathy is reciprocated. When Leamas tells the Tribunal that 'Fiedler's all right' (*The Spy*, p. 226), he does not just mean that Fiedler is 'ideologically sound' (*The Spy*, p. 226), or that he is not, as the East Germans think, a British agent, although he says both of these things, and they are both true. What he means is that Fiedler is a decent man who does not deserve to die.

Here, as elsewhere in le Carré, the value of individual human beings, and of individual human empathy, is emphasised over systems and structures that are inevitably seen as being flawed. But this does not save the lives of Leamas or Fiedler, or of Liz Gold for that matter, because if the value of human life over ideological systems is one key theme in le Carré, injustice and betrayal is another.

---

[34] John le Carré, 'Afterword', in le Carré, *The Spy Who Came in from the Cold*, p. 255. Sisman, *John le Carré*, p. 222, suggests that the 1961 exposure of Heinz Felfe, West Germany's head of Soviet counter-espionage, as a Soviet spy, may also have been an influence.

[35] Garton Ash, 'The Imperfect Spy'. Sisman, *John le Carré*, p. 217, says it was Mundt, not Fiedler, who was originally named Wolff.

[36] Plimpton, 'John le Carré, The Art of Fiction No. 149', p. 161.

[37] Versions of this phrase and their use from Plautus through Montaigne and Hobbes are discussed in Derrida, *The Beast & the Sovereign*, I, 58–62.

The Unconstitutional Detective: *Tinker Tailor Soldier Spy*

Like *The Spy Who Came in from the Cold*, *Tinker Tailor Soldier Spy* also draws on real events for background. Here that historical background concerns the Cambridge spy ring discovered in the 1950s and 1960s, when Kim Philby, Guy Burgess, Donald Maclean, Anthony Blunt and John Cairncross were found to be Soviet agents, recruited during or shortly after their time at Cambridge University in the 1930s. British Intelligence services exhibited an ongoing sense of paranoia after the exposure of the Cambridge spies, continuing to suspect further Soviet infiltration for years afterwards.[38] In a 2008 article, le Carré describes what he calls 'the Great Paranoia Epidemic which ran from the nineteen-fifties into the seventies' when practically everyone in MI5 was suspected of being a Russian spy.[39] Le Carré worked at MI5 in the 1950s, before moving later to SIS, and he describes the atmosphere at the time as being very much as that portrayed in *Tinker Tailor Soldier Spy*.[40]

At the beginning of *Tinker Tailor Soldier Spy*, Smiley is summoned by Oliver Lacon of the Cabinet Office, a figure variously described as 'watch-dog of intelligence affairs' and 'Whitehall's head prefect' (*Tinker Tailor*, p. 32), because there is new evidence of a Russian mole, a spy working from inside the Circus.[41] Smiley and Control had both previously suspected as much. Lacon's problem, as he explains in discussion with Smiley, is how to investigate, given that the instruments of enquiry are all in the Circus's own hands. 'It's the oldest question of all, George', he says. 'Who can spy on the spies?' (*Tinker Tailor*, p. 85). Neither Lacon nor his Minister are prepared to contemplate the orthodox answer of using MI5. Lacon tells Smiley that 'the Minister would rather live with a damp roof than see his castle pulled down by outsiders' (*Tinker Tailor*, p. 85). Having the Circus torn apart by Moscow is in some ways less of a concern than having the job done by another faction of their own.[42] So Lacon turns to Smiley to investigate.

---

[38] On the Cambridge spies, and subsequent paranoia within MI5 in this period, see Andrew, *Defence of the Realm*, pp. 420–41, 503–21.

[39] For allegations against the Director General of MI5, Sir Roger Hollis, see Wright, *Spycatcher*; for a critique of these allegations as conspiracy theory, see Andrew, *Defence of the Realm*, pp. 503–21.

[40] Le Carré, 'The Madness of Spies', but cf. Sisman, *John le Carré*, pp. 193–4. Smiley's 'Circus', is of course SIS (MI6), not MI5.

[41] Le Carré suggests that 'mole' is a genuine KGB term, where most of his other jargon is invented: Bragg, 'The Things a Spy Can Do', pp. 33–4.

[42] On tension between MI5 and MI6, see Sisman, *John le Carré*, pp. 194–6; cf. also le Carré, *The Looking Glass War*, where Control permits a moribund rival agency to mount a doomed operation in order to eliminate his competitors.

In their discussion, Lacon recalls that Smiley had come to him a year previously with a similar suggestion. Lacon had instructed Smiley to abandon his enquiries; Smiley reminds him that he was told they were 'unconstitutional'. Lacon, having come full circle on the matter, now downplays his use of such language as pompous (*Tinker Tailor*, p. 81). Why unconstitutional? As defined by the *OED*, the word means 'not in harmony with, or authorized by, the political constitution; at variance with the recognized principles of the state'.[43] The novel does not elaborate on why Smiley's proposed enquiries might be at risk of such a description, but we might hazard some possibilities.

The most obvious from the context is a possible suspicion on Lacon's part that the Circus was in danger of slipping its leash. Lacon concedes now that he did not trust Smiley's motives at the time of their previous conversation. In general terms, Lacon admits, 'it's a little difficult to know when to trust you people and when not. You do live by rather different standards, don't you? (*Tinker Tailor*, pp. 81–2). More specifically, Smiley's approach to Lacon takes place in the aftermath of a failed operation, codenamed Testify, where a British agent, Jim Prideaux, was shot in Czechoslovakia. 'It's not every day', Lacon says, 'that the head of one's secret service embarks on a private war against the Czechs' (*Tinker Tailor*, p. 83). 'Private war' is an exaggeration on Lacon's part, but it is clear that Testify was both a secret initiative of Control's, and the makings of a substantial crisis: there is a reference slightly later to 'rumours, never officially confirmed, that British troops in Germany had been put on full alert' (*Tinker Tailor*, p. 91). Lacon felt that Control might have put Smiley up to his previous approach as a way of hanging on to power despite this disaster (*Tinker Tailor*, p. 81). Such suspicions indicate that trust between the political class and the leadership of the secret service had broken down, and it is in that context that words like 'unconstitutional' might be used.

The actual investigation that Smiley now undertakes, where a retired spy engages in a covert investigation of his own former agency, might itself be described as somewhat at variance with the recognised principles of the state, however necessary it might be. But we might take a broader view, and recognise that the actions of the Circus as a whole can potentially be viewed in such a light. Such a perspective is offered by the retired policeman, Mendel, who, notwithstanding the assistance he offers to Smiley, holds a jaundiced view of the legitimacy of the Circus and its works, 'an interfering lot of amateurs and college boys' that he considers 'unconstitutional' (*Tinker Tailor*, p. 379). Here, again, we have the word 'unconstitutional': in Mendel's view, it is not

[43] *OED*, s.v. *unconstitutional*, adj., 1.

just a specific activity, but the Circus as a whole that is deserving of the term, though he is prepared to suspend judgment for the sympathetic figures of Smiley and Guillam. There is an even more scathing disregard for the status of secret agents in Mendel's perspective at the end of le Carré's earlier novel, *Call for the Dead*, as he pursues Dieter Frey. Here, for Mendel, 'the frills of Dieter's profession meant nothing' (*Call for the Dead*, p. 128), and Frey is simply another criminal. This is not the only view of Frey offered in *Call for the Dead*: Smiley's position is far more complex and conflicted. Nor is Mendel's suggestion that the Circus is 'unconstitutional' in *Tinker Tailor Soldier Spy* in any way definitive. But in both instances, Mendel's perspective is a reminder that secret services may serve the interests of the state, but the means they use in doing so can be at some remove from the overt principles of the state, as embodied in law. By the time we get to *A Legacy of Spies*, all ambiguity is gone: the police view the Circus as 'a bunch of stuck-up pansies whose mission in life was to break the law' (*A Legacy*, p. 225).

For a long time, Britain's intelligence services occupied a position unrecognised by law. MI5 and SIS (MI6) were established in 1909 as a single organisation, the Secret Service Bureau; its predecessors being the Metropolitan Police Special Branch, which worked in counter-terrorism, and the War Office's MO2 and MO3, which worked in foreign intelligence and counter espionage respectively.[44] Their work was facilitated by passage in 1911 of a new Official Secrets Act, but this Act did not govern the activities of British Intelligence.[45] Legislation to govern domestic and foreign intelligence activities was to come only with the Security Service Act (1989) for MI5, and the Intelligence Services Act (1994) for SIS. In MI5's authorised history, Christopher Andrew comments on the opening words of the Security Service Act ('There shall continue to be a Security Service') as 'elegantly sidestepping the contentious issue of the previous legal basis for the service's operations'.[46] The 1994 legislation governing SIS adopts the same wording: 'There shall continue to be a Secret Intelligence Service … '[47] Even though now positioned firmly within the law, however, section 7 of the Intelligence Services Act is clear that operatives of SIS may be authorised to act outside the law by the Secretary of State.[48] As described by Ian Cobain, the conduct of the UK's crown servants overseas is governed by English law under section

---

[44] Andrew, *Defence of the Realm*, pp. 3, 5; Jeffery, *Secret History of MI6*, p. 3.
[45] Andrew, *Defence of the Realm*, p. 39.
[46] Andrew, *Defence of the Realm*, p. 767.
[47] Intelligence Services Act 1994.
[48] Intelligence Services Act 1994.

31 of the 1948 Criminal Justice Act.[49] But 'as long as the agencies' existence had not been acknowledged, their officers could never be admitted to be crown servants, and so were effectively exempt from that law'. John Major's public acknowledgement of MI6 in 1992 undid that effective exemption; section 7 of the Intelligence Services Act seeks to reinstate that exemption where needed.[50]

In *Tinker Tailor Soldier Spy*, further to the abstract issue of the Circus's legal or constitutional status, there is also a reminder of its resort to extralegal methods, in the form of 'Scalphunters' (or 'Travel' as it is euphemistically known). This is an outfit created at the instigation of Bill Haydon, now headed by Peter Guillam, and exiled to Brixton, 'stabled out of sight behind a flint wall with broken glass and barbed wire on the top' (*Tinker Tailor*, p. 35). It was formed 'in the pioneer days of the cold war, when murder and kidnapping and crash blackmail were common currency', to 'handle the hit-and-run jobs that were too dirty or too risky for the residents abroad' (*Tinker Tailor*, p. 35). We are later told that Guillam 'masterminded the blackest ops this service put its hand to' (*A Legacy*, p. 24).

Given all this potential extralegality of both status and method in the Circus, it is a little ironic perhaps that George Smiley's role in *Tinker Tailor Soldier Spy* is similar to that of a detective, a role not dissimilar to the one he plays in the first two le Carré novels. The espionage novel as a genre is both similar to and indebted to the detective novel, of course, but there is an important difference between them. In the detective story, the detective pursues the truth with a view to bringing criminals to justice. This is true both for the classic form of the detective story (as found in Poe, Conan Doyle, Christie, etc.) and its hard-boiled variation (as found in Chandler, Hammett, etc.). In the latter, the detective's view of justice may be at odds with the view held by the authorities, but it is still justice (however defined) that is the ultimate objective. In the espionage story, however, the protagonist may use the methods of a detective, the format of the story may resemble the detective story, and the immediate objective may be to establish the truth, but the broader objective is a different one. It is not the obtaining of justice, but rather the defence of the realm. 'We're not policemen, Smiley', Maston says at one point in *Call for the Dead*. 'No', Smiley replies, 'I sometimes wonder what we are' (*Call for the Dead*, p. 35).

Before being covertly recalled by Lacon, Smiley is in enforced retirement, having been sacked from the Circus along with Control following the failure

[49] Criminal Justice Act 1948.
[50] Cobain, 'How secret renditions shed light on MI6's licence to kill and torture'; cf. Cobain, *Cruel Brittania*, pp. 247–8, Cobain, *The History Thieves*, pp. 232–3, 240–2.

of Control's covert operation in Czechoslovakia. Control had spent the dying days of his regime trying to determine the identity of his suspected mole, and the disastrous Czech operation was intended to do just that. He had narrowed the list of possible suspects down to the top five people in the Circus: Percy Alleline, Bill Haydon, Roy Bland, Toby Esterhase and Smiley himself. Control had acted alone, sidelining Smiley, who was, of course, one of the possible suspects; but the failure of Testify ended Control's investigation along with his tenure. The fallout from the failed operation, which we will later learn was a trap all along, allows Percy Alleline and his supporters to take over the Circus. Alleline's rise to power has been enabled by his running of an operation that has supplied a steady stream of new high-quality intelligence from a Russian source (or sources), codename Merlin. Alleline had created a separate structure for handling this material, codenamed Witchcraft, citing previous security failings, and effectively using this success to undermine Control's authority.

Following Lacon's tasking of Smiley to investigate new evidence of a possible mole, the plot of the novel resembles a sort of jigsaw puzzle. Various parties hold different pieces, and Smiley assembles a full picture for the most part by interviewing his former Circus colleagues. He supplements their accounts with a trawl through the internal paper trail furnished by Oliver Lacon and Peter Guillam from within the Circus and the Ministry: for Guillam, this involves quietly stealing files from the Circus on Smiley's behalf. What Smiley finds is evidence of a Soviet spy within the Circus, codename Gerald, being run by Cultural Attaché Aleksey Polyakov (whose real name is Colonel Gregor Viktorov), assisted by an embassy driver, Lapin (real name Brod, also known as Ivlov). He discovers that Testify was a trap laid by Moscow for Control. He intuits also that Polyakov is the immediate source of the Witchcraft material that has been so important to Alleline's rise to become head of the Circus. The ultimate source is, of course, Smiley's nemesis, Karla.

Smiley's final interview is with Toby Esterhase, who alone of all his interlocutors is still in post. Esterhase confirms that he and his colleagues (Alleline, Haydon and Bland) are aware that Polyakov is a Soviet agent. However, they believed him to be a double agent loyal to them, providing information from a group of sources, codename Merlin, who now constitute the Circus's major intelligence source. Esterhase also confirms that he was playing the notional role of Merlin's agent inside the Circus, unaware that he and his colleagues were being double-crossed and that there was also a real mole, codename Gerald. There is a rich irony, then, in Percy Alleline's line to Peter Guillam, accusing him of quietly meeting with the fugitive Ricki Tarr: 'There's a *law*, Peter Guillam, against consorting with enemy agents' (*Tinker Tailor*, p. 209).

Guillam is indeed consorting with Tarr, but Tarr, it turns out, is not an enemy agent, though nobody is entirely certain of this at the outset of the novel. Rather, it is Alleline himself and his cronies who have been duped into consorting with Polyakov, in full knowledge that he was a Soviet agent, but incorrectly believing that he had been turned.

The failure of anyone within what is, after all, an intelligence service, to connect these various pieces of partial information is due in part to internal rivalries and loyalties within the Circus. *Tinker Tailor Soldier Spy* is very much an account of the Cold War as office politics. Looking at the files delivered to him by Lacon, Smiley thinks of them as 'a very dull monument' to 'such a long and cruel war' (*Tinker Tailor*, p. 147). We might think for a moment that the war in question is the Cold War, but what he means is the war between Control and Alleline, a conflict so bitter that Alleline at one point suggests that Control had deliberately blown an American plot to Moscow in order to undermine him (*Tinker Tailor*, p. 150).

At the novel's climax, we find that Bill Haydon is the man behind Witchcraft, Alleline's rise, and Control's demise; he is the mole working for Karla inside the Circus.[51] Haydon had been somewhat idolised up to this point, seeming to stand above his colleagues with their dusty files and their intrigues. Some of this is nostalgia for the achievements of a wartime generation now beginning to fade from the scene. Haydon 'had a dazzling war', such that it is possible to compare him with Lawrence of Arabia (*Tinker Tailor*, p. 177), but both the war and Britain's place in the pre-war world are long past – as suggested by the novel's depictions of squalor and decay.[52] Smiley's view of Haydon is more complex than that of his colleagues: pressed by Ann, he admits he does not see Haydon as his own equal (*Tinker Tailor*, p. 167), but he is also unable to view him clearly (*Tinker Tailor*, pp. 177–8).

Haydon is bisexual, and there are suggestions that he may have been Jim Prideaux's lover (*Tinker Tailor*, pp. 257, 302, 393–4)). Sex in general offers the possibility of another sort of secret life, akin to the life of the spy: in the Smiley novels, infidelity means that Ann Smiley also has a secret life, of a different order to her husband's. Homosexual sex, illegal in Britain until 1967, has an even greater sense of the clandestine. Homosexuality and espionage go

---

[51] Hepburn, *Intrigue*, p. 65, comments 'Bill Haydon is Gerald is Merlin'. As I read it, Haydon is Gerald. Karla, with Polyakov as his mouthpiece, is Merlin.

[52] Nicely highlighted in the grimy portrayal of Smiley's hotel and Control's flat in Alfredson, *Tinker Tailor Soldier Spy*. Monaghan, *The Novels of John le Carré*, pp. 47, 48, 85, sees this physical decay as symbolic of spiritual and moral decay, recalling Conrad. Lassner, *Espionage and Exile*, p. 191, reads the portrayal of a ruined London as suggesting the wartime destruction of the home front, and the related sense of homeland.

together in other twentieth-century spy narratives that draw on the story of the Cambridge spies, in part for the obvious reason that Blunt and Burgess were gay.[53] John Banville's espionage novel *The Untouchable* makes clear the potential alignment between illicit sexuality and other forms of deviance: the biography of his protagonist, Victor Maskell, is a blend of Cambridge spy Anthony Blunt and Irish poet Louis MacNeice.[54] Maskell seems untouchable in the sense that he is a member of various excluded castes: a gay man in an era when homosexuality is still illegal, an Irishman (of a complicated sort, claiming, unconvincingly, to belong to a family of turncoat Catholics, with his surname, Maskell, anglicised from that of a hypothetical Mayo clan named O Measceoil (*The Untouchable*, p. 77)), and a spy, a double agent. These various identities seem complementary.[55]

This question of a decision to be taken in a situation of conflicting loyalties is a choice present in several le Carré novels.[56] If the spy is to be entirely effective, they must be completely subjected to the state, free from social loyalties and able to be sacrificed at will. In *The Spy Who Came in from the Cold*, Leamas, in his attachment to Liz, cannot live without sympathy. Smiley, too, is vulnerable on this score: Haydon and Karla identify his love for Ann as 'the last illusion of the illusionless man' (*Tinker Tailor*, pp. 416, 420), an attachment they can use against him. Even Smiley's great enemy, Karla, regarded throughout as a fanatic, has in the end a loyalty that can turn him.[57] Not Haydon. Haydon – for whom many colleagues express feelings of collegiality, of admiration, of friendship and of love – betrays all. In having done so, he seems much reduced. By the end of the novel this once towering figure 'seemed quite visibly to be shrinking to something quite small and mean' (*Tinker Tailor*, p. 415).

The discovery of Haydon's betrayal poses the problem of what to do with him. A trial is never contemplated: here and elsewhere in le Carré,

---

53 Blunt, though not publicly named until 1979, was known by British Intelligence to have been a spy since the 1960s. For similarities between Blunt and Haydon, see Gross, 'The Secret World of John le Carré', pp. 63–4. For similarities between events in *Tinker Tailor Soldier Spy* and Kim Philby's career, see Sisman, *John le Carré*, p. 358.

54 Banville, *The Untouchable*.

55 As it turns out, the *The Untouchable*'s title does not ultimately refer to its protagonist: Maskell is actually the expendable figure sacrificed to protect the man who is truly untouchable. Cf. Hepburn, *Intrigue*, p. 220, on the senses in which Victor, and then Nick, are 'untouchable'; and the broader discussion of Carlston, *Double Agents*, p. 272.

56 On conflict between personal and institutional loyalties, see Plimpton, 'John le Carré, The Art of Fiction No. 149', pp. 149, 158. Sisman, *John le Carré*, p. 135, notes that le Carré's own early career in espionage involved informing on his friends.

57 Le Carré, *Smiley's People*.

bringing the secret world into the courtroom is seen as problematic (*Tinker Tailor*, pp. 350–1, *The Spy*, pp. 148–9). The same is true elsewhere in the literature of espionage: in Graham Greene's *The Human Factor*, a (wrongly) suspected mole is quietly murdered to avoid both the difficulty of a trial and the danger of exposing sources.[58] Instead of facing trial, a proposal is made to trade Haydon for the remaining (and now exposed) British agents behind the Iron Curtain (*Tinker Tailor*, p. 399). This planned exchange never occurs. Haydon, laxly guarded, is killed by the man he betrayed, Jim Prideaux. Within the microcosm of the Circus and its characters, Haydon's personal betrayals are purged by this act of revenge, and order is restored. Alleline is removed, Smiley seeks to be reconciled with his wife (however temporarily), and Prideaux settles into a sort of contentment in his new life.

Writing of *The Spy Who Came in from the* Cold, Allan Hepburn suggests that 'acts of violence merely sustain the status quo'.[59] This is also true for *Tinker Tailor Soldier Spy*; during the Cold War in Europe, the status quo was the best that might be hoped for. Prior to the adoption of a nuclear strategy, a conventional war in Europe was one that the West expected to lose: the first US emergency war plan for Europe assumed that in the event of war, Russia would overrun most of continental Europe in fifty days.[60] From 1954 onwards, NATO's agreed strategy called for the use of tactical nuclear weapons in Europe, a strategy that would have been devastating if conflict had occurred.[61]

But if the status quo is worth preserving, its human cost is severe. In the BBC television adaptation of *Tinker, Tailor, Soldier, Spy*, in the scene where Haydon is unmasked, Guillam accuses him of butchering his agents and asks how many have died since: two hundred, three, four?[62] At the outset, Lacon is able to persuade Smiley to take the job of investigating a possible mole in part because there were vulnerable British agents in the field (*Tinker Tailor*, p. 86). Those exposed networks might have been traded for Haydon, but Haydon's death means that Karla will abandon the deal (*Tinker Tailor*, p. 418). The novel's sequel opens with the Circus appearing to withdraw from its more visible physical manifestations across the globe in what it calls 'a hoods'

---

[58] Greene, *The Human Factor*.

[59] Hepburn, *Intrigue*, p. 180.

[60] May, Steinbruner and Wolfe, *History of the Strategic Arms Competition*, pp. 38, 130–1, 140, 148, 172–3, 343.

[61] For the expected consequences in the UK if a nuclear war had occurred, see Hennessy, *The Secret State*, pp. 121–205.

[62] Irvin, *Tinker, Tailor, Soldier, Spy*. Guillam's outburst is implicit in the novel (*Tinker Tailor*, pp. 396–7).

Dunkirk' (*The Honourable Schoolboy*, p. 463).[63] Only a couple of agents are rescued (*The Honourable Schoolboy*, pp. 499–502). The consequences for the rest are left to the imagination.[64]

Rendering Justice: *A Most Wanted Man*

Most of the principal characters in le Carré's 2008 novel, *A Most Wanted Man*, occupy questionable positions in relation to the law, and the novel's opening circumstance poses a question related to law. Issa Karpov, a Chechen, has fled imprisonment and torture in Russia and Turkey, and has been smuggled to Hamburg, via Stockholm (where he escaped from the custody of the Swedish authorities). His legal status, therefore, might alternatively be that of a refugee fleeing persecution, of an illegal immigrant to Germany, or of an escapee from the legal authorities of several countries: Russia, Turkey, and, most pertinently because of its EU membership, Sweden. Karpov finds shelter with a Turkish family in Hamburg. His potential legal (or illegal) status brings him to the attention of Annabel Richter, a lawyer with a charitable foundation that assists stateless and displaced persons. It also attracts the notice of Günther Bachmann of the Office for the Protection of the Constitution, the German domestic intelligence service. Neither Richter nor the intelligence agents taking an interest in him are particularly confident that Issa Karpov's right to asylum will override the other considerations regarding his potential legal status.

As Richter describes his situation, under the EU's Dublin Convention of 1990, the German authorities must return Karpov to Sweden for deportation (*A Most Wanted Man*, p. 100).[65] German Intelligence has a similar view of Karpov's chances before the law. As an agent explains to Annabel Richter in their initial interview:

> '*Issa Karpov* is an Islamist Russian criminal with a long record of convictions for militant actions. He entered Germany illegally – smuggled by *other* criminals, maybe also Islamist – and has no rights in this country whatever'.
> 'Everyone has rights, surely', Annabel suggested, in gentle reproof.
> 'Not in his situation, Frau Richter. Not in his situation'. (*A Most Wanted Man*, p. 194)

There are aspects of Karpov's biography that demand explanation: particularly that alleged 'long record of convictions for militant actions'. Karpov claims all

---

[63] Le Carré, *The Honourable Schoolboy*.

[64] Le Carré comments angrily in a 1989 interview on the 'gruesome fate' of the British agents betrayed by Kim Philby: 'What Would I Be Like If I Were He?', p. 119.

[65] Convention determining the State responsible for examining applications for asylum lodged in one of the Member States of the European Communities – Dublin Convention 1990.

he is guilty of is being Chechen (*A Most Wanted Man*, pp. 87–8). Erna Frey of German Intelligence is also scathing about the allegations, citing reports from Amnesty International and Human Rights Watch regarding fabrication of evidence and torture of the accused (*A Most Wanted Man*, pp. 127–30). This is torture that has left its mark (*A Most Wanted Man*, p. 16).

Issa Karpov's situation is further complicated by his background. He is the natural son of a Red Army colonel, Grigori Karpov. Grigori Karpov raped Issa Karpov's teenage Chechen mother, who was in turn killed by her family after Issa's birth. Colonel Karpov was involved in organised crime, and he was also a British spy. In return for his co-operation, British Intelligence arranged for Karpov's money to be laundered via a private bank, based in Vienna, owned by a British banker, Edward Amadeus Brue. Brue and Karpov are now both dead, but the illicit accounts still exist at the bank, now based in Hamburg, and headed by Edward's son Tommy Brue. Issa Karpov has nothing but revulsion for his father, denying his heritage to the extent that he will not even bear his name: he goes by Issa Salim Mahmoud, rather than his birth name of Ivan Grigorivich Karpov (*A Most Wanted Man*, pp. 85–7). He has come to Hamburg, however, to explore the possibility of claiming his father's money from Tommy Brue's bank. Brue and Karpov, then, although opposites in terms of age, background and wealth, are both sons dealing with unwanted legacies from their fathers. Brue's father's reckless decision 'to set himself up as Vienna's banker of choice to a bunch of Russian gangsters' (*A Most Wanted Man*, p. 31) first forces the bank to relocate from Vienna to Hamburg, and now, many years later, it allows British Intelligence to blackmail Tommy Brue (*A Most Wanted Man*, pp. 46–7, 247–8).[66]

If Issa Karpov and Tommy Brue occupy questionable positions with regard to the law, the other two major characters in the novel, Annabel Richter and Günther Bachmann, are representatives of the law and the state respectively. If Richter is a lawyer, however, there are certain forms of law, 'law not to protect life, but to abuse it', that she refuses to abide by (*A Most Wanted Man*, pp. 101–2). As Robert Snyder puts it, Richter's view of justice 'encompasses an ethic of empathy'.[67] And if Bachmann is an employee of the state, that does not mean he too does not occupy a questionable position in relation to its laws. Concluding a long introductory speech to his colleagues, he observes:

---

[66] In Corbijn, *A Most Wanted Man*, the father–son theme is accentuated further: here the son of Faisal Abdullah, Bachmann's target, has also been acting as Bachmann's agent. Sisman, *John le Carré*, p. 574, notes the resonance of this motif of troubled father–son relationships with le Carré's own biography.

[67] Snyder, *John le Carré's Post-Cold War Fiction*, p. 103.

> And remember, please, that we are illegal. How illegal, not being a fine
> lawyer like so many of our august colleagues, I don't truthfully know. But
> from all they tell me, we can't so much as wipe our arses without prior
> consent in writing from a board of high judges, the Holy See, Joint Steering
> in Berlin and our beloved Federal Police who don't know spying from shit,
> but have all the powers that the intelligence services are rightly deprived of
> so that we don't become the Gestapo by mistake. (*A Most Wanted Man*,
> p. 68)

Some of this, of course, is rhetoric, and Bachmann is the archetypal maverick
operator with a distrust of authority. But there is some truth here also, in
that (as we have been arguing here) the state uses its intelligence services
to pursue its interests outside the constraints of the law, and this description is not something unique to this particular intelligence service in this
particular novel. Elsewhere in le Carré, for example, we meet Harry Palfrey,
legal adviser to SIS, self-described as 'legal adviser to the illegals'.[68] And the
embrace of illegality is something we see clearly in Bachmann's dealings with
Annabel Richter.

When Bachmann, under an alias, meets Richter at her office, the conversation is preceded by an elaborate acknowledgement of legal niceties (*A
Most Wanted Man*, p. 193). Shortly afterwards, Bachmann has the lawyer
kidnapped in the street (*A Most Wanted Man*, pp. 208–9). The law is against
Bachmann here, as he admits (*A Most Wanted Man*, p. 213). But he can
still manipulate legal process in his favour, threatening Richter with the
arrest of Issa and 'the people who would be seen as his accomplices' – his
Turkish hosts, Brue, even Richter's brother – with consequences for all of
these people, including the possible end of Richter's own legal career (*A Most
Wanted Man*, p. 214).

Günther Bachmann and Erna Frey secure Annabel Richter's co-operation
for a proposed sting, using Karpov and the funds held for him in Brue's bank
as a means of compromising a Dr Faisal Abdullah, a scholar who uses his
charitable roles to conceal funding of terrorist activities. Bachmann wishes to
use Karpov to help him recruit Abdullah as an informant. This is his *modus
operandi*, as he outlines it:

> We are not policemen, we are spies. We do not arrest our targets. We
> develop them and redirect them at bigger targets … If Abdullah is not part
> of a known network, I personally will make him part of one. If need be, I
> will invent a network, just for him. (*A Most Wanted Man*, p. 283)

---

[68] Le Carré, *The Russia House*, p. 47.

The contrast with a law enforcement approach is explicitly drawn here by Bachmann. His strategy is not to arrest those he sees as potential enemies of the state and to bring them to justice, but to manipulate them to best advantage.

Bachmann's difficulty is that suspected Islamic terrorists in Hamburg, post-9/11, attract international interest, and his plan attracts the interest of the CIA (*A Most Wanted Man*, p. 273). Bachmann receives approval for his plan, but finds this authorisation withdrawn at the very last moment (*A Most Wanted Man*, pp. 294, 362–3). His operation is then ambushed by the CIA, who take both Abdullah and Karpov. Here, the Germans, as with the British elsewhere in le Carré, defer to the will of their more powerful ally, the United States, in its furious and undiscriminating pursuit of Islamic terrorism in the aftermath of 9/11. If 'justice has been rendered' here, as the CIA's Newton claims, it is explicitly 'justice with no fucking lawyers around to pervert the course', justice that is rendered in 'some hole in the desert' (*A Most Wanted Man*, p. 370).[69]

Extraordinary rendition is 'the seizure and transportation by authorities of a criminal suspect from one country to another without the formal process of extradition'.[70] In the words of the Open Society Justice Initiative's 2013 report on the practice, it has the specific purpose of placing detainee interrogations 'beyond the reach of the law',[71] and it has been associated with the use of torture. Bachmann's own practice is also perfectly capable of accommodating state kidnapping and a disregard for legal process, as we see in his abduction and recruitment of Annabel Richter. The differences between Bachmann and the CIA in the novel are, of course, substantial. They are, however, differences of degree. What we see in the portrayal of the CIA in *A Most Wanted Man* is a blanket failure to discriminate, to apply due process, or to give heed to the possibility of innocence, together with a lack of concern about proceeding in this way. Abdullah is most likely guilty. Karpov, however, is most likely an innocent man. The Germans are prepared to manipulate and use both men. The CIA, however, simply assumes their guilt, and renders them both.[72]

---

[69] For documentation of the CIA's rendition, detention and interrogation programme, see *The Rendition Project*.

[70] *OED*, s.v. *extraordinary rendition*, n., at *extraordinary*, adj., adv., and n., Additions.

[71] *Globalizing Torture*, p. 5.

[72] Le Carré's plot is partly indebted to the case of Murat Kurnaz, who was detained at Guantánamo Bay in Cuba from 2001 to 2006 (Le Carré, *The Pigeon Tunnel*, pp. 71–6). The background of Issa Karpov's character as the son of a Chechen mother raped by a Russian officer is also based on a real person (Sisman, *John le Carré*, p. 574).

If the political issue of extraordinary rendition is at the heart of le Carré's novel, Anton Corbijn's 2014 film adaptation of *A Most Wanted Man* is less focused on the issue. When the subject is alluded to, the CIA's Martha Sullivan suggests that the US doesn't do that anymore. The power relationship between US and German intelligence remains the same from the book to the film. What is different is Bachmann's individual relationship with Sullivan (named only as Martha in the book). In the film, very much as in the novel, Bachmann (played by Philip Seymour Hoffman) is the archetypal veteran spy, male, middle-aged, maverick, existing on a diet of coffee, cigarettes and alcohol, breaking the rules to save the innocent, indifferent to matters such as civility and collegiality. In the film, as in the novel, that sort of behaviour requires the protection of someone more powerful. In the novel, that person is Michael Axelrod of German Foreign Intelligence. In the film, however, the person who offers Bachmann the latitude to do what he needs is the CIA's Sullivan (played by Robin Wright), a more substantial presence in this version of the story than in le Carré's novel, and the most powerful figure in both. Here, it is possible to read the adverse outcome as a result, not of American duplicity, but of Bachmann's hubris. Sullivan extends him every latitude, but when she asks him in a broader strategy meeting what his objective is should he be allowed (as he wishes) to preserve Karpov and Abdullah, the answer he gives her is a glib repetition of a phrase she has used earlier to him: 'to make the world a better place'. Here, we might think, it is Bachmann's foolish decision to backchat his protector in front of her peers that sinks his operation. This is not the only way to read the film, and it is also possible that we should read the ending as an indication (as in the novel) that Bachmann's wariness of Sullivan throughout was well-judged: we get no direct insight into Sullivan's thinking. Although different from the novel, a scenario where Bachmann misreads Sullivan is nonetheless classic le Carré territory: espionage as office politics. But it also moves the story's emphasis from geopolitics to gender politics. Cold War narratives of espionage, as Timothy Melley argues, are often very much based upon constructions of hypermasculinity and male agency.[73] Corbijn's version of *A Most Wanted Man* seems to suggest that the maverick spy, a model of masculine agency based around an archetype of flawed genius, is an anachronism in the twenty-first century. Bachmann's inability to read the internal politics correctly leaves him wandering around at the end of the film, wondering what happened, as his erstwhile backer cuts him loose and his targets are carried away in the back of a van. But le Carré's own representations of masculinity have always

---

[73] Melley, *Covert Sphere*, pp. 23–7.

been complex, and Bachmann would hardly be the first le Carré leading man to grace either page or screen who finds everything he strives for reduced to ashes by the end.

A Most Wanted Man also touches on concerns visible elsewhere in le Carré's recent work. The figure of Issa Karpov makes it clear that the children of conflicts, recent and past, have the potential to haunt a Europe that would much prefer not to deal with the consequences. Le Carré offered a post-colonial version of some of the same issues in his 2006 novel, *The Mission Song*.[74] Here Bruno Salvador, the son of an Irish Catholic missionary father and a Congolese mother, is a freelance interpreter who works part-time for British Intelligence. Salvador initially assists, and then falls foul of, a shadowy international syndicate that plans to take power in Eastern Congo. This syndicate has arranged a secret conference with a group of East Congolese warlords on an anonymous island in the North Sea. Salvador's masters in British Intelligence have recruited him to act as interpreter at this conference, though his actual role is one of surveillance, and his involvement, he is told, is deniable (*The Mission Song*, p. 45).[75] The syndicate is a self-described 'phil-anthropic offshore venture capital organisation' (*The Mission Song*, p. 115).[76] It is headed by Philip, a consultant, who 'has no rank' and 'is a member of no official service' (*The Mission Song*, p. 49). The syndicate, we are told, has no name: 'This Syndicate is called *Nothing*. It is Nothing Incorporated' (*The Mission Song*, p. 141). This nameless syndicate, located nowhere (simply 'offshore'), headed by a 'consultant' who works for no one, turns out to be not entirely anonymous: its backers include a peer and former minister, as well as elements of British Intelligence, and its objectives are somewhat less philanthropic than originally promised.[77]

Here we can see that our broad argument that the state acts extralegally to defend or pursue its interests, is complicated in the post-Cold War era by the increasing dilution of state power in favour of corporate power, even in matters so fundamental to the state as its security. There are a variety of factors in play here, from ideology to self-interest, but Peter W. Singer argues that privatised military firms are used by Western states after the

---

[74] Le Carré, *The Mission Song*.

[75] Snyder, *John le Carré's Post-Cold War Fiction*, pp. 93–103, locates this motif of surveillance in the context of Foucault's *Discipline and Punish* and the breadth of contemporary state-sponsored surveillance.

[76] On the historic use of US philanthropic foundations for CIA purposes during the Cold War, see Saunders, *Who Paid the Piper?* pp. 129–45.

[77] On parallels between *The Mission Song* and an actual 2004 mercenary plot backed by, among others, Sir Mark Thatcher, see Sisman, *John le Carré*, pp. 560–1.

Cold War to avoid both political scrutiny and domestic legal impediments.[78] Singer suggests that international law offers slim recourse against such firms, which are, in any case, often 'virtual companies' with offshore registration and subcontracted staff, and so easily dissolved.[79] This is certainly the case for Bruno Salvador's 'philanthropic offshore venture capital organization', and we can see something like this again in another recent le Carré novel, *A Delicate Truth*, where Ethical Outcomes, the private contractor behind a disastrous rendition attempt, reconstitutes itself as an entirely different firm, Castle Keep, with 'absolutely no connection visible or otherwise' between the two (Le Carré, *A Delicate Truth*, p. 290).[80]

In *The Mission Song*, Salvador, discovering that all is not quite as it might seem, makes frantic efforts to blow the plot. In return, he finds his own identity cancelled. The powers-that-be arrange for the deportation of his lover and her son, cancel her visa, and inform him that his own British citizenship was never valid (*The Mission Song*, pp. 325–7). Salvador is duly dispatched to a detention camp.[81] He 'is not now and never has been a British subject, loyal or otherwise' (*The Mission Song*, p. 326). He is stateless, pending his eventual acceptance by the Congo. He receives a number to replace his name (*The Mission Song*, p. 330), and when he joins a protest at the detention camp, he receives some broken bones compliments of some 'no name policemen' (*The Mission Song*, p. 333). He has no name, no citizenship, and no rights.[82] The Congo itself, we are told by Salvador's MI5 mentor, Anderson, is 'a rogue country', and hence not entitled to respect under international law (*The Mission Song*, p. 298).

In these twenty-first-century le Carré novels, then, we see the state acting outside the law in what can be described as two complementary strategies of the state in the contemporary West. First, the state itself, when its interests require it, acts outside legal constraints via its intelligence agencies (as in the portrayal of extraordinary rendition by the CIA in *A Most Wanted Man*), or, in some cases, via arm's length partnerships with corporate interests (as in *The Mission Song* and *A Delicate Truth*). Secondly, the state seeks to situate particular individuals outside the reach of the law, whether physically (as with extraordinary rendition) or in terms of their status (as in the indefinite

---

[78] Singer, *Corporate Warriors*, pp. ix–x, 210–11, 214.

[79] Singer, *Corporate Warriors*, pp. 75, 220.

[80] Le Carré, *A Delicate Truth*, p. 290.

[81] On le Carré's post-war role interrogating refugees held in Austrian detention camps, see Sisman, *John le Carré*, pp. 99–101.

[82] On the UK's increasing resort to revocation of citizenship for opponents of the state, see Kadri, 'Short Cuts'.

detention without trial of asylum seekers), in ways that recall the historical phenomenon of outlawry. In *A Most Wanted Man*, Issa Karpov and Faisal Abdullah are abducted and taken to an anonymous location, 'some hole in the desert', to be tortured. In *The Mission Song*, Bruno Salvador has his identity erased, is rendered stateless, and is placed in a detention camp pending his eventual deportation.

The situations that le Carré places these characters in are well grounded in contemporary reality. The UK operates ten immigration removal centres for detaining asylum seekers and individuals to be deported;[83] other European countries, Australia, and the United States also operate substantial immigration detention facilities. While the full extent of the CIA's extraordinary rendition programme is not known, the Open Society Justice Initiative reported in 2013 on 136 individuals rendered by the programme.[84] In short, some of le Carré's recent work highlights the fact that for vulnerable immigrants and individuals suspected of terrorist links, exclusion from the law's protection – outlawry in new and troubling forms – is alive and well in the twenty-first century West.

[83] 'Find an immigration removal centre'.
[84] *Globalizing Torture*, p. 6.

5

'All Plots Tend to Move Deathward':
Plots and Consequences in Don DeLillo

'It's no accident', says Don DeLillo, 'that my first novel was called *Americana*. This was a private declaration of independence, a statement of my intuition to use the whole picture, the whole culture'.[1] This urge to show 'the whole picture', the broad and extended meditation on contemporary America in DeLillo's work, reaches a climax in *Underworld*, an epic portrait of the United States in the latter half of the twentieth century.[2] In looking at 'the whole culture', DeLillo perhaps inevitably shows an enduring interest in both the agents of the state and their opponents.

Such agents are frequently seen or suggested to act either outside or against the law. *Running Dog* features a fully fledged extralegal paramilitary force operating within the forces of the American state, 'run contrary to the spirit and letter of every law, every intelligence directive, that pertains to such matters'.[3] 'Spy work, undercover work', Guy Banister says in *Libra*, 'we invent a society where it's always wartime. The law has a little give' (*Libra*, p. 64). 'A government is a criminal enterprise', Richard Elster suggests provocatively in *Point Omega*, a text concerned among other things with CIA rendition and torture (*Point Omega*, p. 33). And at the heart of DeLillo's body of work is a version of the Kennedy assassination where a coalition of disgruntled former CIA agents set out to make an attempt on the President's life.

From *The Names* onwards, works engaged with these themes are placed in specific historical contexts: the Iran hostage crisis for *The Names*, the Kennedy assassination for *Libra*, the events of 1989 for *Mao II*, the broad backdrop of the Cold War for *Underworld*, the anti-globalisation movement for *Cosmopolis*, 9/11 for *Falling Man*, and the Iraq war for *Point Omega*. DeLillo's engagement with these issues in such contexts offers (like other aspects of his work) what John Duvall calls a 'repeated invitation to think

---

[1] Begley, 'The Art of Fiction CXXXV: Don DeLillo', p. 88.
[2] DeLillo, *Underworld*.
[3] DeLillo, *Running Dog*, p. 81.

historically'.[4] But DeLillo's fiction is often concerned with history of a particular sort, 'a kind of underhistory' as he says of *Underworld*.[5]

'Are They Killing Americans?': *The Names*

In *The Names*, Anne Longmuir writes, 'for the first time, DeLillo plots a novel against a historical intertext', making this novel 'a seminal text that grounds DeLillo's subsequent fiction'.[6] *The Names* poses questions about the *naïveté* of the overseas interventions of US intelligence services – seen as all-pervasive, unknowing, and potentially extremely dangerous – in the context of the Iranian hostage crisis.[7] That crisis, and the Iranian revolution of 1979, might themselves be viewed as the unforeseen long-term outcomes of the CIA's 1953 coup against Iran's Mossadeq regime.[8] The novel's protagonist, James Axton, formerly a freelance writer, has taken a job as a risk analyst with the Northeast Group, a subsidiary of a two-billion dollar conglomerate which Axton knows only as 'the parent' (*The Names*, pp. 47–8). Axton takes the job in order to base himself in Athens: his estranged wife Kathryn is working on an archaeological dig on a Greek island with their son Tap, and he signs up in order to be near them. But Greece is also 'the southeast flank' in the geography of the Cold War (*The Names*, p. 59), and Athens is the relatively safe base from which Axton and his fellow Westerners commute into more dangerous territories.

There are repeated enquiries about Axton's work, from various quarters: his interlocutors find his responses 'vague' (*The Names*, pp. 215, 242). Axton thinks he works in insurance, when in truth his work is something else entirely. There are various descriptions of Axton's 'vague' job as a risk analyst. 'It's just insurance', he tells Kathryn (*The Names*, p. 12). He views his boss, George Rowser, as a man who 'convinced a medium-sized insurance company to sell ransom policies to the multinationals' (*The Names*, p. 46), despite various clues to the contrary. Rowser has three identities, a briefcase packed with technology, and an office outside Washington with elaborate security measures (*The Names*, p. 11, 44). He will not hold work conversations indoors (*The Names*, p. 47). All of this cloak-and-dagger activity should be enough to suggest that something other than insurance is involved here.

---

[4] Duvall, 'Introduction', p. 2.

[5] Echlin, 'Baseball and the Cold War', p. 147.

[6] Longmuir, 'The Language of History', p. 105.

[7] On the Iranian revolution and the hostage crisis, see Weiner, *Legacy of Ashes*, pp. 426–33; Andrew, *For the President's Eyes Only*, pp. 438–42, 448–56.

[8] On which see Weiner, *Legacy of Ashes*, pp. 92–105; Andrew, *For the President's Eyes Only*, pp. 202–6.

But, as Axton's banker friend David Keller tells him, our protagonist is 'a fool, running a fool's errand, in a fool's world' (*The Names*, p. 6).

It is unclear how much others in Axton's circle might know. His friend Charles Maitland ultimately reveals to him, late in the narrative, that he is in fact working, at one remove, for the CIA (*The Names*, pp. 314–16). Maitland professes not to have known all along, but Maitland is, both by his own admission and that of his son, a specialist in pretending not to know things (*The Names*, pp. 41–2, 165). Axton's own air of unknowing, by contrast, is unfeigned.[9] There is a conversation earlier on in the book where Axton offers to enquire with Rowser for a potential role for Maitland. Maitland responds negatively: 'I'm in the world, granted. I've always been in the world. But I don't know that I like it anymore'. Axton takes this as some sort of obscure philosophical statement. 'That's profound, Charles', he replies. But what Maitland may well mean by being 'in the world' is that with his background in international security work, the world (in a quite restrictive sense of the word) he has worked in is quite like the world Axton works in, which turns out to be the world of espionage. It is not clear whether or not this is what is meant, because Axton seems to misunderstand Maitland, and Maitland is unwilling to give any more away (*The Names*, p. 98). But this may be a suggestion that Maitland is on to him early.

David Keller, the banking executive in Axton's circle, supplies him with transcripts of scrambled telexes between bank branches in the region, including confidential information that informs Axton's reports to Rowser (*The Names*, pp. 50, 70). He does this because, as Axton puts it, 'we were serving the same broad ends' (*The Names*, p. 70). When Axton tries to use another American, Roy Hardeman, as a source of information, Hardeman, suspicious, asks who he works for (*The Names*, p. 263). By the 1970s, it seems that Americans overseas with 'vague' professional identities might be routinely suspected of CIA involvement. In Harry Mathews's 'autobiographical novel' *My Life in CIA*, many of his friends and acquaintances suspect him, as an American writer abroad, of being a CIA agent: he then decides to act the part.[10]

The relationship between Axton and Keller reflects the interchangeability of political and corporate interests here: the subject of ironic humour at one point when Keller talks about training for a night drop into Iran, leading 'credit officers with blackened faces' (*The Names*, p. 131). The similarities are highlighted when Axton is mistaken for Keller by Andreas Eliades when the

---

[9] We might note that the CIA failed to see the Iranian revolution coming: Weiner, *Legacy of Ashes*, pp. 426–9; Andrew, *For the President's Eyes Only*, pp. 438–42.

[10] Mathews, *My Life in CIA*.

two first meet. Eliades needles Axton about the actions of US business and political interests in relation to Greece and Turkey; Ann Maitland (who will become Eliades's lover), intervenes to correct his error:

> 'Oh dear', Ann said. 'I think you have the wrong man, Andreas. This is not David Keller. You want David. He's the banker'.
> 'I am James. The risk analyst'. (*The Names*, p. 59)

But perhaps Eliades does not have the wrong man after all, for the interests of American banks and the CIA are interchangeable. Eliades begins to take an interest in Axton, asking questions about him, and his vague job (*The Names*, pp. 240–2). When Keller is shot, Axton suspects Eliades as the instigator, and also suspects that, once again, there might have been a mix-up between him and Keller (*The Names*, p. 327). Whether or not Maitland or Keller have realised the true nature of Axton's role earlier on in the piece, Eliades is certainly wise to Axton's real role long before Axton himself.

The theme of secret intelligence-gathering in a geopolitical context, while important, is far from the full extent of this novel's reach, but the book's other concerns are entwined with its political themes. If language itself is a substantial focus in the book, as Longmuir writes, an emphasis on language that ignores the novel's political backdrop risks missing the point that DeLillo here 'deliberately asks abstract questions of language within a very specific period and location, thereby demonstrating the political implications of these questions and the historical conditions that shape them'.[11] Running in parallel to the gradually unwinding narrative of secret American intelligence gathering in the Middle East is the story of a mysterious cult, a group called *Ta Onómata*, 'The Names' (*The Names*, p. 188). When Kathryn's employer, the archaeologist Owen Brademas, finally locates the cult, they tell him he is a member. He objects, unsuccessfully (*The Names*, p. 298). Like Axton, who finds he has unwittingly become an operative of the CIA, Brademas is in over his head. He stays while the group carry out the ritual murder they are there to commit.

If *The Names* shows James Axton being unwittingly co-opted by US intelligence, such a scenario is a fundamental one for writers during the Cold War. The relationship between writing and espionage in the post-war era is complex. If espionage fiction was an important forum for public understanding of the secret work of the state,[12] and many prominent writers of post-war espionage fiction were themselves former intelligence employees,

---

[11] Longmuir, 'The Language of History', p. 119.
[12] Melley, *Covert Sphere*, p. 9.

the intelligence services were also keen to fight their ideological battles on a broader front by extensively underwriting cultural activities. The Congress for Cultural Freedom, established in 1950, opened offices in thirty-five countries, backed a variety of cultural periodicals, and funded exhibitions, conferences and prizes. The Congress was covertly funded by the CIA, via a number of methods including the use of philanthropic foundations to distribute the funds.[13] The US was in fact somewhat belated in employing such tactics: the Soviet Union had started much earlier.[14] But it did so covertly: 'a central feature of this programme was to advance the claim that it did not exist'.[15] As the CIA's covert funding began to become public knowledge, inevitably many writers in the latter half of the twentieth century were nervous of being compromised.

The Names and the other two DeLillo novels discussed at length below – *Libra* and *Point Omega* – all feature protagonists who have been in some way co-opted by intelligence agencies. None, however, are writers, and in DeLillo's fiction the writer is more likely to be found aligned with the state's opponents. *Mao II*'s novelist character, Bill Gray, embodies the writer as an outcast opposed to the powers-that-be. 'You think the writer belongs at the far margin, doing dangerous things', Charlie Everson says to Gray. 'The state should want to kill all writers' (*Mao II*, p. 97).[16] DeLillo has been clear that Bill Gray is not to be seen as a version of the novelist who created him, but his own views of the role of the writer in society are perhaps not so different. In interview, DeLillo suggests that the role of the writer is to be in opposition:

> This is why we need the writer in opposition, the novelist who writes against power, who writes against the corporation or the state or the whole apparatus of assimilation.[17]

The relationship between art and terror is a major thematic concern of *Mao II*, and here, too, we can see the writer's suspicion of being co-opted, albeit by the other side. But Bill Gray's character ultimately rejects any equation between the artist and the terrorist:[18]

> 'No. It's pure myth, the terrorist as solitary outlaw. These groups are backed by repressive governments. They're perfect little totalitarian states. They

---

[13] Saunders, *Who Paid the Piper?*, *passim*.

[14] Judt, *Postwar*, pp. 222–5.

[15] Saunders, *Who Paid the Piper?*, p. 1.

[16] DeLillo, *Mao II*.

[17] Begley, 'The Art of Fiction CXXXV: Don DeLillo', p. 97.

[18] Auster, *Leviathan*, published a year after *Mao II*, and dedicated to DeLillo, explores similar concerns.

carry the old wild-eyed vision, total destruction and total order'. (*Mao II*, p. 158)[19]

Much as they might both be oppositional, and much as the power of one may ascend as the influence of the other declines, the writer and the terrorist are not kindred souls. If anything, they are opposites. Gray offers a defence of the novel form as 'a democratic shout'; the hostage-taking of terrorist groups, in contrast, is 'the miniaturized form' of the mass terror inherent in the totalitarian state (*Mao II*, pp. 159, 163). If concern about being co-opted, whether by the intelligence agencies or their opponents, is a fundamental one for writers in the second half of the twentieth century, DeLillo's repeated revisitings of the actions of America's secret state and its enemies remain based on his own 'declaration of independence'.

As a portrayal of a naïve American operating in a distant political context, *The Names* recalls in some ways Graham Greene's 1955 novel, *The Quiet American*.[20] Greene's novel is set in Vietnam towards the end of the French occupation, with the United States on the verge of intervening. Aldous Pyle, the quiet American of the title, is a member of the US Economic Aid mission, with, as the Economic Attaché puts it, 'special duties' (*The Quiet American*, p. 23). In other words, like James Axton in *The Names*, he is an undercover intelligence operative. Axton and Pyle each have a more experienced British interlocutor who represents the empire superseded by the rise of the United States: Thomas Fowler in *The Quiet American*, Charles Maitland in *The Names*.[21] Both novels are situated in fragmented and chaotic political situations that draw on real historical circumstance (though Greene's is much more concrete in its description of the politics: DeLillo's book is set against the backdrop of the Iranian hostage crisis, but at some remove, and the overall thrust of DeLillo's novel is less overtly political than Greene's).

The major difference between the American protagonists in each work, however, is that in Greene's novel, it is Fowler, the English journalist, who protests throughout that he is not involved in the conflict, not *engagé*. Pyle believes that US intervention in support of a third force (as he puts it) can result in a western victory in Vietnam. He is mistaken in this, of course,

---

[19] Richardson, *What Terrorists Want*, p. 5, comments that 'terrorism is the act of substate groups, not states', and this is a defining characteristic, though 'this is not to suggest that states do not use terrorism as an instrument of foreign policy'.

[20] Greene, *The Quiet American*.

[21] Neither Pyle's American-ness nor British disengagement from Asia are uncomplicated, however: cf. Piette, *The Literary Cold War*, pp. 153–67, on parallels between the Fowler–Pyle relationship and the relationship between Graham Greene and his brother.

as Fowler continually tries to tell him (though Fowler is also an unreliable narrator who both mistakes the extent of his own involvement and consistently underestimates Pyle's ability and resourcefulness). In DeLillo's book, in contrast, it is Axton, the CIA proxy, who believes he is not involved, whereas Charles Maitland, his more world-weary interlocutor, accepts that he has 'always been in the world'. This makes Axton a less ominous character than Pyle, whose *naïveté* and willingness to overlook means in preference for ends makes him a somewhat terrifying figure, and Axton is much more of a passive actor in the political events playing out around him.

In each novel, however, the activities of Pyle and Axton, Americans operating abroad in contexts they fail to grasp, make them potential targets for assassination. 'Are they killing Americans?' people ask each other in *The Names* (*The Names*, pp. 45, 193). In *The Quiet American*, Pyle is killed, betrayed by Fowler because of a complex series of motivations involving both the love triangle between the two of them and a Vietnamese woman, Phuong, and Fowler's horror at the civilian casualties that result from the bombings that Pyle has helped to organise. In *The Names*, James Axton suspects that the unsuccessful attempt on David Keller's life, most likely organised by their sometime dinner companion Andreas Eliades, might well have been intended for him. Our later discoveries regarding Axton's ultimate employer puts in a new perspective the earlier news that 'our Iranian control was dead, shot by two men in the street' (*The Names*, p. 143). Pyle and Axton's naïve actions have real consequences, sometimes fatal consequences: for others, certainly, and potentially also for themselves.

'We Want to Set up an Attempt on the Life of the President': *Libra*

DeLillo returns to the theme of CIA activity in his ninth novel, *Libra*, an account of the Kennedy assassination. DeLillo has said in interview that 'as I was working on *Libra*, it occurred to me that a lot of tendencies in my first eight novels seemed to be collecting around the dark center of the assassination',[22] and there are a number of allusions to the assassination in previous works. In *Americana*, DeLillo's first book, David Bell's inconclusive journey into America comes to an end in Dallas, at the sites of the assassination and its aftermath.[23] The leading subversive character in *Players* has some history with Lee Harvey Oswald.[24] In *Running Dog*, Senator Percival's wife has been in bed reading the Warren Report for some nine years (*Running Dog*, pp. 77–8). In the latter books, espionage and conspiracy are substantial

---

[22] DeCurtis, '"An Outsider in This Society"', p. 56.
[23] DeLillo, *Americana*, p. 377.
[24] DeLillo, *Players*, pp. 154, 181.

themes, but in *Libra*, the theme of covert activity takes on an entirely different level of seriousness.

The post-war intelligence services of the United States did not exist in a
state of legal limbo as the UK agencies did: the CIA was created initially by
the National Security Act (1947).[25] Rather, the covert sphere, as Timothy
Melley argues, 'has increasingly become a version of the state itself', with
'its own bureaucracies (the intelligence services, shell companies), its own
laws (NSC memorandums, secret authorisation directives, covert rules of
engagement), and its own territories (remote airstrips, Guantánamo Bay,
rendition sites)'.[26] The covert overseas activities of the US intelligence services
did not necessarily in themselves break US laws.[27] Richard Immerman suggests that an 'elastic clause' in the National Security Act allowing the CIA
to perform 'such additional services of common concern as the National
Security Council determines can be more efficiently accomplished centrally'
would serve as 'something of a blank check for the future, justifying the CIA's
involvement in a remarkable range of clandestine and paramilitary operations
few at the time could imagine'. [28] For long-serving CIA lawyer John Rizzo,
the lack of specificity seems deliberate. 'Few federal statutes were meant to
apply to the Agency's activities', Rizzo writes, 'and those that did traced back
to the late '40s and were, by congressional design, cryptic and ambiguously
worded'.[29] But where Rizzo sees congressional design, Immerman suggests
that Congress may have had no appreciation that the legislation contained
such potential.[30] The subsequent CIA Act of 1949 moved the CIA further
towards the covert aspects of its remit: in exempting the CIA from publicly
disclosing its activities, budget and personnel, 'covert and paramilitary operations came to define what the CIA was'.[31]

In part, the latitude available to the CIA and other US intelligence agencies

---

[25] National Security Act 1947. For discussion of this and subsequent legislation, see Snider,
The Agency and the Hill, pp. 137–58.

[26] Melley, *Covert Sphere*, p. 5.

[27] In US law, covert action is 'an activity or activities of the United States Government to
influence political, economic, or military conditions abroad, where it is intended that the
role of the United States Government will not be apparent or acknowledged publicly'. It
must be authorised by a written Presidential finding and reported to the congressional intelligence committees: see 'Presidential Approval and Reporting of Covert Actions'. Scahill,
Dirty Wars, pp. 91–2, notes the contrast with clandestine action, which is a military action
involving operational secrecy.

[28] Immerman, *The Hidden Hand*, p. 19.

[29] Rizzo, *Company Man*, p. 55.

[30] Immerman, *The Hidden Hand*, p. 19.

[31] Immerman, *The Hidden Hand*, p. 28.

derived from the evolution of the separation of powers: the expansion of the executive's powers to gather foreign intelligence, to exercise war powers and to use 'executive privilege' to avoid Congressional scrutiny. Such expanded powers were particularly visible in the early Cold War administrations of Truman and Eisenhower, leading to what the historian Arthur Schlesinger called (in an attack on President Nixon) the 'Imperial Presidency'.[32] But when Congress began to reassert itself against executive power, and in doing so began to scrutinise the intelligence agencies, it suggested that the evolution of the CIA into an agency of covert action might not have been underpinned by legislative intent. The 1976 Church Committee report into intelligence activities, examining the statutory authority for CIA actions, commented that 'authority for covert action cannot be found in the National Security Act', and concluded 'there is no explicit statutory authority for the CIA to conduct covert action'.[33] It conceded, however, that the act did not prohibit such action, and that if Congress, now with full knowledge of CIA covert activity, did not move to restrict it, covert action would effectively be authorised by acquiescence.[34]

The National Security Act and CIA Act may have provided the CIA with legal cover for covert actions. But in specific instances, as when the CIA engaged in domestic surveillance outside its charter,[35] or when it shipped armaments to Iran in exchange for hostages and used the proceeds to fund a covert war in Nicaragua despite a Congressional prohibition,[36] the CIA also broke US law.[37] In more recent times, having learned lessons from Iran-Contra, the US has reportedly used private contractors to avoid legal constraints.[38]

But US intelligence activities in a broad sense also existed outside the law in the sense that they constantly broke the laws of other countries: run-

---

[32] Schlesinger, *The Imperial Presidency*, pp. 130–5, 150–9, 167. Savage, *Power Wars*, pp. 39–44, argues that while Congress sought, after Watergate and Vietnam, to impose checks and balances on Presidential power, the Bush-Cheney administration deliberately sought to redress the balance and expand executive authority.

[33] *Final Report of the Select Committee to Study Governmental Operations*, pp. 128, 508.

[34] *Final Report of the Select Committee to Study Governmental Operations*, pp. 132, 135.

[35] Weiner, *Legacy of Ashes*, pp. 208–9, 223, 329–31, 341–2, 390.

[36] Weiner, *Legacy of Ashes*, pp. 459–77, Andrew, *For the President's Eyes Only*, pp. 478–82, 485–93.

[37] *The Family Jewels*, compiled by the CIA in 1973 and declassified in 2007, summarises prior activities conflicting with the National Security Act of 1947.

[38] Singer, *Corporate Warriors*, pp. 210–11. Cf. the use of shell companies and private contractors to operate the post-9/11 programme of extraordinary rendition: the relevant companies and aircraft are listed by *The Rendition Project*.

ning paramilitary operations abroad, staging coups, sponsoring assassination attempts, engaging in kidnapping, imprisonment and torture.[39] If *The Names* suggests that US intelligence activities overseas may contribute to unexpected dangers ('Are they killing Americans?'), *Libra* brings that message home to the very centre of American power.

For the most part, *Libra* has an alternating narrative structure. One line of the narrative recounts the life of Lee Harvey Oswald, the man whom the Warren Commission judged to be the lone gunman who killed President Kennedy. The second narrative line concerns a plan to make an attempt on the President's life, hatched by disgruntled current and former agents of the CIA and their allies in Cuban radical groups, funded by the Mafia, with multiple and complex motivations, broadly centred on the President's failure to retake Cuba following that country's communist revolution and the subsequent failure of the Bay of Pigs invasion. The book's title, *Libra*, refers to the sign of the zodiac, whose symbol is the scales, and the book's structure holds its accounts of Oswald's evolution as a lone radical and the development of a broader conspiracy in balance for much of the narrative. As well as representing the balance between these two main narrative threads, the word *Libra* refers to Lee Harvey Oswald himself, whose sign it is (*Libra*, p. 315), and who constantly see-saws unsteadily between alternating courses of action. The interest in language games seen in *The Names* repeats here in various plays on possible interpretations of Oswald's aliases: the word *Libra* also contains within it Oswald's first name.

In conspiring against Castro in the first instance, it is clear that the CIA is operating both with and without JFK's knowledge. A complex four-part committee structure is set up to manage US operations against Castro, a level of complexity which allows deniability to the senior staff in the uppermost layer, vis-à-vis the activities of the final grouping, which consists of a CIA agent named Win Everett and three paramilitaries. It is this final group who actually develop and run the covert operations against Castro.[40] Only generalities of these actions are reported back up the committee structure (*Libra*, p. 20). In brief:

> They all knew that JFK wanted Castro cooling on a slab but they weren't allowed to let on to him that his guilty yearning was the business they'd charged themselves to carry out. The White House was to be the summit of unknowing. (*Libra*, pp. 21–2)

[39] Weiner, *Legacy of Ashes, passim*.

[40] For CIA activity against Cuba under President Kennedy, see Weiner, *Legacy of Ashes*, pp. 197–241; Andrew, *For the President's Eyes Only*, pp. 257–66, 274–6, 280–306.

Or, as David Ferrie (one of the conspirators in the plot to assassinate Kennedy) puts it much later: 'CIA is the President's toilet' (*Libra*, p. 335).

In the aftermath of the failed Bay of Pigs operation, this structure is dismantled, and those closest to the covert operations are reassigned. Five of those individuals continue to meet, but are discovered by the CIA's Office of Security. They are reprimanded, and Win Everett is retired (or semiretired, 'a semantic kindness' (*Libra*, p. 17)), suspected not only of heading a group that disobeyed an order to disband, but also of running his own private operation within the CIA's covert anti-Castro activities (*Libra*, p. 24). In DeLillo's novel, it is this group who are behind what will become the attempt on the President's life.[41]

The conspiracy against Castro is reminiscent of Shakespeare. In *Richard II*, Exton kills the imprisoned Richard because he believes Henry IV wishes him to; after the deed, Henry admits he wished Richard dead, but repudiates his murderers (*Richard II*, 5.4.1–11, 5.6.38–44). What happens in *Libra* resembles this, but also goes beyond it. JFK wishes Castro dead, but does not wish to be seen plotting openly against Castro's life. The matter is left to agents of the CIA working with Cuban exiles opposed to Castro. But when US efforts against Castro fail at the Bay of Pigs, at least in part because of a lack of support from the administration, and the servants of the state responsible for those efforts are sidelined, those agents then move from conspiring on behalf of the President to conspiring against him. The actions of the state's covert agencies double back on the state itself. Here we see another version of a paradox of extralegal power also visible in Shakespeare's second tetralogy: the head of state can, and perhaps must, act outside the law to preserve his state. But once he does so, when he begins to act, in a sense, as an outlaw, his own authority becomes vulnerable to extralegal challenge – as much in the twentieth century as in the distant past.[42]

As in *Running Dog* and *The Names*, the CIA is also a quasi-corporate entity

---

[41] There are, of course, a wide variety of competing interpretations of the assassination: for a survey, see Knight, *The Kennedy Assassination*. DeLillo says in interview that 'I chose what I consider the most obvious possibility: that the assassination was the work of anti-Castro elements' (DeCurtis, 'An Outsider in This Society', p. 58).

[42] McCarry, *The Tears of Autumn*, another novel about the assassination, offers a different conspiracy, where Kennedy is killed in revenge for American complicity in the 1963 murder of South Vietnamese President Ngô Đình Diệm and his brother Ngô Đình Nhu, but here, too, Kennedy's death is an unexpected consequence of his own actions. For US involvement in the killings, see Weiner, *Legacy of Ashes*, pp. 243–55. Political assassination was subsequently prohibited by Ford, 'Executive Order 11905: United States Foreign Intelligence Activities'.

here.[43] Larry Parmenter becomes involved in various businesses financed and controlled by CIA, but lines are blurred – 'Parmenter himself could not always tell where the Agency left off and the corporations began' (*Libra*, p. 126) – and this mixing of interests leads to corruption. Parmenter wants Cuba back, not in the national interest, but out of self-interest: he stands to make a fortune from unexplored Cuban oil properties (*Libra*, p. 30). Such corruption is widespread and far-reaching. Carmine Latta, the mafia boss who finances the anti-Castro Cubans, and is therefore indirectly in league with the CIA, is said to have funnelled half a million dollars to the Nixon campaign in 1960 (*Libra*, p. 170). This theme of corruption and criminality in the world around Kennedy and its role in the assassination is one that James Ellroy will take much further in *American Tabloid*, a book explicitly indebted to *Libra*.[44]

Evolving in parallel to this narrative line about a conspiracy being hatched during the course of 1963 by a group within and around the CIA is an account of the career of Lee Harvey Oswald. In interview, when asked why he chose to tell the story from Oswald's point of view, DeLillo says: 'I think I have an idea of what it's like to be an outsider in this society'.[45] Oswald is that from the outset. He is a fatherless boy (*Libra*, p. 4), a boy with a girl's name (*Libra*, p. 7), mocked as a southerner in New York, a Yankee in the South (*Libra*, pp. 7, 33), dyslexic, 'piss-poor' (*Libra*, p. 56). The Warren Commission report emphasises the extent to which the adult Oswald is a solitary figure.[46] In police custody following the assassination, 'the cell was the same room he'd known all his life' (*Libra*, p. 426).

Win Everett's plan requires the invention of a gunman with a history (or histories), and Lee Harvey Oswald, he finds, already has all this (*Libra*, p. 180). It is not clear whether the Oswald of *Libra* is a lone radical, or the creation of US intelligence. Neither the plotters themselves nor the Russians are clear on whether or not Oswald's defection to the Soviet Union was a US project, as his mother claims repeatedly, an option the narrative does not

---

[43] Asked in interview about parallels between *Libra* and evidence at the mid-1980s Iran-Contra hearings, DeLillo mentions *Running Dog* and the process through which (in the interviewer's words) 'terrorism and intelligence become business' (Connolly, 'An Interview with Don DeLillo', pp. 28–9).

[44] Ellroy, *American Tabloid*. DeLillo's influence has been acknowledged many times; see Rich, 'James Ellroy, The Art of Fiction No. 201'.

[45] DeCurtis, 'An Outsider in This Society', p. 59.

[46] *Report of the President's Commission on the Assassination of President John F. Kennedy*, p. 422.

rule in or rule out. Everett asks the question, and Parmenter replies: 'The way we fake our own files, who knows for sure?' (*Libra*, p. 74). Oswald fantasises about being part of the Office of Naval Intelligence false defector programme (*Libra*, p. 164), his former girlfriend thinks he's a spy, and Marina, his wife, has similar suspicions (*Libra*, pp. 203–4). When asked by an FBI agent if he was part of this programme, Oswald replies: 'There are gray areas in ONI. I'm one of those areas' (*Libra*, p. 310).

Nobody in *Libra* is what they seem. 'Everyone was a spook or dupe or asset, a double, courier, cutout or defector, or was related to one' (*Libra*, p. 57). This uncertainty is true of Oswald in particular, who seems to be on every side and none, alternately a possible KGB informant, a possible double-agent for ONI, a possible informant for the FBI and the CIA, a 'soldier for Fidel' (*Libra*, p. 316), and a possible gunman in a Presidential assassination intended to serve anti-Castro interests in the United States. Even in death Oswald is disguised: buried, for security reasons, under an alias (*Libra*, p. 454). As one piece of dialogue between Oswald and the FBI goes:

> 'It goes round and round'.
> 'You seem to pretend'.
> 'But I'm not pretending'.
> 'But you are pretending'. (*Libra*, p. 311)

Aside from Oswald's own 'dizzying history' (*Libra*, p. 303), there are also crude efforts by one of the conspirators, T-Jay Mackey, to plant various Oswald doubles, at least one of whom may actually be Mackey himself (*Libra*, pp. 377–8). But if there are multiple Oswalds, the same seems to be true of many of the novel's characters who have other names or identities (*Libra*, pp. 301–2). This uncertainty of identity extends to Kennedy: on a superficial level, there is the suggestion by the DJ Weird Beard that Kennedy travels with a dozen lookalikes 'when he goes into no man's land' (*Libra*, p. 382). But beyond that there are various hints at Kennedy's secrets and flaws: beneath his charismatic exterior are his adulteries, his use of cortisone and a back brace to compensate for his Addison's disease and his degenerating discs (*Libra*, p. 392), and, most obviously, what various characters regard as his hypocrisies over Cuba.

In the Warren Commission Report on the assassination, there are three shots, all fired from the Texas Book Depository, and Oswald is the assassin: there are no other gunmen. Two of these three shots hit President Kennedy, and the second bullet to hit kills him. One of these two shots that hits the President also hits Governor Connally; the remaining shot (the report does not draw a firm conclusion on whether it is the first, second or third) is likely to have missed.[47] In DeLillo's version of the assassination, likewise, Oswald takes three shots from the Texas Book Depository. Here, the first shot hits Kennedy, but does not kill him. The second hits Governor Connally. In DeLillo's version, however, Oswald's third shot misses, and the shot that kills Kennedy is taken by a second gunman, a Cuban named Ramón (Raymo) Benítez, firing from the grassy knoll (*Libra*, pp. 395–403). Here, Oswald was never intended to be the assassin. He was merely meant to look like the assassin: 'His role was to provide artifacts of historical interest, a traceable weapon, all the cuttings and hoardings of his Cuban career' (*Libra*, p. 386).

The character who directs this successful attempt on Kennedy's life, T-Jay Mackey, is a CIA agent. He is, of course, a rogue agent, having been involved in 'an outlawed group' (*Libra*, p. 23) that continued to plot against Cuba despite being formally disbanded: the same group that plots this assassination. But it is also clear that this is not the only plot to kill the President involving Cuban exiles and the CIA. Prior to the Dallas plot, Mackey becomes aware of a parallel plot to kill Kennedy being planned by a group called Alpha 66, who, Mackey knows, are also supported by elements within the CIA: 'Alpha had CIA mentors. These were men Mackey wasn't even close to knowing' (*Libra*, p. 304). Mackey decides to support this effort as a decoy for his own plan; the plot is leaked (possibly by Mackey) and Kennedy's Miami motorcade is cancelled (*Libra*, pp. 304, 375–7). Another potential plot, this time for Chicago, is thwarted, again with a possible Cuban connection (*Libra*, p. 364). Somewhere in the background, then, are other elements in the CIA, never identified, hostile enough to Kennedy to want him dead.

The clear narrative path DeLillo leads us down is leavened with uncertainties. In the narrative as we have it, the assassination involves Oswald, who seems to be a lone radical, co-opted into a larger plan hatched by disgruntled current and former agents of the CIA and their allies in Cuban radical groups, funded by the Mafia, all of whom nurture resentments against the President centred on the loss of Cuba. Oswald takes part in the assassination attempt, but is not the man who kills the President. This is complex enough, involves multiple motivations on the parts of the actors, and uncertainties on many points of detail. But there are hints of further depths.

The third narrative thread in *Libra* is a metanarratorial structure featuring Nicholas Branch, a retired CIA agent hired as an historian to piece together the secret truth of the assassination. In this narrative line, there are hints of a deeper, untold conspiracy in the subsequent, unexplained deaths of so many

---

[47] *Report of the President's Commission on the Assassination of President John F. Kennedy*, chapter 3.

of the individuals involved (*Libra*, pp. 57–8). Branch, too, alternates between seeing events as coincidence or conspiracy. Though he is certain that the assassination plot was 'a rambling affair that succeeded in the short term due mainly to chance', he is also convinced towards the end that the CIA, who have hired him to get to the truth of events, is nonetheless holding things back from him (*Libra*, p. 441–2). In fact, there is no real chance of finding a single line of truth, for not only is the truth irreducibly complex, we can also see false evidence being manufactured throughout.

If *Libra* is a book about conspiracy, it is also to some degree a book about paranoia. Robert Towers, reviewing the novel, famously described DeLillo as having become 'chief shaman of the paranoid school of American fiction'.[48] As Eva Horn rightly says, however, paranoia 'is neither DeLillo's medium nor his narrative method but his object of study'.[49] It is not that *Libra* endorses paranoia: rather, it shows us that there is no way of distinguishing here between historical fact and the ways in which people succumb to paranoia, because paranoia is a real motivating force in mid-century US politics.[50] 'Do you believe in astrology?' Oswald asks David Ferrie, one of the conspirators. 'I believe in everything', Ferrie replies (*Libra*, p. 315).

Counterpointed against and intertwined with this rampant sense of paranoia is a sort of absolute faith.[51] As portrayed in *Libra*, the CIA has something of a religious aspect; some of the conspirators seem to regard it as both all-knowing and all-forgiving. 'CIA has a picture of my prelapsarian soul in their files', Win Everett says (*Libra*, p. 20). Beryl Parmenter, the wife of the conspirator Larry Parmenter, regards it as 'the best organized church in the Christian world' (*Libra*, p. 260). Both Win Everett and Larry Parmenter believe in the CIA's ability to offer absolution: 'The Agency forgives' (*Libra*, p. 363). DeLillo comments in interview that paranoia in his characters 'operates as a form of religious awe', and intelligence agencies are 'like churches that hold the final secrets'.[52] One of the reasons that the entirely paranoid Guy Banister hates JFK is that Kennedy now seems to hold the secrets,

---

[48] Towers, 'From the Grassy Knoll'.

[49] Horn, *Secret War*, p. 316.

[50] Hofstadter, 'Paranoid Style', argues for paranoia as an important motivating force both in his own time and in American history more broadly; Melley, *Empire of Conspiracy*, p. 2 n. 3 suggests Hofstadter's analysis underestimates paranoia's growing importance in post-war American culture.

[51] Cf. Melley, *Empire of Conspiracy*, p. 8, who suggests that conspiracy theories 'require a sense of quasi-religious conviction, a sense that the conspiracy in question is an entity with almost supernatural powers'.

[52] Begley, 'The Art of Fiction CXXXV: Don DeLillo', p. 106. On the broader role of religion in DeLillo's work, see Hungerford, 'Don DeLillo's Latin Mass'.

secrets that in Banister's view don't belong with the President at all (*Libra*, p. 68).[53] This quasi-religious aspect of the all-knowing agencies of surveillance is embodied above all in the U-2 spy plane, which, Jeremy Green suggests, 'occupies a fantasy vantage point from which all may be seen and known'.[54] In their religious aspect, the intelligence agencies seem transcendent, of a different order to the quotidian workings of state power. If the willingness of the state to act in secret creates uncertainty, and perhaps paranoia, in the world at large, it also gives the intelligence agencies an undeserved aura of inscrutable authority.

After the assassination, there are secrets to be kept. Oswald (like the U-2 pilot Francis Gary Powers) knows too much and has failed to die according to plan. To remedy this, Jack Karlinsky, a mobster representing the man who has financed the Kennedy assassination, approaches Jack Ruby. Karlinsky seeks to persuade Ruby that in Texas, the site of an older, violent version of American values, a revenge slaying will be a form of purgation unlikely to be punished by law. 'It's considered settling things Old West-style', he tells him (*Libra*, p. 431).[55] In fact, for Karlinsky's sponsor, Carmine Latta, shooting Oswald achieves exactly the opposite purpose: it is a means of avoiding judgment for his own association with the President's death.

For all the conspiracy theories about the Kennedy assassination, in DeLillo's version at least, the conspirators do not achieve their ends. Their plan is that the investigation into the President's murder will conclude that Oswald was an agent of Cuba, and that the assassination will provoke the United States into retaking the island. Where in fact what happens is this:

> After Oswald, men in America are no longer required to lead lives of quiet desperation. You apply for a credit card, buy a handgun, travel through cities, suburbs and shopping malls, anonymous, anonymous, looking for a chance to take a shot at the first puffy empty famous face, just to let people know there is someone out there who reads the papers. (*Libra*, p. 388)

The legacy of the Kennedy assassination is not the retaking of Cuba and the redemption of a certain view of America's place in the world, because none of that actually occurs; rather, the assassination's legacy is the random violence

---

[53] On the growth of a culture of secrecy in American government in the twentieth century, see Schlesinger, *Imperial Presidency*, pp. 331–76; for that culture in the twenty-first century, see Savage, *Power Wars*, pp. 350–471; for state secrecy and Agamben's 'state of exception', see Horn, *Secret War*, pp. 37, 93, 95.

[54] Green, 'Libra', p. 106.

[55] For the deep roots of notions of retributive justice and the *lex talonis*, the 'law of repayment in kind', in Western thought and practice, see Kerrigan, *Revenge Tragedy*, pp. 22–5.

of the United States in the later twentieth century.[56] This is something picked up later in DeLillo's work, with the figure of the Texas Highway Killer from *Underworld*. Here, one of the killings is accidentally videotaped by a child, and the tape plays repeatedly on television (*Underworld*, pp. 155–60). The seemingly senseless killing of people riding past in cars, the accidental video footage, the endless playback, the Texan location, the element of uncertainty (one of the killings seems to be a copycat murder): all of these elements echo aspects of the Kennedy assassination and its aftermath, but at the same time the Texas Highway Killer is just another American serial killer, one of the many, an endlessly repeated motif.

By the time we reach *Cosmopolis*, DeLillo's parable of capitalist narcissism run rampant in millennial America, threats to the President are no longer an existential threat to the state. They are a traffic obstruction for billionaires in stretch limousines.[57] This is the egotism of the novel's protagonist, of course, but it also reflects a decisive shift in power away from offices of state and towards the financial markets. What might once have been supposed to be the absolute nature of nation-state sovereignty has now come under severe pressure from the power of international capital. This is a rebalancing, rather than a reversal, of power relations of course: as Derrida says, sovereignty is always divisible and contested,[58] or, as a character in *Underworld* puts it (perhaps too bluntly), 'the state, the nation, the corporation, the power structure, the system, the establishment', are 'all part of the same motherfucking thing' (*Underworld*, p. 575). But the balance of power has moved. Bill Clinton famously captures this rebalancing of power relations between the political and economic establishments with the line: 'You mean to tell me that the success of the program and my reelection hinges on the Federal Reserve and a bunch of fucking bond traders?'[59] In *Cosmopolis*, the notion of a threat to the life of a US President seems antiquated to the billionaire currency speculator Eric Packer:

> 'Do people still shoot at presidents? I thought there were more stimulating targets', he said. (*Cosmopolis*, p. 20)

Here the president (lower-case) of the United States is just another president, a nameless traffic obstacle; and death, when it comes in this story, comes not

[56] Horn, *Secret War*, p. 304, observes that the Kennedy assassination, far from being unique, is followed by the political assassinations of Malcolm X, Martin Luther King and Robert Kennedy.

[57] DeLillo, *Cosmopolis*, p. 11.

[58] Derrida, *The Beast & the Sovereign*, I, 76, 290–1.

[59] Woodward, *The Agenda*, p. 73.

to the President, but to others. Though the President is not named here, the events of *Cosmopolis* take place on a day in April 2000. The President of the United States on that date was Bill Clinton, who, incidentally, met John F. Kennedy at the White House in 1963.[60]

Absence and Loss: *Point Omega*

Point Omega is a spare, thematically complex work, of the sort that, post-*Underworld*, has come to seem characteristic of late-phase DeLillo. Published in 2010, it might be read not only as a standalone piece, but also in relation to two preceding novels. Together, *Cosmopolis*, *Falling Man* and *Point Omega* seem to engage with many of the key issues facing twenty-first century America, from the consequences of unfettered wealth mixed with the rise of technology and global movements of capital, through the events of 9/11, and into the Iraq war and its aftermath. Collectively, these three novels again seem to constitute an invitation to think historically.

Cosmopolis's turn-of-the-millennium concerns with global capital and its opponents seemed on publication to have been quickly eclipsed by the 9/11 attacks, but the global financial crisis and the rise of the Occupy movement would make its concerns seem timely once again when David Cronenberg's film version appeared in 2012.[61] *Falling Man*, published in 2007, is concerned with terrorism and its consequences in the shadow of 9/11.[62] The novel touches on geopolitics, on the motivations of the hijackers, on ways of reading the events of 9/11 historically, and on how art and artists might seek to respond to what happened. But it is primarily a meditation on survival and its consequences; a narrative set for the most part in the long aftermath of the attacks, a story that looks at the differing ways in which a small group of related characters might or might not have coped with what happened. And if *Falling Man* revisits the themes of art and terror, *Point Omega* returns once again to the question of the state and its actions outside the law.

Point Omega's core narrative contains four chapters, set during a period of a few weeks in 2006. Richard Elster, a former 'defense intellectual', is a scholar who has spent two years working for the US government as it prosecutes its war in Iraq. Jim Finley wants to make a documentary film centred on Elster. Elster is reluctant, but invites Finley to join him at his retreat deep in the desert to discuss the project. The discussions drag on for days, without

---

[60] Clinton, *My Life*, p. 62.
[61] Cronenberg, *Cosmopolis*.
[62] DeLillo, *Falling Man*. For DeLillo's multiple responses to 9/11, see Kaufmann, 'The Wake of Terror'.

resolution. Elster and Finley are joined by Elster's daughter Jessie. Then Jessie disappears.

Bookending these four chapters are two sections describing the thoughts of a man viewing Douglas Gordon's artwork, *24 Hour Psycho*, at New York's Museum of Modern Art.[63] Though the narrative never confirms this directly, we presume the narrative voice here to be the voice of Jessie's murderer, a man who is perhaps named Dennis. Two other men whom we see enter and then leave the gallery we take to be Elster and Finley (*Point Omega*, pp. 7–10). The young woman this narrator speaks to towards the end of the novel (*Point Omega*, pp. 105–14), we take to be Jessie: their encounter is reminiscent of the ominous gallery encounter in DeLillo's earlier story 'Baader-Meinhof'.[64] This initial conversation between Jessie and Dennis emerges from an encounter, the day before, between Finley and her father. Finley sees Elster at MoMA, reminds him of his earlier pitch to make a film, and takes him, briefly, to see *24 Hour Psycho*. Elster tells his daughter about the film that evening, and she goes to see it the next day (*Point Omega*, pp. 46–7, 60–1). Finley and Elster, then, inadvertently set in motion the chain of events that will lead to what we assume is Jessie's death in the desert.

Point Omega is a book centred on absences. Elster's career as a 'defense intellectual', which turns out to have him simply occupying 'an empty seat' (*Point Omega*, p. 28), arises because of a text, both present and absent in *Point Omega*, called 'Renditions'. This is an essay written by Elster, a study of the word *rendition* and its meanings, bookended by a brief commentary that makes clear its contemporary application. The essay, we're told, attracts some criticism on the left, but earns Elster an interview at a research institute just outside Washington, with a group including 'the deputy director of a strategic assessment team that did not exist in any set of official records' (*Point Omega*, p. 35). This encounter leads to his two years in government.

DeLillo sketches the contents of the absent essay: a study of the forebears of the word *rendition*, with reference to Middle English, Old French and Vulgar Latin.[65] In dwelling on possible meanings, the (absent) essay cites a potential meaning of *rendering* as a coat of plaster applied to a masonry surface,[66] moving on to discuss a walled enclosure in which an interrogation

---

[63] For the influence of Hitchcock's cinema on the novel, see Cowart, 'The Lady Vanishes', pp. 34–9.

[64] DeLillo, 'Baader-Meinhof'.

[65] *OED*, s.v. *rendition*, n., derives the modern word from fifteenth-century Middle French *rendition*. *MED*, s.v. *rendren*, offers a derivation from Old French *rendre*. All are indebted to Latin *reddere*.

[66] *OED*, s.v. *render*, n., 8(a).

takes place, leading to a surrender – another meaning of *rendition*[67] – by the person being interrogated. Towards the end of the essay, other meanings are considered: interpretation, translation, performance (*Point Omega*, pp. 32–4).[68]

The text of this absent essay, partly quoted and partly summarised in the novel, is itself founded on absence:

> There were footnotes like nested snakes. But no specific mention of black sites, third-party states, or international treaties and conventions. (*Point Omega*, p. 34)

There are also meanings of the word *rendition* that are not canvassed in the essay as summarised here. In particular, there are two potential legal meanings. The first is 'the action of formally delivering a judgment or verdict'.[69] The second is 'the extradition of a fugitive who has fled to another jurisdiction'.[70] But an evolution of this absent definition of *rendition* as extradition is the meaning at the heart of Elster's absent text, in the term *extraordinary rendition*. In early citations, this means the use of irregular measures to return fugitives to face justice; *OED* cites a 1980 entry in the *Virginia Law Journal* stating that '"rendition" encompasses both extradition and irregular recovery of fugitives'.[71] Whatever sins the potential euphemism *irregular* covers here (most likely kidnapping), it is clear that at this stage, the word still means the return of those who seek to escape the law to face justice. By the early twenty-first century, however, the movement was in the opposite direction: individuals were being removed from countries where they might have legal protection (particularly from legal directives on human rights and against torture) to be interrogated in countries where such protections did not apply.[72] Hence *OED*:

> *extraordinary rendition*, n., the seizure and transportation by authorities of a criminal suspect from one country to another without the formal process

---

[67] *OED*, s.v. *rendition*, n., 1(a), 1(b).
[68] *OED*, s.v. *rendition*, n., 5, 7.
[69] *OED*, s.v. *rendition*, n., 6.
[70] *OED*, s.v. *rendition*, n., 3(a).
[71] *OED*, s.v. *rendition*, n., 3(b).
[72] The Eighth Amendment to the US Constitution 1791, prohibits 'cruel and unusual punishments', conventionally understood to include torture. Torture committed overseas by US nationals or by non-US nationals present in the US is punishable under the 'Torture' statute (18 US Code ch. 113c). International conventions to which the US is a signatory include the UN Convention against Torture and other Cruel, Inhuman or Degrading Treatment or Punishment 1984.

of extradition; an instance of this. Sometimes used spec. with reference to moving a terrorist suspect for interrogation in a country considered to have less rigorous regulations for the humane treatment of prisoners.[73]

In the words of the Open Society Justice Initiative's report *Globalizing Torture*:

> Following the terrorist attacks of September 11, 2001, the U.S. Central Intelligence Agency (CIA) commenced a secret detention program under which suspected terrorists were held in CIA prisons, also known as 'black sites', outside the United States, where they were subjected to 'enhanced interrogation techniques' that involved torture and other abuse. At about the same time, the CIA gained expansive authority to engage in 'extraordinary rendition', defined here as the transfer – without legal process – of a detainee to the custody of foreign government for purposes of detention and interrogation. Both the secret detention program and the extraordinary rendition program were highly classified, conducted outside the United States, and designed to place detainee interrogations beyond the reach of the law. Torture was a hallmark of both. The two programs entailed the abduction and disappearance of detainees and their extralegal transfer on secret flights to undisclosed locations around the world, followed by their incommunicado detention, interrogation, torture, and abuse. The administration of President George W. Bush embraced the 'dark side', a new paradigm for countering terrorism with little regard for the constraints of domestic and international law.[74]

In the much more direct language of former CIA agent Bob Baer:

> If you want a serious interrogation, you send a prisoner to Jordan. If you want them to be tortured, you send them to Syria. If you want someone to disappear – never to see them again – you send them to Egypt.[75]

Extraordinary rendition, then, the (absent) sense of rendition at the heart of Elster's absent text, is the removal of individuals beyond the protection of the

---

[73] *OED*, s.v. *extraordinary rendition*, n., at *extraordinary*, adj., adv., and n., Additions.
[74] *Globalizing Torture*, p. 5. Interrogation techniques used by the CIA are described in *Globalizing Torture*, p. 17. Rizzo, *Company Man*, pp. 181–216, notes that the CIA sought and received legal opinions from the Justice Department's Office of Legal Counsel, first in 2002 and again from 2004 to 2007, that 'enhanced interrogation' did not constitute torture, and sought, but did not receive, a Justice Department guarantee that interrogators would not be prosecuted. These Office of Legal Counsel memos were rescinded by President Barack Obama in 2009. For the memoranda and related documents, see *The Torture Database*.
[75] Quoted in Grey, 'America's Gulag'.

law. Both the absences within the essay and the physical absence of the essay from DeLillo's text are also somewhat like *Point Omega* itself, a text that is and is not about the Iraq war, and whose own omega point is also an absence, the disappearance of Elster's daughter Jessie, who is presumed murdered, but whose body remains missing.

The location of the novel's events in the desert also places the narrative in a sort of non-space. Elster's house is 'somewhere south of nowhere in the Sonoran Desert or maybe it was the Mojave Desert or another desert altogether' (*Point Omega*, p. 20). Non-spaces such as this nameless desert are a recurring motif in DeLillo's work. They can be spaces where the protagonists attempt to achieve some sort of self-realisation in a more authentic place outside the urban contemporary (attempts that inevitably fail). This is the case with David Bell's quest to film the heartland of America in *Americana*, or Glen Selvy's retreat from Washington to the West in *Running Dog*.[76] Elster, similarly, characterises his position not as exile, but as 'a spiritual retreat' (*Point Omega*, p. 23).

Alternatively, non-spaces can be the places off the map where things, especially unsavoury things, are hidden away.[77] In *The Names*, when Axton stumbles across the cult he is searching for in the Peloponnese, 'where Europe ends' (*The Names*, p. 180), he is off the map in the literal sense that he has three contradictory maps, none of which may be accurate. Also to be found off the map in this novel are political violence, and, inevitably, oil. In *Underworld*, things reportedly located off the map include weapons research, nuclear testing in remote locations, secret military facilities, secret wars, and a mysterious ship carrying a toxic cargo that no port will accept. In *Point Omega*, Elster's retreat to the desert will come to embody both aspects of the space off the map as found elsewhere in DeLillo. Initially conceived of as a place of retreat in pursuit of meaning, the desert comes instead to be a vast empty space that conceals a murder.

Point Omega does address itself directly to the war in Iraq, though not via an extended, narrative critique of the actions of the state and its agents, as in *The Names* or *Libra*. Elster is aggressively in favour of a war in the abstract. He supports the state's theoretical right to break its own laws and lie to its

---

[76] Longmuir 'Genre and Gender', pp. 137–40, notes that what Selvy arrives at is not an authentic America represented by the West, but rather its representation, the Western.

[77] Weizman, 'On Extraterritoriality', p. 13, describes extraterritorial zones as 'the spatial expression of a series of "states of emergency," or states of exception that are either created through the process of law (through which the law is either severely undermined or annulled) or that appear *de facto* within them. Within these spaces, sovereign power is deposed or challenged'.

own people in self-defence. 'Lying is necessary', he says. 'The state has to lie. There is no lie in war or in preparation for war that can't be defended' (*Point Omega*, p. 28). The opening line of his essay on 'Renditions' reads: 'A government is a criminal enterprise' (*Point Omega*, p. 33).

Elster's brief justification of the war to Finley is full of echoes. 'We need to retake the future', he says, in words that recall the title of DeLillo's own *Harper's* essay following 9/11.[78] 'All they have are old dead despotic traditions. We have a living history and I thought I would be in the middle of it' (*Point Omega*, p. 30). These lines seem to echo Francis Fukuyama's argument at the end of the 1980s that Western liberal democracy was the ultimate end of history, 'the end point of mankind's ideological evolution' and 'the final form of human government', all viable alternatives, and in particular the major twentieth-century challenges of fascism and socialism, having been exhausted.[79] Instead of a living history, though, what Elster participates in is a corporate war: 'in those rooms, with those men, it was all priorities, statistics, evaluations, rationalizations' (*Point Omega*, p. 30). The resident experts are 'the metaphysicians in the intelligence agencies, the fantasists in the Pentagon' (*Point Omega*, p. 19).

Notwithstanding Elster's pro-war stance, then, the novel offers a number of critiques of the state's conduct of the war. There is an adoption of deceit and criminality which Elster is prepared to defend, perhaps even to flaunt, as necessary to the state's self-defence; and a level of arrogance and hubris in the prosecution of the war – 'bulk and swagger' (*Point Omega*, p. 19) – which he is not. But these overt criticisms of the state and its actions are made in passing; asides, almost. More fundamentally, the creation of a text centred on absences and death set against the backdrop of the Iraq war, with an absent text named 'Renditions' partly present in the text, and an absent woman presumed dead at its centre, means that the disappearance of individuals through the process of extraordinary rendition is something woven into the text at a much deeper level.

The novel's focus is on the man himself, and his loss. If this discussion of DeLillo's work opened with the suggestion that DeLillo asks the reader to think historically, we might close by saying that he also asks us to feel empathy. In *Mao II*, Bill Gray thinks of the hostage sitting on a stained mat, chained to a water pipe; he reads his poems, and tries to 'find the places where you converge with him' (*Mao II*, p. 160). Similarly, at around the same time, DeLillo and Paul Auster wrote about Salman Rushdie's life under the Iranian

---

[78] DeLillo, 'In the Ruins of the Future'.
[79] Fukuyama, 'The End of History?', p. 4.

fatwa: 'What can we do? We can think about him. Try to imagine his life. Write it in our minds as if it were the most unlikely fiction'.[80]

Empathy is an important enabling ingredient in the acts of reading, and writing, about other people, real or imagined. Killing, however, is made easier if the possibility of empathy is diminished. In *Libra*, Frank Vásquez describes the 'uncanny' experience of shooting a man from a great distance, using a telescopic sight: the technology removes him from the experience and from an understanding of the action he is carrying out (*Libra*, pp. 297–8). In 'Baader-Meinhof', a story that is in some ways an early DeLillo response to the events of 9/11, there is a male character whose disturbing lack of any feeling when he looks at Gerhard Richter's paintings of the dead might serve as an early warning of what is to come later ('Baader-Meinhof', p. 109).

A lack of empathy also seems an important aspect of DeLillo's characterisation of the 9/11 hijackers in *Falling Man*. Terrorism is often thought of in emotional terms: the word itself suggests that its objective is to create an emotional response, *terror*.[81] Furthermore, terrorists are often assumed to be emotionally motivated. Addressing Congress after the 9/11 attacks, President Bush suggested that those who attacked America 'hate our freedoms'.[82] For DeLillo, however, the defining characteristic of the 9/11 attackers is not the presence of an overwhelming emotion such as hatred, but rather an emotional absence, an inability to empathise. He highlights this in his initial response, in the essay 'In the Ruins of the Future':

> Does the sight of a woman pushing a stroller soften the man to her humanity and vulnerability, and her child's as well, and all the people he is here to kill?
> This is his edge, that he does not see her. Years here, waiting, taking flying lessons, making the routine gestures of community and home, the credit card, the bank account, the post-office box. All tactical, linked, layered. He knows who we are and what we mean in the world – an idea, a righteous fever in the brain. But there is no defenceless human at the end of his gaze.[83]

---

[80] Auster and DeLillo, 'Salman Rushdie Defense Pamphlet'. Rushdie, *Joseph Anton*, p. 400, mentions Auster and DeLillo's support. For the relationship of *Mao II* and the Rushdie affair, see Passaro, 'Dangerous Don DeLillo', pp. 83–4, and Scanlan, 'Writers Among Terrorists'.

[81] Richardson, *What Terrorists Want*, p. 5, comments that 'the whole point is for the psychological impact to be greater than the actual physical act'.

[82] Bush, 'Address to the Joint Session of the 107th Congress', p. 68.

[83] DeLillo, 'In the Ruins of the Future'.

Falling Man's description of the lives of Hammad and his fellow plotters in the United States emphasises this nullification of others, this absence of empathy. In the supermarket, Hammad is invisible to people, and they are becoming invisible to him (*Falling Man*, p. 171). When he asks Amir about the others who will die, Amir denies that other people even exist in any meaningful way (*Falling Man*, p. 176).

What Amir does here is the opposite of what DeLillo claims as the potential of the novel.[84] The terrorist allows the gap between himself and others to justify their deaths. The novelist, in contrast, attempts to use imagination to bridge the distance between himself and others, and asks the reader to do the same. Though DeLillo has indeed long been interested in the dynamic between the state and the terrorist, then, his major fictional response to the most substantial terrorist attack in US history is focused less on politics than on people. But *Falling Man*'s meditation on individual human suffering and endurance, its canvassing of interpretations of events, its documenting of differing reactions over time, and its emphasis on empathy, offers a multilayered response to the events of 9/11 that again seems in line with DeLillo's assertion in *Mao II* that the novel can be a 'democratic shout' against totalitarianism in all its forms.

Point Omega, too, seems ultimately to be about empathy and loss. Judith Shulevitz suggests that Richard Elster is Lear-like,[85] and it is possible to see him this way, pointlessly obsessed with his loss of what he supposed to be power and influence, until confronted with the much greater loss of his child. As so often in DeLillo, the direction of the plot is towards death. 'All plots tend to move deathward', says Jack Gladney in *White Noise*.[86] 'There is a tendency of plots to move towards death', Win Everett thinks in *Libra* (*Libra*, p. 221). And in *Point Omega*, Jim Finley observes of Richard Elster: 'The omega point has narrowed, here and now, to the point of a knife as it enters a body. All the man's grand themes funneled down to local grief, one body, out there somewhere, or not' (*Point Omega*, p. 98). Here the much greater political story of Iraq, of Afghanistan, of extraordinary rendition, of torture, is funnelled down to its human essence, as a story of individual loss.

---

[84] There is a similar meditation on empathy and its absence in Updike, *Terrorist*, pp. 76–7, 252–4, 287–308.

[85] Shulevitz, 'In Search of the Real'.

[86] DeLillo, *White Noise*, p. 26.

6

Unanswered Questions: Ciaran Carson

Ciaran Carson was one of a remarkable cohort of Ulster poets whose work coincided with and, inevitably, engaged with the Northern Ireland Troubles, which saw civil conflict erupt in the late 1960s and endure through to the ceasefires of 1994 and the eventual political settlement of 1998.[1] While Carson's complex and diverse body of work is in no way reducible to its engagement with a contemporary political context, both place and political conflict are nonetheless substantive presences in his writing.[2] The discussion here deals with two selections from Carson's writing. It looks first at poems from the 1980s and 1990s that deal with contemporary Belfast, particularly in the collections *The Irish for No* and *Belfast Confetti*. It then turns to consider three somewhat interlinked post-Troubles works – the poetry collection *For All We Know*, and the novels *The Pen Friend* and *Exchange Place* – that have visible debts to the literature of espionage.[3] All of these works engage with the Troubles as a subject, emphasising in different ways the uncertainties that emerge from any consideration of the conflict.

These uncertainties stem in part from the extent to which both Northern Ireland itself and some of the participants in the conflict existed and acted outside the normal rule of law. Almost from its inception, the Northern Ireland state operated with additional powers as outlined in the Civil Authorities (Special Powers) Act (Northern Ireland) and its associated regulations, initially introduced as a temporary measure in 1922, but regularly renewed and eventually made permanent.[4] After the suspension of the government of Northern Ireland and the imposition of direct rule from London in 1972, the UK government legislated for emergency powers

---

[1] See the important anthology *A Rage for Order*, ed. Ormsby.
[2] For a comprehensive discussion of Carson's work, see Alexander, *Ciaran Carson*.
[3] Reference is to Carson, *Collected Poems* (hereafter *CP*); Carson, *The Pen Friend*; Carson, *Exchange Place*.
[4] Civil Authorities (Special Powers) Act (Northern Ireland) 1922.

via the Northern Ireland (Emergency Provisions) Act 1973.[5] These powers
were then supplemented by a series of temporary provisions for the prevention of terrorism, beginning with the Prevention of Terrorism (Temporary
Provisions) Act 1974.[6] Further to this, various arms of British intelligence
also played a substantial role in the conflict: RUC Special Branch, military
intelligence, and both MI5 and MI6 (whose extralegal status we have discussed in Chapter 4 above).[7]

'The Truth Which is Never Black-and-White': Belfast Poems

Many of Carson's poems from the 1980s and 1990s are about contemporary
Belfast. Carson is a lifelong resident of Belfast, and so some of his subject
matter is first-hand. Looking at a photograph of riot scene, Carson wonders
if he was there that night ('Question Time', *CP* 166); describing a tense interrogation, he is the person under questioning ('Question Time', *CP* 168–70).
There is a kind of anti-Aristotelian dynamic at work here. Carson's writing
does not seek to evoke pity and terror and then domesticate them through
catharsis. For much of his career, pity and terror are present, nightly, on the
streets and on the news. Rather, the work seeks to ask questions about existing in that sort of context.

As Carson comments, discussing these poems in interview:

> My aim was, in that work which deals with the 'Troubles', to act as a
> camera or a tape-recorder, and present things in a kind of edited surreality.
> An ear overhearing things in bars. Snatches of black Belfast humour.[8]

If this means there is a something of a journalistic attitude to Carson's
approach in these poems, that possible affinity between reportage and poetry
is highlighted in his later work. Carson's 2003 collection *Breaking News*
draws on the reportage of the nineteenth-century war correspondent William
Howard Russell; Nina, one of the two primary voices in the 2008 collection
For All We Know, also practises journalism. This is not to suggest that Carson's
Belfast poetry can be straightforwardly identified with reportage. The poems
are a complex mixture of ingredients, formally experimental, broadly allusive,
but rooted in both a specific place and a tradition of storytelling and song: a

---

[5] Northern Ireland (Emergency Provisions) Act 1973.
[6] Prevention of Terrorism (Temporary Provisions) Act 1974.
[7] Andrew, *Defence of the Realm*, pp. 600, 620–1, notes that initially the Metropolitan Police
Special Branch led against the IRA in Britain, RUC Special Branch against the IRA in
Northern Ireland, and MI5 against all other terrorist threats, including loyalist paramilitaries in Northern Ireland; following the imposition of direct rule in 1972, MI5 and MI6
created an Irish Joint Section, with MI6 initially taking the lead role.
[8] Brown, 'Ciaran Carson', p. 148.

kind of postmodern urban *dinnshenchas*.[9] Nor is it to identify reportage as in any way straightforward or neutral. If the Nina character in Carson's novel *The Pen Friend* identifies with the photojournalist Lee Miller, Miller is connected to the group Mass Observation, which was, we're told, a propaganda tool as well as a surrealist exercise (and Nina herself, we will discover, is a sort of spy) (*The Pen Friend*, pp. 131–5, 142–3).

Carson makes a similar observation about the documentary aspect of these 'Troubles' poems in another, later, interview:

> I thought of the poems as snapshots of what was going on, the sometimes surreal circumstances of the violence.[10]

But what *was* going on? As Carson says in the 2002 interview:

> If there's one thing certain about what was or is going on, it's that you don't know the half of it. The official account is only an account, and there are many others. Poetry offers yet another alternative. It asks questions, I think. It asks about the truth which is never black-and-white.[11]

If these poems, then, seek to say what happened during the Troubles, they do so in a way that acknowledges profound uncertainties.

The efforts by various participants in the conflict themselves to understand what is happening is embodied in the constant surveillance we find in these poems:[12]

> everyone is
> watching everybody
>
> in the grey light
> of surveillance. ('Blink', *CP* 442)

Throughout the poems, we come across clandestine devices ('peep-holes, one-way mirrors, security cameras'), radar, binoculars, night-vision telescopes, informers, interrogations, ground patrols, checkpoints, and helicopters

---

[9] Corcoran, 'One step forward, two steps back', p. 196, suggests that the poems seem to aspire not towards literature but rather 'tall tales, ballads, songs, fiddle tunes and flute tunes, reportage and annotation'. *Dinnshenchas* is place-lore – the word is related to *senchas*, lore, or traditional knowledge, and *senchaí*, a storyteller, all of which are relevant terms in thinking about Carson's work: see *Concise Oxford Companion*, ed. Welch, s.v. *dinnshenchas*, *senchaí*.

[10] Carson and Kennedy-Andrews, 'Introduction: For All I Know', p. 17.

[11] Brown, 'Ciaran Carson', pp. 148–9.

[12] For a detailed discussion of surveillance and its implications in Carson's work, see Moore, *Belfast is Many Places*.

hovering overhead (*CP* 100, 139, 144–50, 148, 164, 165–6, 167–70, 177, 184, 204, 220–1, 222–4, 225, 237, 244–5, 255).

The omnipresence of surveillance is suggestive of Jeremy Bentham's Panopticon and Carson makes the comparison directly ('Intelligence', *CP* 185–6). Bentham's Panopticon is a model for a prison, never built as a physical structure, which nonetheless serves as a model for the exercise of political and social authority through total surveillance, particularly via Foucault's influential discussion in *Discipline and Punish*. Bentham's notion is that the individuals in his ideal prison should believe themselves to be potentially under surveillance at all times.[13] Bentham acknowledged that the model was applicable beyond prisons, and might also extend to all establishments of inspection, such as madhouses, hospitals, and schools;[14] it was Foucault who suggested that in practice panopticism extended beyond even these institutions to affect the exercise of power in society as a whole.[15]

If Carson's Belfast resembles a panoptical prison, however, the mode of operation is more complex and multifaceted than conceived of by Bentham.[16] As Eva Horn writes, state paranoia is 'a crisis that runs both ways: as a distrust of the state against its citizens, and as a distrust of the citizens against the state'.[17] In Troubles-era Belfast, if surveillance is omnipresent, it is also mutual. Carson describes listening to the police moving through West Belfast in unmarked cars via short-wave police radio, while sometimes believing that the police might also be able to overhear him.[18] The complexity of mutual surveillance creates a 'mixed mode', where it is difficult to decide whether you are an officer or a prisoner in Bentham's conceptual jail ('Intelligence', *CP* 185), and surveillance, far from providing any sort of certainty, creates instead an echo chamber of paranoia. Everyone here is watching everybody, after all, and power structures, far from being absolute, start to appear slippery.

Surveillance, on all sides, is supplemented by interrogation. Carson

---

[13] Bentham, *Panopticon Writings*, p. 34.

[14] Bentham, *Panopticon Writings*, pp. 33–4.

[15] Foucault, *Discipline and Punish*, p. 216.

[16] If Belfast can be metaphorically represented as a panoptical prison, its literal jails, Carson tells us, are gaps on the map (CP 125, 186). Funder, *Stasiland*, p. 196, likewise describes gaps in a 1984 map of East Berlin where 'entire city blocks and streets in Stasi areas are simply not represented: they are pale orange gaps in the map'.

[17] Horn, *Secret War*, p. 279.

[18] Carson, *The Star Factory*, p. 172. On RUC, MI5 and British army use of technology for surveillance purposes in Northern Ireland, see Dillon, *Dirty War*, pp. 398–417, and cf. Taylor, *Brits*, pp. 300–2. Northern Ireland often saw the early deployment of technologies not seen elsewhere until much later: Dillon, *Dirty War*, pp. 411–12, describes the British Army using unmanned aerial drones for surveillance in 1972.

describes being questioned at gunpoint by the security forces, who check his name and those of his family against their computer records ('Ambition', *CP* 139).[19] In a later text, he is questioned by Republican paramilitaries, who have seen him coming from the Shankill Road, and seek to verify his identity by interrogating his recollections of the disappeared cityscape of his youth ('Question Time', *CP* 170). The black humour Carson alludes to in interview appears on both occasions here. The soldiers may be holding him at gunpoint, but one of them, bored, is also tuned in to the tennis (*CP* 139). His questioning by Republicans concludes with a bleak quip from one of his interrogators – '*a dreadful mistake ... has been made*' – as if, as Carson says, this was a scene from a bad police B-movie (*CP* 170).

Elsewhere in these poems, as in reality, paramilitary interrogation leads to torture. In 'Campaign', the man being questioned has his fingernails pulled out before being taken to some waste-ground and shot nine times, though by now his interrogators have accepted that he is, in fact, innocent: 'someone not involved' (*CP* 98). This, too, is where things start to become very uncertain, for while the bodies of most IRA victims who were executed following interrogation were abandoned (as here) in remote or derelict locations, others were secretly disposed of. The search for the remains of the 'disappeared' was an important aspect of the Northern Ireland peace process, though not all have been found.[20] In a further illustration of the complexity of identities and actions during the Troubles, it emerged in 2003 that one of the men primarily responsible for IRA interrogations for many years, Freddie Scappaticci, the IRA's head of security, was in fact a British agent.[21]

Early in the Troubles, state interrogation methods also included torture. When Northern Ireland introduced internment without trial in 1971, twelve men in August and two more in October were selected from those being interned, and subjected to interrogation methods known as the 'five techniques'. These techniques were deprivation of food, sleep deprivation, hooding, white noise, and 'wall-standing': 'a stress position in which the victim would be forced to stand with his or her legs spread wide apart, leaning forward with arms spread wide and high, with much of their weight supported against a wall on outstretched fingers'.[22] The European Commission

---

[19] Dillon, *Dirty War*, pp. 415–17, describes the army's 'Vengeful' computer system originating in a vehicle registration database in 1974, evolving in the later 1970s for broader intelligence-gathering purposes; Dillon suggests that medical and social services data were also used to build a broad profile of the population.

[20] Moloney, *Secret History of the IRA*, pp. 121–5, 134.

[21] Ingram and Harkin, *Stakeknife*; Moloney, *Secret History of the IRA*, pp. 574–9.

[22] Cobain, *Cruel Brittania*, p. 130, and cf. Taylor, *Brits*, pp. 62–74.

of Human Rights declared in 1976 that this constituted torture; on appeal, the European Court of Human Rights, while agreeing that the UK was in breach of the European Convention on Human Rights, decided that the 'five techniques' constituted 'inhuman and degrading treatment' rather than torture.[23] However defined, the 'five techniques' were in breach not only of European law, but also UK law.[24] Prime Minister Edward Heath told the UK parliament that the 'five techniques' would be banned from future use; Ian Cobain's book on Britain's use of torture, however, states that the 1972 Directive on Interrogation by the Armed Forces in Internal Security Operations, which explicitly banned the techniques, had an unpublished second section which suggested the opposite,[25] and the physical coercion of confessions continued in Northern Ireland for many years.[26] If this was the behaviour of the state, the use of torture in paramilitary interrogations (as in Carson's poem 'Campaign') was both extensive and yet more severe.[27]

Secrecy and silence are the inevitable counterparts of such intelligence gathering, and Carson's poetry, as David Wheatley shows, contains an extensive exploration of 'the poetry of secrets and shibboleths'.[28] 'Whatever you say, you say nothing', as Seamus Heaney puts it, is an imperative in Northern Ireland during the Troubles.[29] This is advice taken by the narrator of 'Queen's Gambit', not talking back to the mirror image of his talkative barber, because a traditional reticence is supplemented in the context of conflict by a concern about where your words might lead:

---

[23] Cobain, *Cruel Brittania*, pp. 159–61. Dickson, *European Convention on Human Rights*, p. 153, argues that subsequent European Court judgments suggest that 'the Court recognised that its decision should have been different'. As Dickson shows, the European Court's arguably deferential approach in allowing states to derogate from the European Convention on Human Rights on the basis of a public emergency is indebted to an early judgment on internment in the Republic of Ireland, *Lawless* v. *Ireland* (pp. 34–8). 'Inestimable damage was done to the credibility of the Convention' in this earlier case, Dickson suggests, damage compounded by the subsequent finding that the UK's 'five techniques' did not constitute torture (p. 363). The US would use this distinction in this judgment between torture and 'inhuman and degrading treatment' to justify its own post-9/11 use of 'enhanced interrogation techniques' (Cobain, *Cruel Brittania*, pp. 231–2). For a firsthand account of the use of similar techniques at Guantánamo Bay, see Slahi, *Guantánamo Diary*, pp. 205 and n., 218, 220, 234–5 and n., 240 and n., 249, 251–2. *Guantánamo Diary* additionally documents physical and sexual assault.

[24] Cobain, *Cruel Brittania*, pp. 153–4.

[25] Cobain, *Cruel Brittania*, pp. 161–5.

[26] Cobain, *Cruel Brittania*, pp. 166–203.

[27] Dillon, *Dirty War*, pp. 362–3.

[28] Wheatley, '"That Blank Mouth"'.

[29] Heaney, *Opened Ground*, p. 132.

And I've this problem, talking to a man whose mouth is a reflection.
I tend to think the words will come out backwards, so I'm saying nothing.
  ('Queen's Gambit', *CP* 149)

Careless talk, after all, can cost lives, and a spray of bullets can send a message into the middle of a conversation:

This night I'm getting it from the horse's mouth, when these two punters
  walk in,
Produce these rods, and punctuate the lunchtime menu: there's confetti
  everywhere.

Which, I take it, was a message. Or an audio-visual aid. At any rate, I
  buzzed off. ('Barfly', *CP* 163)

The speech of informers, especially, has to be clothed in silence, as in this poem from the slightly later collection *First Language*:

They make the place secure for you. It's like a Twilight Zone where they
  exert their Special Powers.
And you make sure you don't repeat yourself. Change the routine ever
So slightly. Tell no one, I mean no one, what you're up to. Never. Never.
  Never. ('Two to Tango', *CP* 223)[30]

Such silences, again, complicate matters.

If these poems are filled with surveillance and interrogation, then, they are also filled with uncertainty and doubt. In 'Queen's Gambit', two plots to raid the Tomb Street GPO, one by a gunman named 'Mad Dog' Reilly, another by a criminal gang wearing cartoon masks, coincide. Security forces are aware of both attempts – an informer has called in Reilly's intentions, and the regular criminals are picked up by surveillance – but the two stories bleed into one another, and the authorities haven't quite managed to piece it together. In the ensuing gunfight, then, Reilly and company escape. The narrator is hearing this from his barber, who thinks it was a set-up, though who was setting up whom, he concedes, is impossible to know ('Queen's Gambit', *CP* 144–50).[31]

This sense of total surveillance and partial knowledge endures into later works. Gabriel remarks to Nina in *The Pen Friend* that it's extraordinary that the

---

[30] On British use of informers within the IRA, see Dillon, *Dirty War*, pp. 309–84; Moloney, *Secret History of the IRA*, pp. 3–6, 24–34, 332–6, 442–3.

[31] Alexander, *Ciaran Carson*, p. 149, in discussing this poem, notes that Carson's poetic narratives are often visibly mediated through other forms of representation – news stories, hearsay, video footage, 'the wider world of disinformation' – and so always subject to multiple viewpoints and interpretations.

Powers that Be seem to know everything about everyone, yet still can't tell who's who or what's what (*The Pen Friend*, p. 146). There are various other examples. 'Ambition' tells how Carson's father was interned in place of his uncle (who Carson, in turn, resembles) ('Ambition', *CP* 141).[32] 'Lima' features surveillance of a 'bunch of hashasheens' taking a drug delivery: here, the case might be open and shut, but only after some editing has been done to produce 'this skewed account' ('Lima', *CP* 334). In 'Trap', a soldier's inability to hear whoever's talking to him on his radio headphones is embodied in the fragmentary form of the poem itself, a few scraps of text, a mere fourteen words in all: the gaps in between suggestive of static, interference, and danger ('Trap', *CP* 434).

On top of all this surveillance and counter-surveillance, all these plots and silences, set-ups and cock-ups, the fragmented nature of the various parties to the conflict adds yet more uncertainty:

> It could have been or might have been. Everything Provisional and Sticky,
> Daily splits and splinters at the drop of a hat or a principle – ('Hairline
>   Crack', *CP* 158)

The 'Provisionals' and 'Stickies' here are the two major Republican para-military organisations, the Provisional IRA and the Official IRA, following their split in December 1969.[33] Further splintering of both Republican and Loyalist groups produced an alphabet soup of paramilitary factions, meaning that any individual incident 'could have been or might have been' committed – provisionally – by a variety of people. Indeed, there was an occasional need by both Republican and Loyalist terror groups to adopt cover names to conceal their involvement in particular killings.

Even now, many years later, in many cases we still lack straight answers for who was who and what was what. Post-conflict Northern Ireland did not follow South Africa's example in setting up a Truth and Reconciliation Commission;[34] many contested issues remain unresolved, and negotiations on dealing with 'legacy issues', as they are termed, continue to the present day.[35] That the truth remains contested is inevitable to some extent, given that truth is, as Carson has said recently in this context, 'a difficult and ambiguous business'.[36] Those difficulties and ambiguities, and the shared interest of

---

[32] This mistake is alluded to again in Carson, *The Star Factory*, p. 117.

[33] On which see Moloney, *Secret History of the IRA*, pp. 68–73; on use of the term 'stick' for a member of the Official IRA, see Moloney, *Secret History of the IRA*, p. 99n.

[34] For South Africa's Truth and Reconciliation Commission, see: <http://www.justice.gov.za/trc/>.

[35] Rowan, 'Northern Ireland's violent past remains unresolved'.

[36] Carson, 'A fusillade of question-marks'.

various former parties to the conflict in avoiding their investigation, are given fictional expression in David Park's 2008 novel *The Truth Commissioner*.[37]

All of this uncertainty and destabilisation of meaning in Carson's writing might suggest that Carson's work has an affinity with the postmodern turn in late twentieth-century writing.[38] It also fits well with a long-standing tendency to obliqueness and a reluctance to commit to certainties in Irish culture. As Bernard O'Donoghue says in a discussion of Paul Muldoon (quoting Kuno Meyer on Early Irish poetry), 'the half-said thing to them is dearest' for traditional Gaelic poetry and the postmodern tradition alike.[39] But outside these cultural contexts, both admittedly important for an understanding of Carson's work, the emphasis on uncertainty here is in part simply a reflection of the chaos of the Troubles and the lack of resolution of key questions in its aftermath. All of this uncertainty means, as Carson says, that when it comes to talking about the Troubles, even now we may not know the half of it.

Uncertain Doublings: *For All We Know*

Carson revisits and reworks some of these themes in three more recent, post-Troubles works, beginning with *For All We Know*, published in 2008. *For All We Know* consists of two mirroring sonnet sequences, each containing thirty-five poems, with mirrored titles: beginning with 'Second Time Around', concluding with 'Zugzwang'.[40] 'Begin' and 'conclude' are not quite right, however, because the first poem opens with an anniversary 'whether first or last', and is, after all, called 'Second Time Around' (*CP* 493). The last, likewise, may follow the death of one of the protagonists, but nonetheless suggests a form of endless return 'as my memories of you recede into the future' (*CP* 587).

To a certain extent, the collection offers elements of a straightforward narrative. Two people meet in Take Two, a Belfast secondhand clothes shop, in the 1970s. They strike up a conversation ('Pas de Deux', *CP* 503–4). As they talk in the street outside, a bomb goes off, seven doors down ('Fall', *CP* 513).

---

[37]   Park, *The Truth Commissioner*, and cf. Cobain, *The History Thieves*, p. 209.

[38]   The question has divided commentators. Corcoran, 'One step forward, two steps back', p. 180, suggests an alignment with 'some theories of the postmodern'. Alexander, *Ciaran Carson*, p. 74, suggests instead a 'dialogue with postmodernism'. Hughes, '"The mouth of the poem"', p. 99, argues that Carson is less a postmodernist than 'a traditionalist who insists that we have misunderstood tradition'; cf. Moore, '"Everything is in the ways you say them"', p. 6, and Longley, *The Living Stream*, p. 60.

[39]   O'Donoghue, '"The Half-Said Thing to Them is Dearest"'.

[40]   *Zugzwang* is both a chess term for a situation where a player is obliged to move but cannot do so without disadvantage (*OED*, s.v. *zugzwang*, n.) and the title of a thriller by Ronan Bennett, *Zugzwang*.

They continue their conversation in the Crown Bar. His name is Gabriel. Hers is Miranda, or Nina. She was born in Ireland, but moved to her father's part of France as a child ('Fall', *CP* 561–2). They begin a relationship. The rest of their story, divided between Ireland and the continent, is told in fragments dispersed across the sequence, and their story is shadowed by various others: a tale of possible collaboration in wartime France, narratives of Stasi surveillance in the former East Germany, Cold War espionage, the firebombing and reconstruction of Dresden, various versions of fairy tale, and, finally, the story of the divide between Nina's parents. The sequence as we have it seems to reflect Gabriel's memories of their relationship, and his retrospective attempts to understand it, following Nina's death in a car crash ('*Je Reviens*', *CP* 585–6).

The book is explicitly indebted to fugue as a musical form; one of its two epigraphs is from Glenn Gould (*CP* 490). The sequence, therefore, is filled with variations, and avoids conclusions. But as Gould's words suggest, this fugue also performs what is 'frequently stealthy work'. Several of the poems concern an inconclusive rendezvous on a snowy night where Miranda (or Nina) is approached by a man pretending to be a salesman ('Redoubt', *CP* 498–9). Here she pretends her name is Juliette ('The Assignation', *CP* 500). She had seen the man first on the train from Berlin to Dresden, and thought for a moment he was Gabriel's *doppelgänger* ('To', *CP* 523–4). She is in Dresden to meet with a professor of music ('Filling the Blank', *CP* 532), who is to slip her a microfilm canister, but never shows ('In the Dark', *CP* 534). She meets the supposed salesman, now explicitly named as an agent, again at breakfast the following morning ('Redoubt', *CP* 545–6); she refuses the pen he offers ('From Your Notebook', *CP* 568).

This encounter is echoed by or mapped onto Nina and Gabriel's relationship several times. Nina, first, thinks the agent looks like Gabriel's *doppelgänger* ('To', *CP* 523–4). Later, Gabriel encounters a woman who reminds him of Nina, which in turn reminds him of Nina's rendezvous story, his own encounter taking place at a railway station where he and Nina are to meet as strangers ('The Assignation', *CP* 547–8). Gabriel subsequently has a vision of his own *doppelgänger*, who for all that he might wish to talk to Nina, finally speaks Gabriel's own words and dreams Gabriel's own dream ('To', *CP* 571–2).

If one of the motifs in *For All We Know* is Cold War espionage, then, Nina, it seems, is an agent of some sort (and Gabriel, it seems, is not):[41]

> It's like this, you said. Those who play the Glass Bead Game don't know
> there's a war on they're so wrapped up in themselves and their Game.

---

[41] Moore, 'We Don't Know the Half of It'.

You know I was in Berlin for a reason. Yes, I chose
to walk that path, as surely as I chose to go with you.

There's no point in going into what else I might have been.
  ('The Shadow', *CP* 557)

Though it's clear that we (and Gabriel) don't know the half of it ('The Shadow', *CP* 556).

If the collection plays with the archetypes of spy narrative, that is not all there is to it: the book is, as Dillon Johnston suggests, something of an 'epistemological thriller'.[42] If the protagonists are uncertain of who is who and what is what, so too are we. Where did that encounter take place: Dresden or Berlin ('To', *CP* 523–4)? Is Nina's interlocutor Gabriel's *doppelgänger*, or is it really Gabriel himself? Is Nina's story of a planned meeting with the music professor a fantasy or a cover story? Interpretation is complicated by the fragmentary nature of the narrative: as we attempt to piece together a coherent whole from the partial (and sometimes contradictory) accounts given in the poems, we find our efforts already anticipated and reflected within those poems in the related figures of the four widow aunts stitching together a patchwork quilt ('Second Time Round', *CP* 493–4) and the East German puzzle-women trying to reconstruct shredded Stasi documents from fragments ('Zugzwang', *CP* 537).

Attempts at interpretation are further complicated by the sense, flagged early on in the sequence, of other identities, deliberately adopted. These poems are full of dressing up, disguising, cross-dressing: Nina and Gabriel meet, after all, intent on dressing up as other people, in a second-hand clothes shop ('Pas de Deux', *CP* 503–4). But if disguise offers a sort of freedom, it also leads to uncertainty. As Elmer Kennedy-Andrews puts it: 'in the dark labyrinths of Carson's poem sequence, identity slips and slides, the disturbance throwing the whole symbolic order into question'.[43]

Nina's narrative of a Cold War-style rendezvous is introduced with lines on being free 'to renegotiate yourself or what you thought you were' ('Redoubt', *CP* 498–9). Indeed, reading that poem, there is a slippage between 'I' and 'you'.[44] The story of the encounter begins 'I found myself this

---

[42] Johnston, 'Voice and Voiceprints', p. 175.

[43] Kennedy-Andrews, 'Carson, Heaney, and the art of getting lost', p. 243.

[44] Johnston's identification of the couple as 'a French performer/scholar of music and an Irish journalist' highlights the difficulty of identifying the identities of the sequence's 'you' and 'I' (Johnston, 'Voice and Voiceprints', p. 175), for while one of the characters does 'what you might call cultural *journalisme*' ('Fall'), we might take that to be Nina, who has already appeared as a writer ('Redoubt'); the music scholar is Nina's rendezvous who fails to show

night approached by a man in a suit' (line 3), and for the next fourteen lines,
'I' is the person approached, and 'you' is the salesman with the fake Mont
Blanc pen. In line 20, however, the first-person pronoun changes referent:
'I' is now the other member of the couple, and 'you' is the person talking
with the salesman ('Redoubt', *CP* 498–9). This movement of 'I' and 'you'
creates (as the title suggests) doubt (there is a similar movement in the second
'Redoubt' poem). Who is who here? Who is 'I'? Who is 'you'? Elsewhere in
the sequence, the characters begin to explicitly blend into one another, in the
imagined cross-dressing of 'Second Time Round':

> You should pretend to be me, you say, picture yourself
>
> In my shoes, whereon I begin to imagine the rest,
> the *broderie anglaise* bodice and the blue pencil skirt. ('Second Time
>   Round', *CP* 539)

Though, as Gabriel asks a few lines later, 'If I'm you, who are you?' (*CP* 540).

If fugue is a musical form, it is also a mental state,[45] 'a kind of trance', as
Carson describes it in interview, 'where the victim walks out the door and,
forgetting who he is, takes up another existence and another name in another
place'.[46]

Several poems come back to the question of whether or not it is really
possible to change identity, to escape the past. In 'Before', Gabriel's hallucinatory vision of Nina is followed by a scene with a nurse, who, like Nina
in the dream, wears a man's sere-cloth jacket. She takes it off, he puts it on. It
fits as if it were made for him. Not so, the nurse tells him:

> It belonged to my grandfather who was shot in the war,
> and buried in a cemetery which no longer exists. ('Before', *CP* 528)

The first 'Birthright' poem suggests that there is no real disguising your identity ('Birthright', *CP* 518). The second, itemising Gabriel's clothing, suggests
perhaps that instead of escaping identity politics, he has merely turned his
coat ('Birthright', *CP* 566).

This endless recurrence of things past is stitched into the sequence in
the constant echoing of earlier poems: the patchwork quilt here recalls the
quilt sewn by Carson's grandmother in previous poems ('The Patchwork
Quilt', 'Patchwork', *CP* 72–3, 119–22); the allusions to Dresden recall the

---

in 'Filling the Blank' and 'In the Dark' (who may or may not be Gabriel, depending on the
extent to which we read the Cold War framing of this rendezvous as reality or fantasy?).

[45] *OED*, s.v. *fugue*, n. 2.

[46] Carson and Kennedy-Andrews, 'Introduction: For All I Know', p. 26.

poem of the same name in *The Irish for No* ('Dresden', *CP* 77–81). We have met the living wearing dead men's clothes before ('Apparition', *CP* 182); there are locations (the Crown Bar) and themes (interrogation, uncertainty) familiar from earlier works. The motifs of fairy tale and song remind us of *The Twelfth of Never*; those of watches and timepieces echo 'Four Sonnets' in *First Language*.[47] Even Nina may be the Miranda from 'S' in *Opera Et Cetera* (*CP* 302).[48] Even that Mont Blanc pen is from 'Two to Tango' (*CP* 223). But truth, we are told, is always shifting ('The Shadow', *CP* 508–9), and stories of the past may or may not be just that ('The Present', *CP* 529–30).

If this sequence is filled with uncertainties, large and small (who is speaking at any given moment; on whose side was Nina's aunt in the war?), it also suggests a number of interrogation scenes, reminiscent of the similar scenes encountered in earlier poems, except here the interrogators are the Stasi ('The Shadow', 'The Fetch', 'Corrigendum', *CP* 508–9, 510, 512).

And again, perhaps, there is surveillance. As Guinn Batten writes:

> Who is that third man, who sells fountain pens and recruits sellers of secrets in the stalemated third world war designated, half a century ago, as 'cold'?[49]

The coldness is present in his association with snow: footprints in the snow, the Mont Blanc pen. Snow has various potential associations here. There is the song, misremembered from Carson's sister's childhood, that provides the book's other epigraph, describing a snowscape. There is also the snow that another Gabriel sees as general all over Ireland at the end of James Joyce's 'The Dead'.[50] But the cold is also associated, as Batten says, with the Cold War, and we recall the emotional numbness required of a le Carré agent before they are allowed to 'come in from the cold' (*The Spy*, pp. 17, 56). So, as Batten suggests, the frozen landscape of a children's song is also here the site of covert activity:

> In For All We Know even, or perhaps especially, the sites of children's songs and stories, embedded in the innocence of snow, become frosty places where the silent ministries perform their stealth.[51]

If the stories here are sometimes versions of *noir* or Cold War thriller, they also play with fairy tale. If Nina is potentially an undercover agent or spy, she is also potentially some sort of apparition: a revenant of sorts, to adapt

---

[47] As noted by Alexander, *Ciaran Carson*, p. 138.
[48] As suggested by Moore, 'We Don't Know the Half of It'.
[49] Batten, 'Love and War', pp. 77–8.
[50] Joyce, 'The Dead'.
[51] Batten, 'Love and War', p. 78.

the title of '*Je reviens*', a spook, in two senses of the word.[52] As Carson says in interview:

> It seemed to me that I was being informed by some kind of *aisling* woman, a creature from another universe which resembled ours and was contiguous to it, but was not our world. So many of the poems are voiced by the woman, with the man responding in a sometimes perplexed manner to her stories or her accounts of their past.[53]

That potentially double identity is suggested by, among other things, a particular location. After the explosion, Nina and Gabriel are in conversation in Belfast's Crown bar ('Fall', *CP* 561). The location carries a suggestion of film *noir*, for some crucial scenes in Carol Reed's 1947 film *Odd Man Out* are set in a Belfast bar which is recognisably a film-set reconstruction of the Crown.[54] But the bar's 'carved heraldic beasts' also serve as a signpost that some of the poems in the sequence will depart for the unreal realm of fairy tale. This supernatural aspect adds further to the sense of ominousness and uncertainty: as Elmer Kennedy-Andrews puts it, 'a recurrent figure of the poems' uncanny returns is that of the doppelganger, the fetch or shadow self, which betokens a sinister form of bilocation, the elusiveness of selfhood'.[55]

If this collection sketches out a much wider world beyond Carson's Belfast, there is a sense here as elsewhere in Carson that these broader perspectives have local resonance. In *For All We Know*, Cold War rendezvous, Stasi interrogation, collaboration or resistance in wartime France, and above all the sense of multiple uncertainties, are brought back to bear upon the recent past in Northern Ireland and its unanswered questions. A brief allusion in 'Through' to 'what passed for the truth' suggests that, during the conflict, official accounts of what was happening were partially true at best ('Through', *CP* 502). Even much later, in the aftermath of conflict, still the truth will not out:

> And all the unanswered questions of those dark days come back
> to haunt us, the disabled guns that still managed to kill,
>
> the witnesses that became ghosts in the blink of an eye. ('Peace', *CP* 533)

There can be no legal redress, the poem tells us, when no one is fit to speak.

---

52 *OED*, s.v. *spook*, n., 1, 2.
53 Carson and Kennedy-Andrews, 'Introduction: For All I Know', p. 22.
54 Reed, *Odd Man Out*, discussed in Carson, *The Star Factory*, pp. 131–3.
55 Kennedy-Andrews, 'Carson, Heaney, and the art of getting lost', p. 243. 'Fetch' here is the supernatural double of a living person: *OED*, s.v. *fetch*, n.[2], 1.

'Second Take' lists a series of witnesses who are dead or disappeared, people whose identity was not what it appeared to be on the first take. If some have new identities, their reason for needing them brings what might have been considered their original identity into question ('Second Take', *CP* 511).[56] For when you take on a false identity, these poems ask, who are you then? For a society where all identities and actions seemed uncertain in the context of conflict, what does all that uncertainty mean in the conflict's aftermath, when so many unanswered questions remain? In the context of so many false witnesses, where might truth, or justice, be found?

Co-option, Collusion and Consequences: *The Pen Friend*

In *The Pen Friend*, published a year after *For All We Know*, but written first,[57] we once again meet a couple named Gabriel and Nina, in a story that is both familiar and different. The Gabriel of this novel has taken early retirement from his post at Belfast's Municipal Gallery. He receives a series of postcards from Nina, his former lover, who he has not heard from in over twenty years. His replies form the text of this epistolary novel, whose plot both is and is not like the basic narrative we intuit behind *For All We Know*.

He is Gabriel Conway, or Angel (he was named for the Angel Gabriel) or Conway-Stewart (like the pen) (*The Pen Friend*, pp. 4–5, 24); the name also seems an echo of Gabriel Conroy from Joyce's 'The Dead', and there is an explicit reference to *Dubliners* later in the novel in a scene set in Mulligan's pub.[58] He first meets Nina at the XL Café in 1982. She has him guess her name, and when he guesses Iris, she tells him he's right, though of course he isn't, and he dubs her Rainbow (*The Pen Friend*, pp. 5, 25). Later she is Miranda Bowyer, or Nina, which she claims as a childhood name when Gabriel buys her an antique Nina Ricci perfume bottle (*The Pen Friend*, pp. 29, 34). Angel and Nina are pet names, but also reminiscent of code-names. Nina's father and his fellows in the Dutch resistance, we're told, adopted *noms de guerre*: his was Harry, and if this was close to his real name, Arie, this is because things are best hidden in plain sight (*The Pen Friend*, pp. 19–20).[59] Later on the N of Nina's signature will remind Gabriel of another N that could stand for Nemo, or Nobody (*The Pen Friend*, p. 225).

Nina works for an organisation called MO2, a government organisation of rather indeterminate status and intent, inspired by the Mass Observation

---

[56] On informers being 'retired' overseas, see Dillon, *Dirty War*, p. 310.
[57] Carson and Kennedy-Andrews, 'Introduction: For All I Know', pp. 22–3.
[58] Joyce, 'Counterparts', and 'The Dead', in Joyce, *Dubliners*, pp. 75–86, 159–204.
[59] In Carson, *Fishing for Amber*, p. 4, Carson's father has a Dutch pen-friend named Arie Kuipers.

movement of the 1930s.[60] Notionally reporting to Home Affairs and the Northern Ireland Office, in practice, they act more independently. Nina's own interview to join the organisation sees her interlocutors ask 'what do you think we do?' (*The Pen Friend*, p. 148). The answer to that question remains somewhat uncertain, though there is the inevitable whiff of espionage. Nina mentions that people suspected the original Mass Observation group of being spies in the 1930s, and when they crop up again later in the story, they have become a propaganda tool (*The Pen Friend*, pp. 47, 133). When Gabriel suggests that Nina's employers are like a spy ring, she agrees, though they are, she says, perfectly open about what they do (*The Pen Friend*, p. 93). Carson's choice of the name MO2 for this successor group also carries a suggestion of espionage, for MO2 was an acronym for one of the early twentieth-century British intelligence offices.[61] Gabriel thinks of them as 'just another of those well-meaning and ultimately pointless local business development agencies' until events cause him to change his mind (*The Pen Friend*, p. 237).

Here again, then, Nina is a spy of some sort, and so too, she suggests, is Gabriel, whether he knows it or not. At one point, the pair encounter a man in a Dublin pub, Hughie Falls, who accuses Gabriel of being 'a Castle Catholic, a collaborator with the occupying forces' (*The Pen Friend*, p. 181). To Gabriel's surprise, Nina suggests that perhaps Hughie Falls is right, and she takes him through the events leading up to his finding a job at the Municipal Gallery, specifically his meeting with John Bradbury, a Gallery Trustee, the week before. Bradbury had mentioned the job. 'That's because John Bradbury is MO2', Nina tells Gabriel, 'And so are you' (*The Pen Friend*, p. 183).[62]

As we found in discussing Don DeLillo, the possibility of being co-opted by government agencies or their opponents is a prominent concern for Western writers during the Cold War and after, for good reason. The same concerns apply in Northern Ireland. Seamus Heaney famously gives an account of being confronted on a train by an IRA member who asks him when he's going to write 'something for us',[63] an interlocutor revealed, many years later, to be Sinn Féin's Danny Morrison.[64] In *The Pen Friend* we see that the state's attempts to win 'hearts and minds' might extend to cultivating and nurturing various cultural activities (*à la* the Congress for Cultural

---

[60] On which see Crain, 'Surveillance Society'.
[61] Andrew, *Defence of the Realm*, pp. 5, 6.
[62] Carson was himself a public servant for many years as Traditional Arts Officer with the Arts Council of Northern Ireland.
[63] Seamus Heaney, 'The Flight Path', in Heaney, *The Spirit Level*, p. 25.
[64] O'Driscoll, *Stepping Stones*, pp. 257–8.

Freedom). But it may also extend to taking, or at least facilitating, action against cultural activities perceived as potentially hostile. And if DeLillo's version of the Kennedy assassination suggests that rogue agents of the state acting outside the law may pose a threat to the state itself, the suggestion here is that collusion between intelligence agencies and terrorist groups may pose a threat to civilians.

If the relationship between Gabriel and Nina in *For All We Know* begins with an explosion, in *The Pen Friend* it ends with one. The book's climax comes with the bombing of an Esperanto class run by Gabriel's father in the upstairs room of the Compass Bar. His father loses a leg, and five others are killed. Why bomb an Esperanto class? Because the ideals of Esperanto involve overcoming division, and there are always those who find it in their best interests to foster hatred (*The Pen Friend*, p. 236). And who might have done such a thing? Those responsible are never identified, but state collusion is suspected:

> No one ever claimed responsibility for The Compass Bar bombing that killed five people, three Catholics and two Protestants. Some said it was a rogue Republican element. Some said it was a rogue Loyalist element. And quite a lot of people said that whoever was responsible, it could not have happened without the collusion of the security forces, whether actively or by omission, that it had been sanctioned at some level in the maze of clandestine operations that lay behind official government policy (*The Pen Friend*, p. 237).

Gabriel Conway's sense of where responsibility might lie is more specific than this. MO2, it seems to him, must have had prior knowledge. Nina intercepted him, delayed him, saved him, but if that were so, she did not save the others (*The Pen Friend*, p. 237).

The literary echoes here are of Graham Greene. Nina's rescue of Gabriel recalls *The Quiet American*: when a public square is bombed, Phuong escapes injury because Pyle, who has advance knowledge, has warned her off. Fowler, however (like Gabriel in *The Pen Friend*), cannot overlook the slaughter of innocents (*The Quiet American*, p. 155). *The Pen Friend* also contains other possible echoes of Greene. *The Confidential Agent* features a character named Mr Muckerji, who is an observer for the 1930s Mass Observation group upon whom Carson has based his organisation MO2.[65] In the same novel, the protagonist has a clandestine meeting at a language school devoted to an artificial language, named Entrenationo, whose purpose is to foster

---

[65] Greene, *The Confidential Agent*.

international communication in place of strife (though the Esperanto theme in *The Pen Friend* also intersects with Carson's biography, for Carson's own father was an Esperantist).[66]

There are also, however, political echoes here, for as well as a variety of controversies about actions directly attributable to British security forces during the Troubles (such as the killing of civilians by undercover Mobile Reconnaissance Force (MRF) troops,[67] the Parachute Regiment's killing of unarmed civilians in Derry on Bloody Sunday,[68] and allegations of a shoot-to-kill policy by the SAS and the RUC's HMSU[69]) there are also long-standing allegations of collusion by members of the security forces in terrorist activities. That collusion occurred is not really in question. Martin Dillon's discussion documents the existence of such collusion at some length: writing in 1990, Dillon noted that over one hundred members of the Ulster Defence Regiment had been convicted of serious offences including murder, attempted murder, causing explosions or possession of explosives.[70] He also documented instances of intelligence files being passed to loyalist terror groups, and of terrorists being given safe passage through security checks.[71] What is open to question is the extent of the collusion. Dillon argued that loyalist terror groups received support from individual members of the security forces rather than the security forces *per se*.[72]

Dillon also commented, however, that some state agencies operated with a latitude that left the police unable to properly investigate incidents involving their personnel:

> Special branch, military intelligence and the security services operate with a freedom which makes it virtually impossible for CID properly to investigate incidents involving personnel from any of their agencies.[73]

The activities of these agencies remain both secret and controversial,[74] with enduring allegations that agents and informants of these agencies were involved in murders that security forces failed to prevent. There has been

---

[66] As discussed in Carson, 'The Language Instinct'. The Carson figure in *Fishing for Amber* also has an Esperantist father (pp. 4, 250–1).

[67] Taylor, *Brits*, pp. 128–31; Dillon, *Dirty War*, pp. 51–7.

[68] On which see Saville, Hoyt and Toohey, *Report of the Bloody Sunday Inquiry*.

[69] Taylor, *Brits*, pp. 208–217, 241–59, 270–85, 298, 303–6.

[70] Dillon, *Dirty War*, p. 220.

[71] Dillon, *Dirty War*, pp. 222–30, 275–7.

[72] Dillon, *Dirty War*, pp. 212, 230, 276.

[73] Dillon, *Dirty War*, p. 459.

[74] Even the authorised history of MI5 concedes that mistakes were made (Andrew, *Defence of the Realm*, pp. 738–9).

particular controversy around the roles of Brian Nelson, the UFF's senior intelligence officer, who, while an agent for a British army intelligence group called the Force Research Unit (FRU) was involved in multiple murders, including that of solicitor Pat Finucane,[75] and Freddie Scappaticci, the IRA's head of security, also a British agent, who was again involved in numerous killings.[76] Such concerns are enduring. In 2015, former Northern Ireland Police Ombudsman Nuala O'Loan, suggested that informers and agents within terrorist organisations might have been responsible for hundreds of deaths.[77] In 2016, media reports suggested that the IRA commander who planned the 1993 Shankill Road bombing that killed nine civilians was a British agent who had passed on intelligence about the bombing prior to its occurrence.[78] Here, again, inevitably, we have an absence of certainty. But both the realities and possibilities of collusion between security forces and paramilitaries during the Northern Ireland Troubles find an echo in the explosion at the heart of Carson's novel.

Double Takes: *Exchange Place*

Carson revisits many of these themes in his subsequent novel, *Exchange Place*. This is a narrative of parallel identity, split between two characters, John Kilfeather and John Kilpatrick, in alternating chapters. Here, again, we have uncertainty, questions of identity, a concern with surveillance, the whiff of espionage and the motif of fugue. The book draws on a range of other texts, including Carson's own writing, sometimes very explicitly, sometimes less so. There are various allusions to and quotations from works by Walter Benjamin, Jean Cocteau, John Donne, Patrick Modiano, Marcel Proust and Arthur Rimbaud, among others. To a large extent, the exchange that occurs within *Exchange Place* is intertextuality, as Carson weaves aspects of his own previous writing and the writings of various others into a new fiction.

In producing a text by assembling a series of quotations from other texts, *Exchange Place* is partly reminiscent of Walter Benjamin's unfinished *Arcades Project*, with which it also shares a number of thematic motifs (the *flâneur*, the collector, fashion, conspiracy, the dream city). Benjamin's book is an explicit presence in the novel: John Kilpatrick, visiting Paris with the intention of writing a book, has transcribed into a notebook passages from Benjamin's text, 'itself one huge notebook' that becomes 'a dream representation of Paris itself, images and phrases intertwining in a vast fugal architecture, echoing

[75] Taylor, *Brits*, pp. 286–96.
[76] Moloney, *Secret History of the IRA*, pp. 574–9.
[77] Moriarty, 'Claim that hundreds of deaths in North happened due to collusion'.
[78] Morris, 'IRA commander at time of Shankill bombing was informer'.

rooms and galleries of language'. The passages that he quotes, on entrances to the underworld and the possibilities of doubles living in parallel worlds, touch at the heart of Carson's plot (*Exchange Place*, pp. 33–4).[79]

Exchange Place also displays certain continuities with the two works just discussed: *For All We Know* and *The Pen Friend*. Like those books, it is concerned with questions of identity, surveillance and uncertainty. It also contains some explicit echoes of its predecessors. When John Kilpatrick dreams about meeting John Bourne in the Crown bar, both are wearing dead men's jackets (*Exchange Place*, pp. 24–5). Later, he bumps into Freddie Gabriel in a café on Rue Daguerre (*Exchange Place*, pp. 54–5), the same street where the Nina of *For All We Know* used to have an apartment ('Rue Daguerre', *CP* 525, 573), and which will later furnish the title of a supposed work-in-progress by Patrick Modiano (*Exchange Place*, p. 101). Freddie Gabriel himself has a surname echoing the Gabriel of the other two books; we notice the Mont Blanc pen before we're told he's a spy (*Exchange Place*, pp. 64, 92). Gabriel invites Kilpatrick to an event at the Hôtel Nevers, which reminds us that the town of Nevers is Nina's destination when she has her fatal car crash in *For All We Know* (*Exchange Place*, p. 83, *CP* 585–6).

If *Exchange Place* has some things in common with *For All We Know* and *The Pen Friend*, its most explicit debt is to a previous unpublished prose text of Carson's, $X + Y = K$. Although unpublished, $X + Y = K$ is described in an essay by Alan Gillis, alongside *The Pen Friend* (also unpublished when Gillis wrote).[80] At the beginning of *Exchange Place*, John Kilfeather finds the text of $X + Y = K$ in his attic, and feels that he 'might be able to recycle some of this material – plagiarising myself, as it were – in this other book that has been at the back of my mind for some years' (*Exchange Place*, p. x). If John Kilfeather and John Kilpatrick are *doppelgängers* here, the novel itself also has a twin of sorts in this unpublished text by Carson, incorporated into *Exchange Place* as an unpublished text by Kilfeather (whoever he is).

Alan Gillis describes the 'Y' section of this unpublished text as follows:

> Kilpatrick visits a 'Consultant Phenomenologist' called Fitzwilliam, who entices him to work for a surveillance project named 'Farset' (a word central to Carson's riffs on the etymology of Belfast). Farset, we are told, is a pun on 'Farsight', the code-name of a CIA surveillance project from the Cold War. Farset is using Farsight's surveillance techniques in Belfast, techniques aimed at accessing 'the matrix': a realm of traces in which 'any and all information about any person, place or thing might be obtained'.

---

[79] Carson quotes Benjamin, *The Arcades Project*, pp. 84, 112, 114.
[80] Gillis, 'Acoustic Perfume'.

Kilpatrick's migraines, it seems, give him special access to this matrix, while these unusual surveillance techniques, the narration points out, make the Farset 'an extended séance'. Section Y ends with Kilpatrick unable to stop his parents' murder in a café bomb in Belfast.[81]

$X + Y = K$, Gillis suggests, takes Carson's infatuation with surveillance to a new level.[82]

Exchange Place takes a very different direction from this unpublished text it's indebted to: there is no reference to CIA surveillance projects, and, unlike *The Pen Friend*, no bombing. But there are similarities nonetheless. Reading the draft of $X + Y = K$ at the beginning of *Exchange Place*, John Kilfeather realises that some of its concerns are the concerns that occupy him now: 'perception, memory, identity, surveillance, disappearance and appearances' (*Exchange Place*, p. x).

Surveillance, in particular, endures. Early on in *Exchange Place*, John Kilpatrick, watching a blind man navigating his way with the aid of a cane, wonders if the man is really blind, or merely conducting surveillance in disguise (*Exchange Place*, p. 2). In a later passage of quotation from $X + Y = K$ incorporated into *Exchange Place*, we have a long list of possible hiding places for bugs and cameras: in phones, door-handles, light fittings, behind curtains, in toilet fixtures, under floorboards, in smoke detectors, behind bar mirrors, or disguised as otherwise innocuous items (*Exchange Place*, pp. 164–5). The list reminds Kilpatrick of a suggestion by John Bourne, owner of a vintage radio, that every new radio bought in Belfast was liable to be bugged. Kilpatrick, reflecting on this, suggests that 'one thing was certain: there was more to everything than met the eye' (*Exchange Place*, p. 165).

Exchange Place has some debts to espionage fiction, explicitly so: Freddie Gabriel is not only a spy, he was once an aspiring John le Carré (*Exchange Place*, pp. 61–2), and John Bourne's name explicitly recalls Robert Ludlum's *The Bourne Identity* (*Exchange Place*, p. 90). But when Gabriel says to John Kilpatrick 'I take it you are one of us?' his meaning is supernatural rather than mundane (*Exchange Place*, p. 173), for *Exchange Place* also has a very different and much more substantial lineage via various fantastical stories of doubling: double lives as in *Dr Jekyll and Mr Hyde*, parallel narratives such as Haruki Murakami's *Hard-Boiled Wonderland and the End of the World*, and divided cities as in China Miéville's *The City & The City*.[83] A turn to the fantastical is

---

81 Gillis, 'Acoustic Perfume', p. 255.
82 Gillis, 'Acoustic Perfume', p. 266.
83 Stevenson, *Dr Jekyll and Mr Hyde*, Murakami, *Hard-Boiled Wonderland*, Miéville, *The City & The City*. Brown, 'Ciaran Carson', p. 148, mentions the Murakami book; Carson, *Until*

by no means an unusual thing in Carson's work. The *aisling*, or dream-vision, is an important motif in Carson's work: he sees it, as he says in interview, as 'an interlingual twilight zone, the place where poetry happens'.[84]

If *Exchange Place* takes a sharp turn from the real into the fantastical, we might have expected as much given the quotations from the *Arcades Project* about entrances to the otherworld and *doppelgängers* occupying parallel realities. One of the other strong intertextual presences in the novel is Patrick Modiano: John Kilpatrick is reading Modiano's *Rue des Boutiques Obscures* (*Exchange Place*, pp. 11, 13–14, 41); later, on the Metro, he feels as if he has entered into a scene from another Modiano novel, *La petite bijou* (*Exchange Place*, pp. 71–2).[85] Kilpatrick's summary of Modiano's books suggests their relevance to *Exchange Place*:

> Though they all seemed to be versions of each other, he was attracted by their fugue-like repetition of themes and imagery, their evocation of a noir Paris in which the protagonists were endlessly in search of their identities. (*Exchange Place*, pp. 13–14)

Rue des Boutiques Obscures, in particular, concerns an amnesiac detective investigating his own forgotten past in the hope of discovering who he really is.

In Carson's novel, Freddy Gabriel suggests to Kilpatrick that Modiano's (French) title is a piece of misdirection: there is no *Rue des Boutiques Obscures* in Paris, rather, it is a translation of a Roman street name (*Exchange Place*, p. 63). But if *Via della Botteghe Oscure* is a real Roman street, it might seem to mean something different in French, for *La Boutique Obscure* is also the title of Georges Perec's dream diary, published in 1973,[86] and so *Rue des Boutiques Obscures* might also be translated as 'Street of Dreams'. As with Carson, then, Modiano's meditation on a man searching for some sort of meaning in his possible identities seems to take place in a space more surreal than real.

The events of *Exchange Place*'s final chapter are fugal in two senses. First, at the end of the novel, the narrator awakes from a fugue in the medical sense, 'a bout of transient global amnesia' (*Exchange Place*, p. 204). Secondly, the final confrontation between John Kilfeather and John Kilpatrick is strongly

---

Before After, p. 121, acknowledges Miéville's novel. For a broad discussion of doubling in fiction, cf. Warner, *Fantastic Metamorphoses, Other Worlds*, chapter 4.

84 Michaud, 'The Exchange: Ciaran Carson'.

85 Modiano, *Missing Person*; Modiano, *Little Jewel*.

86 Perec, *La Boutique Obscure*. Perec is also the author of a partly autobiographical doubled text, *W or The Memory of Childhood* (pronounced 'double-v' or *double vie*, 'double life', in French).

reminiscent of a description, much earlier in the novel, of the end of Glenn Gould's *Contrapunctus XIV* from *The Art of the Fugue* (*Exchange Place*, p. 8). But if this makes the novel fugal both literally and aesthetically, it also means that what we are left with is uncertainty, for, as the epigraph to *For All We Know* told us, a fugue is 'perpetually unfinished' (*CP* 490). At the novel's end, the man who thought he was John Kilpatrick confronts his double, John Kilfeather. After the confrontation, someone, presumably one of them, comes to. But who?

Again, as in *For All We Know*, the complexity of multiple identities brings identity itself into question. 'Take the others who were given a new identity,' as Carson writes there, 'not that we could say for sure who they were in the first place' (*CP* 511). And 'If I'm you, who are you?' (*CP* 540). Here, at the end of *Exchange Place*, the identity of someone whose place has been taken by a double is resolved into ... what? Earlier in the novel, contemplating Blanqui's ideas of infinite worlds and endlessly doubled lives, which make their way into Carson's book via Benjamin's *Arcades Project*, Kilpatrick toys with translating Blanqui's surname as 'Blank Who' (*Exchange Place*, p. 43). Which may turn out to be his own name as well. Like so many other things in Carson's extended meditations on the Troubles and their aftermath, it remains an unanswered question.

7

Contesting the Virtual: William Gibson

Histories of the Future

Even before the Cold War had started to thaw, William Gibson's *Neuromancer* had begun to imagine the contest for the virtual that now preoccupies us. Technology as a driver of social change, and particularly the rise of the virtual, is a major theme in Gibson's work. This enduring concern plays out across a variety of scenarios that draw on the conventions of both science-fiction and the thriller, in settings that are temporally quite different. In *Neuromancer*, Gibson's first novel, explicitly set in a science fiction future, the virtual is a separate reality, a 'consensual hallucination'. By the Blue Ant trilogy, written and set in the approximately now of the early twenty-first century, cyberspace has 'everted', and the virtual and the physical interpenetrate. In all of these scenarios, the virtual appears as a contested space.

In Gibson's earlier works, this contest for the virtual takes place in a world where global corporations and wealthy individuals have acquired powers previously reserved to nation-states. If we have noted slippage in this direction earlier in this discussion, here the nation-state's claim to embody the highest authority is robustly challenged by supranational entities that act as a law unto themselves. If previous chapters here have been about the ways in which sovereign power, latterly embodied in the nation-state, has acted extralegally in pursuit of its interests, in much of Gibson's fiction we are dealing with something else. Extralegal actions here are often less those of states and governments – who barely matter in the worlds of Gibson's earlier fictions – but rather those of global corporations and ultra-wealthy individuals seeking to consolidate and extend their reach in both the real and virtual worlds.

In *Neuromancer* and the two books that follow it, *Count Zero,* and *Mona Lisa Overdrive* (collectively known as the Sprawl trilogy or the Matrix trilogy), the rise of the corporations to global power is something of an optimistic vision, as it portrays a future in which a potential Cold War apocalypse has not come to pass.[1] As Gibson says in interview, from the perspective of the early 1980s, any projected future that does not end in nuclear apocalypse is an optimistic one.[2] The war between the USA and the USSR that *Neuromancer* describes is very limited. We are given glimpses of an American raid on Russia, Bonn has been destroyed in a nuclear attack, but mutual destruction is avoided. The world of *Neuromancer* envisages the United States replaced by a series of smaller political entities, and the nation-state being superseded by global corporations. Gibson suggests in interview that this version of the future was 'kind of backward', in a literal sense at least, in that it was the USSR that collapsed politically in 1989, not the United States.[3] However, the rise of multinational capital, the potentialities of the internet, and the challenges that both pose to the traditional powers of the nation-state remain potent issues in the post-Cold War era.

The fragmentation of the state here is counterpointed by the rise of the global corporation. In the Sprawl trilogy, companies like Hosaka Corporation, Sense/Net, Maas-Neotek and Tessier-Ashpool SA all have global (in the latter case, orbital) reach. Media and organised crime are global too: newsfax is universally that of *Asahi Shimbun*, organised crime run by various franchises of the Yakuza. Power has moved emphatically from the state to the corporation. Instead of future apocalypse, then, the vision of the future offered by Gibson's first trilogy shows the almost unfettered rise to power of global capital.

Such power is accompanied by force. In *Count Zero*, the middle novel of the Sprawl trilogy, Turner is a professional corporate mercenary, his employers 'vast corporations warring covertly for the control of entire economies' (*Count Zero*, p. 4). Much of the novel's plot is concerned with a corporate defection given a treatment akin to a Cold War espionage narrative. Where such a narrative would conventionally involve spies as protagonists and states as their masters, the relevant characters here are mercenaries in the service of global corporations. Turner has been contracted on behalf of the Hosaka Corporation to assist the defection of Maas Biolabs's leading scientist, Christopher Mitchell. However, Turner's boss, Conroy, has been paid off by the billionaire Josef Virek: one qualification to the equation of power with the corporation in these novels is the existence of individual and family wealth associated with the billionaires who serve as Gibson's villains. Conroy double-crosses Hosaka at Virek's instigation, arranging to kill his

[1] Gibson, *Neuromancer*; Gibson, *Count Zero*; Gibson, *Mona Lisa Overdrive*.
[2] Wallace-Wells, 'William Gibson: The Art of Fiction No. 211', p. 220. For the rise of Cold War tensions in the early 1980s, see Fischer, *A Cold War Conundrum*.
[3] Wallace-Wells, 'William Gibson: The Art of Fiction No. 211', p. 221.

entire team (Turner, perhaps, excepted) as cover up (*Count Zero*, pp. 220–1). All concerned then discover that they, in turn, have been played by Mitchell, whose real objective was not to escape, but to free his daughter. Mitchell himself, unsurprisingly, ends up dead.

Gibson's second sequence of novels, the Bridge trilogy, is set in what was the near future when the books were written: the opening book, published in 1993, is set in a fictional 2006.[4] Here, too, we encounter a world where three of the pillars of twentieth-century Western society – the nation-state, the middle class and the nuclear family – have fragmented. California has divided into two states, North and South; there is a president in the White House, but very little other sense of the United States as a political entity; Canada, the USSR and Brazil have likewise fragmented, and there is civil conflict in Europe and New Zealand (*Virtual Light*, pp. 78, 85, 109–10, 227, 284, 289). Russia has a mafia government, the Kombinat (*Idoru*, p. 157). There is a brief mention of rocket attacks and rumours of chemical agents in Mexico, part of an 'obscure and ongoing' struggle (*Idoru*, p. 51).[5]

The nuclear family, likewise, is largely absent. Both the Sprawl trilogy and the Bridge trilogy are filled with orphans and outcasts: 'waifs' as Christopher Palmer terms them, the human equivalents of the *gomi*, or detritus, that also fascinates Gibson.[6] We meet people living in informal family structures with non-relatives, raised by dysfunctional single parents or in juvenile detention centres. Rootlessness is, of course, a key point of the *punk* element in the cyberpunk movement that Gibson is associated with – as Dani Cavallaro observes, 'punk constructed a whole aesthetic out of a reality of socioeconomic alienation and discrimination'[7] – but there is no sense of these fragmented families as being unusual. Also gone is the middle class: Sammy Sal DuPree explains to Chevette Washington that there are two sorts of people, rich and poor; a third category, people in the middle, that previously existed is now gone (*Virtual Light*, p. 146).

Nation-states and their legal apparatuses remain a presence of sorts, still able to deploy physical force, albeit not always effectively, or in their own interests. In *Neuromancer*, the Panther Moderns dupe the security agencies into massacring innocent civilians while inadvertently assisting a daring theft (*Neuromancer*, pp. 79, 86). In *Virtual Light*, the Republic of Desire hack

4 Gibson, *Virtual Light*; Gibson, *Idoru*; Gibson, *All Tomorrow's Parties*.
5 Some of the technology that is described for this politically fragmented near-future world, however, is actually from the 1990s conflict zones of Northern Ireland and Israel: Diggle and Ball, 'An Interview with William Gibson', pp. 96–7.
6 Palmer, '*Mona Lisa Overdrive* and the Prosthetic', pp. 228, 231, 234.
7 Cavallaro, *Cyberpunk and Cyberculture*, p. 20.

the police satellite known colloquially as the Death Star, provoking a police response to a supposed bomb threat and hostage situation from mercenaries (*Virtual Light*, p. 342). This, at least, has the happy effect of rescuing the novel's protagonists. The civic authorities also stage an unexpected rescue at the end of *All Tomorrow's Parties*.

Nation-states also seek to impose legal constraints in areas that seem to pose an existential threat to human society. But even here, attempts at legal prohibition are ineffective. A key theme in the Sprawl trilogy is the rise of Artificial Intelligence. In *Neuromancer*, a legal authority called the Turing police exists to prevent the emergence of sentient AIs. Representatives of the Turing police appear only briefly as an obstacle in the novel: the AI Wintermute has them killed. After achieving their objective, the entity created by the merging of the two AIs Wintermute and Neuromancer conceals their actions by modifying the records of the Turing authorities (*Neuromancer*, pp. 310, 314).

The Bridge trilogy shows a similar concern with the rise of nanotechnology, the possession of which is internationally proscribed, and, as Chia McKenzie is alarmed to discover, carries an automatic life sentence under Japanese law (*Idoru*, p. 211). But while his purposes are subverted by Rei Toei and her confederates, the villain of *All Tomorrow's Parties*, Cody Harwood, does actually succeed in building his global network of nanofaxes in Lucky Dragon convenience stores. Even where the stakes seem highest, then, laws are not successfully enforced.

We meet police officers and lawyers in these novels, but enforcement of state power is rarely their function. In the world of the Bridge trilogy, *Cops in Trouble* is a TV show, but also a diagnosis, as exemplified in the career of Berry Rydell who spirals downwards from being a police officer, to a private security employee of IntenSecure, then an employee of a freelance IntenSecure contractor who works on the wrong side of the law, then in hotel security, and finally as a convenience store security guard. The other police officers Rydell encounters in *Virtual Light*, Svobodov and Orlovsky, are archetypal bent cops who really work for IntenSecure rather than the state.

The semi-ubiquitous use of force in pursuit of private interests through the Sprawl and Bridge trilogies underlines the shift of power away from the state and towards the corporation. Max Weber once defined the state as 'the form of human community that (successfully) lays claim to the monopoly of legitimate physical violence within a particular territory'.[8] Here, the state does not have anything like a monopoly on physical violence, and while some

---

[8] Weber, 'Politics as a Vocation', p. 33.

of the means the corporations possess are clearly illegitimate, clandestine and extralegal, others are not. They are simply the extension of the contemporary privatisation of powers once reserved to the state.[9] Both legitimate and extralegal uses of force here are expressions of the ability of corporations to act with something like impunity in the vacant space created by the shrinking of the state. Even when our friends from the intelligence agencies make their appearance in Gibson's Blue Ant trilogy, they too have been metamorphosed by the influx of corporate contractors into the once-hallowed space of the secret state.

It might seem that in their posited collapse of state power, Gibson's projected futures offer an echo of the past, a refracted version of the fragmentation of authority we saw in medieval England, or of the East India Company's assumption in eighteenth century India of functions normally reserved to states. But as Gibson has said more than once, 'upon arriving in the capital-F Future, we discover it, invariably, to be the lower-case now'.[10] He suggests in interview that his thinking about the rise of corporate power was partly indebted to the representation of Shell Oil in Thomas Pynchon's *Gravity's Rainbow*.[11] The corporations in Gibson's projected futures who supersede nation states and ignore legal boundaries have their roots in the possibilities of twentieth-century capitalism.

Outlaw Cartographies, Virtual and Real

If power in these novels resides within global corporate structures, the books are also populated with a variety of marginal groups, often occupying variations on what may be regarded as outlaw spaces, virtual or real. In *Neuromancer*, the novel's main characters collaborate with a group called the Panther Moderns, 'mercenaries, practical jokers, nihilistic technofetishists' (*Neuromancer*, p. 75). The group's leader is named Lupus Yonderboy (*Neuromancer*, p. 87); later in the novel, *Neuromancer*'s protagonist, Case, will adopt this name, *Lupus*, 'Wolf', for himself (*Neuromancer*, p. 161). In *Count Zero*, an inexperienced Bobby Newmark finds himself collaborating with the members of a hacker subculture who are also practitioners of *vodou*, simultaneously 'a professional priesthood' and 'major dudes, console cowboys, among other things' (*Count Zero*, pp. 77–8). In *Virtual Light*, the hacker group Republic of Desire serve a similar function to the Panther

---

[9] On the privatisation of national security as a transgression of previously understood norms, see Singer, *Corporate Warriors*, p. 7.

[10] Gibson, 'Talk for Book Expo, New York', p. 45. Cf. Wallace-Wells, 'William Gibson: The Art of Fiction No. 211', p. 206.

[11] Diggle and Ball, 'An Interview with William Gibson', p. 104.

Moderns, but are portrayed in less benign terms: the former policeman Berry Rydell, though working with the group, sees them not as 'merry pranksters', but as criminals (*Virtual Light*, p. 338). In *Idoru* and *All Tomorrow's Parties*, we encounter a virtual space called Walled City, also known as Hak Nam, or 'City of darkness' (*Idoru*, p. 182). If the Republic of Desire are portrayed as criminals, the occupants of Walled City are idealists, or, at least, that's the way they tell it, as Zona Rosa explains to Chia McKenzie:

> This is not really how it happened, you understand, but this is how the story is told: that the people who founded Hak Nam were angry, because the net had been very free, you could do what you wanted, but then the governments and the companies, they had different ideas of what you could, what you couldn't do … They went there to get away from the laws. To have no laws, like when the net was new. (*Idoru*, p. 221)

When they appear in *All Tomorrow's Parties*, the representatives of Walled City balk at the suggestion that they are hackers. The term has criminal connotations that they reject, because they represent 'another country', 'an autonomous reality': in short, a virtual outlaw space (*All Tomorrow's Parties*, p. 126). If the virtual in Gibson is a nonspace (*Neuromancer*, p. 81), it is a nonspace that is vigorously contested.

Gibson's fiction also reminds us that not all marginal and/or outlaw groups are progressive in nature. In *Virtual Light*, the Bridge community and the hackers of Walled City are counterpointed with various hard-right groups, including: the video-cult following the Reverend Wayne Fallon; a group named the Revealed Aryan Nazarenes, alluded to but not encountered, who would 'as soon shoot you as look at you' (*Virtual Light*, p. 297); and, crucially, the seven 'heavily armed fundamentalists' from a white racist sect responsible for the murder of James Delmore Shapely, the AIDS saint (*Virtual Light*, p. 349). All of this serves as a reminder that we should qualify Eric Hobsbawm's archetype of the 'social bandit'. That archetype and Hobsbawm's *Bandits* are profoundly useful, of course, but as a Marxist historian, Hobsbawm sought to identify a positive social purpose, and perhaps revolutionary potential, in the figure of the outlaw. Gibson's complex portrayal of a mixture of marginal and oppositional communities in *Virtual Light* serves as a reminder that outlaw communities such as the Bridge community may well be progressive, but the opposite is equally possible. A similar caution about idealising outlaw groups is visible in the Matrix trilogy. David Wills argues that Wigan Ludgate's move to become an anti-Robin Hood, whose hacker career progresses from robbing the (well-protected) rich to robbing the (completely vulnerable) poor in his raid on the digital backwaters of Africa, and the pile of non-virtual corpses that result, represents the return of historical perspective to undercut any utopian notions we might have about this future world of cyberspace.[12]

Outlaw spaces, likewise, are not necessarily progressive, for the rich too have their own outlaw spaces, to different ends. In *Neuromancer*, Freeside is 'brothel and banking nexus, pleasure dome and free port, border town and spa' (*Neuromancer*, p. 125), subject to orbital law, and almost entirely owned by the Tessier-Ashpool clan (*Neuromancer*, p. 95). This is a dynasty whose survival strategy includes cloning, for which the orbital location proves handy:

> There were numerous laws forbidding or otherwise governing the artificial replication of an individual's genetic material, but there were also numerous questions of jurisdiction. (*Mona Lisa Overdrive*, p. 125)

Virtual Light features tax havens in the Channel Islands and data havens in Costa Rica (*Virtual Light*, pp. 77, 296). *Pattern Recognition*, likewise, has offshore tax havens (or *ofshornaya zona*) in Cyprus and Ingushetia (*Pattern Recognition*, p. 280).

The most prominent marginal group in the Bridge trilogy is the Bridge community itself, a collection of San Francisco's homeless who create a world of their own on the Bay Bridge, wrecked by the Little Grande earthquake, and replaced for traffic purposes by a nanomech tunnel (*Virtual Light*, pp. 102–3). The Bridge trilogy constructs an opposition between democratic and corporate space in both the real and virtual worlds. In the physical world, this opposition is represented by the Bridge, on the one hand, and the Sunflower project, a secret corporate plan to rebuild San Francisco against the wishes of its inhabitants (*Virtual Light*, p. 275), on the other. In the virtual world, a similar opposition exists between the net in general, controlled by governments and corporations, and the free space of Walled City. Both Walled City and the Bridge as portrayed by Gibson are indebted to the real space of Kowloon Walled City, a densely occupied enclave in post-war Hong Kong whose contested governance made it, effectively, a lawless zone.[13] As Zona Rosa explains it to Chia McKenzie:

> There was a place near an airport, Kowloon, when Hong Kong wasn't China, but there had been a mistake, a long time ago, and that place, very

---

[12] Wills, *Prosthesis*, pp. 79, 82. Ludgate's virtual raids upon the vulnerable are perhaps echoed again in the temporal 'third-worlding' of Gibson's *The Peripheral*, discussed in Mishan, 'The Future is Here'.

[13] Gibson's account is indebted to Girard and Lambot, *City of Darkness*; an updated edition, *City of Darkness Revisited*, was published in 2014.

small, many people, it still belonged to China. So there was no law there. An outlaw place. And more and more people crowded in; they built it up, higher. No rules, just building, just people living. Police wouldn't go there. Drugs and whores and gambling. But people living, too. Factories, restaurants. A city. No laws. (*Idoru*, p. 221)

If the Walled City of Gibson's novel is a virtual outlaw space, the Bridge is its physical equivalent. The inhabitants of the bridge, Rydell is told, are 'anarchists, antichrists, *cannibal* motherfuckers', who steal children (*Virtual Light*, pp. 165, 166). As Rydell summarises it (sarcastically), the bridge is populated entirely by 'baby-eatin' satanists' (*Virtual Light*, p. 167). The bridge is 'effectively outside the reach of the law', Lucius Warbaby tells Berry Rydell (*Virtual Light*, p. 167). And if the bridge and its community are regarded as dangerous, and effectively outlaw territory, Treasure Island represents those who are exiled yet further: 'wolf-men', 'bad crazies chased off the bridge', 'Mansons out in the bushes' (*Virtual Light*, pp. 190, 226).

But the Bridge is also a sort of bohemia, and across Gibson's fiction, outlaw zones are seen as necessary for creativity and innovation. *Neuromancer* opens with just such a place: Night City, Chiba, 'a narrow borderland of older streets, an area with no official name' (p. 13), a black market space for technology and genetics, 'a deliberately unsupervised playground for technology itself' (*Neuromancer*, p. 19). Gibson is on the record as questioning of whether spaces such as the Bridge are possible any longer in a globally networked culture,[14] and Cody Harwood has a speech in *All Tomorrow's Parties* to much the same effect (*All Tomorrow's Parties*, p. 174). Geography may not be an absolute requirement, however: in *Pattern Recognition*, the first novel of the Blue Ant trilogy,[15] the F: F: F listserv functions (as Gibson observes) as a sort of post-geographic virtual bohemia.[16]

Gibson's fiction, then, repeatedly represents marginal communities, oppositional groups and outlaw spaces who are often outside and at odds with state and corporate power, but his representation of these groups and spaces is complex, incorporating a spectrum of possibilities from bohemians and idealists to cult members and racists. The positioning of his protagonists is similarly nuanced. Gibson's protagonists vary through his later fiction, but all are outsiders of one sort or another. His sometime collaborator Bruce Sterling describes Gibson's work as a 'combination of lowlife and high tech', his characters 'a pirate's crew of losers, hustlers, spin-offs, castoffs, and

---

[14] Wallace-Wells, 'William Gibson: The Art of Fiction No. 211', p. 224.
[15] Gibson, *Pattern Recognition*; Gibson, *Spook Country*; Gibson, *Zero History*.
[16] Wallace-Wells, 'William Gibson: The Art of Fiction No. 211', p. 227.

lunatics'.[17] Gibson himself describes his early heroes with computer chips in their heads as 'information highwaymen';[18] in the fiction works themselves, they are repeatedly called 'cowboys' – wild young men[19] – though not all, of course, are male. In the back cover material for *Mona Lisa Overdrive*, they are 'high-tech outlaws'.[20]

The way in which these protagonists interact with the powerful and the marginal is complex. Outsiders to start with, Gibson's protagonists tend to find themselves recruited by the powerful in pursuit of particular objectives. Case and Molly work for Wintermute, Turner for the corporates, Marly Krushkova for Josef Virek, Angie Mitchell as a simstim star, Berry Rydell for IntenSecure, Colin Laney for SlitScan and then Lo/Rez, Cayce Pollard and Hollis Henry for Hubertus Bigend. In doing so, they enlist the assistance of the various outlaw groups. Almost inevitably, they discover the objectives of their employers, which they then seek to sabotage (the most prominent exception being the protagonists of *Neuromancer*, who succeed in the task they are set). In more than one case, we see a protagonist resolve to conceal their discovery from their employer: not always successfully. Only timing saves Marly Krushkova from inadvertently delivering a lifeline to Josef Virek. Cayce Pollard intends to keep the identity of the Volkovas hidden from Bigend, only to discover that larger forces were always in play. Hollis Henry has more luck in keeping Cayce herself concealed from view. Although outsiders, Gibson's protagonists are co-opted by the powerful, if not entirely complicit in their doings, and consequently find themselves in positions that are at the very least ambivalent.

Aleph and Panopticon

Gibson has noted that he owes his image for 'total artificial reality', 'a point in space that contains all other points', to Jorge Luis Borges's short story 'The Aleph'.[21] This idea of the Aleph, of a totality of information, appears in different guises across the novels. It is particularly apparent in *Mona Lisa Overdrive*, where we meet an unconscious Bobby Newmark strapped to a stretcher and plugged into an object that Cherry Chesterfield and Slick Henry initially think is called an 'LF'. It is, as Thomas Gentry later explains to them, an 'aleph', in a sense an approximation of everything (*Mona Lisa Overdrive*, pp. 45, 141, 154). Gentry himself has been convinced that cyberspace has

[17] Sterling, 'Preface', pp. 11, 12.
[18] Gibson, 'Will We Have Computer Chips in Our Heads?', p. 213.
[19] *OED*, s.v. *cowboy*, n., 3(b).
[20] Gibson, *Mona Lisa Overdrive*, rear cover text.
[21] Wallace-Wells, 'William Gibson: The Art of Fiction No. 211', p. 223; Borges, 'The Aleph'.

a Shape, an overall total form, and he sees Newmark's arrival at the Factory with the aleph as a means for him to progress his search for the shape (*Mona Lisa Overdrive*, pp. 75–6, 108, 178) (Angela Mitchell's final verdict is that Gentry is 'eccentric', 'mad' (*Mona Lisa Overdrive*, p. 284)). In Gibson's work, this idea of a totality of data is an optimistic one, filled with implicit creative potential. We may remember that for Maurice Blanchot, Borges's Aleph is a figure for the literary. 'I suspect Borges of having acquired the infinite from literature', he says. 'The book is in principle the world for him, and the world is a book'.[22] If so, the Aleph is a figure for an infinite universe somehow made finite, and, being booklike, perhaps even readable.

In the Bridge trilogy, the extravagant amount of data generated by individuals in a digital world enables Colin Laney's work as a researcher, tracking 'the sort of signature a particular individual inadvertently created in the net as he or she went about the mundane yet endlessly multiplex business of life in a digital society' (*Idoru*, p. 25). Laney progresses from being an intuitive, savant-like data researcher (like Cayce Pollard in *Pattern Recognition*, a dowser of sorts) to being obsessively immersed in something approximating the totality of the world's data. Partly as a result of being dosed with a drug, 5-SB, in the Gainesville orphanage where he spent his teens, he acquires 'a directly *spatial* sense of something very near the totality of the infosphere', 'the literal shape of all human knowledge', and that immersion in the totality of data comes to constitute who he is (*All Tomorrow's Parties*, pp. 106, 107, 163). This sense of totality sees him move from an ability to predict near-future possibilities for individuals, such as his intuition that Alison Shires, an actor's mistress, will attempt suicide (*Idoru*, pp. 41, 51–8), to an ability to detect patterns in history more broadly. History, that is, as 'stored data, subject to manipulation and interpretation', or, otherwise, 'that *shape* comprised of every narrative, every version' (*All Tomorrow's Parties*, p. 165). Laney achieves this perspective while living (or rather dying) in a cardboard container in a Tokyo subway station, progressing through 'all the data in the world' (*All Tomorrow's Parties*, p. 163).

But the idea of the Aleph, or the shape, a figure for the totality of human knowledge in searchable form, is held in tension in Gibson's work with the awareness that such a totality creates the possibility of surveillance and control: a digital Panopticon. As noted in the previous chapter, Bentham's Panopticon achieved its contemporary prominence as a model for total surveillance via Foucault's *Discipline and Punish*.[23] Writing in the

---

[22] Blanchot, 'Literary Infinity: The Aleph', pp. 93, 94.
[23] Also discussed above, Chapter 6.

1970s, Foucault described the emergence of omnipresent police surveillance in eighteenth-century France via a hierarchised network of thousands of eyes.[24] But if the Panopticon of the state was imaginable in an era when information had to be gathered manually, item by item, via human intelligence, consider the possibilities for panopticism in a society where a totality of data is available electronically. This is very much the world of all three of Gibson's trilogies, and now also our own. At different points in the Sprawl trilogy, then, Bobby Newmark, Marly Krushkova and Kumiko Yanaka find themselves under electronic surveillance, and accordingly face challenges in performing simple tasks without giving themselves away (*Count Zero*, pp. 37, 73, 74–5, *Mona Lisa Overdrive*, pp. 217–18).

In the Bridge Trilogy, again, the idea of the Aleph exists in tension with the idea of the Panopticon, acknowledged as a model for total surveillance here to the extent that chapter 39 of *All Tomorrow's Parties* has the word 'Panopticon' as its title. Colin Laney's work, initially for a tabloid media show called Slitscan, involves surveillance that strays outside legal boundaries:

> 'Some of that was illegal', Laney said. 'You're tied into parts of DatAmerica
> that you aren't supposed to be'.
> 'Do you know what a nondisclosure agreement is, Laney?' (*Idoru*, p. 38)

He does. As the work he is doing involves frequent illegal uses of the enormous DatAmerica database (DatAmerica being 'a law unto itself'), his job requires one (*Idoru*, p. 55).

Throughout Gibson's work, then, there is conflict between power gained and power ceded via the rise of the virtual.[25] That tension remains potent in Gibson's Blue Ant trilogy, set in the early twenty-first century, where surveillance is once again associated with the agents of the state.

Secrecy, Surveillance and the Digital Panopticon

The Blue Ant trilogy differs from the Sprawl and Bridge trilogies in that it is not explicitly science fiction, and is not set in the future: *Pattern Recognition*, in particular, contains a substantial concern with history.[26] But if the Sprawl trilogy is haunted by spectral Artificial Intelligences who sit in the background manipulating events (first Wintermute, then the fragments of the sentient Matrix who manifest as *loa* haunting the virtual realm), the Blue

[24] Foucault, *Discipline and Punish*, p. 214.
[25] Palmer, '*Mona Lisa Overdrive* and the Prosthetic', p. 231.
[26] For a discussion of the historicist positions adopted in the novel, see Easterbrook, 'Alternate Presents'.

Ant trilogy in turn is haunted by intelligence agencies and surveillance systems.

Cayce Pollard's search for the creators of the footage that she is following obsessively online is initially frustrated by Dorotea Benedetti, a former practitioner of industrial espionage and *Pattern Recognition*'s most straightforward villain (*Pattern Recognition*, p. 63). Benedetti's employer is an arm of the security apparatus of a Russian oligarch, Andrei Volkov: Volkov's nieces, Stella and Nora, will turn out to be the objects of Cayce's search. Cayce's borrowed London flat and New York apartment are entered, her phone and email are monitored, her psychologist's records are copied, and there is a brief attempt to physically follow her in Tokyo. Cayce's email is also compromised by Boone Chu, her supposed collaborator, on behalf of their mutual employer, Hubertus Bigend (*Pattern Recognition*, p. 328).

Cayce, in turn, will eventually succeed in identifying the Volkovas through co-opting a former cryptographer, Hobbs-Baranov, now a marginal figure who occasionally trades in signals intelligence (*Pattern Recognition*, p. 219). Such intelligence (as Ngemi explains it to Cayce) is sourced from a system called 'Echelon', that scans all Net traffic (*Pattern Recognition*, p. 244). Volkov's head of security, Wiktor Marchwinska-Wyrwal, on hearing Cayce's none-too-informative account of how she found the Volkovas, quickly identifies this as her source (*Pattern Recognition*, p. 342).

Cayce's response to the footage, and her search for its maker, is entwined with her search for the truth of her father's disappearance. Wingrove Pollard, unexpectedly present in New York on 9/11, is 'a man so thoroughly and quietly missing that it might be impossible to prove him dead' (*Pattern Recognition*, p. 187). Wingrove Pollard, too, had a background in the covert world (*Pattern Recognition*, p. 44), and it was their recognition of Cayce as the daughter of 'this brilliant man, an old opponent' that prompted the ex-KGB elements around Volkov to act against her (*Pattern Recognition*, p. 339). When Cayce finally contacts the Volkovas, she mentions her father's disappearance before saying anything about the footage; Stella's response in turn tells of the loss of her own parents in a bombing (*Pattern Recognition*, pp. 254, 260). In the end, it so happens that the most comprehensive account of Wingrove Pollard's final morning also comes from Volkov's security.

Surveillance remains a key ingredient of *Spook Country*, the next instalment in the trilogy. The novel's villains are rogue contractors who work for the government, except when they don't (*Spook Country*, p. 148): *Spook Country*, like some recent John le Carré novels, here reflects the real and substantial rise in private contractors as part of the intelligence landscape post-9/11.[27] Opposing these contractors is an unnamed old man, a former counterintelligence officer, but himself now 'a renegade, a rogue player'. Deemed mad by some in the Cuban crime family who are assisting him, he remains well connected among other 'old spooks', some retired or forced out, others still in post (*Spook Country*, pp. 147, 319). The book's MacGuffin is a shipping container holding $100 million in cash siphoned from US funds intended for Iraq's reconstruction, still at sea years later. The old man has made it his business to prevent the laundering of the missing money.

Tito, the young Cuban assisting the old man, is being followed; his living space is bugged. The shipping container full of cash is being tracked by a 'geohacker', Bobby Chombo (*Spook Country*, p. 34); Chombo, in turn, is being tracked via a GPS tracking device attached to his truck (*Spook Country*, p. 198). Hollis Henry, pursuing Chombo on behalf of her employer Hubertus Bigend, is also being tracked, both via a GPS tracking device on her phone (*Spook Country*, p. 333) and a bugged Blue Ant figurine (*Zero History*, p. 194).

This obsession with surveillance continues in *Zero History*. London has cameras 'literally everywhere' (*Zero History*, p. 57). There is discussion of technology like Faraday pouches (to prevent data theft) and HERF guns (to erase data from an adjunct location) (*Zero History*, pp. 25, 42). Some of the plot circles around Milgrim's mobile phone, which is being used both to track him and to eavesdrop (*Zero History*, pp. 122–4). Heidi Hyde's room at the bizarre hotel where she and Hollis Henry are staying has a theme that 'seemed to be about spies, sad ones, in some very British sense, and seedy political scandal' (*Zero History*, p. 50). The room's furnishings include a giant china ear; its pair is later discovered in a shopfront window (*Zero History*, pp. 59, 154). This is a novel where rooms and streets literally have ears seeming to listen in.

In these worlds of universal surveillance, anonymity gains a new importance. Milgrim is an outsider to the world of information accumulation. Like Mona in *Mona Lisa Overdrive*, he is something of an innocent standing outside the complexities of the mainstream, who has nonetheless wandered right into the heart of the plot. His ten years as a drug user have left him with no credit rating or address history: 'zero history' as Winnie Tung Whitaker of the Department of Defence describes it (*Zero History*, p. 84). Like Mona, he is so socially marginal as to be almost invisible.

In keeping with this sense of anonymity as desirable, and also the dual sense of 'spook' as undercover agent or spy, but also ghost or apparition,[28]

[27] See Singer, *Corporate Warriors*; Weiner, *Legacy of Ashes*, pp. 591–3.
[28] *OED*, s.v. *spook*, n., 1, 2.

several of the characters of *Spook Country* and *Zero History* appear somewhat spectral, not quite manifest, never fully revealed. This extends all the way down to the level of naming: Garreth is named simply as Garreth. He has a surname, of course, but the one he offers to Bigend is not really his (*Zero History*, pp. 147, 280). The old man, his mentor, is even more mysterious, having no name at all, and in the transition from *Spook Country* to *Zero History* he has moved offstage, no longer physically present, simply a voice from the darknets.

At the end of *Zero History*, we are again reminded that the agents of the state like to stay off-camera (as Wingrove Pollard does so successfully on 9/11). Garreth, in putting together a rescue for the kidnapped Bobby Chombo, acquires from the old man what he describes as 'the ugliest T-shirt in the world'. The garment bears a symbol (or 'sigil', suggesting its quasi-magical properties) that causes London's ubiquitous surveillance cameras to forget both the T-shirt and its wearer (*Zero History*, p. 345). This is technology developed by industry, government, and 'that lucrative sector … that might be either, or both' (*Zero History*, p. 302), in order to facilitate rendition. Garreth and his collaborators set up Chombo's kidnappers to look like terrorists; the police who come to collect them at the end of the novel 'aren't on the books' and take them to 'a special kind of detention' (*Zero History*, p. 395).

The surveillance motif in these recent Gibson novels comes with an explicit contemporary context of an enormous programme of state surveillance by the US's National Security Agency (NSA). As Hollis Henry and Hubertus Bigend comment in conversation:

> 'Wasn't the NSA or someone tapping your phone, reading your e-mail?'
> 'But now we know that they were doing that to everyone'. (*Zero History*, p. 23)

While Gibson is clear that he is not consciously writing from an expressed political philosophy, and in particular he is anxious to avoid political didacticism,[29] the digital Panopticon and the potential power relations inherent in a world gone digital are, of course, very much problems of our current reality. The scale of information being generated and recorded has increased enormously in recent years, and, by 2013, some 98 per cent of that data was being stored digitally: the rise of 'big data', as it is known. As Kenneth Cukier and Viktor Mayer-Schoenberger comment, 'companies such as Google, Amazon, and Facebook – as well as lesser-known "data brokers,"

---

[29] Newitz, 'William Gibson talks to *io9*', p. 196.

such as Acxiom and Experian – are amassing vast amounts of information on everyone and everything', in an explosion of data accumulation which poses substantial privacy concerns, concerns that 'current technologies and laws seem unlikely to prevent'.[30]

To this list of Google, Acxiom and their ilk, we should also add the telephone companies and, particularly in the wake of Edward Snowden's revelations, the intelligence agencies. In May 2013, NSA contractor Edward Snowden revealed the extent of the electronic surveillance conducted by the NSA and its counterparts in the 'Five Eyes' intelligence alliance (which comprises the US, Canada, UK, Australia and New Zealand), with the co-operation of US technology companies. Snowden's revelations about the extent of digital surveillance by intelligence agencies show us the extent to which the tension between these two models of the Aleph and the Panopticon is more than a fictional construct. This is a system of surveillance, as the journalist Glenn Greenwald says, reminiscent of Bentham's Panopticon.[31]

Such surveillance has a legal context. In the US, NSA domestic surveillance is governed by the Foreign Intelligence Surveillance Act (1978).[32] This law, conventionally referred to as FISA, creates a court, known as the FISA Court, to hear applications and grant orders for electronic surveillance. Surveillance activities not covered by FISA are governed by Executive Order 12333, initially issued by President Ronald Reagan.[33] In 2001, the Bush administration authorised a programme called 'Stellarwind', involving warrantless eavesdropping on communications and bulk collection of telephone and email data in violation of both FISA and Executive Order 12333, based on their interpretation of the President's powers as commander-in-chief.[34] A 2004 dispute within the Bush administration about the legality of these programmes saw bulk email collection temporarily suspended; the warrantless wiretapping component of the programme became public in 2005 (in *Spook Country*, Milgrim reads about these revelations in *The New York Times*). These programmes were (in slightly modified form) then brought under the authority of the FISA Court.[35] In 2008, the FISA Amendments Act, in Glenn

---

[30] Cukier and Mayer-Schoenberger, 'The Rise of Big Data'.
[31] Greenwald, *No Place to Hide*, pp. 175–6. For the implications for surveillance in the UK, see Lanchester, 'The Snowden files'.
[32] Foreign Intelligence Surveillance Act 1978 (50 US Code ch. 36).
[33] Reagan, 'Executive Order 12333 – United States Intelligence Activities'.
[34] Greenwald, *No Place to Hide*, pp. 1–2; Savage, *Power Wars*, pp. 180–7. Savage, p. 185, cites a supporting memo that suggests 'an executive order cannot limit a President'.
[35] Savage, *Power Wars*, pp. 190–211.

Greenwald's words, 'effectively legalized the crux of Bush's illegal program'.[36] The Obama administration both continued and expanded these surveillance programmes,[37] though the introduction of the USA FREEDOM Act in 2015 placed some restrictions on NSA data collection.[38]

Though US surveillance programmes now exist in a firmer legal context than they did post-2001 when executive authority was used to override legislative restraint, there are still reasons for concern. First, Glenn Greenwald questions the status of such state surveillance given the Fourth Amendment's guarantees of privacy.[39] Secondly, surveillance is, to a large extent, based on secret law. As David Luban comments:

> Notably, the bulk collection of metadata by the NSA was approved under secret legal interpretations that were reluctantly made public following the Snowden revelations. These interpretations were not merely secret; they were flatly contrary to what many people supposed the law meant. Secret law undermines the rule of law, as legal theorists beginning with Kant have insisted: citizens must be able to know the law under which they are being governed.[40]

Citizens and, we might add, legislators: asked about surveillance of Americans in a public hearing, Director of National Intelligence James Clapper allegedly misled the Senate Intelligence Committee.[41] Thirdly, even where secret surveillance is legally regulated, there is reason to question the effectiveness of such regulation. Wikileaks's Julian Assange and some of his colleagues have been sceptical of the practical possibility of effective legal regulation of bulk data collection: 'the technology is inherently so complex, and its use in practice so secret that there cannot be meaningful democratic oversight'.[42] In practice, we find, several NSA surveillance programmes violated FISA court rules,[43] and other government agencies, it emerged, were also collecting similar data (the DEA's data collection programme was discovered and shut down in 2013).[44] Fourthly, the global nature of telecommunications may offer ways

[36] Greenwald, *No Place to Hide*, p. 74.
[37] Savage, *Power Wars*, pp. 555–626.
[38] USA FREEDOM Act 2015.
[39] Greenwald, *No Place to Hide*, pp. 2–3, and cf. Savage, *Power Wars*, pp. 37, 50, 166, 171, 188, 209, 556, 571–3, 624.
[40] Luban, 'Has Obama Upheld the Law?'. Cf. Horn, *Secret War*, pp. 77–8, on Agamben, Kafka and secret law.
[41] Savage, *Power Wars*, pp. 580–2.
[42] Assange et al., *Cypherpunks*, p. 42.
[43] Savage, *Power Wars*, pp. 165–7, 180–7, 564–6, 571–3.
[44] Savage, *Power Wars*, pp. 600–3.

around regulation: it has been suggested that the US may now be bypassing legal restrictions on domestic data capture via data collection overseas.[45]

William Gibson's views on recent issues of technology and privacy, views which overlap with some of the issues raised in his fictions, are on the record. In a 2010 article, he acknowledges that emergent technologies 'leave legislation in the dust'; we 'necessarily legislate after the fact, perpetually scrambling to catch up, while the core architectures of the future, increasingly, are erected by entities like Google'.[46] In the same article, he acknowledges the Panopticon as a potential model for thinking about digital surveillance, while simultaneously suggesting (as does Ciaran Carson in different circumstances) that contemporary practice requires a somewhat more complex variation on the model.[47]

Gibson is unconvinced, however, that we are on the road to an Orwellian (or Kafkaesque, or Foucauldian) nightmare of the all-seeing state. His view is that increased information transparency will ultimately prove democratic in nature. Talking about *Spook Country* in 2008, Gibson suggests that in the novel, old ideologies shape the initial phases of a long-term change towards information transparency, but that the nature of that change will inevitably leave those ideologies behind, unable to keep up.[48] He had something similar to say in a 2003 essay;[49] and in a 2012 coda to that essay, Gibson affirms his belief in eventual progress to a 'full-on Borgesian digital singularity' in which 'pretty much all will eventually have been revealed'.[50]

There are at least three immediate points to raise against Gibson's optimistic argument for eventual democratic transparency in the digital sphere: one theoretical, one technical and one legal. First, Gibson suggests that technological change will outstrip ideologies of power, but in fact mechanisms of power are adaptable. In an interview with Gilles Deleuze that pre-dates the web, Antonio Negri draws attention to 'three kinds of power: sovereign power, disciplinary power, and above all the control of "communication" that's on the way to becoming hegemonic'. Deleuze agrees, citing Foucault to suggest a move away from disciplinary societies and toward control societies that operate through continuous control and instant communication.[51]

Secondly, a technical point: the data sets available to the broader public

---

[45] Savage, *Power Wars*, pp. 565–6; Wheeler, 'John Bates' TWO Wiretapping Warnings'.
[46] Gibson, 'Google's Earth'.
[47] Gibson, 'Google's Earth'.
[48] Newitz, 'William Gibson talks to *io9*', p. 195.
[49] Gibson, 'The Road to Oceania', p. 168.
[50] Gibson, 'The Road to Oceania', p. 171.
[51] Deleuze, 'Control and Becoming', pp. 174–5.

are very different from the data sets owned by the telephone companies, the financial institutions, the marketing companies, the search engines, and the social media companies, all of which have the potential to assemble far more information on individuals than can be done via publicly available data. There is a sense of corporately owned data being less than transparent in Gibson's Bridge Trilogy, for example, where DatAmerica has possession of data which is not available to the police. In the real world, as we now know via Edward Snowden, security agencies also have very extensive access to corporate data from multiple sources, in addition to their own data gathering and monitoring resources.

Thirdly, a legal issue: this enormous increase in information and its availability is occurring simultaneously with moves towards increased secrecy by Western governments via measures such as secret courts and reporting restrictions. 'Closed material procedures' in the UK's Justice and Security Act (2013) provide for secret court hearings in cases dealing with (among other issues) information relating to national security.[52] Australia's National Security Legislation Amendment Bill (No. 1) (2014) contains penalties for disclosure of information relating to special intelligence operations.[53] In short, big data (and mass surveillance) is already here, but it remains unevenly distributed, and moves to increase secrecy see states seeking to ensure it remains so.

The virtual, then, offers potential for the Aleph and the Panopticon, but the space remains contested. If the net is a formerly non-profit space now dominated by a few large corporations, and both corporations and the state use the net to monitor the activities of its billions of users, the virtual nonetheless remains very much a contested space. To a certain extent, that contest is prosecuted via organisations such as the hacktivist group Anonymous[54] and the freedom-of-information group Wikileaks,[55] though Julian Assange's notion that Wikileaks might be 'the people's intelligence agency'[56] has since been tarnished by suggestions that the group was used by Russian Intelligence to manipulate the 2016 Presidential election in the United States.[57] Other

---

[52] Justice and Security Act 2013. For the use of these procedures in practice, see Cobain, *The History Thieves*, pp. 254–91.

[53] National Security Legislation Amendment Bill (No. 1) 2014.

[54] The evolution of various group activities under the 'Anonymous' umbrella is documented in Coleman, *Hacker, Hoaxer, Whistleblower, Spy*.

[55] As described in Assange et al., *Cypherpunks*, p. 13: 'it is Wikileaks' mission to receive information from whistleblowers, release it to the public, and then defend against the inevitable legal and political attacks'.

[56] Manne, *Cypherpunk Revolutionary*, p. 99.

[57] 'Assessing Russian Activities and Intentions in Recent US Elections'.

contests are being played out also, as mutual intimidation between military powers migrates online: there have been a number of cyberwarfare incidents that have received public attention, such as Russia's 2007 cyberattacks on Estonia, the use of Stuxnet by the US against Iranian nuclear facilities in 2010, and mutual accusations of cyberattacks between the US and China.[58] But the surprising lesson from the suggestions of Russian involvement in the 2016 US election was that 'cyberwarfare' need not be, as we might have expected, an online attack that mimics the effects of real-world physical assault by disabling physical assets and/or networks. Such scenarios are still both plausible and ominous, of course, but what we saw in 2016 was that the online distribution of propaganda and disinformation by intelligence services was in itself effective enough to constitute cyberwarfare – deeply unsettling the power structures of the world's most powerful nation. Digital power relations, then, remain both contested and crucial – the ongoing tension between the simultaneously emerging possibilities of the internet as both a utopian space for knowledge and transparency and a dystopian nightmare of mass surveillance and control of communication by states and corporations remains a fundamental aspect of the contest for the virtual. In the contemporary world, as in Gibson's fiction, the virtual remains contested, and in a world where cyberspace has 'everted' (to use Gibson's term), the contest for the virtual is also very much a contest for the real.

[58] On cyberwarfare in general, see Singer and Friedman, *Cybersecurity and Cyberwar*, pp. 114–65.

Conclusion

This book has sought to pursue four arguments. Firstly, it has sought to show that legal exclusion, in various and related forms, is a tactic of power. Commentators from Maitland, to Keen, to Hobsbawm have suggested that outlawry is a phenomenon of a weak state, and there is some truth to this. Outlawry is sometimes a remedy for the weakness of power in the Middle Ages and afterwards; marginal spaces, likewise, are likely sites for banditry to flourish. But this is only part of the story. As we have argued throughout, legal exclusion is also a proactive tactic of the state, a way of asserting and defending sovereign power, and outlawry serves political as well as legal purposes across the medieval period: from Ine of Wessex's outlawry of his rival Ealdberht in the seventh century, to the outlawry of figures such as William Wallace in support of England's bid for political dominance across the archipelago in the later Middle Ages. This proactive purpose helps to explain both the endurance of outlawry well into the late nineteenth century, and its alignment with other forms of exclusion from law.

If legal exclusion is a tactic of power, it is a tactic that encompasses not only exclusion below the law, but also exclusion above it. The sovereign has extralegal status, albeit a status always debated and contested: hence Kantorowicz's formula, where the medieval English king is *rex infra et super legem*, a king both under and above the law. This is a tension reflected, among other places, at the heart of Shakespeare's *Richard II*. The extralegal status of the sovereign and the outlaw, both excluded from law, one above, one below, leads to unexpected parallels (as noted by both Derrida and Agamben). Sometimes the outlaw's challenge to sovereignty leads to a certain resemblance to the sovereign: Gamelyn is crowned king of the outlaws, and there are suggestive parallels between Robin Hood and the legendary King Arthur. In fourteenth-century Yorkshire, an outlaw named Lionel signs himself 'king of the rout of raveners'; in nineteenth-century Australia, Michael Howe calls himself 'Lieutenant-Governor of the Woods', and Ned Kelly threatens his opponents with outlawry. Sometimes exclusion above and below the law work in tandem. In *Richard II*, after Bolingbroke's return from exile, neither he as outlaw nor Richard as sovereign have status within the law. Sometimes, because outlawry can be a political weapon as well as a legal one, sovereigns and outlaws are somewhat interchangeable figures, as we see in various representations of William Wallace, Robert Bruce, and, again, *Richard II*'s Henry Bolingbroke.

Another tactical form of legal exclusion usefully read in tandem with outlawry is the non-recognition of the sovereign status of neighbouring territories, their rulers, and their legal systems, which are rendered subservient to, and ultimately replaceable by, the legal and governmental systems of the emerging English state. Likewise, if nineteenth-century Australia sees the recurrence of outlawry in its formal legal sense, the use of this tactic against colonial bushrangers is supplementary to the use of much more severe and enduring legal exclusions directed at the country's Indigenous population. In our own era, we see the endurance of this tactic of non-recognition in contemporary political rhetoric concerning 'rogue states'. Outlawry, then, the exclusion of individuals from legal protection, is not merely a reactive gesture by a weak state, or a mode of resistance by those fighting injustice. Rather, outlawry is a tactic of power, one aligned with a range of other forms of exclusion from law, employed in defending, consolidating or extending state or sovereign power.

Our second argument is that if legal exclusion is a tactic of power, it is an enduring one. While outlawry in its legal sense is now an historical phenomenon, exclusion from law as a tactic of power is anything but. One of the most obvious and significant ways in which the contemporary state licences itself to act extralegally is via the creation of secret services, and both Timothy Melley and Eva Horn link this covert sphere to Agamben's theorisation (after Schmitt) of the 'state of exception'.[1] The secret activities of the state, Horn writes, constitute 'a covert but continuous state of exception, the *irregular* side of power itself'.[2] Such agencies play an important role in the international politics of the twentieth and twenty-first centuries, particularly during the Cold War and its aftermath. In the instances discussed here, extralegal actions by these agencies or their personnel include torture, collusion with terrorists to kill civilians, the staging of foreign coups, the operation of secret mass surveillance programmes, and the extraordinary rendition of detainees to third-party states. Here, again, exclusion above and below the law work in tandem: in the twenty-first century practice of extraordinary rendition, for instance (the subject of fictional reflections by John le Carré

---

[1] Melley, *Covert Sphere*, p. 5; Horn, *Secret War*, pp. 37, 93, 95.
[2] Horn, *Secret War*, p. 37.

and Don DeLillo), the US and its allies in the War on Terror detained individuals in territories where they were not subject to legal protections for purposes including torture. Western intelligence agencies were licensed to act outside of various national and international laws prohibiting torture, while the individuals detained had their legal protections against practices such as torture removed.

Extralegal action by the state in the contemporary era occurs in a variety of different ways. In some instances, it occurs because the executive has the power to license extralegal activity by the intelligence services: as in section 7 of the UK's Intelligence Services Act's granting the Secretary of State power to authorise SIS actions outside the law, or 50 US Code 3093's granting Presidential power to approve covert actions. In other cases, as in Northern Ireland, extralegal activity occurs in tandem with the formal adoption of Emergency Powers. Gaps, omissions and contested interpretations of law can prove enabling: examples range from the creation of British intelligence services without any fixed statutory basis, through the American use of executive powers with the force of law to modify and sometimes contradict legislative imperatives. Sometimes the legal justification for the executive's licensing of extralegal action is itself secret: NSA domestic surveillance post-9/11 in violation of FISA and Executive Order 12333 was enabled by classified legal memos arguing Presidential authority. Extralegal activity can occur indirectly – via third-party individuals, companies, or states – in ways that range from hiring contractors to employing extraordinary rendition. It can involve either state intent, or rogue actions by state agents, where the state sometimes fails after the fact to investigate in search of the truth, or to implement the law.[3] But while extralegal action by the state is both historically situated, and tactically variable, it is nonetheless both enduring and substantial. Both the extent of legal exclusion, and its institutionalisation, implies that, as Derrida suggests, in fact all states are rogue states, acting outside the law: 'As soon as there is sovereignty, there is abuse of power and a rogue state'.[4]

Our third argument is that exclusion from law is a shared concern between the literatures of outlawry and espionage, and consequently a key theme in writing about the state and its actions at the heart of a wide range of literary texts in English from the Middle Ages to the present day. Arguing that legal exclusion is a key concern in the literature of outlawry should be straightforward. Exclusion is explicitly the subject matter of these

---

[3] Luban, 'Has Obama Upheld the Law?' says of the Obama administration's decision not to hold CIA operatives accountable for alleged torture, that 'official impunity is, always and everywhere, the archenemy of the rule of law'.

[4] Derrida, *Rogues*, p. 102.

texts – there is no outlaw literature without exclusion. But exclusion's central place in this body of literature can be obscured by an emphasis on the bandit as a figure of resistance. As we saw in Chapter 1, if medieval literary texts do offer a view of outlawry that overlaps substantially with Hobsbawm's model of the 'social bandit', legal texts offer a construction of the outlaw closer to that of Agamben's *homo sacer*. Furthermore, even in the literary texts, a focus on loyalty and community support counterbalances rather than negates the dangers faced by the excluded – if medieval outlaw literature has elements of wish-fulfilment, the dangers of exclusion are always a latent presence. To emphasise exclusion in this way is not simply to replace one archetype (the 'social bandit') with another (the *homo sacer*). As we have seen, both outlawry and its literature can be seen as complex, nuanced and historically situated: as we saw in Chapter 3, for instance, Ned Kelly may be read as 'social bandit', *homo sacer*, Irish rebel and Australian myth. Furthermore, the 'social bandit' archetype retains a certain validity. It does, however, potentially obscure the state's use of legal exclusion, not as an act of weakness, but as an act of power.

The situation with espionage literature is almost the opposite. Exclusion is not so obviously a key theme in these works, but a range of critical writing has highlighted its importance. Timothy Melley and Eva Horn have drawn our attention to the parallels between the covert sphere and Agamben's theorisation of the 'state of exception', and Phyllis Lassner has noted that 'whether enforced or voluntary, exile is endemic to the secret worlds of espionage and to the character of spies'.[5] Throughout Chapters 4 to 7, then, we have encountered numerous examples of espionage paired with exclusion, beginning with John le Carré's Alec Leamas: servant of the state and an entirely excluded figure, as much an outcast as any *homo sacer*. This dual sense of the spy's extralegal exclusion, being potentially both above and below the law, means the medieval parallel between the sovereign and the outlaw is reconfigured in these contemporary texts as a parallel between the spy and a series of excluded figures. Phyllis Lassner notes that elsewhere in le Carré, Elsa Fennan's dual role as Jewish refugee and Cold War spy highlights the exile and exclusion shared by both. Such parallels are revisited in a more recent le Carré novel, *The Mission Song*, where Bruno Salvador begins the novel working for British Intelligence, but ends it in a detention camp, deprived of his name, citizenship and rights. In Don DeLillo's *Libra*, we find a rogue CIA agent, T-Jay Mackey, conspiring with his former colleagues, other interested parties, and the enigmatic figure of Lee Harvey Oswald to carry out a political assassination. In Ciaran Carson's *The Pen Friend*, we find that

---

[5] Lassner, *Espionage and Exile*, p. 3.

MO2's Miranda Bowyer seems to know too much about a bombing where security forces are suspected of colluding with terrorists, and five civilians are killed. In William Gibson's Blue Ant trilogy, ex-spooks like the former cryptographer Hobbs-Baranov and an unnamed former counterintelligence officer aid Gibson's protagonists in navigating a world of total surveillance. The spy, then, or sometimes that doubly excluded figure, the ex-spy, is shown in these works to resemble a number of other pariah figures: the terrorist, the political assassin, the hacker, and the refugee. This archetype of the agent as outcast is important not because it is to be read as realistic, but because it allows espionage literature to both represent and critique the state's very real use of exclusion as a tactic of power.

Our fourth argument is that if exclusion from law is an important theme in writing about the state and its actions from the Middle Ages to the present day, the role of literature in contemplating such action by the state is often to offer critique. Medieval outlaw literature's attacks on the justice system are easily aligned with the extensive later medieval literature of satire and complaint. John le Carré's ethically ambiguous thrillers successfully complicate any potential sense of the Cold War as merely a simple moral conflict between freedom and totalitarianism. Ciaran Carson's writings about the Northern Ireland Troubles seek to ask questions, to offer alternatives to the official account, which 'is only an account, and there are many others'.[6]

In casting their critical eye over events and their official accounts, these texts repeatedly draw our attention to the consequences and risks posed by extralegal action. If Shakespeare's second tetralogy asks whether the sovereign must act outside the law to defend the state, it also asks whether by doing so the sovereign places his own authority at hazard? Don DeLillo's novels offer a contemporary version of the same question, asking whether the work of intelligence agencies, supposedly intended to protect the state and its citizens, instead creates unintended and unforeseen dangers, both from within and without? Le Carré, DeLillo and Gibson all question the implications of corporate involvement in the secret actions of the state, suggesting risks that range from corruption to the hollowing out of state power. Several texts question the extent to which the agents of the state, once licensed to act secretly outside the law, can be either trusted or controlled? Hence Lacon's suspicion of both Control and Smiley in the backstory to *Tinker Tailor Soldier Spy*. Hence too the possibility in *Libra* that CIA agents tasked with killing Fidel Castro might also have been behind killing John F. Kennedy. We see too

---

[6] Brown, 'Ciaran Carson', pp. 148–9.

that the state is prepared to sacrifice not only its agents, but also civilians in pursuit of its ends – from the hostages killed by police fire at the siege of Glenrowan to the suggestion of state collusion in terrorist bombings in *The Pen Friend.*

Extralegal action also leads to a real sense of uncertainty around events that occur covertly in an enduring atmosphere of secrecy and deception. The questioning of such uncertainties is particularly acute in the work of Ciaran Carson, with its emphasis on unanswered questions, uncertain events and unstable identities, but is also visible more broadly across these texts. In these literary works, but also in the reality they reflect, people are killed, and we are left with uncertainties about who has killed them, or why? What were the circumstances behind the secret murder of the Duke of Gloucester at Calais before the events of *Richard II*? Was the Kelly Gang's accomplice Aaron Sherritt killed because he betrayed the Kellys, or because the police were using him as bait? Who was responsible for Liz Gold's death on the Berlin Wall in *The Spy Who Came in from the Cold*? Are there, as CIA historian Nicholas Branch intuits, further depths to the account of the Kennedy assassination offered in *Libra*? Who bombs the Compass Bar in *The Pen Friend*? Elsewhere, in *A Most Wanted Man* and *Point Omega*, people disappear, or, more accurately, are disappeared. Where have they been taken? What has happened to them?

In such contexts, identities, too, may prove uncertain. Where the powerful constantly seek to co-opt the marginal, who is really working for whom? In *The Names*, James Axton eventually discovers that he is working, at arm's length, for the CIA. Even the conspirators who are using him do not know whether *Libra*'s Lee Harvey Oswald is a lone radical or the creation of US intelligence. In *The Pen Friend*, Gabriel Conway is shocked to be told that he, too, is MO2. William Gibson's outsider protagonists almost always find themselves working both for and against their manipulative patrons. In the works of Carson and Gibson, such manipulation occurs in a context of omnipresent (and often mutual) surveillance. Who is listening in on whom? And what are they hearing? Uncertainties about the covert actions of the state contribute, of course, to the increasing importance of paranoia as a cultural phenomenon in the post-war West. Such paranoia is hardly diminished in the internet era by our knowledge not only of the world of espionage, but also of an emerging, extensive, but still largely invisible surveillance state.

In its critique of the state's extralegal actions, literature shares with law a demand for justice. The writer as intellectual in the modern era, Foucault suggests, may in some sense be 'an offspring of the jurist', a descendant of 'the man of justice, the man of law', who counterposes to power 'the universality

of justice and the equity of an ideal law'.[7] Desire for justice is a key characteristic of Hobsbawm's 'social bandit'.[8] As we have seen, real medieval outlaw
bands were more socially diverse and considerably less ethically exemplary
than their literary equivalents and, in a literary example, the hard-right marginal groups lurking at the edges of some of William Gibson's fictions offer us
a futuristic reminder that outlaw gangs may be anything but progressive. But
as suggested at the outset of our discussion, even if Hobsbawm's comments
on justice cannot always be upheld for the practice of outlawry, they have a
certain validity when applied to its literature. In *A Gest of Robyn Hode*, it is
Robin Hood, rather than corrupt legal officials, who is a source of justice.
Ned Kelly claims 'there never was such a thing as justice in the English laws
but any amount of injustice to be had' (*The Jerilderie Letter*, pp. 16–18),
claiming elsewhere 'If I get justice I will cry a go'.[9] Le Carré says in interview:
'I see in what I write a constant progress towards individual values and an
anger that is growing more intense towards injustice'.[10]

If, as Eva Horn suggests of espionage fiction, such critique makes these fictions political,[11] we might ask how politically effective they are? John le Carré
wryly comments on the differences between fictional and real discussions of
espionage practice, saying: 'How much our poor beleaguered spies must be
wishing that Edward Snowden had done the novel instead'.[12] But le Carré's
comment requires context: it concludes a series of anecdotes about spies-
turned-novelists (W. Somerset Maugham, Compton Mackenzie and Graham
Greene) threatened with breach of the Official Secrets Act.[13] If literature were
politically impotent, the state would hardly be so keen to influence, censor or
suppress accounts of its secret workings. In DeLillo's *Mao II*, Charlie Everson
suggests to Bill Gray that 'the state should want to kill all writers' (*Mao II*,
p. 97). This, thankfully, is not quite the reality in the West (though there
are many other states where it is).[14] But if, as we have argued here, literature
is often a means of both representing and critiquing extralegal action by the
state, such critique can be not only political, but also politically risky. Some
texts discussed above, such as the medieval outlaw romance *Gamelyn*, are

[7] Foucault, 'Truth and Power', p. 128; Foucault is specific in locating each of these figures
historically.
[8] Hobsbawm, *Bandits*, pp. 29–30, 46–51, 58–62.
[9] Kelly, *The Cameron Letter*.
[10] Assouline, 'Spying on a Spymaker', p. 89.
[11] Horn, *Secret War*, p. 41.
[12] Le Carré, *The Pigeon Tunnel*, p. 21.
[13] Le Carré, *The Pigeon Tunnel*, pp. 19–21.
[14] See PEN International's annual Case List of detained and persecuted writers: <https://pen-
international.org/who-we-are/case-lists>.

careful to contain the subversion they represent: the poem's challenges to authority are safely absorbed into a model of ultimate loyalty to the monarch. Other texts proved politically dangerous: Shakespeare's *Richard II* acquired a likely unintended association with Essex's Rebellion; Ned Kelly's two polemics, the *Cameron Letter* and *Jerilderie Letter*, were both suppressed. As Frances Stonor Saunders has shown at length, Western states have sought not only to censor but also to influence writers during the 'cultural cold war'.

The state may not wish to silence all writers, and not all writers wish to oppose the state. But the state does often wish to act extralegally, in secret, and with impunity, and literary texts continue to play an important role in questioning and critiquing such actions. If exclusion from law continues to be an enduring tactic of state power in the twentieth and twenty-first century West, the role of literature in representing, questioning and critiquing such actions remains of enduring value.

Bibliography

Primary Texts – Literature

Auster, Paul, *Leviathan* (London: Faber, 1992).

Auster, Paul and Don DeLillo, 'Salman Rushdie Defense Pamphlet', <http://perival. com/delillo/rushdie_defense.html>

Banville, John, *The Untouchable* (London: Picador, 1998).

Barbour, John, *The Bruce*, ed. and trans. A. A. M. Duncan, corrected ed. (Edinburgh: Canongate, 2007).

Barr, Helen (ed.), *The Piers Plowman Tradition* (London: Dent, 1993).

Benjamin, Walter, 'Critique of Violence', in Walter Benjamin, *Reflections*, ed. Peter Demetz, trans. Edmund Jephcott (New York: Schocken, 1978), pp. 277–300.

Benjamin, Walter, *The Arcades Project*, trans. Howard Eiland and Kevin McLaughlin (Cambridge, MA and London: Harvard University Press, 1999).

Bennett, Ronan, *Zugzwang* (London: Bloomsbury, 2007).

Blanchot, Maurice, 'Literary Infinity: The Aleph', in Maurice Blanchot, *The Book to Come*, trans. Charlotte Mendel (Stanford: Stanford University Press, 2003), pp. 93–6.

Blind Harry, *The Wallace*, ed. Anne McKim (Edinburgh: Canongate, 2003).

Bliss, A. J. (ed.), *Sir Orfeo*, 2nd edn (Oxford: Oxford University Press, 1966).

Borges, Jorge Luis, 'The Aleph', in Jorge Luis Borges, *Collected Fictions*, trans. Andrew Hurley (New York: Viking, 1998), pp. 274–86.

Bullough, Geoffrey (ed.), *Narrative and Dramatic Sources of Shakespeare*, 8 vols (London: Routledge and NY: Columbia University Press, 1957–75).

Burgess, Glyn S. (ed. and trans.), *Two Medieval Outlaws: Eustace the Monk and Fouke Fitz Waryn* (Cambridge: Brewer, 1997).

Carey, Peter, *True History of the Kelly Gang* (St Lucia: University of Queensland Press, 2000).

Carson, Ciaran, *The Star Factory* (London: Granta, 1997).

Carson, Ciaran, *Fishing for Amber: A Long Story* (London: Granta, 1999).

Carson, Ciaran, 'The Language Instinct', *The Guardian*, 1 May 2004.

Carson, Ciaran, *Collected Poems* (Oldcastle: Gallery, 2008).

Carson, Ciaran, *For All We Know* (Oldcastle: Gallery, 2008).

Carson, Ciaran, *Until Before After* (Oldcastle: Gallery, 2009).

Carson, Ciaran, *The Pen Friend* (Belfast: Blackstaff, 2009).

Carson, Ciaran, *Exchange Place* (Belfast: Blackstaff, 2012).

Carson, Ciaran, 'A fusillade of question-marks: Ciaran Carson on Troubles art', *Irish*

Times, 26 June 2015, <http://www.irishtimes.com/culture/books/a-fusillade-of-question-marks-ciaran-carson-on-troubles-art-1.2262817>.

Carson, Ciaran and Elmer Kennedy-Andrews, 'Introduction: For All I Know', in *Ciaran Carson: Critical Essays*, ed. Elmer Kennedy-Andrews (Dublin: Four Courts, 2009), pp. 13–27.

Casement, Roger, 'The Language of the Outlaw', *New England Review* 25:1/2 (Winter–Spring 2004), pp. 155–8.

Chaucer, Geoffrey, *The Riverside Chaucer*, ed. Larry D. Benson (Boston: Houghton Mifflin, 1987).

Chesterton, G. K., *The Man Who Was Thursday: A Nightmare* (Melbourne: Penguin, 2013 [1908]).

Childers, Erskine, *The Riddle of the Sands* (London: Penguin, 2007 [1903]).

Conrad, Joseph, *The Secret Agent: A Simple Tale*, ed. Michael Newton (London: Penguin, 2007 [1907]).

Conrad, Joseph, *Under Western Eyes*, ed. Stephen Donovan (London: Penguin, 2007 [1911]).

DeLillo, Don, *Americana* (London: Penguin, 2006 [1971]).

DeLillo, Don, *Players* (London: Vintage, 1991 [1977]).

DeLillo, Don, *Running Dog* (London: Picador, 1999 [1978]).

DeLillo, Don, *The Names* (London: Picador, 1987 [1982]).

DeLillo, Don, *White Noise* (London: Picador, 1985).

DeLillo, Don, *Libra* (London and New York: Penguin, 1988).

DeLillo, Don, *Mao II* (London: Vintage, 1992).

DeLillo, Don, *Underworld* (London: Picador, 1998).

DeLillo, Don, 'In the Ruins of the Future', *The Guardian*, 22 December 2001 (first published in *Harper's Magazine* (December 2001)).

DeLillo, Don, 'Baader-Meinhof', in Don DeLillo, *The Angel Esmeralda: Nine Stories* (London: Picador, 2011), pp. 105–18 (first published in *The New Yorker*, 1 April 2002).

DeLillo, Don, *Cosmopolis* (London: Picador, 2003).

DeLillo, Don, *Falling Man* (London: Picador, 2007).

DeLillo, Don, *Point Omega* (New York: Scribner, 2010).

Drewe, Robert, *Our Sunshine* (Sydney: Pan Macmillan, 1991).

Ellroy, James, *American Tabloid* (New York: Vintage, 2001 [1995]).

Gibson, William, *Neuromancer* (London: Voyager, 1995 [1984]).

Gibson, William, *Count Zero* (New York: Penguin, 1987).

Gibson, William, *Mona Lisa Overdrive* (New York: Bantam, 1989).

Gibson, William, *Virtual Light* (New York: Bantam, 1994).

Gibson, William, *Idoru* (London: Penguin, 1997).

Gibson, William, *All Tomorrow's Parties* (London: Penguin, 2000).

Gibson, William, *Pattern Recognition* (London: Penguin, 2004).

Gibson, William, *Spook Country* (London: Penguin, 2008).

Gibson, William, *Zero History* (London: Penguin, 2010).

Gibson, William, 'Google's Earth', *New York Times,* 31 August 2010, <https://www.nytimes.com/2010/09/01/opinion/01gibson.html>.

Gibson, William, 'Talk for Book Expo, New York', in William Gibson, *Distrust that Particular Flavor* (London: Penguin, 2012), pp. 43–8.

Gibson, William, 'The Road to Oceania', in William Gibson, *Distrust that Particular*

Flavor (London: Penguin, 2012), pp. 165–72 (first published in *The New York Times*, 25 June 2003, <http://www.nytimes.com/2003/06/25/opinion/the-ro ad-to-oceania.html>).

Gibson, William, 'Will We Have Computer Chips in Our Heads?' in William Gibson, *Distrust that Particular Flavor* (London: Penguin, 2012), pp. 211–17 (first published in *Time*, 19 June 2000).

Gibson, William, *The Peripheral* (London: Penguin, 2014).

Gould, Mica (trans.), *Two Tales of Owain Glyndwr*, in *Medieval Outlaws: Twelve Tales in Modern English Translation*, ed. Thomas H. Ohlgren, revised edn (West Lafayette, IN: Parlor, 2005), pp. 248–63.

Green, Richard Firth, '*The Hermit and the Outlaw*: An Edition', in *Interstices: Studies in Middle English and Anglo-Latin Texts in Honour of A. G. Rigg*, ed. Richard Firth Green and Linne R. Mooney (Toronto: University of Toronto Press, 2004), pp. 137–66.

Greene, Graham, *The Confidential Agent* (London: Vintage, 2006 [1939]).

Greene, Graham, *The Quiet American* (London: Vintage, 2004 [1955]).

Greene, Graham, *The Human Factor* (London: Vintage, 1999 [1978]).

Hamer, Richard (ed. and trans.), *A Choice of Anglo-Saxon Verse* (London: Faber, 1970).

Heaney, Seamus, *The Spirit Level* (London: Faber, 1996).

Heaney, Seamus, *Opened Ground: Poems 1966–1996* (London: Faber, 1998).

James, Henry, *The Princess Casamassima*, ed. Derek Brewer (Harmondsworth: Penguin, 1986).

Joyce, James, 'Counterparts', in James Joyce, *Dubliners*, ed. Hans Walter Gabler with Walter Hettche (London: Vintage, 2012 [1914]), pp. 75–86.

Joyce, James, 'The Dead', in James Joyce, *Dubliners*, ed. Hans Walter Gabler with Walter Hettche (London: Vintage, 2012 [1914]), pp. 159–204.

Joyce, James, *A Portrait of the Artist as a Young Man* (Harmondsworth: Penguin, 1960 [1916]).

Joyce, James, *Ulysses*, ed. Hans Walter Gabler with Wolfhard Steppe and Claus Melchior (London: Penguin, 1986 [1922]).

Kaufman, Alexander L. (trans.), *The Hermit and the Outlaw* in *Medieval Outlaws: Twelve Tales in Modern English Translation*, ed. Thomas H. Ohlgren, revised edn (West Lafayette, IN: Parlor, 2005), pp. 338–55.

Kelly, Ned, *The Cameron Letter*, <https://web.archive.org/web/20150302141652/ http://prov.vic.gov.au/whats-on/exhibitions/ned-kelly/the-kelly-story/euroa/ edward-kelly-gives-statement-of-his-murders-of-sergeant-kennedy-and-others-and-makes-other-threats>.

Kelly, Ned, *The Jerilderie Letter*, ed. Alex McDermott (Melbourne: Text, 2001).

Kingsnorth, Paul, *The Wake* (London: Unbound, 2014).

Kipling, Rudyard, *Kim* (London: Vintage, 2010).

Knight, Stephen and Thomas Ohlgren (eds), *Robin Hood and Other Outlaw Tales* (Kalamazoo, MI: Medieval Institute, 2000).

Langland, William, *Piers Plowman: The C Text*, ed. Derek Pearsall (York, 1988).

Le Carré, John, *Call for the Dead* (London: Penguin, 2012 [1961]).

Le Carré, John, *A Murder of Quality* (London: Penguin, 2011 [1962]).

Le Carré, John, *The Spy Who Came in from the Cold* (London: Penguin, 2010 [1963]).

Le Carré, John, *The Looking Glass War* (London: Penguin, 2012 [1965]).

Le Carré, John, 'To Russia, with Greetings', *Encounter* 26:5 (May 1966), pp. 3–6.
Le Carré, John, *A Small Town in Germany* (London: Penguin, 2011 [1968]).
Le Carré, John, *The Russia House* (London: Hodder, 1990).
Le Carré, John, *The Mission Song* (London: Hodder, 2006).
Le Carré, John, *A Most Wanted Man* (London: Hodder, 2008).
Le Carré, John, 'The Madness of Spies', *The New Yorker*, 29 September 2008.
Le Carré, John, *Smiley versus Karla: Tinker Tailor Soldier Spy, The Honourable Schoolboy, Smiley's People* (London: Hodder, 2011).
Le Carré, John, *A Delicate Truth* (London: Penguin, 2013).
Le Carré, John, *The Pigeon Tunnel: Stories from My Life* (London: Penguin, 2017, first published London: Viking, 2016).
Le Carré, John, *A Legacy of Spies* (New York: Viking, 2017).
Mathews, Harry, *My Life in CIA: A Chronicle of 1973* (Normal, IL and London: Dalkey Archive, 2005).
McCarry, Charles, *The Tears of Autumn* (Carlton North: Scribe, 2008 [1974]).
Miéville, China, *The City & The City* (London: Macmillan, 2009).
Modiano, Patrick, *Missing Person*, trans. Daniel Weissbort (Boston: Verba Mundi, 2015 [1980]).
Modiano, Patrick, *Little Jewel*, trans. Penny Hueston (Melbourne: Text, 2015).
Murakami, Haruki, *Hard-Boiled Wonderland and the End of the World*, trans. Alfred Birnbaum (London: Harvill, 2001).
Murray, Les, *Waiting for the Past* (Collingwood: Black Inc., 2015).
Ondaatje, Michael, *The Collected Works of Billy the Kid: Left Handed Poems* (London: Picador, 1989 [1970]).
Ormsby, Frank (ed.), *A Rage for Order: Poetry of the Northern Ireland Troubles* (Belfast: Blackstaff, 1992).
Park, David, *The Truth Commissioner* (London: Bloomsbury, 2008).
Percy, Thomas (ed.), *Reliques of Ancient English Poetry*, 3 vols (London, 1765).
Perec, Georges, *La Boutique Obscure: 124 Dreams*, trans. Daniel Levin Becker (Brooklyn, NY and London: Melville House, 2012).
Revard, Carter (trans.), *The Outlaw's Song of Trailbaston* in *Medieval Outlaws: Twelve Tales in Modern English Translation*, ed. Thomas H. Ohlgren, revised edn (West Lafayette, IN: Parlor, 2005), pp. 151–64.
Rushdie, Salman, *Joseph Anton: A Memoir* (London: Jonathan Cape, 2012).
Scott, Walter, *Rob Roy* (London: Penguin, 1995 [1817]).
Scott, Walter, *Ivanhoe*, ed. Graham Tulloch (London: Penguin, 2000 [1820]).
Shakespeare, William, *King Richard II*, ed. Charles R. Forker (London: Arden, 2002 [1597]).
Shakespeare, William, *King Henry IV Part I*, ed. David Scott Kastan (London: Arden, 2002 [1598]).
Shakespeare, William, *The Second Part of King Henry IV*, ed. A. R. Humphreys (London: Arden, 1981, repr. 2007 [1600]).
Shakespeare, William, *King Henry V*, ed. T. W. Craik (London: Arden, 1995, repr. 2005 [1600]).
Shakespeare, William, *King Henry V*, ed. Andrew Gurr, updated edn (Cambridge: Cambridge University Press, 2005 [1600]).
Shakespeare, William, *The Merchant of Venice*, ed. Jay L. Halio (Oxford: Oxford University Press, 1993 [1600]).

Skeat, Walter W. (ed.), *Specimens of English Literature from the 'Ploughmans Crede' to the 'Shepheardes Calender'*, A.D. 1394 – A.D. 1579 (Oxford: Oxford University Press, 1871).

Stevenson, Robert Louis, *Dr Jekyll and Mr Hyde and other stories* (London: Vintage, 2007 [1886]).

Stewart, Douglas, *Ned Kelly* in *Three Australian Plays* (Ringwood: Penguin, 1985).

Swanton, Michael (trans.), *The Deeds of Hereward* in *Medieval Outlaws: Twelve Tales in Modern English Translation*, ed. Thomas H. Ohlgren, revised edn (West Lafayette, IN: Parlor, 2005), pp. 28–99.

Tolkien, J. R. R. and E. V. Gordon (eds), revised by Norman Davis, *Sir Gawain and the Green Knight*, 2nd edn (Oxford: Oxford University Press, 1967).

Updike, John, *Terrorist* (New York: Knopf, repr. Ballantine, 2006).

Wright, Thomas (ed. and trans.), *The Political Songs of England from the Reign of John to that of Edward II* (London: Camden Society, 1889).

Yeats, W. B., *Collected Poems*, ed. Augustine Martin (London: Vintage, 1992).

Primary Texts – Film and Television

Corbijn, Anton, *A Most Wanted Man*, Lionsgate (first screened United States, 19 January 2014), Film.

Cronenberg, David, *Cosmopolis*, Entertainment One (first screened France, 25 May 2012), Film.

Jordan, Gregor, *Ned Kelly*, Universal (first screened Australia, 22 March 2003), Film.

Richardson, Tony, *Ned Kelly*, MGM (first screened United Kingdom, 1 July 1970), Film.

Reed, Carol, *Odd Man Out*, Rank/Two Cities Films (first screened United Kingdom, 30 January 1947), Film.

Dobson, Kevin James and George Miller, *The Last Outlaw*, Seven Network (first screened Australia, 15 October 1980), Television.

Tait, Charles, *The Story of the Kelly Gang*, National Film and Sound Archive, 2007 (first screened Australia, 26 December 1906), Film.

Irvin, John, *Tinker, Tailor, Soldier, Spy*, BBC (first screened United Kingdom, 10 September 1979), Television.

Alfredson, Tomas, *Tinker Tailor Soldier Spy*, Universal (first screened Italy, 5 September 2011), Film.

Primary Texts – Legal

Administration of Justice (Miscellaneous Provisions) Act 1938.

An Act to Suppress Robbery and Housebreaking and the Harbouring of Robbers and Housebreakers 1830, <http://www.legislation.nsw.gov.au/acts/1830-11a.pdf>.

An Acte for punishment of Rogues Vagabonds and Sturdy Beggars 1597, in *The Statutes of the Realm*, vol. IV part 2 (1819), pp. 899–902.

Boumediene v. *Bush* (553 US 723) (2008), <https://www.law.cornell.edu/supct/html/06-1195.ZS.html>.

Calendar of the Close Rolls preserved in the Public Record Office. Edward I. Vol. V. A.D. 1302–1307 (London: HMSO, 1908).

Calendar of Various Chancery Rolls, A.D. 1277–1326 (London: HMSO, 1912).

Civil Authorities (Special Powers) Act (Northern Ireland) 1922, <http://cain.ulst. ac.uk/hmso/spa1922.htm>.

Civil Procedure Acts Repeal Act 1879 in *The Public General Statutes passed in the Forty-Second and Forty-Third Years of the Reign of Her Majesty Queen Victoria, 1879* (London, 1879), pp. 296–306.

Convention against Torture and other Cruel, Inhuman or Degrading Treatment or Punishment 1984, <https://treaties.un.org/Pages/ViewDetails.aspx?src= TREATY&mtdsg_no=IV-9&chapter=4&lang=en>.

Convention determining the State responsible for examining applications for asylum lodged in one of the Member States of the European Communities – Dublin Convention 1990, <http://eur-lex.europa.eu/legal-content/EN/ALL/?uri= CELEX:41997A0819(01)>.

Criminal Justice Act 1948, <http://www.legislation.gov.uk/ukpga/Geo6/11-12/58/ enacted>.

Crown Proceedings Act 1947, <http://www.legislation.gov.uk/ukpga/Geo6/10-11/44/enacted>.

Eighth Amendment to the US Constitution 1791, <https://www.law.cornell.edu/ constitution/eighth_amendment>.

Espionage Act 1917 (18 US Code ch. 37), <https://www.law.cornell.edu/uscode/ text/18/part-I/chapter-37>.

Felons Apprehension Act (NSW) 1865, <http://www.legislation.nsw.gov.au/session alview/sessional/act/1865-2a.pdf>.

Felons Apprehension Bill 1878, in *The Argus*, 31 October 1878, <http://trove.nla. gov.au/newspaper/article/5919191>.

Foreign Intelligence Surveillance Act 1978 (50 US Code ch. 36) <https://www.law. cornell.edu/uscode/text/50/chapter-36>.

Hamdan v. *Rumsfeld* (548 US 557) (2006), <https://www.law.cornell.edu/supct/ html/05-184.ZS.html>.

Hamdi v. *Rumsfeld* (542 US 507) (2004), <https://www.law.cornell.edu/supct/ html/03-6696.ZS.html>.

Intelligence Services Act 1994, <http://www.legislation.gov.uk/ukpga/1994/13/ crossheading/the-secret-intelligence-service>.

Justice and Security Act 2013, <http://www.legislation.gov.uk/ukpga/2013/18/ contents/enacted>.

Mabo v. *Queensland (No 2)* (1992), <http://www.austlii.edu.au/cgi-bin/sinodisp/au/ cases/cth/high_ct/175clr1.html?stem=0&synonyms=0&query=~mabo>.

National Security Legislation Amendment (No 1) 2014, <http://www.aph.gov.au/ Parliamentary_Business/Bills_Legislation/Bills_Search_Results/Result?bId= s969>.

National Security Act 1947 (50 US Code ch. 44) <https://research.archives.gov/ id/299856>.

Nixon v. *Fitzgerald* (457 US 731) (1982), <https://supreme.justia.com/cases/federal/ us/457/731/case.html#F39>.

Northern Ireland (Emergency Provisions) Act 1973, <http://www.legislation.gov. uk/ukpga/1973/53/contents/enacted>.

Official Secrets Act 1989, <http://www.legislation.gov.uk/ukpga/1989/6/contents/ enacted>.

'Presidential Approval and Reporting of Covert Actions' (50 US Code 3093), <https://www.law.cornell.edu/uscode/text/50/3093>.

Prevention of Terrorism (Temporary Provisions) Act 1974, <http://www.legislation.gov.uk/ukpga/1974/56/contents/enacted>.

Rasul v. *Bush* (542 US 466) (2004), <https://www.law.cornell.edu/supct/html/03-334.ZO.html>.

Torture (18 US Code ch. 113c), <https://www.law.cornell.edu/uscode/text/18/part-I/chapter-113C>.

USA FREEDOM Act 2015, <https://www.congress.gov/bill/114th-congress/house-bill/2048/text>.

Attenborough, F. L. (ed. and trans.), *The Laws of the Earliest English Kings* (Cambridge: Cambridge University Press, 1922).

Drew, Katherine Fischer (trans.), *The Laws of the Salian Franks* (Philadelphia: University of Pennsylvania Press, 1991).

Liebermann, Felix (ed.), *Die Gesetze der Angelsachsen*, 3 vols (Halle: Max Niemeyer, 1898–16).

Mommsen, Theodor (ed.), *Iustiniani Digesta,* <https://droitromain.univ-grenoble-alpes.fr/#4>.

O'Brien, Bruce (ed.), *Leges Edwardi Confessoris*, version 1, <http://www.earlyenglishlaws.ac.uk/laws/texts/ECf1/>.

Stubbs, William (ed.), rev. H. W. C. Davis, *Select Charters and Other Illustrations of English Constitutional History*, 9th edn (Oxford: Oxford University Press, 1921).

Vincent, Nicholas (ed.), *Assize of Clarendon*, <http://www.earlyenglishlaws.ac.uk/laws/texts/Ass-Clar/>.

Watson, Alan (ed.), The *Digest of Justinian*, 4 vols, revised edn (Philadelphia: University of Pennsylvania Press, 1998).

Woodbine, G. E. (ed.), S. E. Thorne (trans.), *Bracton: On the Laws and Customs of England*, 4 vols (Cambridge, MA: Harvard University Press, 1968–77).

Primary Texts – Historical and Political

'Assessing Russian Activities and Intentions in Recent US Elections' (Office of the Director of National Intelligence, 6 January 2017), <https://www.dni.gov/files/documents/ICA_2017_01.pdf>.

'DSMA – Notice 03: Military Counter-Terrorist Forces, Special Forces and Intelligence Agency Operations, Activities and Communication Methods and Techniques', <https://dsma.uk/notice/military-counter-terrorist-forces-special-forces-and-intelligence-agency-operations-activities-and-communication-methods-and-techniques/>.

The Family Jewels (Washington, DC: Central Intelligence Agency, 1973), <https://www.cia.gov/library/readingroom/collection/family-jewels>.

Final Report of the Select Committee to Study Governmental Operations with respect to Intelligence Activities, United States Senate, together with Additional, Supplemental, and Separate Views (Washington, DC: US Government Printing Office, 1976), <https://archive.org/details/finalreportofsel01unit>.

'Find an immigration removal centre', <https://www.gov.uk/immigration-removal-centre/>.

'Governor Phillip's Instructions' (1787) <http://www.foundingdocs.gov.au/resources/transcripts/nsw2_doc_1787.pdf>.

'The Mansfield Murderers', *The Argus*, 18 December 1878, p. 6, <http://trove.nla.gov.au/newspaper/article/5925149>.

PEN International Case Lists: <https://pen-international.org/who-we-are/case-lists>.

Recognising Aboriginal and Torres Strait Islander Peoples in the Constitution: Report of the Expert Panel (Canberra: Commonwealth of Australia, 2012), <https://www.pmc.gov.au/resource-centre/indigenous-affairs/final-report-expert-panel-recognising-aboriginal-and-torres-strait-islander-peoples-constitution>.

The Rendition Project, <http://www.therenditionproject.org.uk/>.

Report of the President's Commission on the Assassination of President John F. Kennedy (Washington, DC: United States Government Printing Office, 1964), <http://www.archives.gov/research/jfk/warren-commission-report/>.

Royal Commission on Police: The Proceedings of the Commission, Minutes of Evidence, Appendices, Etc. (Melbourne: John Ferres, 1883), <https://digitised-collections.unimelb.edu.au/handle/11343/21369>.

Second Progress Report of the Royal Commission of Enquiry into the circumstances of the Kelly Outbreak, the present state and organisation of the Police Force, etc. (Melbourne: John Ferres, 1881), <https://digitised-collections.unimelb.edu.au/handle/11343/21368>.

The Torture Database, <https://www.thetorturedatabase.org/>.

The Universal Declaration of Human Rights, <http://www.un.org/en/universal-declaration-human-rights/index.html>.

Aquinas, St Thomas, *Summa Theologiae*, ed. T. Gilby and others, 61 vols (London: Blackfriars, 1964–81).

Aristotle, *The Politics*, trans. T. A Sinclair, rev. Trevor J. Saunders (London: Penguin, 1992).

Barney, Stephen A., W. J. Lewis, J. A. Beach and Oliver Berghof, with the collaboration of Muriel Hall (trans.), *The Etymologies of Isidore of Seville*, corrected edn (Cambridge: Cambridge University Press, 2010).

Bentham, Jeremy, *The Panopticon Writings* (London and New York: Verso, 1995 [1791]).

Buchanan, George, *De Jure Regni aped Scotos or, A Dialogue, Concerning the due Priviledge of Government in the Kingdom of Scotland. Betwixt George Buchanan and Thomas Maitland* (London: Richard Baldwin, 1689).

Bush, George W., 'Military Order of November 13, 2001: Detention, Treatment, and Trial of Certain Non-Citizens in the War Against Terrorism' (13 November 2001), <https://fas.org/irp/offdocs/eo/mo-111301.htm>.

Bush, George W., 'Address to the Joint Session of the 107th Congress', in *Selected Speeches of President George W. Bush 2001–2008*, p. 68, online at <https://georgewbush-whitehouse.archives.gov/infocus/bushrecord/documents/Selected_Speeches_George_W_Bush.pdf>.

Clinton, Bill, *My Life* (London: Arrow, 2005).

Curtis, Edmund and R. B. McDowell (eds), *Irish Historical Documents 1172–1922* (London: Methuen, 1968 [1943]).

Douglas, David C. and G. W. Greenaway (eds), *English Historical Documents 1042–1189* (London: Eyre & Spottiswoode, 1975).

Ehrenberg, John, J. Patrice McSherry, José Ramón Sánchez, Caroleen Marji Sayej (eds), *The Iraq Papers* (New York: Oxford University Press, 2010).

FitzNigel, Richard, *Dialogus de Scaccario*, ed. Charles Johnson, F. E. L. Carter and D. E. Greenway (Oxford: Oxford University Press, 1983).

Ford, Gerald R., 'Executive Order 11905: United States Foreign Intelligence Activities' (18 February 1976), <https://fas.org/irp/offdocs/eo11905.htm>.

Given-Wilson, Chris (trans. and ed.), *Chronicles of the Revolution 1397–1400: The Reign of Richard II* (Manchester: Manchester University Press, 1993).

James I, *The True Law of Free Monarchies and Basilokon Doron*, ed. Daniel Fischlin and Mark Fortier (Toronto: Centre for Reformation and Renaissance Studies, 1996 [1598, 1599]).

John of Salisbury, *Policraticus: Of the Frivolities of Courtiers and the Footsteps of Philosophers*, ed. and trans. Cary J. Nederman (Cambridge: Cambridge University Press, 1990).

McNeill, John T. and Helena M. Gamer (eds), *Medieval Handbooks of Penance: A translation of the principal libri poenitentiales and selections from related documents* (New York: Columbia University Press, 1990 [1938]).

Musson, Anthony, with Edward Powell (eds), *Crime, Law and Society in the Later Middle Ages* (Manchester: Manchester University Press, 2009).

Nechayev, Sergey, *The Revolutionary Catechism* (1869), <https://www.marxists.org/subject/anarchism/nechayev/catechism.htm>.

Obama, Barack, 'Executive Order 13526 – Classified National Security Information' (29 December 2009), <https://www.archives.gov/isoo/policy-documents/cnsi-eo.html>.

Reagan, Ronald 'Executive Order 12333 – United States Intelligence Activities' (4 December 1981), <https://www.cia.gov/about-cia/eo12333.html>.

Rothwell, Harry (ed.), *English Historical Documents, 1189–1327* (London: Eyre & Spottiswoode, 1975).

Lord Saville of Newdigate, William L. Hoyt and John L. Toohcy, *Report of the Bloody Sunday Inquiry*, 10 vols (London: The Stationery Office, 2010), <https://www.gov.uk/government/publications/report-of-the-bloody-sunday-inquiry>.

Slahi, Mohamedou Ould, *Guantánamo Diary* (Edinburgh: Canongate, 2015).

Standish, Frederick Charles, 'Captain Standish to the Chief Secretary re: Secret service money' (1880), <https://web.archive.org/web/20150302122555/http://prov.vic.gov.au/whats-on/exhibitions/ned-kelly/the-kelly-story/jerilderie/secret-service-money>.

Strachey, John (ed.), *Rotuli Parliamentorum; ut et Petitiones et Placita in Parliamento ab Anno Decimo Octavo R. Henrici Sexti ad Finem eiusdem Regni*, 6 vols (London, 1767–77).

Tench, Watkin, *1788*, ed. Tim Flannery (Melbourne: Text, 2012 [1789, 1793]).

Wittes, Benjamin, 'Jeh Johnson Speech at the Oxford Union', 30 November 2012, <http://www.lawfareblog.com/2012/11/jeh-johnson-speech-at-the-oxford-union/>.

Wright, Peter, with Paul Greengrass, *Spycatcher: The Candid Autobiography of a Senior Intelligence Officer* (Richmond, VIC: Heinemann, 1987).

Works of Reference

Dolan, Terry (ed.), *A Dictionary of Hiberno-English: The Irish Use of English*, 2nd edn (Dublin: Gill & Macmillan, 2004).
Macquarie Dictionary, <https://www.macquariedictionary.com.au/>.
Middle English Dictionary, <https://quod.lib.umich.edu/m/med/>.
Oxford English Dictionary, <http://www.oed.com/>.
Ó Muirithe, Diarmaid, *Words We Use* (Dublin: Gill & Macmillan, 2006).

Secondary Texts

Globalizing Torture: CIA Secret Detention and Extraordinary Rendition (New York: Open Society Foundations, 2013).
Kelly Culture: Reconstructing Ned Kelly (Melbourne: State Library of Victoria, 2003).
'List of intelligence agencies', <http://en.wikipedia.org/wiki/List_of_intelligence_ agencies>.
'List of secret police organizations', <http://en.wikipedia.org/wiki/List_of_secret_ police_organizations>.
Sidney Nolan's Ned Kelly: The Ned Kelly paintings in the National Gallery of Australia (Canberra: National Gallery of Australia, 2002).
Agamben, Giorgio, *Homo Sacer: Sovereign Power and Bare Life*, trans. Daniel Heller-Roazen (Stanford: Stanford University Press, 1998).
Agamben, Giorgio, *State of Exception*, trans. Kevin Attell (Chicago and London: University of Chicago Press, 2005).
Agamben, Giorgio, *The Use of Bodies*, trans. Adam Kotsko (Stanford: Stanford University Press, 2016).
Ai Weiwei, 'Ai Weiwei: to live your life in fear is worse than losing your freedom', *The Guardian*, 21 June 2012, <http://www.theguardian.com/commentisfree/2012/jun/21/ai-weiwei-living-life-fear-freedom>.
Alexander, Neal, *Ciaran Carson: Space, Place, Writing* (Liverpool: Liverpool University Press, 2010).
Alford, John A., 'Literature and Law in Medieval England', *PMLA* 92:5 (1977), pp. 941–51.
Alford, John A., 'The Idea of Reason in *Piers Plowman*', in *Medieval English Studies Presented to George Kane*, ed. Edward Donald Kennedy and others (Woodbridge: Brewer, 1988), pp. 199–215.
Alford, Stephen, *The Watchers: A Secret History of the Reign of Elizabeth I* (London: Allen Lane, 2012).
Almond, Richard and A. J. Pollard, 'The Yeomanry of Robin Hood and Social Terminology in Fifteenth-Century England', *Past & Present* 170 (2001), pp. 52–77.
Andrew, Christopher, *For the President's Eyes Only: Secret Intelligence and the American Presidency from Washington to Bush* (New York: HarperCollins, 1995).
Andrew, Christopher, *The Defence of the Realm: The Authorized History of MI5*, revised edn (London: Penguin, 2010).
Arendt, Hannah, *The Origins of Totalitarianism* (London: Penguin, 2017 [1951]).
Arthurson, Ian, 'Espionage and Intelligence from the Wars of the Roses to the Reformation', *Nottingham Medieval Studies* 35 (1991), pp. 134–54.

Assange, Julian, with Jacob Appelbaum, Andy Müller-Maguhn and Jérémie Zimmermann, *Cypherpunks: Freedom and the Future of the Internet* (New York and London: OR Books, 2012).

Assouline, Pierre, 'Spying on a Spymaker', in *Conversations with John le Carré*, ed. Matthew J. Bruccoli and Judith S. Baughman (Jackson: University Press of Mississippi, 2004), pp. 86–9 (first published in *World Press Review* 33 (August 1986), pp. 59–60).

Bailey, Mark, *The Decline of Serfdom in Late Medieval England: From Bondage to Freedom* (Woodbridge: Boydell, 2014).

Bartlett, Robin, *England Under the Norman and Angevin Kings* (Oxford: Oxford University Press, 2000).

Batten, Guinn, 'Love and War: The Collaborative Art of Ciaran Carson', *An Sionnach* 4:2 (2008), pp. 72–9.

Begley, Adam, 'The Art of Fiction CXXXV: Don DeLillo', in *Conversations with Don DeLillo*, ed. Thomas DePietro (Jackson: University Press of Mississippi, 2005), pp. 86–108 (first published in *The Paris Review* 128 (Fall 1993), <http://www.theparisreview.org/interviews/1887/the-art-of-fiction-no-135-don-delillo>).

Bellamy, J. G., 'The Coterel Gang: An Anatomy of a Band of Fourteenth-Century Criminals', *English Historical Review* 79:313 (1964), pp. 698–717.

Bellamy, J. G. [John Bellamy], *Crime and Public Order in England in the Later Middle Ages* (London: Routledge, 1973).

Bellamy, J. G., *The Law of Treason in England in the Later Middle Ages* (Cambridge: Cambridge University Press, 2004 [1970]).

Bender, Abby, 'The Language of the Outlaw: A Clarification', *James Joyce Quarterly* 44:4 (2007), pp. 807–12.

Boswell, Anna, 'Cross-Cultural Comparison and the Making of Outlaws: A Cautionary Tale', *Journal of New Zealand Literature* 24:2 (2007), pp. 185–204.

Blok, Anton, 'The Peasant and the Brigand: Social Banditry Reconsidered', *Comparative Studies in Society and History* 14:4 (1972), pp. 494–503.

Blum, Gabriella and Philip B. Heymann, *Laws, Outlaws, and Terrorists: Lessons from the War on Terrorism* (Cambridge, MA and London: MIT Press, 2010).

Bossy, John, 'Trust the Coroner', *London Review of Books*, 28:24 (14 December 2006), p. 14.

Bragg, Melvyn, 'The Things a Spy Can Do: John le Carré Talking', in *Conversations with John le Carré*, ed. Matthew J. Bruccoli and Judith S. Baughman (Jackson: University Press of Mississippi, 2004), pp. 33–7 (pp. 33–4) (first published in *The Listener*, 22 January 1976, p. 90).

Brand, Paul, 'Jews and the Law in England, 1275–90', *English Historical Review* 115 (2000), pp. 1138–58.

Brown, John, 'Ciaran Carson' in John Brown, *In the Chair: Interviews with Poets from the North of Ireland* (Cliffs of Moher: Salmon Publishing, 2002), pp. 141–52.

Brown, Max, *Australian Son: The Story of Ned Kelly* (Melbourne: Georgian House, 1948).

Burnside, Julian, 'R v Edward (Ned) Kelly', <http://www.julianburnside.com.au/law/r-v-edward-ned-kelly/>.

Bynum, Caroline Walker, *Metamorphosis and Identity* (New York: Zone Books, 2005).

Canning, J. P., 'Law, Sovereignty and Corporation Theory, 1300–1450', in *The*

Cambridge History of Medieval Political Thought, ed. J. H. Burns (Cambridge: Cambridge University Press, 1988), pp. 454–76.

Carlston, Erin G., *Double Agents: Espionage, Literature, and Liminal Citizens* (New York: Columbia University Press, 2013).

Cavallaro, Dani, *Cyberpunk and Cyberculture: Science Fiction and the Work of William Gibson* (London: Athlone, 2000).

Chomsky, Noam, *Rogue States: The Rule of Force in World Affairs* (Cambridge, MA: South End Press, 2000).

Cobain, Ian, 'How secret renditions shed light on MI6's licence to kill and torture', *The Guardian*, 15 February 2012, <http://www.theguardian.com/world/2012/feb/14/mi6-licence-to-kill-and-torture>.

Cobain, Ian, *Cruel Brittania: A Secret History of Torture* (London: Portobello, 2013).

Cobain, Ian, *The History Thieves: Secrets, Lies and the Shaping of a Modern Nation* (London: Portobello, 2016).

Coleman, Gabriella, *Hacker, Hoaxer, Whistleblower, Spy: The Many Faces of Anonymous* (London and New York: Verso, 2014).

Condren, Conal, 'Understanding Shakespeare's Perfect Prince: Henry V, the Ethics of Office and the French Prisoners', *The Shakespearean International Yearbook* 9 (2009), pp. 195–213.

Connolly, Kevin, 'An Interview with Don DeLillo', in *Conversations with Don DeLillo*, ed. Thomas DePietro (Jackson: University Press of Mississippi, 2005), pp. 25–39 (first published in *The Brick Reader*, ed. Linda Spalding and Michael Ondaatje (Toronto: Coach House Press, 1991), pp. 260–9).

Cooper, John, *The Queen's Agent: Francis Walsingham at the Court of Elizabeth I* (London: Faber, 2011).

Corcoran, Neil, 'One step forward, two steps back: Ciaran Carson's *The Irish for No*', in Neil Corcoran, *Poets of Modern Ireland: Text, Context, Intertext* (Cardiff: University of Wales Press, 1999), pp. 177–97.

Corfield, Justin, *The Ned Kelly Encyclopaedia* (South Melbourne: Lothian, 2003).

Corish, Patrick J., 'The Cromwellian Regime, 1650–60', in *A New History of Ireland III: Early Modern Ireland 1534–1691*, ed. T. W. Moody, F. X. Martin and F. J. Byrne (Oxford: Oxford University Press, 2009 [1976]), pp. 353–86.

Cowart, David, 'The Lady Vanishes: Don DeLillo's *Point Omega*', *Contemporary Literature* 53:1 (2012), pp. 31–50.

Crain, Caleb, 'Surveillance Society: The Mass-Observation movement and the meaning of everyday life', *The New Yorker*, 11 September 2006, <http://www.newyorker.com/magazine/2006/09/11/surveillance-society>.

Creed, Barbara, *Stray: Human-Animal Ethics in the Anthropocene* (Sydney: Power Publications, 2017).

Crook, David, 'Some Further Evidence Concerning the Dating of the Origins of the Legend of Robin Hood', in *Robin Hood: An Anthology of Scholarship and Criticism*, ed. Stephen Knight (Cambridge: Brewer, 1999), pp. 257–61 (first published in *English Historical Review* 99 (1984), pp. 530–4).

Cukier, Kenneth Neil and Viktor Mayer-Schoenberger, 'The Rise of Big Data: How It's Changing the Way We Think About the World', *Foreign Affairs* 92:3 (May/June 2013), <https://www.foreignaffairs.com/articles/2013-04-03/rise-big-data>.

Curry, Anne, 'The Military Ordinances of Henry V: Texts and Contexts', in *War, Government and Aristocracy in the British Isles, c. 1150–1500: Essays in Honour of Michael Prestwich*, ed. Chris Given-Wilson, Ann J. Kettle and Len Scales (Woodbridge: Boydell, 2008), pp. 214–49.

Curthoys, Ann, 'Expulsion, Exodus and Exile in White Australian Historical Mythology', *Journal of Australian Studies* 23:61 (1999), pp. 1–19.

Curtin, Tansy, Leanne Fitzgibbon and Karen Quinlan, *Imagining Ned* (Bendigo: Bendigo Art Gallery, 2015), <https://web.archive.org/web/20180313041855/http://www.bendigoartgallery.com.au/files/36779ae0-1c8f-4d9b-bf55-a46701126170/Imagining_Ned.pdf>.

Davies, John R., 'The Execution of William Wallace: The Earliest Account', <http://www.breakingofbritain.ac.uk/blogs/feature-of-the-month/may-2011-the-execution-of-william-wallace/>.

Davies, R. R., 'The Law of the March', *Cylchgrawn Hanes Cymru/Welsh History Review* 5:1 (1970), pp. 1–30.

Davies, R. R., 'Kings, Lords and Liberties in the March of Wales, 1066–1272', *Transactions of the Royal Historical Society* 29 (1979), pp. 41–61.

Davies, R. R. [Rees Davies], 'Frontier Arrangements in Fragmented Societies: Ireland and Wales', in *Medieval Frontier Societies*, ed. Robert Bartlett and Angus MacKay (Oxford: Oxford University Press, 1989), pp. 77–100.

Davies, R. R., *The Revolt of Owain Glyn Dŵr* (Oxford: Oxford University Press, 1995).

Davies, R. R., *The First English Empire: Power and Identities in the British Isles 1093–1343* (Oxford: Oxford University Press, 2000).

Davis, Norman, Douglas Gray, Patricia Ingham and Anne Wallace-Hadrill, *A Chaucer Glossary* (Oxford: Oxford University Press, 1979).

DeCurtis, Anthony, '"An Outsider in This Society": An Interview with Don DeLillo', in *Conversations with Don DeLillo*, ed. Thomas DePietro (Jackson: University Press of Mississippi, 2005), pp. 52–74 (first published in *South Atlantic Quarterly* 89:2 (1990), pp. 281–304).

Deleuze, Gilles, 'Control and Becoming', in Gilles Deleuze, *Negotiations, 1972–1990*, ed. Martin Joughin (New York: Columbia University Press, 1990), pp. 169–76.

Derrida, Jacques, *Rogues: Two Essays on Reason*, trans. Pascale-Anne Brault and Michael Naas (Stanford, CA: Stanford University Press, 2005).

Derrida, Jacques, *The Beast & the Sovereign*, ed. Michel Lisse, Marie-Louise Mallet, Ginette Michaud, trans. Geoff Bennington, 2 vols (Chicago and London: The University of Chicago Press, 2009, 2011).

Dickson, Brice, *The European Convention on Human Rights and the Conflict in Northern Ireland* (Oxford: Oxford University Press, 2010).

Diggle, Andy and Iain Ball, 'An Interview with William Gibson: *Virtual Light* Tour', in *Conversations with William Gibson*, ed. Patrick A. Smith (Jackson: University of Mississippi Press, 2014), pp. 96–107.

Dillon, Martin, *The Dirty War* (London: Arrow, 1991).

Duvall, John N., 'Introduction: the power of history and the persistence of mystery', in *The Cambridge Companion to Don DeLillo*, ed. John N. Duvall (Cambridge: Cambridge University Press, 2008), pp. 1–10.

Easterbrook, Neil, 'Alternate Presents: The Ambivalent Historicism of *Pattern Recognition*', *Science Fiction Studies* 33:3 (2006), pp. 483–504.

Echlin, Kim, 'Baseball and the Cold War', in *Conversations with Don DeLillo*, ed. Thomas DePietro (Jackson: University Press of Mississippi, 2005), pp. 145–51 (first published in *The Ottawa Citizen*, 28 December 1997).

Evans, Ruth, '*Sir Orfeo* and Bare Life', in *Medieval Cultural Studies: Essays in Honour of Stephen Knight*, ed. Ruth Evans, Helen Fulton and David Matthews (Cardiff: University of Wales Press, 2006), pp. 198–212.

Farrell, Michael, *Writing Australian Unsettlement: Modes of Poetic Invention, 1796–1945* (New York: Palgrave Macmillan, 2015).

Feldman, Noah, 'Crooked Trump?' *New York Review of Books*, 24 May 2018, <https://www.nybooks.com/articles/2018/05/24/crooked-trump-legal-swamp/>.

Fischer, Benjamin B., *A Cold War Conundrum: The 1983 Soviet War Scare* (Washington, DC: Central Intelligence Agency, 2007), <https://www.cia.gov/library/center-for-the-study-of-intelligence/csi-publications/books-and-monographs/a-cold-war-conundrum/source.htm>.

Fitzmaurice, Andrew, 'The genealogy of *Terra Nullius*', *Australian Historical Studies* 38:129 (2007), pp. 1–15.

Foucault, Michel, *Discipline and Punish: The Birth of the Prison*, trans. Alan Sheridan (London: Penguin, 1991 [1977]).

Foucault, Michel, *The History of Sexuality: The Will to Knowledge*, trans. Robert Hurley (London: Penguin, 1998 [1978]).

Foucault, Michel, 'Truth and Power', in *Power/Knowledge: Selected Interviews and Other Writings 1972–1977*, ed. Colin Gordon, trans. Colin Gordon, Leo Marshall, John Mepham, Kate Soper (New York: Vintage, 1980), pp. 109–33.

Foucault, Michel, '*Society Must Be Defended*': *Lectures at the Collège de France, 1975–76*, ed. Mauro Bertani, Alessandro Fontana, trans. David Macey (London: Penguin, 2004).

Frame, Robin, *The Political Development of the British Isles 1100–1400* (Oxford: Oxford University Press, 1995).

Fukuyama, Francis, 'The End of History?' *The National Interest* 16 (Summer 1989), pp. 3–18.

Funder, Anna, *Stasiland* (Melbourne: Text, 2002).

Garton Ash, Timothy, 'The Imperfect Spy', *New York Review of Books*, 26 June 1997.

Garton Ash, Timothy, *The File: A Personal History*, revised edn (London: Atlantic Books, 2009).

Giancarlo, Matthew, 'Murder, Lies, and Storytelling: The Manipulation of Justice(s) in the Parliaments of 1397 and 1399', *Speculum* 77:1 (2002), pp. 76–112.

Gillis, Alan, 'Acoustic Perfume', in *Ciaran Carson: Critical Essays*, ed. Elmer Kennedy-Andrews (Dublin: Four Courts, 2009), pp. 254–74.

Girard, Greg and Ian Lambot, *City of Darkness: Life in Kowloon Walled City* (Chiddingfold: Watermark, 1993).

Girard, Greg and Ian Lambot, *City of Darkness Revisited* (Chiddingfold: Watermark, 2014).

Gohn, Jack Benoit, '*Richard II*: Shakespeare's Legal Brief on the Royal Prerogative and the Succession to the Throne', *Georgetown Law Journal* 70 (1982), pp. 943–73.

Gosling, Daniel Frederick, *Church, State, and Reformation: The Use and Interpretation of Praemunire from its Creation to the English Break with Rome* (PhD, University of Leeds, 2016).

Gray, Douglas, 'The Robin Hood Poems', in *Robin Hood: An Anthology of Scholarship and Criticism*, ed. Stephen Knight (Cambridge: Brewer, 1999), pp. 3–37 (first published in *Poetica* (Tokyo) 18 (1984), pp. 1–18).

Green, Jeremy, 'Libra', in *The Cambridge Companion to Don DeLillo*, ed. John N. Duvall (Cambridge: Cambridge University Press, 2008), pp. 94–107.

Green, Richard Firth, *A Crisis of Truth: Literature and Law in Ricardian England* (Philadelphia: University of Pennsylvania Press, 1999).

Greenblatt, Stephen, 'Invisible Bullets', in Stephen Greenblatt, *Shakespearean Negotiations: The Circulation of Social Energy in Renaissance England* (Berkeley and Los Angeles: University of California Press, 1988), pp. 21–65.

Greenblatt, Stephen, 'Martial Law in the Land of Cockaigne', in Stephen Greenblatt, *Shakespearean Negotiations: The Circulation of Social Energy in Renaissance England* (Berkeley and Los Angeles: University of California Press, 1988), pp. 129–63.

Greenblatt, Stephen, *Will in the World: How Shakespeare became Shakespeare* (New York and London: Norton, 2004).

Greenblatt, Stephen, 'Shakespeare in Tehran', *New York Review of Books*, 2 April 2015, <http://www.nybooks.com/articles/2015/04/02/shakespeare-in-tehran/>.

Greenwald, Glenn, *No Place to Hide: Edward Snowden, the NSA and the Surveillance State* (London: Penguin, 2014).

Grey, Stephen, 'America's Gulag', *New Statesman* (17 May 2004).

Gross, Miriam, 'The Secret World of John le Carré', in *Conversations with John le Carré*, ed. Matthew J. Bruccoli and Judith S. Baughman (Jackson: University Press of Mississippi, 2004), pp. 60–71 (first published in *The Observer*, 3 February 1980, pp. 33, 35).

Gross, Oren and Fionnuala Ní Aoláin, *Law in Times of Crisis: Emergency Powers in Theory and Practice* (Cambridge: Cambridge University Press, 2006).

Guldi, Jo and David Armitage, *The History Manifesto* (Cambridge: Cambridge University Press, 2014).

Halpern, Richard, 'The King's Two Buckets: Kantorowicz, *Richard II* and Fiscal *Trauerspiel*', *Representations* 106 (2009), pp. 67–76.

Hamilton, Donna B., 'The State of Law in *Richard II*', *Shakespeare Quarterly* 34:1 (1983), pp. 5–17.

Hanawalt, Barbara, 'Economic Influences on the Pattern of Crime in England, 1300–1348', *American Journal of Legal History* 18:4 (1974), pp. 281–97.

Hanawalt, Barbara [Barbara A. Hanawalt], 'Fur-Collar Crime: The Pattern of Crime among the Fourteenth-Century English Nobility', *Journal of Social History*, 8:4 (1975), pp. 1–17.

Hanawalt, Barbara [Barbara A. Hanawalt], 'Ballads and Bandits: Fourteenth-Century Outlaws and the Robin Hood Poems', in *Robin Hood: An Anthology of Scholarship and Criticism*, ed. Stephen Knight (Cambridge: Brewer, 1999), pp. 263–84 (first published in *Chaucer's England: Literature in Historical Context*, ed. Barbara A. Hanawalt (Minneapolis: University of Minnesota Press, 1992)).

Hand, G. J., *English Law in Ireland, 1290–1324* (Cambridge: Cambridge University Press, 1967).

Harding, Alan, 'The Revolt Against the Justices', in *The English Rising of 1381*, ed. R. H. Hilton and T. H. Aston (Cambridge: Cambridge University Press, 1984), pp. 165–93.

Harding, Alan, *Medieval Law and the Foundations of the State* (Oxford: Oxford University Press, 2002).

Harriss, Gerald, *Shaping the Nation: England 1360–1461* (Oxford: Oxford University Press, 2005).

Hennessy, Peter, *The Secret State: Whitehall and the Cold War*, revised edn (London: Penguin, 2003).

Hepburn, Allan, *Intrigue: Espionage and Culture* (New Haven and London: Yale University Press, 2005).

Hilton, R. H., 'The Origins of Robin Hood', in *Robin Hood: An Anthology of Scholarship and Criticism*, ed. Stephen Knight (Cambridge: Brewer, 1999), pp. 197–210 (first published in *Past and Present* 14 (1958), pp. 30–44).

Hobsbawm, Eric, *Bandits,* 4th edn (London: Abacus, 2001; first published London: Weidenfeld and Nicolson, 1969).

Hofstadter, Richard, 'The Paranoid Style in American Politics', *Harper's Magazine* (November 1964), pp. 77–86.

Holt, J. C., 'The Origins and the Audience of the Ballads of Robin Hood', in *Robin Hood: An Anthology of Scholarship and Criticism*, ed. Stephen Knight (Cambridge: Brewer, 1999), pp. 211–32 (first published in *Past and Present* 18 (1960), pp. 89–110).

Holt, J. C., *Robin Hood*, revised edn (London: Thames and Hudson, 1989).

Honan, Park, *Christopher Marlowe: Poet and Spy* (Oxford: Oxford University Press, 2005).

Horn, Eva, *The Secret War: Treason, Espionage, and Modern Fiction*, trans. Geoffrey Winthrop-Young (Evanston, IL: Northwestern University Press, 2013).

Hughes, Eamonn, '"The mouth of the poem": Carson and place', in *Ciaran Carson: Critical Essays*, ed. Kennedy-Andrews, pp. 86–105.

Hughes, Robert, *The Fatal Shore: A History of the Transportation of Convicts to Australia, 1787–1868* (London: Harvill, 1986).

Hungerford, Amy, 'Don DeLillo's Latin Mass', *Contemporary Literature* 47:3 (2006), pp. 343–80.

Hutson, Lorna, 'Imagining Justice: Kantorowicz and Shakespeare', *Representations* 106 (2009), pp. 118–42.

Immerman, Richard H., *The Hidden Hand: A Brief History of the CIA* (Oxford: Wiley Blackwell, 2014).

Ingram, Martin and Greg Harkin, *Stakeknife: Britain's Secret Agents in Ireland* (Dublin: O'Brien, 2004).

Jeffery, Keith, *The Secret History of MI6* (London: Penguin, 2011; first published London: Bloomsbury, 2010).

Johnston, Dillon, 'Voice and Voiceprints: Joyce and recent Irish Poetry', in *The Oxford Handbook of Modern Irish Poetry*, ed. Fran Brearton and Alan Gillis (Oxford: Oxford University Press, 2012), pp. 161–80.

Jones, Ian, *Ned Kelly: A Short Life*, revised edn (Sydney: Hachette, 2008).

Jones, Radhika, 'Peter Carey, The Art of Fiction No. 188', *The Paris Review* 177 (Summer 2006), <http://www.theparisreview.org/interviews/5641/the-art-of-fiction-no-188-peter-carey>.

Jones, Timothy S., *Outlawry in Medieval Literature* (New York: Palgrave Macmillan, 2010).

Jones, W. R., 'The Court of the Verge: The Jurisdiction of the Steward and Marshal of the Household in Later Medieval England', *Journal of British Studies* 10:1 (1970), pp. 1–29.

Judt, Tony, *Postwar: A History of Europe Since 1945* (London: Vintage, 2010 [2005]).

Jussen, Bernhard, '*The King's Two Bodies* Today', *Representations* 106 (2009), pp. 102–117.

Kadri, Sadakat, 'Short Cuts', *London Review of Books* 37:12 (18 June 2015), <http://www.lrb.co.uk/v37/n12/sadakat-kadri/short-cuts>.

Kaeuper, Richard W., 'Law and Order in Fourteenth-Century England: The Evidence of Special Commissions of Oyer and Terminer', *Speculum* 54 (1979), pp. 734–84.

Kaeuper, Richard W., *War, Justice, and Public Order: England and France in the Later Middle Ages* (Oxford: Oxford University Press, 1988).

Kantorowicz, Ernst H., *The King's Two Bodies: A Study in Mediaeval Political Theology* (Princeton, NJ: Princeton University Press, 1997 [1957]).

Kaufmann, Linda S., 'The Wake of Terror: Don DeLillo's "In the Ruins of the Future," "Baader-Meinhof," and *Falling Man*', *Modern Fiction Studies* 54:2 (2008), pp. 353–77.

Keane, Damien, 'Quotation Marks, the Gramophone Record, and the Language of the Outlaw', *Texas Studies in Literature and Language*, 51:4 (2009), pp. 400–15.

Keen, Maurice, *The Laws of War in the Late Middle Ages* (London: Routledge, and Toronto: University of Toronto Press, 1965).

Keen, Maurice, *English Society in the Later Middle Ages 1358–1500* (Harmondsworth: Penguin, 1990).

Keen, Maurice, *The Outlaws of Medieval Legend*, revised edn (London: Routledge, 2000).

Kennedy-Andrews, Elmer, 'Carson, Heaney, and the art of getting lost', in *Ciaran Carson: Critical Essays*, ed. Elmer Kennedy-Andrews (Dublin: Four Courts, 2009), pp. 227–53.

Kerrigan, John, *Revenge Tragedy: Aeschylus to Armageddon* (Oxford: Oxford University Press, 1996).

Kerrigan, John, *Archipelagic English: Literature, History, and Politics 1603–1707* (Oxford: Oxford University Press, 2008).

Kiberd, Declan, *Inventing Ireland: The Literature of the Modern Nation* (London: Vintage, 1996).

Knight, Peter, *The Kennedy Assassination* (Edinburgh: Edinburgh University Press, 2007).

Knight, Stephen, *Robin Hood: A Complete Study of the English Outlaw* (Oxford: Blackwell, 1994).

Knight, Stephen, *Robin Hood: A Mythic Biography* (Ithaca and London: Cornell University Press, 2003).

Kruse, Ursula and Horst (trans.), 'What Would I Be Like If I Were He?' in *Conversations with John le Carré*, ed. Matthew J. Bruccoli and Judith S. Baughman (Jackson: University Press of Mississippi, 2004), pp. 112–21 (first published in *Der Spiegel* no. 32 (7 August 1989), pp. 143–8).

Lanchester, John, 'The Snowden files: why the British public should be worried about GCHQ', *The Guardian* (3 October 2013), <http://www.theguardian.com/world/2013/oct/03/edward-snowden-files-john-lanchester>.

Laqueur, Walter, *Terrorism* (London: Weidenfeld and Nicolson, 1977).

Lassner, Phyllis, *Espionage and Exile: Fascism and Anti-Fascism in British Spy Fiction and Film* (Edinburgh: Edinburgh University Press, 2016).

Leerssen, Joep, *Mere Irish and Fíor-Ghael: Studies in the Idea of Irish Nationality, its Development and Literary Expression prior to the Nineteenth Century*, 2nd edn (Cork: Cork University Press in association with Field Day, 1996 [1986]).

Lemon, Rebecca, *Treason by Words: Literature, Law, and Rebellion in Shakespeare's England* (Ithaca, NY: Cornell University Press, 2006).

Lewis, Ewart, 'King Above Law? "Quod Principi Placuit" in Bracton', *Speculum* 39:2 (1964), 240–69.

Lieberman, Max, *The Medieval March of Wales: The Creation and Perception of a Frontier, 1066–1283* (Cambridge: Cambridge University Press, 2010).

Longley, Edna, *The Living Stream: Literature & Revisionism in Ireland* (Newcastle upon Tyne: Bloodaxe, 1994).

Longmuir, Anne, 'The Language of History: Don DeLillo's *The Names* and the Iranian Hostage Crisis', *Critique* 46:2 (Winter 2005), pp. 105–22.

Longmuir, Anne, 'Genre and Gender in Don DeLillo's *Players* and *Running Dog*', *Journal of Narrative Theory* 37:1 (Winter 2007), pp. 128–45.

Luban, David, 'Has Obama Upheld the Law?' *New York Review of Books*, 21 April 2016, <https://www.nybooks.com/articles/2016/04/21/has-obama-upheld-the-law/>.

Martin, F. X., 'Diarmait Mac Murchada and the Coming of the Anglo-Normans', in *A New History of Ireland II: Medieval Ireland, 1169–1534*, ed. Art Cosgrove (Oxford: Oxford University Press, 1993), pp. 43–66.

Martin, F. X., 'Overlord becomes Feudal Lord, 1172–85', in *A New History of Ireland II: Medieval Ireland, 1169–1534*, ed. Art Cosgrove (Oxford: Oxford University Press, 1993), pp. 98–126.

McCarthy, Conor, 'Injustice and Chaucer's Man of Law', *Parergon* 20:1 (2003), pp. 1–18.

McCarthy, Conor, *Marriage in Medieval England: Law, Literature and Practice* (Woodbridge: Boydell, 2004).

McClennen, Sophia A. and Alexandra Schultheis Moore, 'Aporia and Affirmative Critique: Mapping the Landscape of Literary Approaches to Human Rights Research', in *The Routledge Companion to Literature and Human Rights*, ed. Sophia A. McClennen and Alexandra Schultheis Moore (London and New York: Routledge, 2016), pp. 1–20.

McCrum, Robert, 'The 100 best novels: No 100 – True History of the Kelly Gang by Peter Carey (2000)', *The Observer*, 16 August 2015, <http://www.theguardian.com/books/2015/aug/16/100-best-novels-true-history-kelly-gang-peter-carey>.

McDermott, Alex, 'The Apocalyptic Chant of Edward Kelly', in Ned Kelly, *The Jerilderie Letter*, ed. Alex McDermott (Melbourne: Text, 2001), pp. v–xxxiv.

McFarlane, K. B., *The Nobility of Later Medieval England: The Ford Lectures for 1953 and Related Studies* (Oxford: Oxford University Press, 1973).

McGrath, Ann, 'Shamrock Aborigines: The Irish, the Aboriginal Australians and their children', *Aboriginal History* 34 (2010), pp. 55–84.

McIntosh, Marjorie K., 'Immediate Royal Justice: The Marshalsea Court in Havering, 1358', *Speculum* 54:4 (1979), pp. 727–33.

Macintyre, Stuart and Anna Clark, *The History Wars* (Melbourne: Melbourne University Press, 2003).

MacNiocaill, Gearóid, 'The Contact of Irish and Common Law', *Northern Ireland Legal Quarterly* 23:1 (1972), pp. 16–23.

McQuilton, John, *The Kelly Outbreak 1878–1880: The Geographical Dimension of Social Banditry* (Melbourne: Melbourne University Press, 1987).

Maley, Willy, 'The Irish Text and Subtext of Shakespeare's English Histories', in *A Companion to Shakespeare's Works. Volume II. The Histories*, ed. Richard Dutton and Jean E. Howard (Oxford: Blackwell, 2003), pp. 94–124.

Manne, Robert, *Cypherpunk Revolutionary: On Julian Assange* (Collingwood: Black Inc., 2015).

May, Ernest R., John D. Steinbruner and Thomas W. Wolfe, *History of the Strategic Arms Competition, 1945–1972*, ed. Alfred Goldberg (Washington, DC: Office of the Secretary of Defense Historical Office, 1981).

Melley, Timothy, *Empire of Conspiracy: The Culture of Paranoia in Postwar America* (Ithaca, NY: Cornell University Press, 2000).

Melley, Timothy, *The Covert Sphere: Secrecy, Fiction, and the National Security State* (Ithaca, NY: Cornell University Press, 2012).

Meron, Theodor, *Henry's Wars and Shakespeare's Laws: Perspectives on the Law of War in the Later Middle Ages* (Oxford: Oxford University Press, 1993).

Michaud, Jon, 'The Exchange: Ciaran Carson', *The New Yorker*, 18 May 2009, <https://www.newyorker.com/books/page-turner/the-exchange-ciaran-carson>.

Milsom, S. F. C., *Historical Foundations of the Common Law*, 2nd edn (London: Butterworths, 1981).

Mishan, Ligaya, 'The Future is Here', *New York Review of Books* (2 April 2015), <https://www.nybooks.com/articles/2015/04/02/william-gibson-future-is-here/>.

Moloney, Ed, *A Secret History of the IRA*, 2nd edn (London: Penguin, 2007).

Monaghan, David, *The Novels of John le Carré: The Art of Survival* (Oxford: Blackwell, 1985).

Moore, Ross, '"Everything is in the ways you say them": Traditional Music and Story-telling in the Works of Ciaran Carson', *ROPES – Review of Postgraduate Studies (NUI Galway)* 8 (2000), pp. 5–10.

Moore, Ross [Alexander Ross Moore], *Belfast is Many Places: Contemporary Poetry and the City* (unpublished doctoral thesis, National University of Ireland, Galway, 2005).

Moore, Ross, 'We Don't Know the Half of It', <http://www.culturenorthernireland.org/features/literature/we-don't-know-half-it>.

Moriarty, Gerry, 'Claim that hundreds of deaths in North happened due to collusion', *Irish Times*, 29 May 2015, <http://www.irishtimes.com/news/ireland/irish-news/claim-that-hundreds-of-deaths-in-north-happened-due-to-collusion-1.2230050>.

Morris, Allison, 'IRA commander at time of Shankill bombing was informer', *Irish News*, 25 January 2016, <http://www.irishnews.com/news/2016/01/25/news/the-ira-commander-at-time-of-shankill-bombing-was-a-police-informer-393891/>.

Mulryne, J. R., 'Kyd, Thomas (bap. 1558, d. 1594)', *Oxford Dictionary of National Biography* (Oxford: Oxford University Press, 2004).

Musson, Anthony and W. M. Ormrod, *The Evolution of English Justice: Law, Politics and Society in the Fourteenth Century* (London: Macmillan, 1999).

Nagy, Joseph Falaky, 'The Paradoxes of Robin Hood', in *Robin Hood: An Anthology of Scholarship and Criticism*, ed. Stephen Knight (Cambridge: Brewer, 1999), pp. 411–25 (first published in *Folklore* 91 (1980), pp. 198–210).

Nayar, Pramod K., *The Postcolonial Studies Dictionary* (Chichester: Wiley Blackwell, 2015).

Neal, David, *The Rule of Law in a Penal Colony: Law and Power in Early New South Wales* (Cambridge: Cambridge University Press, 1991).

Nederman, Cary J., 'A Duty to Kill: John of Salisbury's Theory of Tyrannicide', *The Review of Politics* 50 (1988), pp. 365–89.

Nederman, Cary J., *Lineages of European Political Thought: Explorations along the Medieval/Modern Divide from John of Salisbury to Hegel* (Washington, DC: Catholic University of America Press, 2009).

Neville, Cynthia J., *Violence, Custom and Law: The Anglo-Scottish Border Lands in the Later Middle Ages* (Edinburgh: Edinburgh University Press, 1998).

Newitz, Annalee, 'William Gibson talks to *io9* about Canada, Draft Dodging, and Godzilla', in *Conversations with William Gibson*, ed. Patrick A. Smith (Jackson: University Press of Mississippi, 2014), pp. 194–7 (first published on *io9.com*, 10 June 2008, <https://io9.gizmodo.com/william-gibson-talks-to-io9-about-canada-draft-dodging-5015137>).

Ó Ciardha, Éamonn, 'Tóraíochas is Rapairíochas sa Seachtú hAois Déag/Tories and Rapparees in the Seventeenth Century', *History Ireland*, 2:1 (Spring, 1994), pp. 21–5.

O'Donoghue, Bernard, '"The Half-Said Thing to Them is Dearest": Paul Muldoon', in *Poetry in Contemporary Irish Literature*, ed. Michael Kenneally (Gerrards Cross: Colin Smythe, 1995), pp. 400–20.

O'Driscoll, Dennis, *Stepping Stones: Interviews with Seamus Heaney* (London: Faber, 2008).

O'Farrell, Patrick, *The Irish in Australia, 1788 to the Present*, 3rd edn (Sydney: University of New South Wales Press, 2000).

O'Reilly, Nathaniel, 'The Voice of the Teller: A Conversation with Peter Carey', *Antipodes* 16:2 (2002), pp. 164–7.

Otway-Ruthven, Jocelyn, 'The Request of the Irish for English Law, 1277–80', *Irish Historical Studies* 6:24 (1949), pp. 261–70.

Otway-Ruthven, Jocelyn, 'The Native Irish and English Law in Medieval Ireland', *Irish Historical Studies* 7:25 (1950), pp. 1–16.

Owst, G. R., *Literature and Pulpit in Medieval England*, 2nd edn (Oxford: Blackwell, 1966).

Palmer, Christopher, '*Mona Lisa Overdrive* and the Prosthetic', *Science Fiction Studies* 31:2 (2004), pp. 227–42.

Passaro, Vince, 'Dangerous Don DeLillo', in *Conversations with Don DeLillo*, ed. Thomas DePietro (Jackson: University Press of Mississippi, 2005), pp. 75–85 (first published in *The New York Times Magazine*, 19 May 1991).

Phillips, Helen, 'Bandit Territories and Good Outlaws', in *Bandit Territories: British Outlaw Traditions*, ed. Helen Phillips (Cardiff: University of Wales Press, 2008), pp. 1–23.

Phillips, John H., *The Trial of Ned Kelly* (Sydney: The Law Book Company, 1987).

Piette, Adam, *The Literary Cold War, 1945 to Vietnam* (Edinburgh: Edinburgh University Press, 2009).

Plimpton, George, 'John le Carré, The Art of Fiction No. 149', in *Conversations with John le Carré*, ed. Matthew J. Bruccoli and Judith S. Baughman (Jackson: University Press of Mississippi, 2004), pp. 145–61 (first published in the *Paris Review* 143 (Summer 1997), pp. 50–74, <https://www.theparisreview.org/interviews/1250/john-le-carre-the-art-of-fiction-no-149-john-le-carre>).

Pollock, Frederick and Frederic William Maitland, *The History of English Law Before the Time of Edward I*, 2nd edn, 2 vols (Cambridge: Cambridge University Press, 1968).

Prassel, Frank Richard, *The Great American Outlaw: A Legacy of Fact and Fiction* (Norman and London: University of Oklahoma Press, 1993).

Prestwich, Michael, *Edward I* (Berkeley and Los Angeles: University of California Press, 1988).

Prestwich, Michael, 'Gilbert de Middleton and the Attack on the Cardinals, 1317', in *Warriors and Churchmen in the High Middle Ages: Essays presented to Karl Leyser*, ed. Timothy Reuter (London: Hambledon, 1992), pp. 179–94.

Price, Adrian, 'Welsh Bandits', in *Bandit Territories: British Outlaw Traditions*, ed. Helen Phillips (Cardiff: University of Wales Press, 2008), pp. 58–72.

Rauchut, E. A., 'Hotspur's Prisoners and the Laws of War in *1 Henry IV*', *Shakespeare Quarterly* 45:1 (1994), pp. 96–7.

Reynolds, Henry, *The Law of the Land*, 2nd edn (Ringwood: Penguin, 1992).

Reynolds, Henry, *Forgotten War* (Sydney: University of New South Wales Press, 2013).

Rich, Nathaniel, 'James Ellroy, The Art of Fiction No. 201', *The Paris Review* 190 (Fall 2009), <https://www.theparisreview.org/interviews/5948/the-art-of-fiction-no-201-james-ellroy>.

Richardson, Louise, *What Terrorists Want: Understanding the Enemy, Containing the Threat* (New York: Random House, 2006).

Riggs, David, *The World of Christopher Marlowe* (London: Faber, 2004).

Rizzo, John, *Company Man: Thirty Years of Controversy and Crisis in the CIA* (New York: Scribner, 2014).

Rose, Deborah Bird, 'Ned Kelly Died for Our Sins', *Oceania* 65:2 (1994), pp. 175–86.

Rowan, Brian, 'Northern Ireland's violent past remains unresolved', *Irish Times*, 16 January 2016, <https://www.irishtimes.com/news/politics/northern-ireland-s-violent-past-remains-unresolved-1.2498749>.

Saul, Nigel, *Richard II* (New Haven and London: Yale University Press, 1997).

Saunders, Corinne, *The Forest of Medieval Romance: Avernus, Broceliande, Arden* (Cambridge: Brewer, 1993).

Saunders, Frances Stonor, *Who Paid the Piper? The CIA and the Cultural Cold War* (London: Granta, 1999).

Savage, Charlie, *Power Wars: Inside Obama's Post-9/11 Presidency* (New York: Little, Brown, 2015).

Scahill, Jeremy, *Dirty Wars: The World is a Battlefield* (London: Serpent's Tail, 2013).

Scanlan, Margaret, 'Writers Among Terrorists: Don DeLillo's *Mao II* and the Rushdie Affair', *Modern Fiction Studies* 40:2 (1994), pp. 229–52.

Scattergood, V. J., *Politics and Poetry in the Fifteenth Century* (London: Blandford, 1971).

Scattergood, V. J. [John Scattergood], '*The Tale of Gamelyn*: The Noble Robber as

Provincial Hero', in John Scattergood, *Reading the Past: Essays on Medieval and Renaissance Literature* (Dublin: Four Courts, 1996), pp. 81–113.

Schlesinger, Arthur M. Jr, *The Imperial Presidency* (Boston: Houghton Mifflin, 1973).

Schmitt, Carl, *Political Theology: Four Chapters on the Concept of Sovereignty*, trans. George Schwab (Chicago and London: University of Chicago Press, 2005).

Schulz, Fritz, 'Bracton on Kingship', *English Historical Review*, 60:237 (May 1945), pp. 136–76.

Scott-Warren, Jason, 'Was Elizabeth I Richard II? The Authenticity of Lambarde's "Conversation"', *Review of English Studies* 64:264 (2013), pp. 208–30.

Seal, Graham, *The Outlaw Legend: A Cultural Tradition in Britain, America and Australia* (Cambridge: Cambridge University Press, 1996).

Seal, Graham, 'The Robin Hood Principle: Folklore, History, and the Social Bandit', *Journal of Folklore Research*, 46:1 (2009), pp. 67–89.

Seal, Graham, *Outlaw Heroes in Myth and History* (London and New York: Anthem, 2011).

Seed, David, 'The Well-Wrought Structures of John le Carré's Early Fiction', in *Spy Thrillers: From Buchan to le Carré*, ed. Clive Bloom (London: Macmillan, 1990), pp. 140–59.

Shulevitz, Judith, 'In Search of the Real', *Slate* (7 February 2010), <https://slate.com/culture/2010/02/don-delillo-s-point-omega.html>.

Singer, Peter W., *Corporate Warriors: The Rise of the Privatized Military Industry* (Ithaca and London: Cornell University Press, 2003).

Singer, Peter W. and Allan Friedman, *Cybersecurity and Cyberwar: What Everyone Needs to Know* (New York: Oxford University Press, 2013).

Sisman, Adam, *John le Carré: The Biography* (London: Bloomsbury, 2015).

Slaughter, Joseph R., *Human Rights, Inc.: The World Novel, Narrative Form, and International Law* (New York: Fordham University Press, 2007).

Smith, Brendan, 'The Concept of the March in Medieval Ireland: The Case of Uriel', *Proceedings of the Royal Irish Academy* 88C (1988), pp. 257–69.

Smith, J. Beverley, *Llywelyn ap Gruffudd, Prince of Wales*, new edn (Cardiff: University of Wales Press, 2014).

Smyth, Heather, 'Mollies Down Under: Cross-Dressing and Australian Masculinity in Peter Carey's *True History of the Kelly Gang*', *Journal of the History of Sexuality* 18:2 (2009), pp. 185–214.

Snider, L. Britt, *The Agency and the Hill: CIA's Relationship with Congress, 1946–2004* (Washington, DC: Center for the Study of Intelligence, 2008).

Snyder, Robert, *John le Carré's Post-Cold War Fiction* (Columbia, MO: University of Missouri Press, 2017).

Sokol, B. J. and Mary (eds), *Shakespeare's Legal Language* (London: Athlone, 2000, repr. London: Continuum, 2004).

Spraggs, Gillian, *Outlaws & Highwaymen: The Cult of the Robber in England from the Middle Ages to the Nineteenth Century* (London: Pimlico, 2001).

Sterling, Bruce, 'Preface', in William Gibson, *Burning Chrome and other stories* (London: Voyager, 1995 [1986]), pp. 9–13.

Stones, E. L. G., 'The Folvilles of Ashby-Folville, Leicestershire, and Their Associates in Crime, 1326–1347', *Transactions of the Royal Historical Society* 7 (1957), pp. 117–36.

Strayer, Joseph, 'The Historical Experience of Nation-Building in Europe', in

Medieval Statecraft and Perspectives of History: Essays by Joseph Strayer, ed. John F. Benton and Thomas N. Bisson (Princeton, NJ: Princeton University Press, 1971), pp. 341–8 (first published in *Nation-Building*, ed. K. W. Deutsch and W. J. Foltz (New York: Atherton, 1963), pp. 17–26).

Strohm, Paul, 'Saving the Appearances: Chaucer's "Purse" and the Fabrication of the Lancastrian Claim', in Paul Strohm, *Hochon's Arrow: The Social Imagination of Fourteenth-Century Texts* (Princeton, NJ: Princeton University Press, 1992), pp. 75–94.

Strohm, Paul, *England's Empty Throne: Usurpation and the Language of Legitimation, 1399–1422*, paperback edn (Notre Dame, IN: Notre Dame University Press, 2006).

Strong, Tracy B., 'Foreword. The Sovereign and the Exception: Carl Schmitt, Politics, Theology, and Leadership', in Carl Schmitt, *Political Theology: Four Chapters on the Concept of Sovereignty*, trans. George Schwab (Chicago and London: University of Chicago Press, 2005), pp. vii–xxv.

Tardif, Richard, 'The "Mistery" of Robin Hood: A New Social Context for the Texts', in *Robin Hood: An Anthology of Scholarship and Criticism*, ed. Stephen Knight (Cambridge: Brewer, 1999), pp. 345–61 (first published in *Word and Worlds: Studies in the Social Role of Verbal Culture*, ed. S. Knight and S. J. Muckherjee (Sydney: Sydney Association for Studies in Society and Culture, 1983)).

Taylor, Joseph, '"Me longeth sore to Bernysdale": Centralization, Resistance, and the Bare Life of the Greenwood in *A Gest of Robyn Hode*,' *Modern Philology* 110:3 (2013), pp. 313–39.

Taylor, Peter, *Provos: The IRA and Sinn Fein* (London: Bloomsbury, 1997).

Taylor, Peter, *Brits: The War Against the IRA* (London: Bloomsbury, 2001).

Tierney, Brian, 'Bracton on Government', *Speculum* 38:4 (1963), pp. 295–317.

Tillyard, E. M. W., *Shakespeare's History Plays* (Harmondsworth: Penguin, 1962; first published London: Chatto and Windus, 1944).

Towers, Robert, 'From the Grassy Knoll', *The New York Review of Books*, 18 August 1988.

Ullmann, Walter, *A History of Political Thought: The Middle Ages*, revised edn (Harmondsworth: Penguin, 1970).

Ullmann, Walter, *Law and Politics in the Middle Ages: An Introduction to the Sources of Medieval Political Ideas* (London, 1975).

Ullmann, Walter, 'Historical Jurisprudence, Historical Politology, and the History of the Middle Ages', in Walter Ullmann, *Jurisprudence and the Middle Ages* (London: Variorum, 1980), II, 199–201.

Vaughan, Paul, 'Le Carré's Circus: Lamplighters, Moles, and Others of That Ilk', in *Conversations with John le Carré*, ed. Matthew J. Bruccoli and Judith S. Baughman (Jackson: University Press of Mississippi, 2004), pp. 53–9 (first published in *The Listener*, 13 September 1979, pp. 339–40)).

Wallace-Wells, David, 'William Gibson: The Art of Fiction No. 211', in *Conversations with William Gibson*, ed. Patrick A. Smith (Jackson: University Press of Mississippi, 2014), pp. 198–228 (first published in *Paris Review* 197 (Summer 2011), 106–49, <https://www.theparisreview.org/interviews/6089/william-gibson-the-art-of-fiction-no-211-william-gibson>).

Warner, Marina, *Fantastic Metamorphoses, Other Worlds: Ways of Telling the Self* (Oxford: Oxford University Press, 2002).

Watt, J. A., 'The Anglo-Irish Colony under strain, 1327–99', in *A New History of Ireland II: Medieval Ireland, 1169–1534*, ed. Art Cosgrove (Oxford: Oxford University Press, 1993), pp. 352–96.

Weber, Max, 'Politics as a Vocation', in Max Weber, *The Vocation Lectures*, ed. David Owen and Tracy B. Strong, trans. Rodney Livingstone (Indianapolis: Hackett, 2004).

Weber, Thérèse (ed.), *Outlawed! Rebels, Revolutionaries, and Bushrangers* (Canberra: National Museum of Australia, 2003).

Weiner, Tim, *Legacy of Ashes: The History of the CIA* (London: Penguin, 2008; first published London: Allen Lane, 2007).

Weizman, Eyal, 'On Extraterritoriality', in *Arxipèlag D'Excepcions: Sobiranies de l'extraterritorialitat* (Barcelona: Centre de Cultura Contemporània de Barcelona, 2007), pp. 13–20.

Welch, Robert (ed.), *The Concise Oxford Companion to Irish Literature* (Oxford: Oxford University Press, 2000).

Wheatley, David, '"That Blank Mouth": Secrecy, Shibboleths, and Silence in Northern Irish Poetry', *Journal of Modern Literature* 25 (2001), pp. 1–16.

Wheeler, Marcy, 'John Bates' TWO Wiretapping Warnings: Why the Government Took Its Internet Dragnet Collection Overseas', <https://www.emptywheel.net/2013/11/20/john-bates-two-wiretapping-warnings-why-the-government-took-its-internet-dragnet-collection-overseas/>.

Williams, Bernadette, 'The Sorcery Trial of Alice Kyteler,' *History Ireland* 2:4 (1994), pp. 20–4.

Wills, David, *Prosthesis* (Stanford, CA: Stanford University Press, 1995).

Woodward, Bob, *The Agenda: Inside the Clinton White House* (New York: Simon & Schuster, 2005 [1994]).

Wotherspoon, Gary, 'Gay Men', *Dictionary of Sydney* (2008), <https://dictionaryofsydney.org/entry/gay_men>.

Wright, Clare and Alex McDermott, 'Ned's Women: A Fractured Love Story', *Meanjin* 69:2 (2010), <https://meanjin.com.au/essays/neds-women-a-fractured-love-story/>.

All web links last accessed 5 March 2019.

Index